LIBRARY OF HEBREW BIBLE/ OLD TESTAMENT STUDIES

562

Formerly Journal for the Study of the Old Testament Supplement Series

Editors
Laura Quick, Oxford University, UK
Jacqueline Vayntrub, Yale University, USA

Founding Editors
David J. A. Clines, Philip R. Davies and David M. Gunn

Editorial Board
Sonja Ammann, Alan Cooper, Steed Davidson, Susan Gillingham,
Rachelle Gilmour, John Goldingay, Rhiannon Graybill, Anne Katrine Gudme,
Norman K. Gottwald, James E. Harding, John Jarick, Tracy Lemos,
Carol Meyers, Eva Mroczek, Daniel L. Smith-Christopher,
Francesca Stavrakopoulou, James W. Watts

HATE AND ENMITY IN BIBLICAL LAW

Klaus-Peter Adam

LONDON • NEW YORK • OXFORD • NEW DELHI • SYDNEY

T&T CLARK

Bloomsbury Publishing Plc

50 Bedford Square, London, WC1B 3DP, UK

1385 Broadway, New York, NY 10018, USA

29 Earlsfort Terrace, Dublin 2, Ireland

BLOOMSBURY, T&T CLARK and the T&T Clark logo are trademarks of Bloomsbury Publishing Plc

First published in Great Britain 2022
Paperback edition published 2024

Copyright © Klaus-Peter Adam, 2022, 2023

Klaus-Peter Adam has asserted his right under the Copyright, Designs and Patents Act, 1988, to be identified as Author of this work.

For legal purposes the Acknowledgments on p. xi constitute an extension of this copyright page.

All rights reserved. No part of this publication may be reproduced or transmitted in any form or by any means, electronic or mechanical, including photocopying, recording, or any information storage or retrieval system, without prior permission in writing from the publishers.

Bloomsbury Publishing Plc does not have any control over, or responsibility for, any third-party websites referred to or in this book. All internet addresses given in this book were correct at the time of going to press. The author and publisher regret any inconvenience caused if addresses have changed or sites have ceased to exist, but can accept no responsibility for any such changes.

A catalogue record for this book is available from the British Library.
Library of Congress Control Number: 2021951976

ISBN: HB: 978-0-5676-8189-8
PB: 978-0-5677-0649-2
ePDF: 978-0-5676-8190-4

Series: Library of Hebrew Bible/Old Testament Studies, volume 562
ISSN 2513-8758

Typeset by Trans.form.ed SAS

To find out more about our authors and books visit www.bloomsbury.com and sign up for our newsletters.

Contents

List of Tables ix
Acknowledgments xi

Chapter 1
INTRODUCTION 1
  1. Definitions of Blood Feud 2
  2. Functional vs. Evolutionary Theories of Conflict Settlement 3
  3. Feuding and Conflict Settlement in Ancient Israel
      in Evolutionary Legal Theory 6
  4. Hatred and Enmity in the Old Testament: A Proposal 18

Chapter 2
"IF TWO ARE QUARRELING WITH EACH OTHER...":
LONG-TERM ENMITY IN THE COVENANT CODE 23
  1. Enmity in the Covenant Code 23
  2. Exodus 21:13aα: "he has not intended..." 32
  3. Exodus 21:13aβ: "The God" Initiating Homicide—
      A Legal Fiction 33
  4. Reading Exodus 21:14 through a Redaction Critical Lens 34
    4.1. "My altar" in Verse 14b 34
    4.2. Verse 12 in its Relation to Verses 13-14 35
    4.3. The Relevance of the Parties' Social Status
        in the Compositional Logic of 21:12-34 36
    4.4. רע – Everyday Neighbor 39
    4.5. *זיד/זוד Exodus 21:14 (Proverbs 21:14; Psalm 86:14) 42
    4.6. Conclusion: The Relevance of Enmity for Procedural Law 43
  5. Injury Law 45
    5.1. Exodus 21:18-19 45
    5.2. Reworking of Exodus 21:18-19 48
    5.3. Reception History of Exodus 21:18-19 52
  6. Exodus 22:1-2 as a Test Case for Long-term Enmity 55
  7. Long-term Enmity in the y^eshallem-laws of Exodus 21:33–22:14 59
  8. Enmity Legislation in Exodus 23:4-5 and Proverbs 25:21-22 63
    8.1. Exodus 23:4-5 in Exodus 23:1-8 63
    8.2. Legal Procedure between Opponents in Exodus 23:1-8 66
    8.3. Proverbs 25:21-22 69

9. Conclusion: Intentionality and Long-term Enmity	72
9.1. Intentionality in Ancient Near Eastern Law	74
9.2. חמד: Intentionality and Long-term Enmity in the Decalogues	76
9.3. Early Judaism	80
9.4. Summary and Outlook	81

Chapter 3
LONG-TERM ENMITY AND LEGAL PROCEDURE IN DEUTERONOMIC LAW

	85
1. Private Long-term Enmity: A Legal Construct and Its Implications	85
2. Hate and Enmity as Themes of the Composition Deuteronomy 19 and 21	87
3. Deuteronomy 19:1-12 (19:2a, 3b, 4, 5, 6, 11-12)	94
3.1. Translation, Source Criticism, Outline	94
3.2. The Continuous Nature of the Slayer–Victim Relation	97
3.3. Subcase I (v. 4b)	99
3.4. The Case Law (v. 5)	102
3.5. Subcase II (vv. 11-12)	104
3.6. Conclusion	105
4. "Hate" as a Legal Category in Deuteronomy and Beyond	105
4.1. Deuteronomy 22:1-4 as Interpretation of Exodus 23:4-5	106
4.2. Marriage Law in Deuteronomy 22:13-21a; 24:1-4	110
4.3. "Hate" in Biblical Marriage Law and in "Wifehood" Documents from Elephantine	119
4.4. Inheritance Law in Deuteronomy 21:15-17	122
4.5. Conclusion	123
5. Cultural and Literary Historical Contexts: Deuteronomy 19:4, 11 (אח, רע)	124
5.1. Fictive Kinship	127
5.2. The Singular "Your Brother" in Witness Law	129
5.3. Kinship Ethos and Social Justice	129
5.4. Private Enmity as a Result of Economic Injustice	130
5.5. Brother Ethos and Honor: Deuteronomy 25:1-3	133
5.6. Conclusion	134
5.7. Excursus: "Neighbor" in Proverbs	135
5.8. Deuteronomy 19:3b: רצח – "to kill in a community"	139
5.9. Conclusion	140
6. Outlook: Deuteronomy 19 as Response to an Agonistic Society?	142

Chapter 4
ENMITY AND HATE IN PRIESTLY LAW:
NUMBERS 35 (DEUTERONOMY 4; JOSHUA 20)

	145
1. Source Criticism: Enmity in Priestly Law	145
2. Outline and Legal Thought	155
3. Numbers 35 and Deuteronomy 19:1-12: Parallels, Modifications, Clarifications	157

4. Legal Categories	158
4.1. בשגגה – "Inadvertently" or "Tragically"?	159
4.2. Distinction of Tools and Modes of Action in *trauma ek pronoias*	163
4.3. Nominalizations and Modes of Action as Evolutions of Homicide Law	167
4.4. Modes of Action: To Push, to Throw and to Drop, to Slay	167
4.5. איבה, שנאה	168
4.6. צדיה	170
4.7. Conclusion	172
5. Legal Procedure and Social Background	174
5.1. Israelite, Metic, Settler	174
5.2. Jurisdiction of the עדה	180
5.3. The Local Congregation as Jury and עיר מקלט as "City of Refuge"	185
5.4. Verses 25-29 as Regulatory Statutes	187
5.5. Asylum Cities as Places of Refuge in Classical Athens and in the Hellenistic Era	190
6. Reception History (Deuteronomy 4; Joshua 20)	193
7. Conclusion	196

Chapter 5
BROTHERLY LOVE IN LEVITICUS 19:11-18

1. Brotherly Love	199
1.1. The Composition of Leviticus 19:11-18	203
1.2. Prohibitive Rows and their Themes	205
1.3. Themes Relevant to the Community of H	207
2. Leviticus 19:11-18 in Leviticus 19	212
3. Conflict Settlement, Patriarchal and Communal Authority	215
3.1. Verses 11-12	215
3.2. Verses 13-14	217
3.3. Verses 15-16	219
3.4. Verses 17-18	225
4. Outlook—Religious Historical Parallels	240
4.1. Hate and Urban Carnage	240
4.2. Conflict Settlement and Enmity in Religious Associations	242
4.3. Conclusion	249

CONCLUSION	251
Bibliography	254
Index of References	274
Index of Authors	293
Index of Hebrew Terms	297
Index of Subjects	299

Tables

Table 2.1	46
Table 2.2	61
Table 2.3	66
Table 3.1	92
Table 3.2	94
Table 3.3	100
Table 3.4	101
Table 3.5	104
Table 3.6	107
Table 3.7	111
Table 3.8	116
Table 3.9	124
Table 3.10	131
Table 3.11	133
Table 4.1	153
Table 4.2	154
Table 4.3	168
Table 4.4	169
Table 4.5	170
Table 4.6	187
Table 4.7	194
Table 4.8	196
Table 5.1	204
Table 5.2	214
Table 5.3	217
Table 5.4	222

ACKNOWLEDGMENTS

The present book has been in the working since, more than a decade ago, the theme of private enmity and the interweaving of law and narrative caught my attention in the Saul–David narratives. I am grateful for comments on presentations in papers and earlier drafts of chapters I have received from many colleagues, among others, Corrine L. Carvalho, Simeon B. Chavel, Thomas B. Dozeman, Shalom E. Holtz, William S. Morrow, Wolfgang Oswald, Eckart Otto, Bernd Schipper, Brent A. Strawn, Bruce Wells, Jacob L. Wright, and the SBL Law section. Any remaining errors remain my own. Parts of Chapter 5, 4.2. appeared in a previous version in "Purity and Holiness in P: Lev 19:11–18 and the Decalogues", in *Eigensinn und Entstehung der Hebräischen Bibel. Erhard Blum zum siebzigsten Geburtstag*, ed. Joachim J. Krause, Wolfgang Oswald, and Kristin Weingart (Mohr Siebeck: Tübingen, 2020), 147–62.

My thanks go to the Henry Luce Foundation and the Association of Theological Schools for an annual Henry Luce III-Fellowship in Theology during the academic year 2016/17, which allowed me to draft the lion's share of this book. The German Academic Exchange Service (DAAD) sponsored a stay as visiting scholar at the Fachbereich Evangelische Theologie at the Ludwig-Maximilians-University Munich in the summer of 2016, upon the generous invitation of Friedhelm Hartenstein. Finally, I am grateful for the sabbaticals at the Lutheran School of Theology at Chicago in 2012, 2016/17, and in 2020. For invaluable help with the bibliography during the Covid pandemic I owe thanks to the librarians of the JKM library at LSTC and MTS, namely Emilie Pulver and Barry Hopkins. Chingboi Guite proofread and helped with the bibliography. Ole Schenk carefully and insightfully twice edited the entire text and made many valuable improvements. Many thanks to the anonymous reviewer and to the previous LHBOTS serial editors, Claudia V. Camp and Andrew Mein.

Chicago, January 2021

Chapter 1

INTRODUCTION

Hate between individuals was a universal phenomenon in the ancient world. Nonetheless, the essence of private enmity between two individuals is complex to determine and continues to challenge scholarship. On the surface, this challenge is due to the historical differences between the notions of enmity in the contemporary and in the ancient world. On a deeper level, hate and its opposite, friendship, between individuals in antiquity occurred in a social context quite different from modern Western societies with distinct mechanisms of continuous malevolence or benevolence between two private individuals. Any portrayal of the procedures of opponents in a kinship-based society with roots in tribal structures, such as ancient Israel and Judah, is thus a complex endeavor with many historical aspects. This study describes and conceptualizes enmity and hateful conflict settlement on the basis of selected laws. It probes how biblical law reflects patterns of conflict settlement and hateful relationships in kinship-based societies and it demonstrates how facets of hatred, such as vicious slander, defamatory public speech, and the undisguised thirst for blood revenge provide the conceptual backdrop of many biblical laws.

This attempt to describe enmity as a construct that informs law reacts to a twofold need in biblical scholarship. First, the need to define the nature of private enmity as a regular pattern of social interaction and thus as a fundamental category of everyday conflict settlement in Ancient Israel. Many areas of the Old Testament, such as the Psalms of the Individual, reflect this commonplace constellation, yet a precise definition of the nature of private enmity is lacking. This functional analysis of enmity in the kinship-based society of ancient Israel and Judah seeks to fill this gap. It reflects on contexts in which this construct is most apparent, in blood feud, and it discusses this definition with the area of legal studies that has most thoroughly reflected on it, legal anthropology. At its outset, this study thus describes the nature of private enmity as legal anthropology defines it in its analysis of blood feud. A second goal is to precisely map this definition of enmity in the reconstruction of the development of biblical law.

1. *Definitions of Blood Feud*

Legal anthropology describes systems of law, including the nature and settlement of disputes between two opponents, traced in their cultural settings.[1] Analyzing mechanisms of hatred removed from the public–private dichotomy of modern society, it reconstructs legal thought and clarifies the mechanisms of violence in contexts that lack the formative influence of a central power that would have regulated and informed the legal concepts. In other words, legal anthropology provides greater descriptive precision for cultural contexts lacking a formal textual and bureaucratic system of regulation. The present approach seeks to describe hatred as a legal-historical and sociological syndrome through exposing patterns of enmity in the biblical contexts against the backdrop of the kinship-based society in which they are set. It seeks to deepen the understanding of typical rules and dynamics of conflicts between enemies, to describe namely the facets of institutional and non-institutional patterns of dispute settlement. Attaining more precision in these areas helps to more sharply define the nature of enmity as a social construct which follows the patterns and rules of dispute settlement. Leaving aside all stereotypical description in ancient sources about enemies, distinct acts committed by an opponent can then be recognized with greater contextual detail. Beyond examining those single acts, this study suggests biblical law implicitly conceptualizes the social construct of enmity as the context of a series of hateful acts, a status to which it ascribes tangible legal consequences. With this analytical category, it seeks to describe the nature of the interaction between opponents as communities perceive it and as it informs the patterned behavior between individual enemies in a conflict. Derived from the source texts, with this category, this study seeks to reconstruct the social reality that informs the texts.

For heuristic and practical purposes of this study, the textual basis for the reconstruction of conflict settlement procedure will predominantly focus on homicide law and blood feud. Blood feud arises around revenge, understood as "the attempt at some cost or risk to oneself, to impose suffering on those, who have made one suffer, because they have made one suffer."[2] More specifically it is blood revenge, the necessity to kill a person in an act of revenge, that legal anthropology describes as part of a feuding pattern: "Feud is a state of conflict between two kinship groups within a society, manifest by a series of unprivileged

---

1. Cf., for instance, N. Rouland, "The Settlement of Disputes," in *Legal Anthropology*, trans. P. G. Planel (Stanford: Stanford University Press, 1994), 255–86, and bibliography on 287–90.

2. J. Elster "Norms of Revenge," *Ethics* 100, no. 4 (1990): 862–85, here 862. See also R. Verdier, G. Courtois, and J.-P. Poly, *La Vengeance. Études d'ethnologie, d'histoire et de philosophie*, 4 vols. (Paris: Cujas, 1980–84), and, in particular, R. Verdier, "Le système vindicatoire," in vol. 1, 13–42. On the contexts of modern law, see Verdier, "Le désir, le devoir et l'interdit: masques et visages de la vengeance," *Déviance et Société* 8, no 2 (1984): 181–93.

killings and counter-killings between the kinship groups, usually initiated in response to an original homicide or other grievous injury."[3] Blood feud is not the only dynamic at play in conflicts in kinship-based societies, but it is the most serious. This extreme case of the mechanism of challenge and riposte most clearly demonstrates how opponents in diverse kinship-based societies would live out private conflicts. It thus serves a particular clarifying purpose for the present study. The respective laws expose the patterns of conflict settlement so typical for Israelite and Judean society, and therefore beginning with the case of blood feud best serves heuristically the purpose of the study. Furthermore, it is in the nature of counter-vengeance or feuds that social norms give rise to describable behavior patterns of the opponents involved, because the act of revenge itself is an affront that must be avenged. Indeed, legal anthropology suggests feuding behavior followed procedural rules. Societies in which feuds or vendettas followed rules are, for instance, found in medieval Iceland, the Balkans, and other Mediterranean countries, as well as South American tribes.[4] Feuding may sometimes be perceived as an uncoordinated form of conflict settlement, when it is in fact typically regulated, if not highly so. Consistent with this internally structured character, feuding procedure follows expected patterns: "What constitutes an affront that must be avenged? Who is allowed or is required to exact revenge? What means could legitimately be used when taking revenge? How soon is vengeance allowed or required? Whose death shall expiate an affront? What fate is reserved for those who fail to take revenge when the norms require it?"[5] The description of the precisely regulated patterns of feuding as the essence of conflict settlement has allowed legal anthropology to compare conflict mechanisms across many societies. And thus this functional lens of legal anthropology on feuding procedure as conflict settlement has also opened the view for a more broad comparison of a wide variety of forms of conflict settlement. With their precise functional analysis of feuding, legal anthropologists then came to question established perceptions of ideal-typical evolutionary theories of law leading from feuding to more advanced conflict settlement forms; a developmental view that has also been relevant for the reconstruction of the history of biblical law and thus requires brief attention.

2. *Functional vs. Evolutionary Theories of Conflict Settlement*

Homicide and ensuing blood feud are prominent areas of conflict that histories of law have used to analyze dispute-settlement mechanisms. In the nineteenth

---

3. E. A. Hoebel, "Feud: Concept, Reality and Method in the Study of Primitive Law," in *Essays on Modernization of Underdeveloped Societies*, vol. 1, ed. A. R. Desai (Bombay: Thacker, no year), 500–513, here 506, original italics.

4. Elster, "Norms," 866. While typically associated with pre-modern societies, it occurs in kinship-based societies until the present time.

5. Elster, "Norms," 867.

and early twentieth centuries these studies typically followed a trend of reconstructing developments in law and legal systems along evolutionary patterns. This is particularly relevant for the analysis of patterns of hateful behavior between individuals. Ethnographers typically would perceive conflict settlement systems along evolutionary patterns, often of unilinear nature. These evolutionary schemas typically reconstructed a unilinear development and ascribed feuding to premodern societies, associated with premodern, obsolete legal systems. Bronislaw Malinowski's 1926 *Crime and Custom in Savage Society*[6] molded one of the most effective rejections of evolutionary theories. It was also seminal in helping to establish legal anthropology as a separate field of ethnography rather than of legal studies, as Malinowski deliberately cut ties with the traditional field that hitherto had been called legal history. Methodologically, this redefinition of legal anthropology brought about a watershed. Since then the field has employed the functional theories of social anthropology[7] and most English-language scholarship began to base interpretations of law on anthropological research.[8]

Anthropology, and within it a fraction of ethnographers, generally remain critical toward evolutionary theories of human societies. Moving beyond models that argue along evolutionary lines, a plethora of legal anthropology studies would now highlight sub-themes, such as power development, male domination and many others. What these sub-themes offer is in fact a clarification of patterns of interactions and a description of the respective associated roles of players, or the explanation of honor–shame concepts. This had an effect on legal anthropological scholarship. Only a few attempts re-combined legal anthropology with evolutionary models. The fundamental difference between evolutionary or functional theories in anthropological research has conceptual implications. Unlike preceding ethnography, structuralism in particular remains critical toward evolutionary trajectories of societies and their implicit concepts of superiority. Along these structural lines of thought, legal anthropology would assess feud and conflict settlement by way of reflecting on their functionality in relation to their respective societal backgrounds[9] and, consequently, the fruit of these attempts

---

6. B. Malinowski, *Crime and Custom in Savage Society* (London: Kegan Paul, Trench & Trubner, 1926).

7. See, for instance, U. Wesel, *Frühformen des Rechts in vorstaatlichen Gesellschaften. Umrisse einer Frühgeschichte des Rechts bei Sammlern und Jägern und akephalen Ackerbauern und Hirten* (Frankfurt am Main: Suhrkamp, 1985), 16.

8. German legal historical approaches continued to adhere to a strictly legal historical paradigm; see the summary in Wesel, *Frühformen*, 16.

9. Social anthropology and legal history combine evolutionary and functional theories in a plethora of historical and ethnographic studies. Particularly relevant are the cultural historical examples of conflict settlement modes including Middle Eastern North African (MENA) cultures. On feuding structures in Proverbs, see, for instance, J. J. Pilch, *The Cultural Life Setting of the Proverbs* (Minneapolis: Fortress, 2016), 175–76, 189–93. On conflict settlement in classical Athens, see below. Cultural historical studies on kinship-based societies, include, for instance: on Montenegro, C. Boehm, *Montenegrin Social*

therefore inform the present study. In an attempt to describe the fundamental nature of hateful relations, social anthropology clarified the "axiom of amity" in kinship systems as a complementary phenomenon of enemy feud. It would specify the typical kinship mechanisms, namely the interconnection between kinship and polity in tribal societies. Ultimately, it asserts that "kinship concepts, institutions, and relations classify, identify, and categorize persons and groups," all of which contribute to "a general principle of kinship morality that is rooted in the familial domain and is assumed everywhere to be axiomatically binding…the rule of prescriptive altruism…the principle of kinship amity."[10] This perspective on patterned behavior along the alternatives of amity among kin to which enmity is the opposite state offers an invaluable heuristic perspective, as this study will demonstrate. Namely, for the study of biblical law, the two analyses of kinship-based societies through the paradigm of functional models of dispute settlement and the examination of amity among kin offer an effective vantage point to more accurately conceptualize the essence of conflict settlement and feuding in Ancient Israel and Judah. The present approach, rather than aiming at a synthesis of conflict settlement theory, balances a source-critical reading and the resulting evolutionary perspectives on biblical law with a perspective on enmity in the kinship-based society of Ancient Israel and Judah through the lens of legal anthropology. It describes the structural patterns of the social construct of private enmity and points to its fundamental relevance in biblical law, ascertaining its distinct phenotypes in historically diverse moments. Throughout, the backdrop of this status of enmity appears to be the society in Ancient Israel and Judah that on the local level operated as a segmentary, kinship-based society. In the various historical settings, the present study argues that biblical law would recognize that two opponents engaging in feud would acquire the social status of enmity that had substantial legal ramifications. This study demonstrates how biblical law conceives of enmity analogous to any other social status, such as marriage,

Organization and Values: A Political Ethnography of a Refuge Area Tribal Adaptation (New York: AMS Press, 1983); C. Boehm, *Blood Revenge: The Enactment and Management of Conflict in Montenegro and Other Tribal Societies*, 2nd ed (1984; repr. Philadelphia: University of Pennsylvania Press, 1987); nineteenth-century Corsica, S. Wilson, *Feuding, Conflict and Banditry in Nineteenth Century Corsica* (Cambridge: Cambridge University Press, 1988). See also, on conflict settlement among shepherds in Sardinia, J. L. Ruffini, "Disputing over Livestock in Sardinia," in *The Disputing Process: Law in Ten Societies*, ed. L. Nader and H. F. Todd (New York: Columbia University Press, 1976), 209–47, here from: *Law and Anthropology: A Reader*, ed. S. F. Moore (Blackwell: Boston, 2005), 135–53. For an overview on anthropological research on dispute, see S. Roberts, "The Study of Dispute: Anthropological Perspectives," in *Disputes and Settlements. Law and Human Relations in the West*, ed. J. Bossy (Cambridge: Cambridge University Press, 1983), 1–24.

10. Meyer Fortes, *Kinship and the Social Order. The Legacy of Lewis Henry Morgan* (1969; repr. with a new introduction by Lionel Tiger, New Brunswick NJ: Transaction Publishers, 2006), 231–32.

widowhood, adultery, patriarchal, detention, enslavement or the leadership status of the *pater familias* in a kinship-based society. As any status, as for instance, enslavement, in detail would undergo many historical changes in the history of law, an essential legal relevance of the status of enslavement would persist.

3. *Feuding and Conflict Settlement in Ancient Israel in Evolutionary Legal Theory*

The new lens on the functionality of kinship-based "segmentary" or "acephalous" societies has challenged many assumptions of biblical law. The present study puts the focus on the social construct of enmity as it shapes the patterns of interaction in conflict settlement. It reconstructs how individuals in Ancient Israel and Judah would have interacted during conflicts in what this study assumes to be the social framework of some laws from the Covenant Code and more prominently in Deuteronomy and priestly sources. In light of the fragmentary character of biblical law collections as sources, it refrains from sketching out an overall historical arc of legal thought or legal institutions. Rather, it contributes to retrieve the historical background at exemplary moments in time and to describe how the concept of private enmity influenced and informed legal institutions, for instance, marriage law in Deuteronomy. The specific shape of homicide and asylum law in Num 35 reveals how, at a particular point in time, Judah secured practices around legal institutions based on concepts of private enmity as they are typical for kinship-based societies.

With these legal-anthropological and source-critical historical insights, this study in new ways clarifies legal thought and practices against the backdrop of the largely acephalous, segmentary, or kinship-based society of Ancient Israel and Judah. In comparison, perspectives on conflict settlement that previously had assumed only central legal organs could prevent chaos in a community; such approaches certainly sharpened the view on a variety of concurrent uses of centralized patterns of institutional litigation alongside feud-like conflict settlement. They have necessarily also posed the question about the role of professional local legal experts, institutions of law enforcement, and central government. Yet, at times they may have reconstructed a fundamentally unilinear evolution of legal institutions. This poses the question whether the history of law and legal institutions would be better reconstructed as a complex trajectory seen against the backdrop of multiple coexisting conflict settlement institutions and conflict settlement modes. The present study largely brackets out the reconstruction of the trajectory of legal institutions, limiting itself to the reconstruction of law and legal thought.

This study's functional perspective on private enmity contributes mainly to the reconstruction of legal thought. In detail, when determining the evolution of law as a development of legal thought and when describing the relevant functional perspectives for a particular era, many fundamental challenges for any reconstruction of legal procedure on the literary level still remain. Consider, for instance, the complex relationship between literary texts and the reconstructions of legal procedure.[11] Any reconstruction of legal procedure on the literary level, not as descriptions of legal practice, undisputedly provides pivotal historical clarifications of legal thought. While this reconstruction may still be prone to an evolutionary theory from kinship-based law toward local or more centralistic legal organization,[12] some of its results point to opposite developments.

The increasing relevance of feuding patterns in biblical law is an astonishing result in a field in which the prejudices about evolutionary theories of feuding as archaic at times may drive the scholarly reconstruction of compositional and editorial processes. Two exemplary glances into the scholarship of biblical law[13] illustrate such underlying general evolutionary theories and reveal how historical events or assumptions of the development of the legal system build their backdrop. Consider for instance the description of kinship-based law placed within the overall histories of biblical law. H. J. Boecker in broad terms reconstructs authoritative patriarchal conflict settlement. As to Boecker, the Hebrew Bible rarely explicitly refers to patriarchal conflict settlement and, consequently, he suggests it to be typical for the "nomadic period."[14] Detached from feuding that he associates with the nomadic period, following L. Köhler, Boecker subsequently associates kinship-based law with the local assembly of the elders in the

---

11. Methodologically, the evolution of legal institutions according to the law collections must be separated from the assumption that this development parallels faithfully the evolution of legal procedure in Ancient Israel. Histories of law rely on evolutionary developments and the reconstruction of such developments from its beginning is intertwined with the source-critical analysis of biblical law. As an example of a brief synthesis on the literary historical and of the source-critical work on the collections of law, see E. Otto, *Theologische Ethik des Alten Testaments* (Stuttgart: Kohlhammer, 1994), 19–24 on CC; 175–80 on Deuteronomy.

12. The current approach assumes developments of legal thought and legal institutions but it does so in light of the fragmentary character of the sources of biblical law only in certain areas while remaining skeptical towards reconstructions of unilinear evolutionary theories from kinship-based to centralistic systems and legal institutions. The category of private enmity as a legal construct in a kinship-based society remains valid even during a period of strengthened centralistic institutions. Furthermore, this study clarifies the relevance of kinship-based institutions for the polity of Judah. Laws could reflect the attempt to secure the autonomy that kinship-based laws required. Institutions relevant to feuding could thus become tokens of autonomy in times when Judah found itself dependent from a suzerain; see below Chapter 4, part 5. Enmity and its opposite, mutual benevolence ("amity"), among kin members are essential legal categories in the rules of close-knit communities; see the interpretation of Lev 19:11-18 in analogy with rules of religious associations in Chapter 5, part 4.2.

13. The following brief summary of scholarship is based on Otto, *Ethik*, 20–24.

14. H. J. Boecker, *Law and the Administration of Justice in the Old Testament and the Ancient Near East* (London: SPCK 1980), 29–30.

gate as the paramount legal institution in Ancient Israel.[15] Seen through this lens, blood-feud remained an exempt form of conflict settlement that institutions in the nascent sedentary society of Ancient Israel, such as the local courts in the gate, could seemingly neither eliminate nor integrate.[16] Boecker essentially perceives feuding as typical for the pre-sedentary, nomadic epoch.[17] This evolutionary theory thus informs the analysis of the literary sources in their relevance for the reconstruction of a history of biblical law.

Another example of a late twentieth-century synthesis of legal institutional development is Eckart Otto's reconstruction of the eighth-century Covenant Code (CC) origins broadly as a development from the pre-monarchic to the monarchic era. He describes this evolutionary theory as "a tendency to detach law from the realm of the kinship and to increasingly connect it with judicial institutions, with enhanced institutionalization and more nuanced procedure..."[18] Source-critically,

---

15. Boecker, *Law*, 31. Such meeting places were reserved for the representatives of kin who possessed land, property, and honor – women, children, slaves, as well as sojourners, were exclude (32).

16. Boecker, *Law*, 36–37. In a brief synthesis, Boecker downplays the royal administration as limited to military affairs as well as to cases at the royal court proper without infringing on the rights of the local courts; Boecker, *Law*, 43, with reference to C. Macholz, "Die Stellung des Königs in der israelitischen Gerichtsverfassung," *ZAW* 84 (1972): 157–82, here 177. Boecker also refers to exceptions, such as Jer 26:1-19, where the "officers/princes of Judah" in v. 10 was extended to local interests of the city states; *Law*, 44. Likewise, he suggests 2 Kgs 6:26-30 presents a case from a situation of siege and is therefore of national concern and to be ruled by the king; 2 Sam 15:1-6 falls under royal military jurisdiction; see Boecker, *Law*, 47. The college of judges in Jerusalem according to 2 Chr 19:8-11 essentially provided "official assistance" to the local court, and presented only one significant extension of the royal jurisdiction in that it included the cases of bloodshed (v. 10); see Boecker, *Law*, 49.

17. At the same time, his reconstruction of legal institutions acknowledges the limited authority of a central court. Deuteronomy 17:8-12 establishes the superior authority of the central court only as a supplementary judicial agency to the local court, without reference to the king. Boecker, *Law*, 49. More subtly, evolutionary trajectories would also inform literary-historical analyses. Consider, for instance, Schwienhorst-Schönberger's suggestion of a core of collections of secular, casuistic laws in 21:12 and 21:18–22:13, secondarily enlarged in 21:31-36* and subsequently augmented in various stages in their context through Israelite schools of scribes into a context of theology. In this context, laws on debt slavery laws and altar laws (20:24-26*; 21:2-11) were placed in front of CC, and other laws were inserted, such as 21:13-17, 20-27*, 30; 22:1-2, 9-10, 15-16. A Dtr redaction interpreted CC in light of the Ten Commandments (Exod 20:23; 22:19b; 23:13) and adjusted it to Deuteronomy; see L. Schwienhorst-Schönberger, *Das Bundesbuch (Ex 20,22–23,33)* (Berlin: de Gruyter, 1990), 234–38.

18. E. Otto, *Wandel der Rechtsbegründungen in der Gesellschaftsgeschichte des antiken Israel. Eine Rechtsgeschichte des „Bundesbuches" Ex XX 22–XXIII 13* (Leiden: Brill, 1988), 2 (my translation), cf. 65–66.

Otto assumes analogous theories of an evolution when he describes the development of law from small collections of cuneiform laws to large collections; in this particular case, the corresponding evolution of laws about private conflicts. These small collections about private conflicts, suggests Otto, constitute the core of the legislation of CC in its current form. At their basis is kinship law. These small collections included the quintessential forms of firstly casuistic sentences that would have originated from inter-kin-conflict resolution, together with secondly apodictic laws such as the prohibitives, as they are also known from the Decalogue, and furthermore death sentences, curses and incest prohibitions which intended to secure norms through sanctions within a kinship group. Thirdly, and finally, laws on cultic affairs that had first been collected in two small collections were added.[19] Kinship-based law thus marks the point of origin in an evolutionary theory of biblical law.

These two examples of Boecker and Otto illustrate the relevance which scholars of law assign to kinship structure for the reconstruction of legal thought and for the redaction of biblical law respectively.[20] In both distinct theories, kinship law relates to a social reality that has left its vestiges in laws from later periods. With these two factors the relevance of kinship structure for legal thought or its relevance for the redaction of biblical law clarified, such scholars can then place into view related additional factors pertaining to compositional determinants. For instance, in the context of an evolutionary theory, they determine the purpose of law collections for scribal education, comparable to cuneiform law collections from Eshnunna or of the Old Babylonian law of Hammurapi.

---

19. Otto suggests the core of the CC composition consists of two collections, each one itself composed of two sub-collections that include in the first case a law of death within a lineage or kin (Exod 21:12-17), cases of physical injury (Exod 22:18-32) with the talionic command and, finally, property law (Exod 21:33–22:14). Including a programmatic priestly-theological reworking in 20:24–22:26* as a law of the royal God Yahweh, this first collection is one of the two oldest roots of CC that urges protection of and solidarity with the weak.

20. Rather than arguing for a structure of the laws based on pre-existing collections, E. Otto sought to elucidate the final collection of CC as developed out of a twofold set of collections of laws. First, Exod. 21:12–22:19a; 23:1-8, which was bookended by a six- or seven-law collection about slavery in 21:2-11; 23:10-12. Its two core units go back to two independent collections of law in 20:24-26; 21:2–22:6* (collection I). Collection II is a compilation of laws that puts the divine privilege in the center, namely in the six- or seven-law structure (22:28–23:12) under the assumption of a divine selection for Yahweh (Exod. 22:28-29; 23:10-12) that serves the purpose to support a collection of rules of procedural law in 23:1-3, 6-8, including the command to love an enemy (vv. 4-5). See E. Otto, *Das Gesetz des Mose* (Darmstadt: Wissenschaftliche Buchgesellschaft, 2007), 122–23; and, in more detail, Otto, *Wandel*, 12–53; and Otto, "Book of the Covenant," in *The Oxford Encyclopedia of the Bible and Law*, ed. B. A. Strawn (Oxford: Oxford University Press, 2015), 1:68–77.

This study ascertains the continuous relevance of kinship structure in legal thought, including other aspects that inform it, such as honor–shame concepts, as an essential backdrop of much of biblical law and details their changing facets across periods and traditions.[21] It traces feud-like systems of legal dispute between individuals at the local level in the kinship-based, segmentary societies of Israel and Judah at a point in time when centralized law likely also played a role in particular fields. It challenges both the reconstructions of legal institutions of Israel and Judah along a theory of an evolutionary arc and the understanding that feuding on the local level would by default be in tension with other forms of adjudication. Functional approaches to conflict settlement that draw from legal anthropology excavate out the various developments of conflict settlement patterns in the sources with more accuracy than evolutionary theories that associate kinship-based law with a more archaic stage of legal thought.

Generally speaking, ideal-typical reconstructions of the development and the arrangement of Deuteronomic law have associated to some extent kinship law as pertinent to a more archaic phase of legal development. Evolutionary theories of Deuteronomic law, while often more complex than those seeking to describe CC, still tend to be informed by the overall notion of an increasingly strengthened centralized legal system.[22] In other ways, too, reconstructions of biblical law may be prone to preconceived evolutionary notions. Such notions necessarily inform, for instance, how the legal corpus of Deuteronomy to a large extent "updates" law from CC.[23]

While source-critical analyses allow scholars to determine how judicial reflection and conflict settlement forms may be reflected in law collections, they also presuppose and develop evolutionary models of historical judicial institutions. For instance, reconstructions of the history of biblical law seem to perceive Deuteronomy's legislation against the backdrop of a rule of the Judean kings rather than kinship law. In Otto's view, Deuteronomy in its core presents itself as a program of brotherly solidarity and a form of religious identity with the law of cult centralization in 12:13-27, that is followed by a request for mutual loyalty among community members in Deut 13:2-12* and a corresponding part in the

---

21. The impact of kinship-based contexts becomes more fully evident when considering individual laws against their societal backdrop. See also the cultural context approach of Pilch, *Cultural Life Setting*, 203–204.

22. On the origin of the law of Deuteronomy with either Levitical priestly circles, prophetic circles or scribal circles at the royal court that would best explain the overlap with wisdom tradition, see D. I. Block, "Deuteronomic Law," in Strawn, ed., *The Oxford Encyclopedia of the Bible and Law*, 1:182–95, here 184.

23. The specific assumptions about the authority of the preceding text in comparison to the following text are a complex field. See, for instance, M. Fishbane, *Biblical Interpretation in Ancient Israel* (Oxford: Oxford University Press, 1985), 5–19, and on the scope and content of biblical law as factor in the emergence of exegesis, 91–106.

1. Introduction

curses of 28:15, 20-44*.[24] In this redaction-critical analysis, cult centralization and unrestrained loyalty to Yahweh serve as the polemic counter-program to the contemporary Assyrian ideology of the empire and as the hermeneutical keys for the collection of laws in which the altar law from CC in Exodus is now replaced with the centralization law.[25]

That said, a caveat of this study are the many historical contexts of laws that it largely brackets out. Consider, for instance, the process of the Davidic dynasty's central structures as it developed a system of courts in major Judean cities and how and when these courts would have become active in conflict settlement.[26] Ideal-typical histories of law seek to embed this centralizing process into larger evolutionary theories, suggesting the gradual loss of the relevance of local kinship structure, with laws prior to this point in time leaving room for a more dominant local kinship structure, while assuming after the installation of central courts an adjudication through professional judges. Before the installation of central courts, the scarcely developed central institutions in Judah would have been incapable to regulate consistent forms of feud and barely could have managed the eruptions of violence among Judean citizens. This historical scenario thus essentially perceives feuding as a conflict settlement mechanism typical for a period in which more "archaic" kinship structures have gained dominance that would again become more relevant after the decay of the monarchy.[27] Alternatively, scholars

---

24. Otto, *Gesetz des Mose*, 127. For more detail on the interweaving of social ethics, family law and legal procedure in a fan-concatenation in Deuteronomy, see E. Otto, *Deuteronomium 12,1–23,15* (Freiburg: Herder, 2016), 1526 on 16:18–21:23; 1786 on 22:1–24:5; and E. Otto, *Deuteronomium 23:16–34:12* (Freiburg: Herder, 2017), 1830 on 24:6–25:12. On the arrangement, see W. S. Morrow, "The Arrangement of the Original Version of Deuteronomy According to Eckart Otto," *ZABR* 25 (2019): 195–206, here 196–97 and 201–202.

25. At the same time, Otto also mentions the dissolution of traditional kinship structures, the Assyrian crisis in the late eighth century, and subsequently in 701 BCE, which builds the backdrop of Deuteronomy's development of its fictive kinship ideology; cf. Otto, *Gesetz des Mose*, 133.

26. Cf. the installation of professional judges in Deut 16:18–17:13. In a source-critical reading Gertz concludes that arguably under Josiah, the deuteronomic legislator, installed a secular professional group of judges (Deut 16:18aαb; 17:8 [without בֵּין־דָּם...רִיבֹת], 9 [without הַלְוִיִּם], 10a, 12abα) in order to adjust the judicial system of conflict settlement in the capital Jerusalem to the larger territory of Judah. Therefore, the law mentions provisions about authorities of the community, namely the court secretaries (שֹׁטְרִים) and the judges (שֹׁפְטִים) that are installed in the entrenched provincial cities of Judah (שְׁעָרֶיךָ) in order to decide cases there. Their relationship to traditional kinship authorities in the second half of the seventh-century Judah remains unclear; cf. J. C. Gertz, *Die Gerichtsorganisation Israels im deuteronomischen Gesetz* (Göttingen: Vandenhoeck & Ruprecht, 1994), 28, 228–29.

27. For instance, Gertz, *Gerichtsorganisation*, 231–32, as a result of a source-critical reading of the elders laws, interprets them as texts for religious edification that

of law would describe a development of legal thought and procedure along an urban–rural divide and associate vengeance patterns with "the clan structure" in rural areas, assuming they were in stark contrast to "adjudication" in court as "not clan based at all. On the contrary, it is unabashedly urban, with no hint at a role for the clan as a unit."[28] The underlying assumptions of this urban–rural divide and the coupling of rural areas with the rulership of clans in contrast to centralized law in urban spaces must be questioned.

The current attention of legal studies to kinship-based law and feuding clearly invites a comprehensive synthesis of the history of feuding and of legal institutions in Israel and Judah. Legal anthropological approaches to the study of law have yielded much explanatory value in approaches to other ancient Near Eastern cultures of law. More modestly, the goal of the present approach is to specify the prevalence of structured feuding patterns, while presupposing their use alongside with and through other institutions, for instance, local courts.[29] Suffice for now to refer to two areas that support the systemic relevance of feuding, namely, first, ancient Near Eastern and, second, classical Athenian law. Studies in ancient Near Eastern law have included a plethora of legal documents, in particular court and trial records, that widen the perspective on feuding elements in conflict settlement. These sources show how constructs of enmity between individuals shape the backdrop of legal thought that may allow for more complex relationships between "adjudication" and mechanisms of kinship-based feuding.[30] Indeed, the absence of institutions of adjudication in CC, for instance, has led scholars to assume that the participial provision in the laws of CC reflected a law that was essential to secure norms for survival of the family (kin), while

consequently do not reflect historical institutions of the elders in the jurisdiction of Judah under Josiah, but rather reflect the kinship leaders' gain of authority of adjudication after the fall of the monarchy.

28. R. Westbrook, "Reflections on the Law of Homicide in the Ancient World," in *Ex Oriente Lex: Near Eastern Influences on Ancient Greek and Roman Law*, ed. D. Lyons, K. Raaflaub, and R. Westbrook (Baltimore: Johns Hopkins University Press, 2015), 194–219, here 213; originally *Maarav* 13 (2006): 143–47, 152–73.

29. Legal anthropology has described models of legal pluralism in which societies would concurrently avail themselves of diverse types of conflict settlement that it finds are practically not mutually exclusive; cf., on conflict settlement among shepherds in Sardinia, Ruffini, "Disputing over Livestock." In other cases, local communities continued feuding patterns through legal institutions created by a colonial power; see, for instance, Wilson, *Feuding, Conflict and Banditry*, 14–16, 265–93.

30. See the examples in G. Pfeifer and N. Grotkamp, ed., *Außergerichtliche Konfliktlösung in der Antike. Beispiele aus drei Jahrtausenden* (Frankfurt: Max Planck Institute for European Legal History, 2017). With regard to the biblical evidence, CC mentions virtually no institutions, with the exception of the *hapax legomenon* פלילים (Exod 21:22) and the deity as adjudicative authority (Exod 22:7-8); B. Wells, "Competing or Complementary? Judges and Elders in Biblical and Neo-Babylonian Law," *ZABR* 16 (2010): 77–104.

casuistic law was then attached to inter-family disputes that were brought to local courts. The local court was originally the institution of conflict settlement between different local kin – it had no coercive powers; rather, its verdicts had the status of recommendations. Implementing sanctions would be reserved to the *pater familias*, suggests Otto.[31] Positioning himself close to Otto, B. S. Jackson frames the relevance of both apodictic and casuistic laws for conflict settlement as processes of "self-execution," conceiving of law in a less institutional manner than Otto, without the mediation of any court as a third party, but instead as realized in "pre-institutional forms of dispute settlement."[32] The current discourse on the potential modes of implementation of biblical law is of utmost relevance for the reconstruction of conflict settlement. Kinship-based communities in Ancient Israel supposedly would affirm the emergence of local modes of inter-kin conflict settlement, a setting that strongly suggests that this included feuding mechanisms between kin.[33]

For good reason, the questions about the nature of the jurisdiction and the coercive power of the kin in biblical law are particularly relevant for the case of homicide law. Also, the inclusion of ancient Near Eastern law within the critical consideration of these texts has added to the complexity and to the clarification of conflict-settlement patterns in kinship-based societies. Consider P. Barmash's comparative approach to conflicts around homicide, which she labels as "feuding patterns." Indeed, a more comprehensive and comparative understanding of feuding as a conflict settlement pattern of kinship-based societies illustrates many of the specifics of dispute settlement that are also extent in Mesopotamian legal texts and trial records. By way of these records, taken with a view to patterns, Barmash can then demonstrate how legal texts attest to the complex local realities that may differ from impressions primarily gained on the basis of collections of laws.[34] Barmash paints a nuanced, complex picture of feuding patterns, namely

31. E. Otto, *Wandel*, 31–33, 63 and 64, on the lack of coercive powers Exod 22:15-16 and see below in Chapter 2, under 1.

32. B. S. Jackson, *Wisdom-laws: A Study of the Mishpatim of Exodus 21:1–22:16* (Oxford: Oxford University Press, 2006), 58. Otto, conceiving of the legal institution as a third party, otherwise confirms the overlap between both on the relevance of biblical law in conflict settlement without assuming any notion of a "positive" law; cf. E. Otto, "Gesellschaftsstruktur in der Hebräischen Bibel," in *Strafe und Strafrecht in den antiken Welten unter Berücksichtigung von Todesstrafe, Hinrichtung und peinlicher Befragung*, ed. R. Rollinger, M. Lange, and H. Barta (Wiesbaden: Harrassowitz, 2012), 233–47, 235 n. 12.

33. The historical reconstruction of developments of courts in the epoch of the monarchy must be bracketed out; cf. the brief overview on how professional judges and the local elders may have functioned simultaneously, in Wells, "Competing or Complementary?," 78–80, and note in particular reconstructions of legal pluralism (n. 29 above).

34. P. Barmash, *Homicide in the Biblical World* (Cambridge: Cambridge University Press, 2005); see, in particular, her legal anthropological approach to feuding as it applies to biblical conflict settlement (23–27).

on detailing the relevance of the kin, and its juxtaposition to what she in a dichotomy refers to as "state control." Driving home two characteristic aspects of feuding, its local nature and its rule-bound essence,[35] Barmash describes essentials of the procedure, detailing the underlying legal thought of blood feud.[36] She identifies the avenger of blood, a close family member (Deut 19:5; Josh 20:5; Num 35:12), as the pivotal remedying institution for homicide and a standard element of the feuding mechanism.[37] Already the terminological equivalent to

35. Barmash, *Homicide*, 23.

36. Barmash's nuanced and detailed description of interface between central authority and feuding as seen in trial records sheds new light on various historical contexts of conflict settlement. The overall synthesis, namely the assumption of a stark contrast between kin-based social structures in ancient Israel and the development of only limited elements of centralization point to the relevance of kinship law; see Barmash, *Homicide*, 45–47. At the same time, the approach is not free from stereotypes, for instance, when Barmash contrasts Israelite law as kinship-based against the more "urban" structures mirrored in Mesopotamian law, concluding, for instance, that Mesopotamian law would (typically) allow revenge outside the victim's family (Code of Hammurapi 1, see Barmash, *Homicide*, 27–28), and then suggesting that Mesopotamian trial records show differences in their handling of homicide when comparing primarily urban centers of Mesopotamian society, represented in late third-millennium Ur-III documents, with early second-millennium Old Babylonian records of legal handling of homicide; see also earlier P. Barmash, "Blood Feud and State Control: Differing Legal Institutions for the Remedy of Homicide During the Second and First Millennia B.C.E.," *JNES* 63 (2004): 183–99, here 184. In spite of the small sample of documents, Barmash assumes "the Mesopotamian adjudication of homicide differed radically from that in biblical Israel" mainly because of her perception of much of Mesopotamia culture as an "urban and centralized" space (Barmash, "Blood Feud," 199; idem, *Homicide*, 45), where, in general, the victim's family had a claim but, in the end, would have to give in to the state authorities, while the legislation in Deut 19, Num 35, and Josh 20 would seemingly suggest a predominantly feuding character of conflicts around homicide in Ancient Israel; see Barmash, "Blood Feud," 194. Her understanding of "urbanism" as "organized hierarchically along territorial or political lines, not along lines of kinship" (Barmash, "Blood Feud," 194) that uses different forms of homicide legislation may overestimate the scattered evidence from the cases. Another caveat of the comparative perspective is a lack of equivalents of biblical trial records. The notable exception of the text from Meṣad Ḥashavyahu corrects the record to some extent. The unremarkable character of the case of a stolen garment demonstrates that petitions written for a claimant seeking to retrieve an object by means of accusing a thief in a hierarchic system were not uncommon. As a consequence, institutional help with conflict settlement may not always have been uncommon in Israelite contexts either; cf. the interpretation of the ostracon as an extrajudicial petition of the document by F. W. Dobbs-Allsopp, "The Genre of the Meṣad Ḥashavyahu Ostracon," *BASOR* 296 (1994): 49–55. Clearly, the case demonstrates aspects of the administration of conflict settlement.

37. Barmash, "Blood Feud," 185, and see the affirmation on feuding in the review of P. Barmash, *Homicide* by B. Wells, *JNES* 69 (2010): 102–103, esp. 102.

the "blood avenger" in Mesopotamian law, *bēl damê*, used for both the killer or for the representative from the claimant's family, points to the analogy of feuding in Mesopotamian contexts. Barmash interprets the equivocal use of the term for both functions as one sign of the clans' complex involvement in homicide conflict settlement procedure.[38]

The present study agrees with Barmash's consideration on feuding in Mesopotamian contexts. Beyond the lexicographic support for feuding structures, source documents on ancient Near Eastern legal procedure also point to feuding mechanisms in conflict settlement. Consider by way of example, from among the vast evidence, the specific debt obligation after a homicide case ADD 618 from the Neo-Assyrian context, in which the (original) killer was himself killed in revenge and yet the debt of blood money owed now to the first killer's village is still requested from the second killer's kinsmen. The case illustrates the authority of the clans in blood-feuding mechanisms allowing for nuanced patterns of responses of the two parties in conflict settlement. The victim's clan could decide whether they would focus on retribution in money or on taking revenge. ADD 321 is another example for this alternative that locates the decision on the level of the kin: "(2-6') It is now mutually agreed: the one who shall give Amat-adimri, the daughter of Attar-qāmu, to Shamash-kēnu-uṣur, the son of Samaku (who was killed) in place of blood(-money) and wash the blood way. (6'-8') If he does not give the woman, they will kill him on top of Samaku's grave..."[39] This text demonstrates again the regulating power of clans to mediate between exchanges themselves, deciding the manner of recompense for vengeance. Cases from the Middle Assyrian laws likewise illustrate the role of the victim's family within these exchanges.[40]

The biblical record confirms these results and indicates similar scenarios of homicide legislation in which the parties would negotiate a payment of a

---

38. Barmash, "Blood Feud," 190. The involvement of the royal and central state authorities is found in an Old Babylonian text CT 29 42, which reports a case in which a private individual had originally launched a lawsuit which was then pursued by the authorities. Another case from Neo-Babylonian Uruk, TCL 12 117, is a document about an attempted murder of the royal commissioner of the temple, typically a document that was of interest to the state authorities. In a case from fifteenth-century Alalaḫ, the slayer's property was confiscated by the palace. See the discussion of *Alalaḫ* 17 in Barmash, "Blood Feud," 191.

39. Quoted from Barmash, "Blood Feud," 188.

40. MAL A 10 reserves the right to choose between killing the slayer and enforced payment: "[If either] a man or a woman enters [another man's] house and kills [either a man] or a woman, [they shall hand over] the killers [to the head of the household]. If he chooses, he shall take [their property]. And if there is [nothing of value to give from the house] of the killers, either a son [or a daughter]..." quoted from Barmash, "Blood Feud," 189. The families could choose between a penalty of either execution or compensation. As Barmash indicates, it was the right of the family and the centralized legal institutions had to respect their decision; Barmash, "Blood Feud," 189.

ransom in lieu of extradition of clan members. Consider, for instance, the explicit exclusion of ransom (כפר) in Num 35:31 which points to the general availability of this option. In the conflict between the Gibeonites and David, the extradition of the seven sons of Saul in 2 Sam 21:1-6 may serve as a textbook example for two hallmarks of enmity in kinship-based societies. The negotiations between the feuding parties about the expiation after homicide illustrate the typical flexibility and variation in the game of challenge and riposte. The conflict between David and the Gibeonites also demonstrates the principle of heritability of private enmity from one generation of the clans to the next, as the Gibeonites' claim originally refers to the blood guilt of the house of Saul.

Barmash's reconstruction of the wide-ranging use of feuding patterns thus merits serious attention, and some of the subsequent repudiation of her results from scholars in biblical law demonstrates their reluctance to fully acknowledge the relevance of feuding in ancient Israel and Judah. See, for instance, the criticism based on the notion that biblical law would *de facto* limit structures of feuding to the field of homicide law, whereas the "laws of P and D on other serious crimes such as wounding, rape, and adultery rigorously, at least on the surface, exclude any reference to private initiative and revenge. Their forum is the local urban court and their language of punishment is impersonal or by collective action, as if the clan did not exist."[41] This *argumentum e silentio* against feuding patterns is indicative of a tendency in the reconstruction of biblical legal thought that downplays the relevance of feuding patterns based on their alleged absence in law collections. The criticism neglects, however, the fact that such patterns inform not only blood feud, but beyond, these patterns of private enmity widely underlie forms of conflict settlement in their setting of kinship-based societies. Typically, their social setting would inform laws and for this very reason it would not be expected to always appear explicitly in the law collections.[42]

Having thus pointed to the fundamental relevance of feuding patterns as Barmash highlights them, it must also be noted that legal anthropology suggests that feuding patterns may remain in place throughout periods of centralization and in urban societies in antiquity. Barmash's alleged contrast between a Mesopotamian "centralized, bureaucratic, and specialized"[43] urbanism which inhibits local kin-based feuding patterns on the one hand, and local feuding in a decentralized Israel on the other, may not be free from bias either. Interestingly, this contrast that undergirds Barmash's analysis is in tension with legal anthropological studies and studies in Attic law. Reconstructions of conflict settlement in the city democracy of Classical Athens that are informed by legal anthropology

---

41. Westbrook, "Reflections," 213.

42. Notably, in a review of Barmash, Westbrook refers to 2 Sam 21 by way of pointing instead to the ruler's general capacity of negotiating between ransom or humans as "suitable objects for revenge" (Westbrook, "Reflections," 205), rather than pointing to the extradition as an obvious example for typical revenge-driven mechanism in kinship-based societies.

43. Barmash, *Homicide*, 44.

point to patterns of interpersonal feuding that by default would also use the courts as institutions of the mechanisms of dispute settlement. This use of court proceedings for dispute settlement in Athens fundamentally challenges evolutionary theories of law. Courts may in general be associated with an objective "rule of law," yet the use of courts for feuding purposes fundamentally questions this notion. Consequently, scholars of Attic law have been rejecting evolutionary legal theory that would associate the famous Aristotelian idiom of "the rule of law" with a seemingly self-evident trust in the city's judicial institutions. David Cohen even refers to the contested interpretation of the idiomatic rule of law in antiquity itself.[44] Indeed, studies of individual cases of conflict settlement widely argue that feud-like structures constitute a hallmark not only of the archaic legal system in Athens but also beyond. The readings of Attic fifth–fourth-century forensic oratory, including violent conflict settlement modes, detail how feuding conflict settlement remained in place at a point in time when Athens had courts as institutions of litigation.[45] The larger defining structures and the organizing principles of Athenian agonistic society, such as an honor–shame value system, suggest that, generally speaking, conflict settlement in Athens is best described in analogy to feuding. This insight significantly shapes Cohen's understanding of dispute resolution between private enemies. His clarification of the relationship between institutional feud-like conflicts and other centralized legal institutions rejects the notion of law as "some impersonal truth-finding mechanism, which 'evolves' to produce 'justice' from the chaos of dispute."[46] Rather, societies and their leadership created legal systems that served multiple purposes, from settling disputes to fueling the escalation of lawsuits, from ideals of social justice to the strife for economic superiority. In this system, the courts in Athens may be understood as yet another forum in which community members would pursue their feuds.

---

44. In an unusual interpretation of the idiomatic Aristotelian "rule of law," D. Cohen, *Law, Violence, and Community in Classical Athens* (Cambridge: Cambridge University Press, 1995), 35, suggests that it does not programmatically exclude kinship feud in Athenian political theory. In his view Aristotle's understanding of the nature of political community includes the ability of human beings to form political associations (*Politics* 1253a10-18) and to scrutinize one's own acts from a moral point of view as either good or bad in a discourse. Without such a discourse, communities cannot endure. "On the other hand, justice, which is judgment concerning the just, is an ordering (*taxis*) of the political community" (Aristotle, *Politics*, 1253a32-40; cf. Cohen, *Law*, 37), while "order" (*taxis*) needed to be implemented in order to keep unscrupulous and savage tendencies of humanity at bay. "The word taxis implies a regulation or arrangement, that is an artificial order that is imposed to control that element of human nature which tends towards excess and savagery" (Cohen, *Law*, 37).

45. This is in spite of their lack of literal quotes from laws that have been omitted in the speeches' transmission history.

46. Cohen, *Law*, 23.

Consequently, conflict settlement that follows feuding patterns is not limited to a particular stage in an evolutionary pattern, nor is it a typically rural behavior that could be contrasted to the adherence to the principles of a rule of law.

The insight into concurrent use of feuding patterns through other institutions of conflict settlement, such as public trials in Athens, is in itself a significant result of legal historical research. It illustrates the concurrent relevance of feuding patterns in a polity together with established courts. And it demonstrates that feuding patterns would determine the acting out of enmity as concise, adaptable social constructs that, in the case of Athens, would inform the reality of an agonistic society. This conceptualization of enmity in antiquity in a feuding society offers itself as a potential analogy for other legal traditions. Fifth- to fourth-century BCE conflict settlement in Athens is even more instructive as the cases of forensic oratory as sources of trial procedure substantiate and nuance the social construct of private enmity and the concise hallmarks of the legal status of enemies. What is more, the principal lexicographic distinction between πολέμιοι, "public enemies, enemies of the state, the enemy (in war)," and ἐχθροί, ἔχθρα, "private enemies/enmity," helps to clarify matters in Judah and Israel. Biblical legal texts implicitly also draw this distinction between public and private enemies, independent from the use of the same Hebrew root איב which serves as designation for either category of opponent[47] depending on the respective context. Furthermore, Attic forensic oratory demonstrates the continuous effect of the feuding character of enmity constellations on the city democracy as the public square. Since Athenian trial procedure showcases the construct of private enmity, it offers itself as a model for clarifying both legal procedure and conflict settlement mechanisms as they play out at the interface of the private dispute in the public square.[48] In general, it illustrates how in an urban space feuding principles could remain in place and could permeate and dominate trial procedure in the courts.

4. *Hatred and Enmity in the Old Testament: A Proposal*

Enemies unequivocally describe their opponents as vicious and unfair. In individual scenarios of conflict settlement, private enemies accuse each other of having committed a variety of different acts and of availing themselves with an array of specific malevolent behaviors. Narrative tradition boldly mirrors these

---

47. D. D. Phillips, *Avengers of Blood. Homicide in Athenian Law and Custom from Draco to Demosthenes* (Stuttgart: Franz Steiner, 2008), 15. On the private–public distinction, see D. Cohen, "Crime, Punishment and the Rule of Law in Classical Athens," in *The Cambridge Companion to Greek Law* ed. M. Gagarin, D. Cohen (Cambridge: Cambridge University Press, 2005), 211–35, esp. 214–19.

48. The present approach assumes a structural analogy between concepts of private enmity in various historical contexts. On the influence of concepts known from Greek law in the late Persian-period biblical law, see Chapter 4.

patterns of hateful behavior between opponents. Beyond that, it is telling that the Hebrew language offers a plethora of terms for personal opponents. Four variants dominate the multi-faceted lexicography for enmity in the Hebrew Bible: איב ("enemy"),[49] שנא ("hater"), צר ("challenger"); in individual laments one may add רדף ("persecutor"). Rather than deriving a theory of enmity directly from these terms[50] and by way of exclusion of narrative[51] and poetic[52] tradition, this study evaluates the Hebrew lexicography on the basis of a socio-historical theory of private enmity. It seeks to reconstruct hatred or enmity, using these terms interchangeably as designations of a social construct with its legal implications.[53] It does so in light of legal historical considerations, which must be bracketed

49. The Greek translation (LXX) renders איב usually as ἔχθρος.

50. For a lexicographic study, see A. J. Riley, *Hate in the Ancient Near East: A Lexical and Contextual Analysis* (Piscataway NJ: Gorgias, 2017).

51. Both poetic and narrative sources are beyond the scope of this study. Suffice it to point to the complexity of the compositional framework of narratives on enmity and consider the example of the narratives of pursuit with the intent of homicide (1 Sam 24:8-21; 26:17-25); cf. J. Burnside, "Flight of the Fugitives: Rethinking the Relationship between Biblical Law (Exodus 21:12-14) and the Davidic Succession Narrative (1 Kings 1–2)," *JBL* (2010): 418–31.

52. The separation of the general, more common features of the terms for enemy from their more specific features are a burning question in the exegesis of the Psalms of the Individual that this study cannot address. The lexicography for enmity echoes the hallmarks of enmity of public declaration, of a flexibility and variation when acting out enmity, as well as reciprocity of actions between enemies; escalation of the conflict, its expansion onto other society members. A critical task is separating the common features of the terms for an opponent in the Psalms from their more specific, legal features. The lexicography for enemies has often been assessed in detailed lists, see already H. Gunkel and J. Begrich, *Introduction to the Psalms: The Genres of the Religious Lyric of Israel*, trans. J. D. Nogalski (Macon GA: Mercer, 1998), Chapter 6: "Individual Complaint Songs"; see furthermore the comprehensive study of O. Keel, *Feinde und Gottesleugner. Studien zum Image der Widersacher in den Individualpsalmen* (Stuttgart: Katholisches Bibelwerk, 1969), 93–98; cf. B. Janowski, *Arguing with God: A Theological Anthropology of the Psalms* (Louisville: Westminster John Knox, 2013), 97–127. Unsurprisingly, the lexicography for enmity in individual laments poses some interpretive resistance. Terminologies typically overlap in poetry that is built on the principle of parallelism. Keel, in his 1969 hallmark study *Feinde und Gottesleugner*, suggested two distinct semantic groups of designations, the צדיק/רשע related lexicographic group and the צר/איב group; yet a recent investigation into רשע in the Psalms is lacking. Possibly the two distinct groups simply represent subsequent phases of enmity terminology. The רשע-type in some instances is seemingly a secondarily applied derogatory label for an individual that was seen in contrast to the "pious/just" (צדיק).

53. For reasons of space it largely excludes its opposite, "love, friendship" (אהב), but see Chapter 5 on Lev. 19:18; see also the thorough study of S. M. Olyan, *Friendship in the Hebrew Bible* (New Haven: Yale University Press, 2017).

out from further examination for the purposes of this study; specifically, the aforementioned clarification of scholarship on the orators' forensic speeches from Classical Athens about the nature of hate as the construct of a social status in which an individual would find themselves when in conflict with another community member.[54]

In summary, the status of enmity was known in the local communities in Israel and, comparable to reconstructions of this status from Attic law including the forensic orators, it (1) implied a form of public declaration or overtly acting out enmity.[55] Furthermore, (2) it included acting out enmity in ways that allowed for flexibility and variation, i.e., opponents could act out their enmity in various ways. In addition, (3) acting out enmity was a reciprocal process and (4) the reciprocity between the enemies usually escalated and could reach its climax in one party's attempt to kill their foe. Finally, (5) private enmity was transitive: a person at enmity with another would naturally expect their friends' solidarity.[56]

These five hallmarks of enmity provide the coordinates along which we can define the nature of enmity in biblical law. Enmity is a social construct that is essential to the patterns of acting out dispute. Given the nature of the documents of biblical law, for methodological reasons, this study describes the development of the social construct of enmity on the basis of the sources in the more narrow field of the collections of biblical law. However, it reflects in certain cases on whether and how the construct of enmity may or may not correspond to actual legal practice and it attempts to reconstruct the social life in ancient Israel. It leaves a comprehensive reconstruction to further studies and aims at a more

---

54. This is based on Phillips, *Avengers*, 21–26. Numerous studies on Athenian law have drawn attention to the litigiousness in the city's culture as a facet of an *agonistic* ethos. The reconstructions are based on both law collections and to a large extent the fifth/ fourth-century Attic forensic oratory of Demosthenes, Antiphon, Lysias, Aeschines, and others that allow for the reconstruction of judicial procedure; see S. C. Todd, *Lysias*, trans. S. C. Todd (Austin, TX: University of Texas, 2000); idem, "Law and Oratory in Athens," in *The Cambridge Companion to Ancient Greek Law*, ed. M. Gagarin and D. Cohen (Cambridge: Cambridge University Press, 2005), 97–111; Cohen, *Law*, 61–118; cf. the critical voice of E. M. Harris, "Feuding or the Rule of Law? The Nature of Litigation in Classical Athens: An Essay in Legal Sociology," in *Symposion 2001. Vorträge zur griechtischen und hellenistischen Rechtsgeschichte (Evanston Illinois, 5.-8. September 2001)*, ed. R. Wallace and M. Gagarin (Vienna: Verlag der Österreichischen Akademie der Wissenschaften, 2005), 125–41; M. R. Christ, *The Litigious Athenian* (Baltimore: John Hopkins University Press, 1998), 14–48, on litigation practice in Athens, and 160–92, on private quarrels and public disputes; Phillips, *Avengers*, 13–131. See also the essays in *The Attic Orators*, ed. E. Carawan (Oxford: Oxford University Press, 2007). Further sources include comedy and the fourth-century prose of Xenophon, Isocrates, Plato, and Aristotle.

55. Equally, their public reconciliation would officially terminate their enmity.

56. Besides kin members, friends are demanded to join in the fight against a private opponent. As a consequence of this transitivity, private enmity presented an inherent threat to potentially split an entire community in two confrontational camps.

limited goal. Through the consideration of an array of legal texts it substantiates the tangible legal implications of the social construct of private enmity in biblical law, analogous to being married, demoted or divorced, imprisoned or being impure. Specifically, the prominent variations of homicide law in CC, Deuteronomy and priestly law collections substantiate the backdrop of private enemy relations in a kinship-based society. Consequently, they largely shape the course of this study.

Chapters 2–5, largely independent from each other, sketch out the development of the status of private enmity in biblical law. These studies reconstruct the conceptualization of enmity, injury and revenge and trace how the construct of enmity (and friendship) informs the sources. For pragmatic reasons, the study proceeds along the established source critical order, starting with the CC, continuing with Deuteronomic law and ending with (late) priestly law in Numbers and Lev 19 (H).[57] A plethora of further legal sources would lend themselves to reconstruct developments and to trace the transformations of the construct of enmity throughout biblical law. The current approach limits itself to a small, exemplary reading of a selection of relevant laws rather than a comprehensive coverage of the evidence of private enmity throughout the biblical sources.

Chapter 2 presents a historical reconstruction of hateful relationships between individuals. Much of the re-conceptualization of the status of private enmity is done on the basis of laws that mostly presuppose this social construct without naming it explicitly. It reconstructs the concept of private enmity based on the selection of the earliest sources of biblical law, thus synthesizing this status as it informs an almost random collection of biblical laws. Analyzing the mechanisms of feuding that shape the background of enmity between individuals therefore uncovers the implicit modes of deliberation on private enmity in such diverse areas as homicide law (Exod 21:12-14), burglary and the killing of a nocturnal

---

57. The material for the reconstruction of feuding mechanisms in Ancient Israel and Judah is ample and includes, besides actual laws in law collections, also narratives that this study, for reasons of space, brackets out. Consider narratives reflecting legal history, for instance, at the time of establishment of Judah's central institutions. For the use of narratives as sources for the reconstruction of legal historical developments, see, for instance, Boecker, *Law*, 27–52, or the presentation of narrative sources in D. Patrick, *Old Testament Law* (Atlanta: John Knox, 1984), 189–99. See the distinction between the ideal/typical narrative genres of precedents, juridical parables and legal narratives in R. Westbrook and B. Wells, *Everyday Law in Biblical Israel* (Louisville: Westminster John Knox, 2009), 13–14; F. R. Magdalene and B. Wells, "Law in the Writings," in Strawn, *The Oxford Encyclopedia of the Bible and Law*, 1:485–95, and, in the work, A. Bartor, "Narrative," 2:125–33. Note, for instance, the theme of enmity and feuding plays a role in framing Deuteronomic law as part of an egalitarian concept of the shared experience of the exodus from the slavery in Egypt (Deut 5:6, 15; 6:12, 21; 7:8; 8:14; 13:6, 11; 15:15; 16:12; 24:18, 22 and others); the redemption through Yahweh (Deut. 4:32-40; 11:2-4; 13:6, 11; 15:15; 16:1; 20:1; 21:8; 24:18; 26:8); the endurance of trial at the Horeb (Deut 9:7-12); and the trying in the desert (Deut 8:2-16; 11:5-6; cf. 4:3-4; cf. 29:4-5).

thief (Exod 21:37–22:2), the deposit laws (21:34–22:14), exhortations to fairness in legal procedure (23:1-3, 6-8), and case law relating to private enemies (23:4-5).

Three subsequent chapters describe ways in which biblical law generates significant shifts in the concept of hate and enmity. Chapter 3 analyzes homicide law in Deut 19:1-12, the construct of brotherly behavior (Deut 22:1-4), marriage law (22:13-21), and inheritance law (21:15-17). It considers how a later layer in Deuteronomic law programmatically pushes back against the default tendencies of establishing private hate through references to brotherly love. The latter concept claims mutual benevolence as the expected kinship ethos and sets this ethos of brotherly amity against an ubiquity of hate and enmity.

Chapters 4 and 5 clarify the literary-historical and socio-historical contexts of two traditions of priestly law in which the construct of private enmity plays a pivotal role. In Num 35, firstly, a distinct abstract terminology emerges as a way to specifically designate this construct of enmity and hate. The reading reconstructs the relevance of the jurisdiction in the domain of homicide legislation in the polity and its setting in a theocratic concept of this textual layer in Numbers. Chapter 5 reads the programmatic list of prohibitives in Lev 19:11-18 and traces echoes of priestly lexicography and nomenclature and their refined notion of the social status of enmity and its excesses. Leviticus 19:11-18 describe typical behavioral roles when acting out hate or benevolence between opponents, urging to mutual benevolence. The chapter analyzes the compositional aspects of Lev 19 and how H uses its distinct idiosyncratic lexicography of holiness to create a community identity in its socio-historical context. More specifically, it suggests that the posture expected in interactions with community members in 19:11-18 overlaps with rules of close-knit groups that share the tendencies of the community of H to separate itself from surrounding cultures. The ethos of such groups further contextualizes the ban of constellations of private enmity in H in Lev 19:17-18 and helps to further historically anchor Lev 19:11-18 in the contexts of Second Temple Judah.

Chapter 2

"IF TWO ARE QUARRELING WITH EACH OTHER...":
LONG-TERM ENMITY IN THE COVENANT CODE

1. *Enmity in the Covenant Code*

How does the oldest collection of biblical law, the Covenant Code (CC), conceptualize the social status of quarreling opponents and what is its legal relevance? This chapter analyzes laws from CC that lend themselves to reconstruct the relationship between opponents. It probes in what respect CC[1] considers conflict settlement differently from notions of the contemporary social world and its concept of a public–private sphere. Any such reconstruction of social structures through laws faces methodological caveats. First, the problem of how exactly the laws of CC might represent actual social structures and to what extent they are on the other side purely literary representations of social realities that serve the purpose of law to determine degrees of guilt, can only approximately be answered. Biblical law does not offer immediate access to the social structures it presupposes and this study therefore cannot fully reconstruct them. Furthermore, while this study attempts by indirect ways to reconstruct enmity and its structures in CC, the reconstruction of legal thought in CC is by necessity biased insofar as it must presuppose an evolutionary theory of law and legal thought. In the case of CC, this is more evident than in other traditions of biblical law as it is the oldest law collection that, when considered in the context of later development, comes in view as an early stage to later developments. Finally, scholars agree that any considerations about the practices and the practicability of biblical law can be misleading. This study brackets out legal practice, leaving open ways to best determine the relevance of the biblical collections of laws for everyday interaction. Nevertheless, as for any reconstruction of legal thought, one may

---

1. See a brief scholarship Otto, "Book of the Covenant," 68–77; cf. the scholarship reviews in H. Cazelles, *Etudes sur le Code de l'alliance* (Paris: Letouzey et Ané, 1946); Boecker, *Law*, 141–44; Schwienhorst-Schönberger, *Bundesbuch*, 3–22; R. Rothenbusch, *Die kasuistische Rechtssammlung im "Bundesbuch" (Ex 21,2-11.18-22,16)* (Münster: Ugarit Verlag, 2000), 23–91; Jackson, *Wisdom-Laws*, 1–25.

acknowledge some form of practicability of the laws in the sense that they render precise narrative images and can be read as such. Based on semantics and on syntax,[2] laws evoke specific situations and particular constellations between opponents as actors in a social context, constellations that legal anthropology seeks to clarify, for instance, when it considers roles of opponents in a feuding pattern. Consequently, a pivotal question for understanding the laws of CC is their alleged social background.[3]

If set in a kinship-based society, arguably, no centrally authorized jurisdiction such as court-appointed judges would rule on everyday conflicts between individuals. Rather, on the local level, typical institutional and non-institutional contexts of a kinship-based society would have jurisdiction.[4] In such a context, the fear of conflict escalation informs the significance of the fragility of neutral neighborly relationships. Such relationships could easily deteriorate into continuous hostility, ongoing violent confrontation, and, when leading to the death of one of the opponents, escalate into extended feuding.[5] The following readings of selected laws from CC thus in particular seek to determine how

---

2. Cf. the theory that informs Jackson, *Wisdom-Laws*, 25. As will be demonstrated, I assume the semantics and the syntactical structures play a critical role.

3. The present study aligns itself with current critical appraisals of the reconstruction of the origins of the laws of the CC that explain its similarities with other ancient Near Eastern laws as grounded in "general or specific traditions, preserved orally and reflected in inherited legal practice" (D. P. Wright, *Inventing God's Law: How the Covenant Code of the Bible Used and Revised the Laws of Hammurabi* [Oxford: Oxford University Press, 2009], 4). Yet it would not date such practices particularly to the second millennium BCE, nor would it assume cuneiform scribal schools that imported Mesopotamian legal tradition to Syria-Canaan as responsible for disseminating Mesopotamian practices which were subsequently handed down in the first millennium BCE primarily in oral form (Wright, *God's Law*, 4). Rather, the present approach neither assumes that the CC indeed "reflects actual legal practice in Israel or Judah" (Wright, *God's Law*, 5), nor that the Covenant Code depends literally on Mesopotamian law, for instance, of the Code of Hammurapi. It does not demonstrate literary dependence, but instead considers to what extent private enmity between individuals represents a social construct that informs the laws in the Covenant Code, independent from the question whether it also formed the backdrop of the laws of Hammurapi.

4. This has implications on the hermeneutics of biblical law. Far from "positive law" or the notion of "the rule of law," biblical law is relevant to reconstruct legal procedure; cf. the legal hermeneutics in Jackson, *Wisdom-Laws*, 24.

5. Legal anthropology acknowledges the seriousness of this risk; see among others, Wesel's summary on forms of conflict settlement in segmentary societies, along with considerations on conflict settlement among the Nuer and on the elaborate system of conflict settlement among the Lele. Wesel suggests most differences between individuals were seemingly calmed peacefully by way of negotiation and mediation. The reasons for a peaceful ending were, among other things, social pressure as well as the fear of the outbreak of violence; cf. Wesel, *Frühformen*, 329.

laws conceive of the constellation of opponents in a conflict and explain their pacifying tendency. The theoretical basis on which these readings seek to analyze this constellation between two enemies in biblical law is to interpret laws in analogy to "narrative images" to a state of affairs to which the laws relate. The following readings understand the constellations in law as comparable to "the formulation 'narrative typification of action', the social constructs which manifest the universal human inclination towards meaning in narrative form."[6]

The following readings do not presuppose a fundamental evolutionary theory of law. Yet, starting with homicide law, these readings must take as their point of departure one pivotal distinction in legal thought, namely the shift from strict liability to fault-based liability.[7]

This suggests on the level of the alleged source-critical reconstruction of CC, according to current critical readings, that the slayer's intent or premeditation to be the oldest criterion for judging homicide was fault-based liability.[8] Legal history indeed describes the procedural and the institutional development of homicide law in Exod 21:12-14 as an example for the transition from strict

---

6. Jackson, *Wisdom Laws*, 25 n. 115. On the background of this model in semiotic theory, see Jackson, *Semiotics and Legal Theory*, 12–13, and his contribution to a semiotic model of law, 283–310.

7. The alleged hypothetical literary development is not to be understood as an evolutionary development of legal thought as such from a more primitive to a more sophisticated mode. The reason why Exod 21:13-14 introduces fault-based liability may be of pragmatic nature; for instance, it may be the result of the specific context of the individual law in the collection. This interpretation of the Covenant Code allows for concurrently existing legal thought and does not align a version of biblical law to a particular stage of legal thought and does not subscribe to a unilinear evolutionary pattern for biblical law in general. "For example, several scholars see a development from self-help customary law reflective of a simpler sociological situation to more elaborate regulations connected with village, town, and eventually state interests. The Covenant Code has been viewed as fitting into this developmental scheme. Its presumed early redactional layers reflect a relatively primitive stage of law, and the Covenant Code as a redacted whole reflects a more developed politico-judicial context" (Wright, *God's Law*, 6). In the view of the present study, the combination of Exod 21:12 with vv. 13-14 does not necessarily reflect a historical development in legal thought, as much as it represents a literary development in biblical law.

8. See, for instance A. Phillips, *Ancient Israel's Criminal Law* (Oxford: Clarendon, 1970), 100; Barmash, *Homicide*, 120; Jackson, *Wisdom-Laws*, 123; idem, *Essays in Jewish and Comparative Legal History* (Leiden: Brill, 1975), 91–92; F. C. Fensham, "Liability in Case of Negligence in the Old Testament Covenant Code and in Ancient Legal Traditions," in *Essays in Honour of Ben Beinart: Jura Legesque Antiquiores Necnon Recentiores*, ed. B. Beinart and W. De Vos (Cape Town: Juta, 1978), 283–94, here 285; R. Westbrook, *Studies in Biblical and Cuneiform Law* (Paris: Gabalda, 1988), 77; C. Houtman, *Das Bundesbuch: Ein Kommentar* (Leiden: Brill, 1997), 111; Otto, *Wandel*, 32–33, 64. See on the relevance of "intention" below under 9.

liability,[9] that is, from a general application of the *mot-yumat*-law independent from the successful impact of the slayer, toward fault-based liability, that is, depending on the slayer's intention. Scholars may refer to this development of legal reasoning as a step in an overarching evolutionary theory of law, yet for the purpose of this study, the shift to fault-based liability is only relevant to determine the slayer–victim relationship. The principle of fault-based liability alters legal reasoning. Intention[10] is a mental state and, as such,[11] its evidence is more complicated to prove. It thus can be expected that this development of legal thought would have required procedural adjustments and institutional changes, namely a local institution capable of and entrusted with implementing legal procedure with a distinction between intentional and accidental homicide.[12]

When considering whether intentionality is pivotal for homicide law and whether it might also form the backdrop of other areas of law, injury law is of particular interest. Injury law in Exod 21:18-19 is a twin case of adjudication, closely related to homicide. Physical injury from an assault could lead to a fatal outcome. By the same token, homicide is a sub-case of injury. For injury or assault law in general it is relevant whether the attack had been carried out with long-term premeditation that was likely part of a long-term relationship between slayer and victim, or whether it was a spontaneous act. Exodus 21:18-19 is thus the second typical case to consider. A third related form of a physical attack that this chapter considers is the assault on a nocturnal burglar of Exod 22:1-2.

---

9. Otto, *Wandel*, 33, "Erfolgshaftung." Note, however, that the alleged source-critical development in CC may not allow to reconstruct a unilinear development of social reality and legal practice that is hypothetically associated with it.

10. One may also call it "premeditation"; Jackson, *Wisdom-Laws*, 121.

11. The procedural questions raised by the sentence are complex. See, for instance, Martin Buss, "Logic and Israelite Law," *Semeia* 45 (1989): 49–65, here 56, who draws conclusions for legal procedure. He suggests that the penalty is authorized by the community or by its head who would also execute or delegate the execution to a representative; the phrase "he must surely die" should then be more adequately translated "he is liable to the death penalty," which would leave open the possibility of repayment by composition as in Hittite law.

12. The nature of such institutions naturally is a matter of debate. See further above Chapter 1, under 3. Theoretically, this could suggest a shift of the institution of blood revenge away from the authority of a trial in the kin toward another form of adjudication, yet it is plausible that adjudication of 21:12-15 on a local level remained the responsibility of the kin. For instance, Otto, *Wandel*, 64, sees the participial construction v. 12 as part of an early system of kinship enforced law through the *pater familias*, before legal proceedings in a local institution would decide along the criteria of vv. 13-14, and as a first step towards shifting the monopoly on punitive sanctions away from the kin; see also idem, 'Gesellschaftsstruktur,' esp. 233, and above in Chapter 1, under 3. Cf., earlier, E. Gerstenberger, *Wesen und Herkunft des „apodiktischen Rechts"* (Neukirchen-Vluyn: Neukirchener Verlag, 1965), 110–17, placing the origins of a significant number of apodictic formulations in the family or kin.

Here too, as will be analyzed below, the question is whether this law essentially perceives intent as a form of premeditated revenge as a legal category distinct from spontaneous killing. In all assault cases, intentionality necessarily plays a role to determine fault-based liability of the slayer. A question this study puts to the forefront is whether CC perceives homicide in the context of the slayer's enduring adversarial relationship to his victim. If so, this hateful relationship between the opponents could be the criterion to adjudicate homicide and physical injury. The assumption of a social status of long-term enmity between two adversaries would have to be demonstrated in other CC laws. If a long-term relationship between two opponents indeed played a role, its relevance will be apparent in cases of neighbors in a conflict seeking retribution or demanding penalty. The *yeshallem*-laws, procedural law in Exod 23:1-8 and comparable evidence in Prov 25:21-22 all reflect such cases and it is therefore critical whether these passages presuppose a construct of long-term enmity.

The present considerations have questioned the relevance of intentionality as isolated criterion. Rather, they have highlighted the social context of any potential slayer, namely the nature of the slayer–victim relationship as pivotal for the evaluation of homicide. Considering laws against the backdrop of the mechanism of long-term feuding and the specific slayer–victim relationship as a narrative image thus challenges the established shift from the criterion of strict liability to fault-based liability as the decisive criterion for the development of legal thought. This criterion of the slayer's intentionality seemingly holds true for any law collection, as examples demonstrate from the oldest laws on homicide in Exod 21:12-14, to Deut 19:1-12, 4:42-43, Num 35:9-34 and Josh 20. Intentionality of the agent was seemingly the decisive criterion throughout the reconstruction of a unilinear development of biblical homicide law, suggesting a dual outcome of either intentionality or inadvertence: the slayer was either acting intentionally and was incurring blood guilt, or he killed accidentally and was granted asylum. And, expectedly, biblical law would distinguish between granting and denial of asylum along the lines of intentionality and inadvertence. This same criterion was also used in legal cultures across the ancient Mediterranean from the early second millennium BCE Old Babylonian Code of Hammurapi (CH) §206-207 to the mid-second-millennium Hittite Laws and to Drakon's law of 621/620 B.C.E. Athens.[13] Yet the broad consensus with regard to the slayer's intentionality as a decisive criterion for homicide law is relatively astonishing when looking at the sources. For instance, Drakon's law requires the killer to be forced out of the

---

13. See Phillips, *Avengers*, 49–57; D. M. MacDowell, *Athenian Homicide Law in the Age of the Orators* (Manchester: Manchester University Press, 1963); E. Ruschenbusch, "Φόνος: Zum Recht Drakons und seiner Bedeutung für das Werden des athenischen Staates," *Historia* 9 (1960): 129–54, repr. in E. Ruschenbusch, *Kleine Schriften zur griechischen Rechtsgeschichte* (Wiesbaden: Harrassowitz, 2005), 32–53; E. Carawan, *Rhetoric and the Law of Draco* (Oxford: Clarendon, 1998); M. Gagarin, *Drakon and Early Athenian Homicide Law* (New Haven: Yale University Press, 1981); R. S., Stroud, *Drakon's Law on Homicide* (Berkeley: University of California Press, 1968), 5–7.

country into exile, whether he killed intentionally or unintentionally: "Even if a man unintentionally kills another, he is exiled."[14] CH features no general rule on intentional homicide. Only indirectly do laws allude to an aggressor's intention or premeditation.[15] CH's surprising reluctance toward a general criterion of intentionality is even more striking in light of CH's consistent reference to the slayer–victim relationship. This preliminary result thus questions any unilinear reconstruction of the development of biblical law that is based solely on the intentionality of the slayer as an indication for fault-based liability. The following thus considers whether a re-reading of other laws in CC may possibly substantiate the questions vis-à-vis a unilinear reconstruction of the development of biblical law and may further clarify the slayer–victim relationship.

The analysis must therefore begin with the showcase example for the criterion of intentionality in biblical law: Exod 21:13-14 presents a homicide case under the heading of the apodictic clause of v. 12 – "If a man slays a man so that he dies, he shall surely be put to death" – as a binary arrangement of intentional and of unintentional killing. Remarkably general in its wording, נכה[16] describes a

---

14. The inscription from Dreros from the seventh and sixth century is the supposedly oldest inscriptional evidence in *Inscriptiones Graecae, Inscriptions Atticae Euclidis Anno Anteriores*. Vol. 1, *Decreta et Tabulae Magistratuum*, ed. D. Lewis, 3rd ed. (Berlin: de Gruyter, 1981), 104; cf. M. Gagarin, *Early Greek Law* (Los Angeles: University of California Press, 1986), 87, on the bibliography see n. 18; see further the recent treatment in Z. Papakonstantinou, *Lawmaking and Adjudication in Archaic Greece* (London: Duckworth, 2008), 85. For an alternative meaning of the second half as "he stand trial," see Phillips, *Avengers*, 51 n. 74.

15. Wright, *God's Law*, 157–58. Wright suggests a number of cases that may imply intentionality, among them CH 210: if a man strikes a pregnant woman (lit. the daughter of a man) to death, his own daughter is to be put to death. Further examples include the laws about the collapsing of a house in LH 229-230 that involve negligence and rule the builder's death; the false charge of homicide in CH 1 which is a capital crime; a creditor's negligent beating and killing of a son of a debtor who was seized to pay a debt which requires the execution of the creditor's son CH 116 and, a woman who has killed her husband, is to be impaled CH 153. Interestingly, the abstract category of intentionality is nowhere mentioned.

16. The verb puts the emphasis on the process of killing, while death as effect of the slaying is often pointed out separately with the addition of מות; cf. Deut 21:1; 2 Sam 14:6-7; Lev 24:17, 21; Exod 21:20; 22:1 (*hoph*). For intentional homicide, see 2 Sam 4:7; 20:10; 2 Kgs 19:37; attempted homicide, 1 Sam 18:11; 19:10; 20:33; based on personal motives, 2 Sam 12:9; homicide law, Deut 19:4, 11; Num 35:11, 15-18, 21, 24, 30; Josh 20:3, 5, 9; homicide as penalty or revenge, 2 Sam 1:15; 3:27; 2 Kgs 14:5-6 and Gen 4:15b; Deut 19:6; as personal revenge, Exod 2:12; 2 Sam 13:28; as penalty for other violations like idolatry, Num 25:14-15, 18 (*hoph*); to punish political enmity, 2 Kgs 25:21; Jer 29:21. See the overview of D. Conrad, נכה, *TDOT* 9 (Grand Rapids: Eerdmans, 1998), 415–23, esp. 417–19.

stroke or blow, as the result of which, it is implied, death occurred. The following v. 13 offers a first subcategory, "non premeditated homicide," and evaluates the slayer's chance of being granted asylum. Verse 14 denies asylum for premeditated homicide:

SUPERSCRIPTION: GENERAL CASE
[12] Who ever slays a man must be put to death.
SUBCASE 1
[13] But if he did not intend,
but the God has led his hand,
I will set you a place where he can flee.
SUBCASE 2
[14] But if a man has been lying in wait against his neighbor to kill him in an ambush,
you shall take him from my altar, to kill him.[17]

Syntactically, v. 13 rules an exception to Exod 21:12: "but if he did not intend..." The protasis is a relative clause that introduces a condition with the adversative conjunction *waw* followed by the negated verb, "to intend." Two clauses with explanatory intent follow: the first is again introduced with an adversative conjunction, "*and/but/however* God has led his hand." A twofold apodosis follows. First, in the form of a YHWH-speech: "then I will designate a place for you," which is followed by a relative clause, "where he can flee," mentioning a place.[18] Altogether, v. 13 demonstrates the protection of a killer who has slain his victim without intention and who, now seeking asylum, is granted a secure place. Hence, intentionality serves as a criterion for the eligibility of asylum. As to the content of both sentences, the idiom "the God has led his hand" introduces a legal fiction, shifting the liability from the slayer to God and, in what seems to be a logical consequence, the manslayer is to be granted asylum. The second clause of the current arrangement, v. 14, substantiates the counter-case of the denial of asylum: v. 14 adds a כי-sentence as second phrase, "And if a man plots against his neighbor to kill him intentionally," and adds the apodosis, "You shall take him from my altar in order to kill him."

---

17. Translations are my own, unless otherwise noted.

18. שים is widely used with "the place" with the emphasis on the quality and specific appropriateness, i.e., a place that would allow for permanence and for security, not so much the providing of the space as such; cf. in 2 Sam 7:10; 1 Kgs 8:21. D. F. Murray, "MQWM and the Future of Israel in 2 Sam VII," *VT* 40 (1990): 309–19, here 315, with reference to Deut 19; Num 35; and Josh 20, suggests that this is not a reference to the altar but to a town. The "place of security and refuge" is then mainly a reference to the nature and the purpose rather than to its location that is left open here; cf. the overview on p. 311 regarding the use of the term in the Deuteronomistic History that does not so much refer to the sanctuary or the altar but to the city of Jerusalem (Josh 9:27; 1 Kgs 8:16, 29, 44, 48; 9:3, 7, 13, 32, 36; 14:21; 2 Kgs 21:4, 7; 23:27).

This second case introduces the relationship between slayer and victim: the slayer has "laid in wait" for an occasion to kill his adversary, a criterion to deny him asylum. As opposed to a spur-of-the-moment decision, בערמה implies in general premeditation and in particular emphasizes the slayer's malicious intent in a plot or guile.[19] It may be helpful to imagine a situation in which such assault would have occurred. Notably, the slayer does not target a stranger but a particular person he is acquainted with. He premeditated a killing within a pre-existing relationship when he has "maliciously plotted against his רע." The victim's designation as רע[20] is critical for the understanding of the opponents' relation to each other. It designates an individual the slayer personally knew in an unspecific way as a "neighbor" or "companion." This neighborly relationship between slayer and victim as רע determines the case categories. In the current arrangement of v. 14, different from Exod 21:13, the relationship between the manslayer and his victim as "a man and his רע" provides the main criterion to decide whether or whether not blood guilt had incurred. Intentionality is only a sub-criterion and of secondary relevance. In conclusion, Exod 21:14 specifies intentional homicide in a particular case between individuals who have known each other long before. Furthermore, the long-term relationship and the intentionality of the killer as criteria are situated on different levels. Intentionality or premeditation concerns the slayer's attitude, while the designation of aggressor and victim as "a man and his רע" introduces a category of social interaction between both parties involved.

This preceding analysis then sheds new light on how Exod 21:14 conceives of what is called "fault-based liability" as the main criterion of the slayer. Far from self-evident, homicide law needed to exactly define the criterion on which it would ground fault-based liability. Thus, from a legal anthropological point of view, when seeing Exod 21:14 as a reflection of how a kinship-based society could clarify legal responsibility for homicide, this rule would be required to distinguish intent or premeditation from an accident,[21] and in order to do so, it needed to mark the exact social context in which homicide occurred. Insofar as any further consideration of this case includes a hypothetical element, for methodological reasons it is not possible to fully specify the exact nature of the relationship between the slayer and the victim in Exod 21:12-14. Yet there are a number of descriptors that point to the presupposition of a slayer–victim

---

19. Cazelles, *Code*, 51, noting that the term occurs five times in the Bible, three times with a positive connotation. Proverbs 1:4 and 8:5 put the noun in contrast to simple mindedness, which suggests strategic thoughtfulness as a meaning. According to Prov 8:12, the wisdom "dwells in craftiness." With the negative connotation of guile, it is used in Josh 9:4 of the Gibeonites. Jackson, *Wisdom-Laws*, 124, following Houtman, *Bundesbuch*, 111, suggests "extreme subtlety"; Wright, *Inventing*, 158, "craftily, with planning."

20. See on this below 4.4.

21. Jackson, *Wisdom-Laws*, 124–25, rightly distinguishes as a third option besides premeditated and accidental, a spur-of-the-moment, sudden quarrel that this law does not cover separately.

relationship as the narrative image of this law.[22] The following reconstruction primarily clarifies the signals that point to a slayer–victim relationship and secondarily ponders how and when this relationship would then become relevant in Exod 21:12-14 and in its context Exod 21:12-25. While this reconstruction remains skeptical vis-à-vis any unilinear reconstruction of legal texts, the analysis considers a tentative date and suggests a plausible source-critical growth, namely for vv. 13-14. It seeks to demonstrate that the earliest understanding of fault-based liability by necessity presupposes a long-term relation between slayer and victim. This includes a hypothetical element yet both semantic and formal elements suggest this, while this differentiation is irrelevant for Exod 21:12. I first consider how and why 21:13 and 14 could point to a long-term slayer–victim relationship.[23] Based on this reconstruction other laws that may also presuppose a slayer–victim relationship and that thus may refer to analogous behavioral patterns between two opponents come into view. For instance, the inadvertent homicide of a nocturnal thief (Exod 22:1-2) that does not incur blood guilt on the slayer. Once the evidence for a slayer–victim relationship in these laws of CC is laid out, a survey of Exod 23:4-5 and passages from Proverbs allows further clarification of the legal relevance of the social status of enmity.

22. Taking further the legal anthropological perspective, on the literary level of Exod 21:13-14 we can assume that a homicide happened between two different kin. The law's main intent would then either be to determine the slayer's exact fault for the sake of punishment as sanction (this is the understanding of E. Otto as he reads 21:13-14 in light of injury law; see his *Körperverletzungen in den Keilschriftrechten und im Alten Testament. Studien zum Rechtstransfer im Alten Orient* [Neukirchen/Kevelaer: Neukirchener, Butzon und Bercker 1991], 135–37, where this has also a function as deterrent), or its main intent can be seen in pacifying the involved kin after a homicide. I assume that in the case of homicide in a local context the law was more concerned about the agreement between the involved kin to secure subsequent life in a community after a homicide of a member than it was concerned about one individual's punishment. From the perspective of the future life of the kin, determining fault-based liability in homicide law was only one necessary step on the way toward an agreement between the kin at enmity. Its unequivocal criterion was the nature of the slayer–victim relationship, in particular if no witnesses were present. Kin members of the slayer and victim would have naturally been aware of this relationship and able to immediately determine it. Their joint determination was the only way to obtain a fast, unequivocal, trusted agreement between the kin of the slayer and the victim. In light of an imminent feud in a community caused through homicide, this future relationship between the two kin may have weighed out the relevance of the specific sanction for one individual.

23. A thorough theory of the redaction of CC is beyond the scope of this study, yet the analysis suggests that a long-term relationship between slayer and victim in the current form of 21:13-14 is likely the product of a reworking of a hypothetical older version; see below, Chapter 3, Section 5, Table 3.9.

2. *Exodus 21:13aα:* "*he has not intended...*"

The following seeks to demonstrate why v. 13 presupposes a slayer–victim relationship and therefore not intentionality as such, but intentionality in a slayer–victim relationship is decisive to create a narrative image for the homicide case. I first consider subcase 1 that entitles the slayer to asylum in case of accidental homicide:

> [13] But if he did not intend,
> but the God has led his hand,
> I will set you a place where he can flee.

Introduced with an adversative conjunction ו and a relative clause, this subcase in v. 13aα points to intentionality as decisive for judging about the entitlement to asylum in the case of accidental homicide. The syntactic addition with a relative sentence that discerns a subcase from the participial sentence in Exod 21:12[24] suggests its secondary character, namely when compared to v. 12, as it references the negation of intent and the clarifying legal fiction of the deity causing homicide.

Other aspects of the specification of v. 13aα become apparent in its semantic elaboration. The clause designates "intent" with the term צדה in a perfect form. צדה, "to intend," in v. 13aα, expresses the intent of putting a person to death with a remarkable reference to a specific situation of intentional killing in a narrative, thus suggesting a focus of this term on homicide.[25] The parallels of the noun all specifically denote intentionality in such cases.[26] This contextual specificity of the use of the term suggests that the expression of intent is not used on the same level as the remainder of the law, and the terms in the description of intentionality sheds light on its specific character. In other contexts, the rare term designates a long-term slayer–victim relationship.[27]

---

24. When assuming an eighth-century core layer of the CC one would expect a broad inner-biblical reception history of the verb; the clearest evidence for its reception is the cognate צדיה in late layer in Priestly tradition, Num 35:20, 22. Its rare use in itself in the context of an attempted homicide is neither a marker for a particularly early, nor for a particularly late date.

25. This is the meaning of the verb in the only other biblical reference that uses this verb – 1 Sam 24:12b, in the context of intended homicide. Later, priestly asylum law in Num 35:22 uses the abstract noun צדיה. For the aspect of "planning," see, among many others, Barmash, *Homicide*, 23, and Wright, *Inventing*, 158.

26. They appear in later homicide legislation. Namely, the noun is twice used in paralellism with the abstract noun איבה (Num 35:21-22); the latter is used altogether five times in the Hebrew Bible (Gen 3:15; Ezek 25:15; 35:5).

27. The late reception history leaves open a number of questions. It suggests a relative date for Exod 21:13aα at an earlier point in time than Num 35. Yet, as *terminus ante quem* it does not allow establishing an absolute date for Exod 21:13aα. On Num 35,

3. *Exodus 21:13αβ:* "*The God*" *Initiating Homicide—A Legal Fiction*

Already the semantics of v. 13aα have suggested that the law uses descriptors that seem to suggest that the slayer had a long-term relationship with the victim. This long-term relationship would thus situate intentionality as one aspect of the social construct of enmity between two opponents, namely the continuous attempt to hurt an opponent. For a fault-based analysis, intent would be pivotal, while, on the other hand, accidental homicide would be free from guilt. Verse 13aβ suggests that in this latter case, intent may still have played a role, but on another level. The positive specification, "but the God let him fall into his hand" or "but the God has led his hand,"[28] is generally understood as encroachment of the deity. Its purpose is explanatory, to give a reason for a pure accident.[29] The rationale behind the reference to the deity's agency is a religious reflection on the principle of guilt and, as such, it is of immediate relevance when determining fault-based liability. The legal rationale for the deity's interference plays out on the procedural level when in a trial about this case the slayer was required to provide evidence for the accidental nature of the homicide.[30] The character of a legal fiction with God as initiator of homicide justifies the deity's granting of asylum at the local sanctuary.

Source critically, v. 13 was suggested to be an addition to v. 12.[31] Notwithstanding this relative dating of the legal clause in relation to v. 12, two semantic markers in v. 13 point to it as reflection on homicide law. אנה, possibly to be translated "to encounter," is used in conjunction with "evil" and "death" as

---

see Chapter 5 below. For a source-critical evaluation, see R. Achenbach, "Numeri und Deuteronomium," in *Das Deuteronomium zwischen Pentateuch und Deuteronomistischem Geschichtswerk*, ed. E. Otto and A. Achenbach (Göttingen: Vandenhoeck & Ruprecht, 2004), 123–34, here 134, suggesting Num 35 to be a third set of additions to Numbers after the Hexateuch redaction and the Pentateuch redaction. He sums them up as "theocratic reworking," based on the fact that it rules that the central sanctuary will not be in charge of asylum tasks, and, instead, the assembly is subordinated to operate under the High Priest.

28. D. Daube, "Direct and Indirect Causation in Biblical Law," *VT* 11 (1961), 249–69, here 254–55: "but God let it happen to his hand."

29. Jackson, *Wisdom-Laws*, 123; C. M. Carmichael, *The Origins of Biblical Law: The Decalogues and the Book of the Covenant* (Ithaca: Cornell University Press, 1992), 102 n. 37; E. Otto, "Biblische Rechtsgeschichte als Fortschreibungsgeschichte," *Bibliotheca Orientalis* 56 (1999), 5–14, here 33: "höhere Gewalt."

30. Otto, *Wandel*, 33; idem, "Rechtshermeneutik in der Hebräischen Bibel. Die innerᵐ biblischen Ursprünge halachischer Bibelauslegung," *Zeitschrift für Altorientalische und Biblische Rechtsgeschichte* 5 (1999): 75–98, here 468, refers to the parallel in the Roman Law of the twelve tables: *si telum manu fugit magis quam iecit*, "if the weapon rather fled from the hand than he (consciously) threw it."

31. See F. C. Fensham, "Das Nicht-Haftbar-Sein im Bundesbuch im Lichte der altoriᵉ entalischen Rechtstexte," *JNSL* 8 (1981): 17–22, 19, and idem, "The Role of the Lord in the Legal Sections of the Covenant Code," *VT* 26 (1976): 262–74.

its object,³² thus the semantic profile associates this verb with evil and death. The idiomatic use of the definite article with the deity, "but the god,"³³ features prominently in Chronicles, Ezra, Nehemiah, Qoheleth, Jonah³⁴ and in late layers of Deuteronomy,³⁵ pointing to a context in which the reference to the deity is an act of self-perception of Israel within the wider context of other surrounding cultures.³⁶

4. Reading Exodus 21:14 through a Redaction Critical Lens

4.1. *"My altar" in Verse 14b*

Before considering the redaction of the law in detail, I first assess the content of Exod 21:12-14 in the collection 21:12-32 about the violation of an individual's

---

32. It is used in Prov 12:21 ("the righteous may not encounter evil/death"), Ps 91:10 ("to encounter evil/death"; *pual*); 2 Kgs 5:7 (*hitp.* participle: "to encounter to bring evil/death"); see Fensham, "Nicht-Haftbar-Sein," 20. The parallels hardly support a pre-exilic origin.

33. The specific combination with the conjunction as "and/but the God" of the conditional clause (21:13a) is found in the heading of Gen 22:1; Exod 19:19; 1 Chr 28:3; 2 Chr 13:15; Eccl 3:14-15.

34. The Old Testament uses the form 366 times; cf. in Exod 20:20-21; 21:6; Exod 22:7-8; Exod 24:11, 13; see further 1 Chr 6:33-34; 9:11, 13, 26-27; 13:5-8, 12, 14; 14:11, 14-16; 15:1-2, 15, 24, 26; 16:1, 6, 42; 17:2, 21, 26; 21:7-8, 15, 17; 22:1-2, 19; 23:14, 28; 24:5; 25:5-6; 26:20, 32; 28:12, 21; 29:7; 2 Chr 1:3-4; 2:4; 3:3; 4:11, 19; 5:1, 14; 7:5; 8:14; 9:23; 10:15; 11:2; 13:12; 15:18; 18:5; 19:3; 22:12; 23:3, 9; 24:7, 9, 13, 16, 20, 27; 25:7-9, 24; 26:5, 7; 28:24; 29:36; 30:12, 16, 19; 31:13-14, 21; 32:16, 31; 33:7, 13; 35:8; 36:16, 18-19; Ezra 1:3-5; 2:68; 3:2, 8-9; 6:22; 8:36; 10:1, 6, 9; Neh 4:9; 5:13; 6:10; 7:2; 8:6, 8, 16, 18; 9:7; 10:29-30; 11:11, 16, 22; 12:24, 36, 40, 43; 13:1, 7, 9, 11; Job 1:6; 2:1, 10; Qoh 2:24, 26; 3:11, 14, 17-18; 4:17; 5:1, 5-6, 17-19; 6:2; 7:13-14, 26, 29; 8:12, 15, 17; 9:1, 7; 11:5, 9; 12:7, 13-14; Dan 1:2, 9, 17; 9:3, 11; Jon 1:6; 3:9-10; 4:7.

35. See Deut 4:35, 39; cf. H. Ringgren, אלהים, *TDOT 1* (Grand Rapids: Eerdmans 1974), 267–84, here 283–83.

36. This wording in Exod 21:13 may hint to an origin not before the sixth/fifth century with the idiomatic "the God" in the contexts of incomparability discourses. Two source-critical options for Exod 21:13 present themselves. A pre-exilic core unit of CC in which an earlier version of this verse did not contain this legal fiction of the deity as subject of accidental homicide who would then, as a consequence, grant asylum for the precise reason of his divine interaction. Alternatively, v. 13 in its current form was not part of an eighth-century CC. The comparative evidence is relevant when dating Exod 21:13 relative to Exod 21:12; cf. Fensham, "Nicht-Haftbar-Sein," 21. While the term צדיה is only attested in Second Temple period texts, the fact that CH 206-208 and Hittite Laws 3-4 also differentiate premeditation from unintentional killing points to early precursors of the legal thought.

physical integrity.³⁷ The passage can be outlined in three distinct categories – vv. 12-17, 18-27, 28-32 – beginning with the most extreme outcome of homicide, and the curse with the consequence of inferring blood guilt vv. 12-17. In a close reading, leaving aside source-criticism, the following verses, vv. 18-27, collect violations of physical integrity that do not cause (immediate) death; vv. 28-32 refer to a domestic animal threatening and hurting the physical integrity of a community member. In the current textual arrangement this thematic outline is fairly obvious, but the literary development of vv. 12-14 remains yet to be clarified. Did the altar law Exod 20:24-26 precede Exod 21:12-14*³⁸ and did Exod 20:24 inspire the terminology for the "place" in v. 14b? With many others, Schwienhorst-Schönberger suggests a pre-deuteronomic altar law and, in a pragmatic effort, reduces the complexity of hypothetical reworking, and assumes that Exod 21:13-14 and the altar law represent the same literary pre-deuteronomic stratum.³⁹

4.2. Verse 12 in its Relation to Verses 13-14

Returning to the relationship between strict liability Exod 21:12 and limited liability, 21:13-14 read like a subdivision that appears to be an addition to 21:12.⁴⁰ The ideal-typical scholarly source-critical reconstruction can easily be explained when seen through the lens of legal procedure. These additions became necessary at a moment in time when (local) forensic institutions needed to decide on intentional homicide⁴¹ which included handling the proof of evidence to determine fault-based liability. It would be interesting to understand how Exod 21:12-14 was composed and to reconstruct whether the development of this law reflects stages of the history of law. In the redaction process of the law collection, Schwienhorst-Schönberger suggests v. 12 ultimately came to stand as a heading of vv. 12-17 by inserting the casuistic vv. 13-14 and 21:15-17. The verse creates an artistic composition with a four-partite row of crimes to be punished with death, of which v. 12 and v. 15 begin with a participle and an object: מכה אביו/מכה איש. Two reasons buttress this sequencing that leads to the placement of v. 12 as the heading of 21:13-14. First, arranging more portentous sentences in front of a unit is a technique in Hittite law.⁴² Second, looking at the outline of the legal corpus, the principle of Exod 21:12 legitimizes mechanisms of blood revenge without

---

37. Houtman, *Bundesbuch*, 102–103.
38. See, for instance, J. Stackert, *Rewriting the Torah: Literary Revision in Deuteronomy and the Holiness Legislation* (Tübingen: Mohr Siebeck, 2007), 36–37.
39. Schwienhorst-Schönberger, *Bundesbuch*, 42. On the possibility that an older form of v. 14 was at the same level as Exod 20:24, which then prompted mentioning the altar v. 14b, see below.
40. Schwienhorst-Schönberger, *Bundesbuch*, 230.
41. Gertz, *Gerichtsorganisation*, 125.
42. Schwienhorst-Schönberger, *Bundesbuch*, 230 with reference to V. Korošec [and others], "Gesetze," in *RLA* III 1966, 289.

considering their institutional background. Hence, in this respect, this summative apodictic sentence functions as a heading that evokes the image of blood revenge and, at the same time, the non-deathly injuries in 21:18-19 present a counter-case in which the same type of hateful opponents interact: the insertion of 21:13-14 opens up the context of 21:12 and 18-19.

The most likely assumption of a development is that in 21:12-14, v. 13 is not on the same level as v. 12.[43] Together with 21:13, the arrangement follows the typical composition of a case/counter-case arrangement with "granting" versus "denial" of asylum as the basic distinction that is also formative in subsequent homicide legislation (Deut 19:1-12), in reverse order, denial – granting asylum, in Num 35.

4.3. *The Relevance of the Parties' Social Status in the Compositional Logic of 21:12-34*

Reconstructing a slayer–victim relationship for the laws of CC is highly dependent on the social world it presupposes. Whether features of its form and semantics may be used as markers of the social world these laws presuppose remains an open question. Yet, syntactic and semantic aspects, such as the use of the root צדה as designation of a long-standing intent to kill, have precisely pointed to the underlying slayer–victim relationship that informs Exod 21:13-14. On the semantic level, in Exod 21:14 the use of "your neighbor" also indicates a long-term relationship of the slayer to the victim. Rather than referencing a random individual, in its current form, the law in 21:14 uses a relational term, thus possibly referring to a long-term opponent driven by a continuous intent.[44]

An observation of the context further supports the significance of this specific terminological choice. This argument draws on the composition of the laws in 21:12-34. Verses 12-34 mention three times the category "neighbor" in the context of a fatal injury through a human (v. 14); an injury through a human (v. 18); and a fatal injury caused by a goring ox (v. 35).[45] Altogether, the rules

---

43. The idiom "the place" in Exod 21:13 is a reference to the altar law and as such dependent on Exod 20:24; see Schwienhorst-Schönberger, *Bundesbuch*, 40–41. Alternatively, it was on the same literary level as the law collection in CC; see Stackert, *Rewriting*, 37, following D. P. Wright. Reconstructing the development of Exod 21:13-14, whether it is a later, post-dtr, post-priestly addition (as M. Anbar, "L'influence deutéronomique sur le Code d'Alliance: le cas d'Exode 21:12-17," *ZABR* 5 [1999]: 165–66, argues), or, more likely, that multiple stages of additions should be assumed in its growth, is beyond the scope of this study.

44. In a hypothetical neutral form of Exod 21:14, using for instance, "man" instead of "neighbor," the only exclusion of a long-term relationship to the victim would be the case of the slayer being a robber or a highwayman lying in wait for any indiscriminate victim.

45. Taken by itself, this is not a satisfactory criterion that allows assuming a coherent redactional reworking of the passage. On the other hand, the category of the neighbor is critical for understanding this particular rule on homicide law.

on general physical assault and injury in 21:12-35 may be broken down into four parts:[46]

12-17	(physical)[47] assault, curse, kidnapping, which are to be avenged by death
18-27	physical assault without death as a consequence
28-32	physical assault caused by livestock
33-36	physical harm caused by negligence (unaware or aware) of the owner of an animal

The coherence of this collection can be seen on various levels and there have been multiple attempts to structure the laws in Exod 21:12-27.[48] One suggestion to make sense of the arrangement of casuistic law in vv. 18-35 is the distinction of two typical quarrels: quarrels between equal free men (vv. 18-19, 22-24), which includes the talionic formula for physical injuries and disciplinary laws between two equal men, and, on the other hand, quarrels between a man and his slave (vv. 20-21, 26-27).[49] This distinction is based on the slayer–victim relationship as criterion. As to the compositional logic, the apodictic sentences follow this categorization of different groups of victims:[50] v. 12, a man; v. 15, (slay) father/mother; v. 16, a free man (kidnapped and sold); v. 17, the curse of father/mother. Beyond a physical assault and a curse in vv. 12-17, the slayer–victim relationship is also a possible principle for the arrangement in Exod 21:20. This becomes evident when considering the categories. Implicitly, slaves are listed separately,

---

46. See the outline of vv. 15-32 in Houtman, *Bundesbuch*, 102–103.

47. The curse in v. 15 is not a physical assault.

48. See, for instance, B. L. Eichler, "Exodus 21:22–25 Revisited: Methodological Considerations," in *Birkat Shalom: Studies in the Bible, Ancient Near Eastern Literature, and Postbiblical Judaism Presented to Shalom M. Paul on the Occasion of His Seventieth Birthday: Volume 1*, ed. C. Cohen et al. (Winona Lake, IN: Eisenbrauns, 2008), 11–29, here 25, who divides the text as follows: (A) capital crimes (vv. 12-17) – homicide (vv. 12-14), striking parents (v. 15), abduction (v. 16), reviling parents (v. 17); (B) noncapital crimes – assault and battery (vv. 18-27), including (1) exemptions from capital liability (vv. 18-19, 20-21, 22-23), and (2) noncapital criminality (vv. 24-25, 26-27); cf. idem, "Literary Structure in the Laws of Eshnunna," in *Language, Literature, and History: Philological and Historical Studies Presented to Erica Reiner*, ed. F. Rochberg-Halton (New Haven: American Oriental Society, 1987), 71–84.

49. This outline that divides between non-fatal injuries to free men (vv. 18-19, 24-25) and the fatal and non-fatal injuries to dependents – the pregnant woman (vv. 22-23) and the slave (vv. 20-21, 26-27) – is suggested by Jackson, *Wisdom-Laws*, 172.

50. The arrangement of these cases suggests a development from the cases towards the heading. The cases were summarized with the headings in Exod 21:12, 15, 17. The cases collect older material that the apodictic sentences arrange in categories. As suggested below, the distinction between a random victim and long-term enemy is critical for the arrangement of Exod 21:12-14, 15-17, 18-32.

given their social status that is defined through a long-term relation to their master.⁵¹ Apodictic clauses include:⁵²

Exod 21:12	איש	מכה
Exod 21:15	אביו	מכה
Exod 21:16	איש	גנב
Exod 21:17	ועמו אביו	מקלל

Casuistic clauses:
13-14:   v. 13: undefined status of slayer/victim
         v. 14: a man and his <u>neighbor</u>
18-19:   v. 18: men, a man and his <u>neighbor</u> quarreling and striking each other
20-21:   v. 20: slave owner
22-25:   v. 22: men wrestling
26-27:   v. 26: man and his slave
28-32:   v. 28: ox gores man/woman
33-34:   v. 33: a man
35-36:   v. 35: a man's ox gores its <u>neighbor</u>'s ox; v. 36: known for 'long time'

This leads to the following conclusions of a hypothetical principle of the arrangement of these laws in which the social status of the agent or driving force and their victim are of relevance:

First, the arrangement of apodictic sentences follows the social status of the individuals involved and this status is of legal relevance. As a rule, the casuistic sentences list groups of people with whom the slayer or the driving force has been acquainted over a long period of time.⁵³ For 21:12-13 and 21:14, which leave the social status of the individuals involved undefined, we may assume that these laws refer to free men. That said, the arrangement demonstrates that the collection describes the legal status in different categories and the nature of the slayer–victim relationship was of relevance to the law.

Second, one may pose the question whether "neighbor/companion" (vv. 14, 18, 35) should also be understood as a distinct social category. In favor of this interpretation is that the laws perceive "neighbor/companion" as comparable to other social statuses, such as slave. There are good reasons that it refers to the established relation, specifically to the long-term acquaintance between slayer and their injured opponent, as will be specified below. Consider in 21:35 the law about the ox goring. The reference to a neighbor's ox qualifies the involved parties as "a man and his neighbor" (v. 35), adding the adjective "(for) a long

---

51. The law on the goring ox in vv. 28-32 does not use the term "neighbor." This is plausible if it is (except for the additions in vv. 30 and 31) old traditional Mesopotamian law.

52. Cf. Otto, *Wandel*, 31.

53. Exceptions are found in vv. 22, 33, 35-36.

time" in v. 36 to specify this aspect of the owner's negligence in the context of a long-term relationship.⁵⁴

Taken together, do the arrangement and the classification of the parties as "neighbors/companions" point toward the construct of long-term relationships that informs this law? It remains a question whether the law collection uses this term to express a long-term relationship and this interpretive question cannot be fully resolved here. Clearly, it is critical whether slayer and victim were in a long-term relationship in which both opponents would have acted out hatefully and thus have achieved a social status as opponents. The following limits itself to specify why the category of the neighbor/companion as a term possibly implies the continuous nature of a relationship and, consequently, when seen through a legal anthropological lens, this may suggest that the slayer and their enemy have been acting out as private opponents in a feuding pattern.

4.4. רע – *Everyday Neighbor*

רע in biblical law describes a correlation that, depending on the context, extends from "companion, fellow, friend, beloved" to "neighbor."⁵⁵ רע in the latter sense describes a community member in immediate vicinity to another individual with whom one would get in contact by sharing everyday life,⁵⁶ usually in visible or in

---

54. A third aspect requires further consideration. On a compositional level, when reading the *yiqtol* forms as an indication of an iterative mode of action, this may potentially contribute to the notion of a long-term relation. In particular, when 21:14 is read with 21:18, they add further correspondences between the laws in 21:14, 18, pointing to their connection to each other. Both use *yiqtol* forms in their protases: 21:14a has "to plan maliciously," and 21:18 uses the technical term for "to quarrel," ריב *yiqtol*. A third passage, 21:22-24, detailing the *talio* for revenge in the different steps of a process, also uses the *yiqtol* to describe physical dispute settlement between two enemies.

55. רע is attested 187 times in the OT, see D. Kellermann, רע, *TDOT*, vol. 8 (Grand Rapids: Eerdmans, 2004), 522–32; the least specific meaning is simply "another." Biblical law uses this term four times in the Decalogues, Exod 20:16, 17; Deut 5:20, 21. The *mishpatim* in CC use it ten times, mostly in casuistic sentences with 3rd pers. masc. sing. suffix (Exod 21:18, 35; 22:6, 10, 13), with the 2nd pers. masc. sing. used in 22:25. Deuteronomy 12–26 uses 15 times, with 3rd pers. masc. sing. found in 15:2 (2×); 19:4, 5 (2×), 11; 22:24, 26; 27:17, 24; and 2nd pers. masc. sing. used in Deut 19:14; 23:25-26 (3×); 13:7, with the meaning "friend". H uses it four times in the 2nd pers. masc. sing. (Lev 19:13, 16, 18); and once 3rd pers. masc. sing. (Lev 20:10); cf. the overview in J. J. Fichtner, "Der Begriff des Nächsten im AT," *WuD* 4 (1955): 23–52, 36, reprinted in idem, *Gottes Weisheit. Gesammelte Schriften zum Alten Testament*, ed. K. D. Fricke (Stuttgart: Calwer Verlag, 1965), 88–114, here 99.

56. This general meaning is evident in the word's wider use, in particular in Proverbs. For Proverbs as a source that notes these everyday encounters with a neighbor, see the definition in Fichtner, "Begriff," 95–96. A more bland, less nuanced meaning is the idiomatic "fellow human"; for instance, in Gen 11:3, 7, and also the use for individuals in a

audible distance. One would have met a neighbor randomly, and this individual would be identifiable; one may exchange greetings[57] with them and would expect to receive help[58] from them and at other times expect being prompted to forgive.[59] One may consider to pledge[60] for a neighbor, lead a lawsuit[61] against them, slander about them or swear falsely against[62] such a person. It is thus plausible that with the term רע used for a community member in the immediate vicinity, Exod 21:14 would describe a long-term slayer–victim relationship. Different from a foreigner or a stranger,[63] as a community member, a neighborly relationship, while volatile and unstable compared with the trustworthy status of a friend or a clan member,[64] would by default be continuous. Along this line of thought, consequently, this could easily mislead to adopt overly trusting behavior. In a critical situation, one might falsely assume a neighbor to be a reliable friend and pledge for them, while in fact the relationship is non-committal.

While it is not possible to fully clarify the use of "neighbor/companion" at the time of the laws of CC, a look at the use of "companion/neighbor" in the book of Proverbs supports the meaning of "neighbor/companion" as a long-term relationship. Proverbs points to a neighbor's freedom to withdraw and to act as an untrustworthy "stranger" (זר) and shamelessly exploit a carelessly given vow holding captive someone who gave a pledge.[65] Further, Proverbs perceives the

collective (1 Sam 10:11; 2 Kgs 2:3); cf. also the corresponding animal parts in Gen 15:10. See also the excursus on the term in Proverbs below, Chapter 3, 5.7.

57. Greetings of peace; cf. Pss 28:3, 122:8; Prov 27:14.
58. Sir 29:20.
59. Sir 28:2.
60. Prov 6:1, 3; 17:18; cf. Fichtner, "Begriff," 95.
61. Prov 18:17; 25:8-9.
62. Prov 11:9, 12; cf. 27:14, cursing; 29:5, flattering; Prov 24:28, witnessing against a neighbor; 25:18, false witness.
63. רע designates a random individual of one's own nation to whom one can talk in the local idiom (1 Sam 10:11).
64. A poor person will be hated by his neighbor/companion (Prov 14:20). Proverbs 27:10 relates the "neighbor" as being less close than the kin but as potentially more important in immediate problems: "Better is a neighbor who is nearby than kindred who are far away." The type of relation between neighbors can be gathered from Proverbs, which uses רע in the sense of "neighbor" or "friend." A loving neighbor (רע) will ideally remain favorable at all times, but "a brother is born for distress" (Prov 17:17).
65. In particular, passages in Prov 1–9 lead a discourse on trust towards one's neighbor; cf. Prov 6:1-2a, 5. Proverbs 6:1 points to the volatility of the relationship, comparing them with a stranger and warning against contractual agreements. This advice continues with the urge to free oneself from this pledge (v. 5): "Deliver yourself like a gazelle from a hand and like a bird from the hand of the fowler!" Usury was not allowed among community members; thus, the neighbor seemingly functioned as guarantor for a person he does not know. The neighbor forces the person who has secured the loan to pay the money back. In such cases, a neighbor as a member of one's own ethnicity will not

neighbor as a potential future adversary conceivably using the hateful techniques of slanderous speeches[66] and false testimony.[67]

These literary contexts confirm רע as a personally acquainted individual and member of the community in close vicinity, which also applies to the quarreling opponents in Exod 21:18. The volatility of a neighborly relationship and prospective conflicting interests are apparent in law too, for instance when comparing the quarreling of opponents in Exod 21:18 and negligence laws Exod 21:33-34, 35. In this case, the relationship to the aggrieved party remains unspecified and the laws do not use the term "neighbor." The law imposes no penalty in case of negligence, but the owner of the pit or of the ox must restitute for incurred damage. Even in the case of negligence when the owner knew his ox was goring, he would have to restitute the aggrieved party. Unlike in these negligence cases, laws concerning quarreling opponents intend mediation between the injuring and the aggrieved party. Typically, as the later law Lev 19:17-18 illustrates, this would happen among members of a community or polity and it specifically refers to the conclusion of revengeful patterns between the partners.[68] This reception history is in line with the concept of רע as an identifiable, personally known individual who is neither a member of one's own kin nor a

tolerate any delay on the payment. Verse 3 may be a later transitional verse leading over from the protasis to the apodosis: "go, stormily tread(?), storm against your neighbor…" The imp. *hitp.* התרפס is unclear: "to stamp, tread, foul by stamping"; all these are directed against the unfaithful neighbor. On the difficulties of the interpretation of vv. 1-6, see J. A. Loader, *Proverbs 1–9* (Leuven: Peeters, 2014), 256–57. Ben Sira also partakes in the discourse about the trustworthiness of a neighbor, with Sir 29:14-16 encouraging to trust the neighbor, while 29:17-20 point to the dangers of giving sureties. Cf. also the case of Prov. 17:18 that equally highlights neighborly instability: "A man lacking in understanding claps a hand, he takes on a pledge before his neighbor." In this case, the neighbor has misused the confidence that a person afforded him when he was called to testify; see also Prov 22:26.

66. Prov 25:8, 9; see also the swearing of a false oath against a neighbor in 24:28; 25:18; and on the infamous speaking of a neighbor, see 11:12; on the urge to bless a neighbor, see Prov 27:14.

67. Prov 11:9. The fact that Prov 3:29 reject wrongful intentions points to the likelihood of such interactions. On the conflicts with the neighbor, see below, Chapter 3, 5.8.

68. The passage mentions רע three times in vv. 13, 16, 18 and it is limited to these instances and Lev 20:10 in H. Leviticus 19:11-18 use it together with "compatriot" (עמית, vv. 11, 15, 17), sons of the people (עם, vv. 16, 18), brother (v. 17). The later command of the love of the stranger (גר) in 19:34 as an element in a sequence with the love of the neighbor indirectly supports this ethnic connotation; see also E. Gass, "Zum syntaktischen Problem von Lev 19,18," in *"Ich werde meinen Bund mit euch niemals brechen!" (Ri 2,1). Festschrift für Walter Gross zum 70. Geburtstag*, ed. E. Gass and H.-J. Stipp (Freiburg im Breisgau: Herder, 2011), 197–216, here 203, and see below, Chapter 5.

foreigner, but an everyday communication partner.[69] This term's meaning in homicide law already in Exod 21:14 remains naturally hypothetical. It would signal a slayer–victim relationship as the category that determines the fault-based liability in homicide. Following this understanding, the opponents were acquainted members of the same community that permanently settled in close vicinity, as opposed to random strangers.

4.5. *זיד/זוד* Exodus 21:14 (Proverbs 21:14; Psalm 86:14)
Along this vein of thought of a presupposed long-term relationship between slayer and victim, other aspects of Exod 21 require attention. The lexicographic profile of Exod 21:14 relates in multiple ways to רע as a permanent acquaintance in immediate vicinity. One is the activity of "lying in wait" to kill a neighbor/companion (רע), obviously a member of one's own community. Exodus 21:14, וְכִי־יָזִד, describes the willful attempt to trespass a legal order.[70] יָזִד, derived from זיד,[71] hi. designates malicious intent. The connotation of the verb implies the vicious nature of the attempt of overcoming a neighbor.[72] Parallels from four areas point to this attitude as being generally incompatible with Judean/Yahwistic law and its institutions. In Psalms, this root often takes on an ethical meaning of arrogance, for instance, of an opponent insisting on exceptional claims.[73] Second Temple period prophecy in Isa 13:11 and Jer 43:2 compare the זדים with the רשעים[74] as intentional transgressors of the law, rejecting the prophetic word, "presumptuous, impudent, fool hardy."[75] The cognate זדון designates a fool's

---

69. 1 Sam 30:5; Exod 11:2: Typically they are members of an ethnic community, in this case, the Egyptians in a number of distinct social situations that build the respective backdrop of רע in Proverbs, Exodus, Deuteronomy, Leviticus, Job and, Ben Sira; see the term below in Chapter 3 on Deut 19:1-12.

70. Whether the *yiqtol* in this context indicates a repeated activity mode of the slayer requires further consideration.

71. J. Scharbert, *זיד/זוד*, *TDOT*, vol. 4 (Grand Rapids: Eerdmans, 1980), 45–51, here 47, distinguishes two separate roots based on Arabic.

72. It is twice used in the *qal*: Exod 18:11 uses the verb with the Egyptians as subject to describe the collective as paradigmatically presumptuous, as does Jer 50:29. In the *hi.* the verb can also designate the general disregard for God; cf. Deut 1:43; 17:13; 18:20.

73. J. Scharbert, *זיד/זוד*, 48 on Ps 86:14 (the same clause Ps 54:5 [conjecture]). The psalm refers to enemies as "the presumptuous (who) raised above me and an assembly of the wicked (who) threatens my life." The passage first highlights the Psalmist's enemies; a third stich, "and they do not set you before them," qualifies them religiously as ungodly in nature. Cf. similar aspects found in Ps 119:51, 69, 78, 85, 122; v. 78 characterizes the presumptuous' behavior as "unjust" (עות) and "oppressive" (עשק). LXX Exod 21:14 ἐπιτίθημι similarly associates this with arrogance.

74. Isa 13:11; Jer 43:2; Mal 3:15, 19.

75. Mal 3:15, 19 support a Persian or Hellenistic date for their lament of a reversal of "wickedness" and "evil doers" as praiseworthy, exposed to YHWH's final judgment:

audacious or overly self-confident behavior as leading to quarrel and, ultimately, to shame.⁷⁶ Proverbs 21:24 lists a triad of vicious characters first the "presumpe tuous," before repeating this root at the end as a form of excessive, willful "insolence" or "aggression."⁷⁷ Presumptuousness also designates the rebellion against the authority of legal institutions.⁷⁸

In conclusion, the root pair *זיד/זוד adds the bias of willful homicide; it does not necessarily presuppose a long-term slayer–victim relationship. It classifies "acting out enmity" together with the notion of Deut 17:12-13 as "disloyalty," comparable to a form of "disrespect" vis-à-vis the central priestly or Levite legal authority and expertise in the central sanctuary which ensues capital punishment. These latter laws presuppose a pivotal role of the central institution at the temple, that is, under priestly or Levite legal authority.

4.6. Conclusion: The Relevance of Enmity for Procedural Law

The preceding analysis makes the case that it is possible that already the law in CC may have envisioned a long-term relationship between slayer and victim,

---

Mal 3:15, "And now we praise the זדים blessed, those who do evil are built up, they also believe in God and they will be saved"; Mal 3:19 (MT; Mal 4:1 ET), "But, see, the day comes (on which) an oven burns, and all the זדים and the evil doers will stubble, the day that comes shall burn them up, says YHWH of hosts, so that it will leave them neither root nor branch." The root designates the willful, presumptuous claims of prophets in Deut 18:22 and, more generally, it designates the rejection of God's religious order (Jer 50:29; Dan 5:20; Neh 9:16, 29; Sir 3:16).

76. Prov 21:24.

77. "Presumptuous, haughty, non-compliant his name, he does insolence in excess." Wisdom psalms describe the opposition of the "haughty" specifically in opposition to YHWH's law. The terms vary in detail: Ps 119:21 (מצות), vv. 51, 85 (תורה), vv. 69, 78 (פקודים). Another clarification is their acting as "oppressors" in v. 122 (עשק), cf. v. 121. The Psalmist self-identifies as YHWH-"servant," claiming for himself to act out "justice and righteousness" (צדק משפט), pleading not to be left at the mercy of his oppressors. Along comparable lines, Ps. 19:14, a Wisdom Psalm, rejects presumptuousness as ethically similar to "great sin" (פשע רב). Presumptuousness is the rejection of judicial authority in Deut 17:12a.

78. The significance of זדון as presumptuousness becomes especially apparent in cases of physical injury, homicide and rebellion against priest or judge (Deut 17:12a), at a point in time when cases of assault, conflicting claims, and blood guilt needed to be turned over to the central authorities in Jerusalem. זדון (Deut 17:12a) is the presumptuousness of rejecting the decision of a priest or a judge made in the deity's name, ensuing capital punishment. This harsh punishment points to the degree of danger such individuals would carry (Deut 17:13 זדה hi.). Gertz, *Gerichtsorganisation*, 71, suggests a basic layer of 17:12a.*bα and 17:8a*b.10a; ascribing the noun to the older Deuteronomic layer, which led to the insertion of the root in v. 13; cf. also Otto, *Deuteronomium*, 1429–30, ascribing most of v. 12 to an early Deuteronomic layer.

especially in Exod 21:14. This result remains hypothetical since the laws do not fully allow the classification of the slayer–victim relationship. If the category "neighbor/companion" refers to a long-term opponent, it clearly would differ categorically from an enemy in a spontaneous brawl. Two aspects in the current form of the law specify and substantiate the permanence of the status between two opponents. First, Exod 21:14 potentially suggests the longevity of such a status if one assumes permanent quarrels that also point to the ongoing nature of the conflict between the opponents, resulting in a particular relationship of enmity. Further, substantiation is given if רע as the term for an opponent does imply the notion of a continuing hateful relationship. Seen through a legal anthropological lens, at a moment in time when "neighbors" or "companions" would turn into opponents, this transformation was as such relevant for legal procedure. By definition the opponents had previously known each other for a long time and, consequently, the likelihood of their involvement in a long-term quarrel was significantly increased. Expectedly, in a trial between the two kin, a proof of evidence would be needed if the parties were indeed at enmity, especially before a fatal assault happened (Exod 21:14).

Second, the law seems to presuppose a long-term status, when it suggests that legal procedure would be adjusted accordingly, namely the removal of the intentional slayer from the altar. With this, the procedure addresses the relevance of the long-term relation between the opponents in this homicide case once the case is considered in retrospect. This would not be surprising, but is expectable. Analogously, other laws in CC also recognize the status of long-term friendship and the resulting loyalty with one party as the reason for a bias in a trial. Befriended witnesses would twist the evidence in favor of their allies in a trial. This default mutual support is the background of the explicit ban of a witness in trial who could side with "the wicked" or with the more influential party.[79] A slayer–victim relationship thus is the expected default in a feuding context. Seen through a legal anthropological lens, the opponents would thus adopt the social status of private enemies from different kin and act out this status accordingly. Naturally in these social systems, any individual would side with their allies and would act as false witness or plaintiff in their ally's favor.

14 וְכִי־יָזִד אִישׁ עַל־רֵעֵהוּ לְהָרְגוֹ בְעָרְמָה
מֵעִם מִזְבְּחִי תִּקָּחֶנּוּ לָמוּת:

But if a man has been lying in wait against his neighbor to kill him in an ambush, you shall take him from my altar, to kill him.

In both Exod 21:13 and 14 willfulness and treachery are the decisive criteria to distinguish between eligibility and denial of asylum. Beyond this, with the continuous act of lying in wait with the intention to hurt an enemy Exod 21:14

---

79. Cf. Exod 23:1-2 and see below, 8.1.

describes an ongoing relation between two individuals, that is, a long-term enmity. This detail allows stating more precisely the criterion for asylum in Exod 21:14 in contrast to accidental homicide.[80] Prior to the accident, the slayer would by default not have known the victim, or known this person only randomly. Exodus 21:14 implies the community's awareness of a dispute or feud between the two parties prior to the homicide. The law thus suggests that a kinship-based society would recognize "private enmity" as a legally relevant status. A kinship-based society would judge parties that fulfill the criteria of this social status differently than spontaneous slayers. A man publicly known to be an enemy of another man (his "neighbor") who killed his opponent would be put to death. If no such long-term conflict would be known, Exod 21:14 does not apply. Assuming a long-term slayer–victim-relationship, while only indirectly retrievable, would be in line with the apodictic sentences in Exod 21:12-36 that specify a distinct status of one of the parties involved (v. 15). Also, in part, the casuistic sentences either define a distinct status of the players involved (vv. 14, 20, 26, a slave), or they leave it unspecified (vv. 12-13, 18-19, 22-24).

5. *Injury Law*

5.1. *Exodus 21:18-19*
The continuous, publicly lived out relationship vis-à-vis an opponent, while only hypothetical, has proven to be critical for the interpretation of homicide law in Exod 21:14. Yet in the present study homicide law and the ensuing blood feud serve only as a quintessential case to more clearly analyze how such structures of feuding patterns and the social construct of long-term private enmity might indeed inform laws of CC. Expectably thus, this ongoing hateful relationship and the social construct of a private enemy could also be of relevance in other cases and possibly might form the backdrop of other laws of CC. Though limited in scope, this study now considers the injury law in Exod 21:18-19. It is in form and content closely related to homicide law, reflecting on two enemies engaged in physical quarrels. In the situation of mutual injury, the relevance of opponents acting out in hate against each other is apparent. Seen through a legal

---

80. The description of an explicit slayer–victim relationship in 21:14 may be the product of a reworking. An earlier shorter sentence may have excluded the 3rd person masc. sing. suffix from the following object and used instead of a *yiqtol* form of *זיד/זוד a *qatal* to describe the killing, with its mode of action highlighting an individual encounter rather than a long-term slayer–victim relationship: וכי איש הרגת בערמה מעם מזבחי תקחנו למות. The use of the *yiqtol* in 21:14a should then be seen in connection with 21:18, 22a. If in the latter two cases the *yiqtol* may be interpreted as conveying an iterative mode of action, this would further substantiate a series of actions between opponents and thus enhance the notion of a continuous quarrel in 21:18, 22a. Whether in analogy, this iterative action mode should also be applied to the *yiqtol* 21:14a is beyond the scope of this study.

anthropological lens, it seems relevant to a community that it would clarify the presupposed slayer–victim relationship. If at enmity, both opponents by nature would intentionally fight against each other, and each at their own risk engage in a feuding pattern. It is plausible that for such relationships between enemies other rules would apply than for spontaneous assault. Yet at which point in time and how exactly laws would consider such quarrels as ongoing and whether and how they reflect at all on the status of private enemies, requires attention. In the case of injury law in CC this requires both a look at the law itself and at its current arrangement in its sub-collection.

Injury law is compositionally closely related to the sub-collection of the *yeshallem*-laws[81] that otherwise reflect on deposits in Exod 22:6-14 with the *yeshallem* phrases that serve as a paradigm for other case law in CC. Later additions to CC include 21:33–22:14. In this passage of the law, suggests Otto, the notion of negligence would demand punishment rather than compensation.[82]

Moving away from negligence laws, another segment was integrated in the laws of physical injury in 21:18-32. In this collection in Exod 21:20-21, 26-27, 32, clauses concerning free individuals alternate with those concerning slaves and death penalty laws.[83] Thus the arrangement of laws in this collection most likely reflects the relevance of the nature of the slayer–victim relationship. Beyond this, on a more formal level, injury law relates to homicide law. It will thus be necessary to determine whether these two laws are intentionally related to each other as injury with and without fatal outcome. Moreover, it will be relevant to determine if injury law perceives the slayer–victim relationship in the context of feuding patterns between long-term enemies.

The law on physical injury in 21:18-19 shows formal parallels to laws of intentional homicide and injury that are of relevance in light of the distinction between intended and involuntary homicide. The juxtaposition demonstrates the idiomatic and structural parallel between homicide and injury law.

Table 2.1

21:14	21:18-19
"When (וכי) a man is lying in wait, against his neighbor	[18] "When (וכי) men are quarreling, and the one man slays his neighbor, with a stone or with the fist,
in order to kill him…"	but he does not die, but falls in bed,

---

81. Otto considers the *yeshallem* phrases to be the oldest source of CC; see Otto, "Book of the Covenant," 72.

82. It makes sense to assume the severe punishment was imposed in light of the two parties' long-term relation.

83. Otto, "Book of the Covenant," 72.

	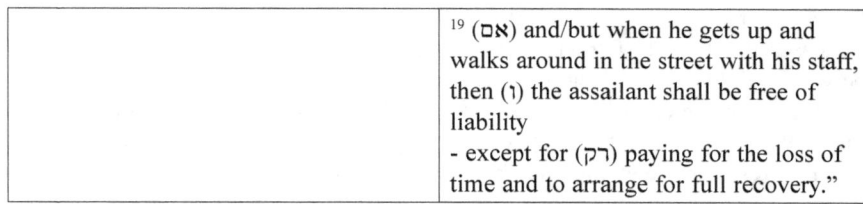 ¹⁹ (אם) and/but when he gets up and walks around in the street with his staff, then (ו) the assailant shall be free of liability - except for (רק) paying for the loss of time and to arrange for full recovery."

The formal rendering of this case is relevant for its interpretation. The protasis in both laws features a parallel introduction with a conditional phrase introduced with *waw* and with the conjunction *ki*, "when." In both clauses, a *yiqtol* form describes the slayer's action. Verse 18 specifies the aggressor's assault with either a stone or a fist. Both clauses mention the victim's death, either as the slayer's intention or as the avoided outcome ("he does not die," v. 18). Verse 19 then specifies as a second outcome that the victim may fall sick but would not die. In this case it details the victim's subsequent recovery and a consequence, introduced with *waw*, that the slayer would be free of liability. It then adds as an exception a second consequence, introduced with "except" (רק), ruling the payment for the loss of time and the arrangement of full recovery.

With regard to the content, the two foremost points of comparison with homicide law are the term רע and the consequences it specifies. First, as pointed out above, the term רע in Exod 21:14, 18, 36 may indeed suggest a long-term relation between slayer and victim as neighbors/companions. This category differs from other slayer–victim long-term relationships, to father/mother in 21:15, 17 or to a slave in 21:20. Yet it shares with them their emphasis on the long-term character. As proposed for 21:14, this longevity of the connection between a slayer and a victim is inherent as a precise narrative image in the current form of the clause. This seems to also be the case in 21:18, as will be explained below. A second point of comparison relates to the content of the law, especially the consequences involved. The collection of laws in Exod 21:18-32 gathers content of related cases which either suggest a death punishment or refer to related conflicts between an aggressor and a victim.

While it is plausible to assume that both Exod 21:12-17 and 18-32 reflect a shift of legal procedure towards the relevance of proof, this does not imply they would abandon family or kinship law and instead adopt the rules of a court of the central government.[84] In Exod 21:13-14 the requirement of a proof of evidence

---

84. Otto, *Wandel*, 33–34, suggests that penalty law which had its original place in a family or kin-related trial gradually shifted into the authority of the local courts. See also, Otto, *Gesellschaftsstruktur*, 237. The alternatives of ascribing death law either as being generally part of family law were considered by G. Liedke, *Gestalt und Bezeichnung alttestamentlicher Rechtssätze. Eine formgeschichtlich-terminologische Studie* (Neukirchen-Vluyn: Neukirchener Verlag, 1971), 131–35, and the ascription of death law as uniquely ruled by local courts was suggested by H. Schulz, *Das Todesrecht im Alten Testament. Studien zur Rechtsform der Mot-Jumat-Satze 114* (Berlin: de Gruyter, 1969), 85–87.

for inadvertence is in line with the need for public dispute settlement. Some of the cases in 21:18-32 likewise focus on an extended slayer–victim relationship between neighbors (v. 18) or to a slave (vv. 20, 26) in which an injury occurs. The injuries are more complex and therefore require more detailed regulation. As is the case in 21:14, a dispute between the parties in Exod 21:18 was of relevance in trial procedures and thus needed to be assessed. The injuries from quarrels over time are relevant for the reconstruction of the particular dispute settlement.

5.2. *Reworking of Exodus 21:18-19*

As is the case in homicide law in Exod 21:14, injury law in its current form reflects a continuous enmity between two opponents. Exodus 21:18-19 suggest a form of dispute settlement that balances claims of the victim with those of the slayer in the case of an injury. Injury is a close parallel to homicide insofar as the victim could potentially die, which is the first of two main scenarios of injury. The death may cause the aggrieved party to start a blood feud, and the pacifying tendency of the law thus makes sense.[85] The clause in v. 19 includes this possibility with the preposition אם in v. 19a which has a temporary function: "*as soon as* he gets up and walks around outside on his cane." This is critical since it indicates that the aggressor would probably have to hide until he knew the aggrieved party got up and walked around outside, and until then he did not know whether he would be the target of vengeance.

In the other case of the victim's recovery the law offers two internally inconsistent outcomes. ונקה המכה ("and the slayer goes free," v. 19aβ) suggests the slayer has no obligations or liabilities toward his victim.[86] Another interpretation is that the slayer was free from blood guilt and could not be claimed to be killed by the deceased man's kin. This interpretation implies the victim's initial recovery and the possibility of a later subsequent death.[87] The criterion for this outcome was the aggrieved party's ability to walk around outside, to act in public and, in short, to fully participate in public life, thus indicating the end of the slayer's obligations. However, in the case of the second consequence, the payment for the victim's idleness and illness, v. 19b stipulates differently than v. 19aβ that the slayer *still* needed to reimburse the victim for having to stay at home and that he still had to provide for the recovery or for his medical costs.

---

85. Cf. Otto, *Gesellschaftsstruktur*, 239, points to the pacifying tendency that he sees achieved through the transfer from the immediate reaction of the victim to a judicial authority that replaces talionic law with a more balanced agreement reached through negotiation.

86. The end of the liability נקה can refer to the end of the fear from blood guilt or it can refer to the end of the actual liability to care for the victim, as the adjective נקי is used for the release from obligations of service or for military duty in Deut 24:5 and in 1 Kgs 15:22; see Schwienhorst-Schönberger, *Bundesbuch*, 55.

87. On this interpretation, see Jackson, *Wisdom-Laws*, 174; for further references, see Houtman, *Bundesbuch*, 152–53.

Verses 19aβ and 19b thus are in stark contrast to each other. The slayer was either free *or* has to pay for the victim. The victim was either dead, and so no payment was to be made, or the victim was alive and payment had to be paid. Of the two consequences, the second, payment for injury, is documented in ancient Near Eastern law. The slayer's payment for the victim's recovery and medical cost is in line with parallels in CH §§206 and Hittite Laws §§10-11. CH and CC both consider the victim's inability to work, and both rule a payment of money for medical care, in CC including payment for recovery, without giving fixed sums of money, unlike the Hittite Laws.

While remaining skeptical to unilinear developments in the history of law and while the source criticism remains hypothetical by nature, clearly, the two contradicting consequences and their corresponding cases of injury or death suggest a reworking of Exod 21:18-19. The outcome in v. 19b, was presumably an older rule for the case of injury in which the victim survived. Verse 19aβ was added later, responding to the case of a temporary convalescence in a severe case that did not cause death that could be attributed to the assault. Originally 18-19aα.b considered a potentially deadly injury, distinguishing between injury as such and injury with homicide; the latter was covered in 21:12. This suggestion of an ongoing dispute has yet another consequence that needs to be addressed. Exodus 21:18-19 consider a different case than CH. A major difference between Exod 21:18-19 and CH is that in the latter the slayer's intentionality plays a major role. The slayer must swear that he did not slay intentionally:

If an *awīlum* strikes another *awīlum* in a fight and injures him,
that *awīlum* shall swear (saying),
"I did not strike him with intent,"
and he shall pay the physician.[88] (CH 206)

While in CH the slayer must swear he has not intended to kill his victim, Exod 21:18 assumes the opposite situation. It implies the assailant's intentionality and in the initial sentence, while not explicitly mentioned, it is possible to interpret this in the sense that it points to the involvement of both in the ongoing quarrel (ריב *yiqtol*). Such continuous engagement with an opponent also implies the latter victim's agreement (rather than fleeing) to enter in a fight. CH shows a great complexity and CC[89] mirrors and modifies it. A hypothetical, reconstructed older form of Exod 21:18-19 may have read as follows:

---

88. Translation from Wright, *Inventing*, 154.
89. Wright, *Inventing*, 157, suggests that CC has in Exod 21:12 changed the context from inadvertent to intentional homicide.

¹⁸ וְכִי־יְרִיבֻן אֲנָשִׁים וְהִכָּה־אִישׁ אֶת־רֵעֵהוּ בְּאֶבֶן אוֹ בְאֶגְרֹף	¹⁸ When a man slays a man[90] with a stone or the fist,
וְלֹא יָמוּת וְנָפַל לְמִשְׁכָּב:	and he does not die, but falls ill,
¹⁹ אִם־יָקוּם וְהִתְהַלֵּךְ בַּחוּץ עַל־מִשְׁעַנְתּוֹ	¹⁹ as soon as he rises and walks around in the street on his cane,
שִׁבְתּוֹ יִתֵּן וְרַפֹּא יְרַפֵּא:	for his recuperation and for his healing he must pay.

The specification of the material that the slayer used in v. 18, stone or fist, and the consequence of the attack on the victim who then, however, recovers, also support a later reworking. In an earlier form, these specifications may have detailed whether the slayer intended to kill his adversary or acted out of the spur of the moment. An injury with a hand or a fist referred to a more spontaneous violent encounter, while a weapon like a stone could be part of the slayer's long planned offensive strategy against his enemy, rather than a means to defend himself,[91] or it could indicate the degree to which the slayer wanted to hurt his victim.

The differences between CH and a reworked final form of Exod 21:18 are as follows:

1. Exodus 21:18 precisely determines the resulting recovery period when the victim was bound to stay home in bed. In line with a hypothetical understanding of a long-term slayer–victim relationship, this indeed makes sense when read in the context of an ongoing quarrel between opponents. Already in the original form of Exod 21:18-19 this sentence intends to limit the slayer's liability: the victim needed not to fully recover, but as soon as he was able to walk around with a cane, this ended the aggressor's liability in the case. This sentence, which is lacking from CH,[92] protects the slayer's interests, not the interests of the injured party, who could easily pretend longer sickness in order to maximize the compensation for personal suffering from the injury. An expected possible course of conduct, this explains the need of the law to protect the slayer from this pretense and claim. Furthermore, the conduct of the injured party makes sense in an ongoing hostile relationship between the two opponents[93] and it illustrates that the public nature of the hateful interaction was essential: the victim could be seen walking around in public. Enemies would naturally seek to hurt each other and the limitation of the slayer's responsibility would restrict the dynamic between the two parties. In favor of the victim, v. 19b rules that the aggressor restitutes for the slayer's medical costs. The law restricts the slayer's liability in that it

---

90. The designation רע for the victim would have replaced a general term that does not include a long-term slayer–victim relationship.
91. Similar Wright, *Inventing*, 166.
92. See also Wright, *Inventing*, 167.
93. See above on the suggestion that the *yiqtol* form in vv. 18, 22a may potentially enhance an iterative action mode.

limits the time for which he pays. Exodus 21:18-19 address the conflict between slayer and victim. The slayer and his kin hoped for a release from obligations which can be seen in the sentence "when he walks outside on a cane" and "the slayer is free from (any further) liability." Verse 19b expresses the victim's claims "except for (the time of) him being sick and for the healing."[94] This setting of the rule presupposes an ongoing conflict between the victim and the slayer in which both tried to secure their interests. In this context of a long-term enmity between slayer and victim, a neighbor, the law limits the slayer's responsibility: he is not "liable." The double sense of this rule, that is, the fact that the slayer is neither guilty nor in charge of helping the victim fiscally, puts the responsibility of the fight back into both parties' authority: as long as no homicide has occurred, both the slayer and his neighbor who were equally engaged in a long-term dispute or enmity are responsible for their losses. If no third party was injured and if neither of them dies from the fight, the regulation is their own and their respective clans' responsibility.

2. Both the specifications of the way of hurting the victim (through stone or fist), on the one hand, and its restriction to only restitute and not to penalize, on the other hand,[95] may equally point to a long-term enmity dynamic between slayer and victim as the context of this law. While not specified in the law, the following scenario would provide a plausible background: once in a status of mutual enmity, the future slayer and his victim continuously would act out their conflict. During the course of their enmity they could choose to hurt each other with a stone or their fist. Typically, such dispute settlement in public would include injuries. CC does not declare the slayer guilty for engaging in a quarrel as such, yet it holds him responsible if a potentially life-threatening injury occurs. Exodus 21:18-19 for the first time in biblical law also differentiates between the weapons the slayer used, potentially already in its basic form. Biblical law would later more precisely identify the particular weapon that caused the injury.[96]

---

94. Both claims are in tension with each other; see Liedke, *Gestalt*, 48; Schwienhorst-Schönberger, *Bundesbuch*, 55.

95. Fensham, "Nicht-Haftbar-Sein," 23, suggests that a penalty may have been cut out at some point.

96. Deut 19:5; Num 35:17-18. It is possible that the distinction between hand/fist and stone in Exod 21:18 was a later addition. Athenian trial records likewise suggest that laws took into account the particular material an aggressor used when hurting his opponent. The choice of the instrument to hurt an opponent played a critical role for institutional aspects of dispute settlement in intended injury (*trauma ek pronoias*) between private enemies in Athenian law. In these cases, fault-based liability would be determined based on the weapon of the slayer as evidence for their intent. See Todd, *Law*, 269; see, in detail, D. D. Phillips, "*Trauma Ek Pronoias* in Athenian Law," *Journal of Hellenic Studies* 127 (2007), 74–105. For instance, in the case of *Lysias* 4, a piece of broken pottery that was readily available served the aggressor as an auxiliary weapon; see Todd, *Lysias*, 53, and see below Chapter 4, 4.2.

Furthermore, formally, "if two men are quarrelling with each other..." uses the term ריב for "quarreling" between the parties, found in law collections and in narratives.[97] Such constellations typically suggest a repeated activity of dispute and dispute settlement as a look at comparable laws from CC suggests. Consider the elements of dispute settlement (ריב) in the procedural law Exod 23:1-8,[98] for instance, the bearing of a fair witness in a lawsuit in v. 2, partiality to the poor in v. 3, or the perversion of justice in v. 6. Similar to apodictic sentences, Exod 23:1-8, placed toward the end of the CC, take into consideration the specific context in which two opponents would hatefully engage against each other. Homicide and injury law in CC leave the slayer–victim relationship open, yet when envisioning these laws as they would mirror typical conflict settlement situations in a kinship-based society, these procedural rules make most sense as addressing a series of actions in a conflict between individuals that knew each other for a long time.

5.3. Reception History of Exodus 21:18-19

For the aim of describing the backdrop of the status of private enmity in feuding patterns, it is now necessary to specify if injury law indeed reflects on such a long-term hateful relationship. If so, injury law would substantiate the social construct of enmity between individuals in its legal relevance; a result that may shed further light on homicide law in 21:12-14. However, injury law poses some interpretive challenges. Whether the above evidence refers to litigation procedure (ריב) in the narrower sense would require further consideration[99] about when and how such "quarreling" exactly would have happened.[100] Methodologically,

---

97. Genesis 13:7-8 reports quarrels between Abraham's and Lot's herdsmen who, as individuals and, at the same time, as members of the collective of their kin, argue about the use of wells. The Philistines in Gen 26:20-21 quarrel with the Israelites about the use of wells; Jacob quarrels with Laban in Gen 31:36 and they settle their dispute in Gen 31:44-45. Harsh accusations against the officials and against the nobles are referred to in Neh 5:7; 13:11, 17, 25.

98. On Exod 23:1-3, 6-8, see below 8.2.

99. Especially, the cultural and historical backdrop of the trial procedures and at what time "leading a trial" may allude to a Greek understanding of enmity. Interestingly, LXX renders the verb with κρίνειν (24× and 1× in Sir); κρίσις 3×; μάχεσθαι (10× and 2× Sir); δικάζειν (8×) and λοιδορεῖν (6×). The noun is rendered 25 times with κρίσις and 7 times δίκη; and 8 times ἀντιλογία; 6× μάχη + 2× Sir; λοιδορία 2× + 4× in Jesus Sirach. λοιδόρησις is the translation of Exod 17:7.

100. To mention a few, Deut 19:17 refers to two parties in a trial that face the priests and the judges and will present their witnesses. Deuteronomy 17:8 refers to a trial "in your gates." According to Deut 21:5, a later addition to the laws of the elders, the priests judge in matters of physical assault. Deuteronomy 25:1 refers to forensic trials. When he was standing in the gate, in 2 Sam 15:2, 4, Absalom claims to be judge in the king's stead. Proverbs 25:8 warns against premature engagement in a lawsuit. Lamentations 3:36

one would have to further distinguish between the literary framing of these laws and the actual social constructs between opponents they refer to to further corroborate the suggestion of reading injury law against the backdrop of a slayer–victim relationship. In light of this interpretive conundrum, a look at the reception history is clarifying. A reflection of Exod 21:18-19 from Hellenistic time highlights the asymmetry between an unexpected victim who is suddenly attacked by a long enemy or an individual who would suddenly engage in hateful action. This reception of Exod 21:18-19 addresses the possibility of a subsequent death of the victim in the phrase "he that struck him shall be clear" (ונקה המכה, Exod 21:19aβ), and refers to a well-known consequence still valid in Hellenistic time. Philo, in reference to Exod 21:18-19, explains the risk of a violent encounter causing death in the following case:

> [104] ...we ought also not to be ignorant of this, that very often unexpected occasions arise in which a person slays a man without having ever prepared himself for this action, but because he has been suddenly transported with anger, which is an intolerable and terrible feeling, and which injures beyond all other feelings both the man who entertains and the man who has excited it; [105] for sometimes a man having come into the market-place on some important business, meeting with some one who is inclined precipitately to accuse him, or who attempts to assault him, or who begins to pick a quarrel with him and engages him in a conflict, for the sake of separating from him and more speedily escaping him, either strikes his opponent with his fist or takes up a stone and throws it at him and knocks him down. [106] And if the wound which the man has received is mortal, so that he at once dies, then let the man who has struck him also die, suffering the same fate himself which he inflicted on the other. But if the man does not die immediately after receiving the blow, but is afflicted by illness in consequence and takes to his bed, and having been properly attended to rises up again, even though he may not be able to walk well without support, but may require some one to support him or a stick to lean upon, in that case the man who struck him shall pay a double penalty, one as an atonement for the injury done, and one for the expenses of the cure. [107] And when he has paid this he shall be acquitted as to the punishment of death, even if the man who has received the blow should subsequently die; for perhaps he did not die of the blow, since he got better after that and recovered so far as to walk, but perhaps he died from some other causes, such as often suddenly attack those who are of the most vigorous bodily health, and kill them.[101]

assumes this corresponds to the people's situation in the land – that they are oppressed in court; see H. Ringgren, ריב, *TDOT* 13 (Grand Rapids: Eerdmans, 2004), 473–79, esp. 477–78.

101. Philo, *De Specialibus Legibus*, 3:104-10, trans. C. D. Yonge, *The Works of Philo Judaeus, the Contemporary of Josephus*, vol. 3 (London: G. Bell & Sons, 1855); see this parallel in Jackson, *Wisdom-Laws*, 175.

Philo first presents a case of unpremeditated homicide triggered by random anger against an individual who provokes a conflict for the sake of having a dispute and then, as the conflict escalates quickly, flees and throws a fist or a stone at his opponent, who subsequently dies. In this case blood guilt has occurred and the slayer must die. In the counter-case, if the person did not die, the slayer has to pay double penalty, as atonement for the injury done, and for the expenses for the surgeon.

The passage distinguishes two cases that follow the logic of the complex rule in 21:18-19 in its final form. This interpretation thus supports Jackson's suggestion that CC combines two originally separate rules in one: first, the victim does not die but keeps to his bed, versus, second, he dies after he has been healthy and the aggressor is cleared of responsibility.[102]

In conclusion, injury law in 21:18-19 was potentially reworked to more fully reflect the backdrop of the status of long-term private enmity in Ancient Israel. The current form of vv. 18-19 shares the social backdrop and the literary context of homicide law in which 21:12 served as a superscription for the two contrasting cases, with 21:13* as the presumably older sentence and 21:14 as the counter case. It became apparent that the laws imply the authority and jurisdiction of the kin and affirm the public nature of dispute settlement with both clans involved in the cases of potentially fatal injury, which corresponds with other casuistic laws that also rule justice in cases of physical harm committed in a community, such as 21:35 and 22:6. The legal institutions and the essentially public character of oppositions to which both injury and homicide refer, point to the social setting of these legal sentences in kinship-based society.[103]

---

102. Jackson, *Wisdom-Laws*, 177. The framing of Exod 21:18-19 poses the question whether the introductory particle in v. 19 (אם) is thought to be a sub-case of v. 18. This is more likely, since the preposition אם nowhere in Exod 21:1–22:6 is an introduction to a co-ordinate clause within a protasis. It commences a protasis which introduces a new case within the paragraph, i.e., this is a case/counter-case arrangement; Jackson, *Wisdom-Laws*, 176. While it has been suggested to read v. 19 and 23-25 as sub-cases, it is more plausible to separate vv. 18-19 from 23-25, because the talion in vv. 23-25 is different from the nature of the restitution of the victim by paying for his time in bed and for his recovery. See especially H. Holzinger, *Exodus* (Tübingen: Mohr Siebeck, 1900), 86. Schwienhorst-Schönberger, *Bundesbuch*, 53. On the intentionality in Philo, see A. Botica, *The Concept of Intention in the Old Testament, Philo of Alexandria and the Early Rabbinic Literature. A Study in Human Intentionality in the Area of Criminal, Cultic and Religious and Ethical Law* (Piscataway, NJ: Gorgias, 2011), 169–317.

103. On the location of the prohibitives in kinship law, see E. Gerstenberger, *Wesen*, 112–3, with reference to Jer 35:6-7 and Lev 18; cf. pp. 115–16. In the cases of blood shedding, the kin was in charge to avenge the dead in Archaic Greece. See, among many others, H. J. Treston, *Poine: A Study in Ancient Greek Blood-Vengeance* (London: Longmans, Green & Co., 1923), 79; Phillips, *Avengers*, 58.

6. *Exodus 22:1-2 as a Test Case for Long-term Enmity*

If injury and homicide law in CC may possibly presuppose the social construct of private enmity, and if such constellations prove to be naturally relevant when judging a case, the reflection on long-term hateful relations in biblical law likely points to a social construct that informs other laws too. Exodus 22:1-2a provides for the case of burglary.[104] In its current setting, its second half raises the suspicion whether this burglary was committed as part of a continuing intention to act out hatefully against another individual of which the homeowner became aware as he fought the intruder. Depending on the interpretation of the clause[105] "if the sun shone," this is possible. It either has a temporal meaning as a reference to strangers that come rummaging in a domicile with unclear intent and that consequently might be treated as burglars or, potentially, that they even intended to kill someone.[106] Alternatively, this phrase may refer to the time of the arrest, not the time of the crime, when it was still unclear whether the defendant will be convicted as a thief and no proof has been given yet.[107] At this point in time, at night, it would be unclear whether the intruder was a thief, which would be clear and visible if the crime had been committed at daylight. The first interpretation of this case seems more plausible, namely, that this passage rules that a thief who is caught nocturnally, i.e., in the moment when he broke in,[108] when slain to death will not incur blood guilt on the slayer:

---

104. The source-critical reconstruction of the law of 21:37–22:3 is disputed; see further below. Unless one reads synchronically and assumes an entirely new case in 22:3, as Westbrook, *Studies*, 118–21, the law must have undergone a redaction. One suggestion is of B. Levinson, "The Case for Revision and Interpolation within the Biblical Legal Copora," in idem, *The Right Chorale: Studies in Biblical Law and Interpretation* (Winona Lake, IN: Eisenbrauns, 2008), 201–23, here 215. The original structure was: general statement of legal principle – multiple damages for slaughter or sale of stolen animals (21:37); first contingency – indenture of the thief unable to pay multiple damages (22:2b); second contingency – lesser damages for simple possession (22:3). "He shall surely pay" in 22:2 is understood as *Wiederaufnahme* from 21:37. In this context it frames an entirely new law about legitimate or illegitimate homicide in the case of housebreaking in 22:1-2a of the Masoretic text attached through the *Wiederaufnahme*. I follow the alternative source-critical reading of Schwienhorst-Schönberger, *Bundesbuch*, 175–82, suggesting that vv. 1-2 are the product of a redaction that inserted them into the preceding law 21:37; 22:3 also references to theft, yet now pondering the difference between a theft at day or at night.

105. W. H. C. Propp, *Exodus 19–40* (New Haven: Yale University Press, 2006), 240.

106. Otto, *Rechtsbegründungen*, 20. Redaction critically, Exod 22:2bα's *šallem yᵉšallem* has been inserted into the blood guilt tradition; v. 2bβ relates to 21:37 and not to 22:1-2a. The text without 22:1-2a makes perfect sense in the context of retribution.

107. Schwienhorst-Schönberger, *Bundesbuch*, 177.

108. See also Jer 2:34: "Also on your skirts they have been found, the lifeblood of the innocent poor; you did not find them while breaking in."

¹ If a thief is found breaking in and is beaten to death,
no blood(guilt) is incurred;
² but if it happens after sunrise, bloodguilt is incurred.
²ᵇ – He has to pay retribution.
If he has none, he shall be sold for his theft.

If this case may be understood as a general rule about potentially murderous assault at night, defense against nocturnal intruders would *de facto* be interpreted as self-defense and, accordingly, the slayer would not be culpable. The counter-case would be the same act committed in daylight, which would thus be intentional homicide. In this interpretation of nocturnal intrusion, the context of long-term enmity does not play a role. This possible reading of the passage seems especially likely for the first sentence. Acting at night was the typical behavior for thieves and slayers alike, as passages such as Job 24:14, 16 demonstrate:

> The murderer rises in the dark, that he may kill the poor and needy, and in the night he is as a thief… In the dark they dig through houses, by day they shut themselves up; they do not know the light.[109]

The first half of this passage fully explains the tactics of slaying an enemy at night and it would not require the addition of the counter-case about burglary and subsequent slaying of someone during daytime. The first case of a nocturnal intruder sufficiently covers self-defense.[110]

For yet another reason the second case adds a situation that differs from immediate, spontaneous killing of the intruder. The guiding principle of the arrangement of the sentences with the subcase of the burglar is the incurrence of bloodguilt or the lack thereof. The two cases are thus arranged as a case/counter-case sequel: either no bloodguilt incurred or bloodguilt incurred. While the meaning of 22:2, including the rule for retribution in v. 2bα, that echoes 21:37, and 2bβ has been disputed,[111] it is a safe starting point to assume that the theft has occurred and is immediately redressed (v. 1), and that v. 2a refers to the same case of an occurred theft, only that the victim of the burglary kills a convicted thief in the morning after the theft.[112] Following this compositional logic of case and counter-case, the passage rules in the first case that the victim has not incurred blood guilt, while in the second case, the victim of the burglary has committed premeditated homicide and, as a consequence, has incurred blood guilt on

---

109. See Jackson, *Wisdom-Laws*, 26.

110. Furthermore, the context of this case in the *yeshallem*-laws points to the relevance of these laws, even though not in light of restitution between two individuals; cf. Jackson, *Wisdom-Laws*, 301; Wright, *Inventing*, 258–64.

111. See the discussion in Schwienhorst-Schönberger, *Bundesbuch*, 177. B. S. Jackson, *Theft in Early Jewish Law: An Historical Perspective* (Oxford: Clarendon, 1972), 157, suggests it made a difference whether the thief was apprehended at night or at day.

112. Schwienhorst-Schönberger, *Bundesbuch*, 177.

himself.¹¹³ Independent from the potential bloodguilt of the slayer, v. 2b adds the thief's principal responsibility for retribution, which originally had immediately followed 21:37.

The legal reasoning presupposes the distinction between homicide in the heat of the moment at night or deliberately on the morning after the nocturnal burglary, that is, after the immediate threat of the burglar's presence. This second subcase fulfills the criteria for an intentional, long-term enmity relationship. The succinct style of this rule omits additional details that we may imagine. For instance, that the victim may have planned at night to slay the thief the following day, may have prepared a weapon, or may possibly have asked friends to join him. "After sunrise" in v. 2a indicates that the victim has acted out of premeditation when he killed the convicted thief in the morning. In the context of the legal consideration of private enmity, this premeditation marked the beginning of a long-term enmity between victim and burglar. The meaning of Exod 21:14 presents itself as analogous case: the victim of the theft in Exod 22:2a was maliciously "lying in wait" to overcome the thief and with this long-term aspect, the legal consequences of homicide change.¹¹⁴ The second case (Exod 22:2a) thus presupposes a long-term enmity relationship between the slayer and his victim.

Given the secondary inclusion of 22:1-2,¹¹⁵ another parallel would be the rigorous restriction for killing a thief at night in early Greek Drakon's law. It

---

113. Exodus 22:1-2 rules homicide committed in the spur of the heat as differently from long-term meditated homicide; see Jackson, *Theft*, 154–61; idem, *Wisdom-Laws*, 26, with reference to Job 24:14, 16: typically, thefts occur at night. This is presupposed in Exod 22:1-2. Jackson rightly remarks that the interpretation of the second verse as a restriction of slaying the intruder only to nocturnal incidents would be a misleading "literal" reading; see also Schwienhorst-Schönberger, *Bundesbuch*, 175–82; and Gertz, *Gerichtsorganisation*, 129–30.

114. Exodus 22:2a implies the victim's premeditation to kill the thief, yet it does not explicitly mention this secondary criterion for the judgment of homicide, but, instead, refers to the time as the decisive factor of the enmity.

115. Redaction critically, for our purpose it is sufficient to conclude that there are good reasons to assume 22:1-2 were secondarily inserted into the *šallem yᵉšallem*-collection, mainly for the reason that they focus on injury law and incurred blood guilt (Exod 22:1-2a; Wright, *Inventing*, 260), rather than on restitution, the collection's actual theme and of relevance in long-term relationships to neighbors; see B. Baentsch, *Exodus-Leviticus-Numeri* (Göttingen: Vandenhoeck & Ruprecht, 1903), 197; Schwienhorst-Schönberger, *Bundesbuch*, 179, attributes 22:1-2 to the same redactor; Otto, *Wandel*, 19–20, with v. 2bα as the original continuation of 21:37; Levinson, "Revision," 215; Rothenbusch, *Rechtssammlung*, 344; Wright, *Inventing*, 261, leaves it open whether vv. 1-2a originally interrupted vv. 6b-7 or whether CH formulated the burglary law along with vv. 6-7 and it came into its current position in the final composition. The insertion of the law on spontaneous killing of a nocturnal intruder on the one side and the counter-case of homicide in a long-term relationship into a sequel of laws on animal theft in which 21:35 mentions the "neighbor," has led scholars to read Exod 22:1-2a as a comment in comparison with CH

runs along the same lines as Exod 22:1-2a: "If he stole anything, however small, by night, the person aggrieved might lawfully pursue and kill or wound him, or else put him into the hands of the Eleven, at his own option."[116] The sentence that probably also rules daylight theft[117] restricts the victim's self-defense to the thief's immediate pursuit, with an optional forensic litigation. It states an exception, as Athenian law allowed for lawful homicide only in extreme cases, namely in defense of oneself or one's property.[118] Aeschines 1.91 suggests a general rule:

8: an insolvent thief could be put to death. In this line of thought, it was suggested to read v. 2a on the basis of v. 2b. As a consequence, 22:1-2a rules a thief may never be killed, even if he is not able to restitute the stolen good. In the case of theft, homicide of the thief may in general not be understood as adequate response; cf. Schwienhorst-Schönberger, *Bundesbuch*, 181. On the other hand, Exod 22:1-2a have been compared to CH 21 and the Codex Eshnunna §13: "A man who is seized in the house of a commoner, within the house, at midday, shall weigh and deliver 10 shekels of silver; he who is seized at night within the house shall die, he will not live"; see Wright, *Inventing*, 258.

116. εἰ δέ τις νύκτωρ ὁτιοῦν κλέπτοι, τοῦτον ἐξεῖναι καὶ ἀποκτεῖναι καὶ τρῶσαι διώκοντα καὶ ἀπαγαγεῖν τοῖς ἕνδεκα, εἰ βούλοιτο. Reconstructed from Demosthenes 24.113 *Against Timocrates*; cf. Ruschenbusch, "Φόνος," 49.

117. Ruschenbusch, "Φόνος," 50, suggests that theft at daytime was ruled similarly: they permitted the killing of the thief. Aristotle, *Athenaion Politeia* 52.1: "They also appoint the Eleven, officers chosen by lot to superintend the persons in the prison, and to punish with death people arrested as thieves and kidnappers and footpads that confess their guilt, but if they deny the charge to bring them before the Jury-court, and if they are acquitted discharge them, but if not then to execute them" (from *Aristotle in 23 Volumes*, vol. 20, trans. H. Rackham [Cambridge, MA: Harvard University Press; London: William Heinemann, 1952]). See Ruschenbush, "Φόνος," 50. See also Aeschines 1.91; Demosthenes 24.65 *Against Timocrates*: "Inasmuch, therefore, as the laws provide that evil doers of other kinds shall upon confession be punished without trial, you, men of Athens, have a right to give your verdict against this man without allowing him to speak or giving him a hearing, now that he has been caught in the act of maltreating the laws; for by proposing this law in contravention of the former law, he has pleaded guilty" (translation from *Demosthenes*, with an English translation by A. T. Murray (Cambridge, MA: Harvard University Press; London: William Heinemann, 1939); cf. Aeschines 1.113.

118. Drakon's law requires exile even for unintentional homicide; see above, the inscription from Dreros, *IG* 1 (3rd ed.), 104. In Athenian law intentional killers who went into exile presumably suffered confiscation of property, unlike in the case of unintentional homicide; cf. "Even if someone kills without premeditation, he shall be exiled." W. T. Loomis, "The Nature of Premeditation in Athenian Homicide Law," *The Journal of Hellenic Studies* 92 (1972): 86–95, further refers to Demosthenes 21.43; Lysias 1.50; Aristotle, *Ath. Pol.* 47.2. Loomis, "Premeditation," 89, and D. M. MacDowell, *Athenian Homicide Law in the Age of the Orators* (Manchester: Manchester University Press, 1963), 38, suggest "unintentional" as a distinction may be based not on the intent to kill but on the intent to physically harm. As a consequence, only if the slayer intended no harm, it was unintentional. See also on intentionality and premeditated wounding in Chapter 5.

"Robbers or paramours or killers ... who are caught in the act, if they admit it, are immediately punished by death."[119] Similarly, Demosthenes 23.50 declares these conditions: "If one kills immediately in defense of one's property a man carrying or leading it away by force unjustly, he is to be killed with impunity." In his following defense speech, Demosthenes puts the emphasis on the two decisive criteria that allow for lawful homicide: if it happens "immediately" and if it happens "in defense of one's property."[120]

Athenian law offers a striking parallel to Exod 22:1-2a and thus supports the relevance of some form of a social interaction between the opponents that this law possibly presupposes. A thief may only either be killed immediately or alternatively must be turned over to the respective judicial institutions. These rules evidently prohibit the execution of a thief if time had lapsed after the burglary. The time lapse would de facto create the situation of a long-term enmity between slayer and victim. In conclusion, Exod 22:1-2a, 2b seem to distinguish analogously between spontaneous homicide and some form of a long-term enmity relationship[121] between two opponents, a legal difference that would align with Drakonion law in similar cases of property defense. This is further evidence that the nature of the relationship between the two opponents may by nature have been critical in the case of homicide.

7. Long-term Enmity in the yᵉshallem-laws of Exodus 21:33–22:14

The current analysis of homicide law has suggested that other laws in CC may indicate that in a long-term relationship between opponents' premeditated homicide would categorically be ruled differently from spontaneous killing, whether accidental or erupting during a spontaneously kindled brawl. Could the distinction between a spontaneous and an intentional act in a long-term hateful relation inform other laws in Exod 21:33–22:14, besides homicide law? The rules on payments of restitution that assess an individual's responsibility and the influence of higher power are natural parallels.[122] Content-related and redaction-critical analyses illustrate the relevance of restitution law in the context of long-term enmity relationships.

Content-related, the yᵉshallem-laws of Exod 21:33–22:14[123] break down into two subsets. A first subset of negligence laws in 21:33-36, animal theft in 21:37+22:2b-3, crop destruction in 22:4-5, and the case of a spontaneous,

---

119. Translation from MacDowell, *Homicide*, 75: Aeschines 1.91, οἱ μὲν ἐπ' αὐτοφώρῳ ἁλόντες, ἐὰν ὁμολογῶσι, παραχρῆμα θανάτῳ ζημιοῦνται.

120. Demosthenes 23.60-61 *Against Aristokrates*; MacDowell, *Homicide*, 76.

121. This does not suggest any immediate influence.

122. Independent from their potential function as guideline in the institutionalized local courts to judge on these cases, the question is whether they presuppose a theoretical category of long-term hate as opposed to spontaneous homicide; Otto, *Wandel*, 23–24.

123. See on this collection in Otto, *Wandel*, 19–20.

accidental homicide in a burglary (Exod 22:1). This first subset was inserted into the collection before and after 22:1-2a. The subject matter of the second subset, vv. 6-14, is deposits and borrowing, with three categories: first, deposits of silver or tools; second, deposits of animals at the neighbor's house; and, third, borrowing from the neighbor. Differing from the laws in the first half of the y^eshallem-laws (21:37), the laws in 22:2b-3, 4-5 instead address cases between *neighbors*. The typical introduction of the general cases is "a man and his neighbor" (איש ורעהו). The terminology is the same as in Exod 21:14 where רעהו expresses the long-term notion. In what follows, I propose that the semantic profile of the neighbor-laws in 22:6-14 points to a context between neighbors or members of the same community with whom a person could identify. The semantic profile designates the stance of neighbors that have settled in a common vicinity, as opposed to strangers. The context would then allow for a translation of the term רעהו as "companion" or "trustworthy friend."

Redaction historically, two diachronic models reconstruct an earlier stage of these laws. Schwienhorst-Schönberger suggests, based firstly on the parallelism between vv. 9 and 13 with the verbs שאל, שבר, מות, נתן, and, secondly, based on the lack of an object of שאל in v. 13, a contrast between the deposit and the borrowing of animals.[124] Along this line of thought, he suggests vv. 11-12 are secondary while 22:9*, 10*, 13* were arranged as original case (נתן) and counter-case (שלם). When depositing an animal at a neighbor's house, no retribution is suggested, while when borrowing, retribution will be asked for. This model operates on the basis of a strict difference between depositing and borrowing animals and it eliminates vv. 6-7 from an original collection.[125]

From a tradition-historical point of view, on the other hand,[126] Otto suggests the difference between deposit and borrowing is not of paramount nature and that both cases share much more similarities.[127] He assumes vv. 6, 7aα, 9a, 11-12, 13, 14a constitute a basic layer, and vv. 7aβ, 8, 9b, 10 represent a secondary interpretation that introduces the idea of a (divine) judgment[128] and 14b as further addition. Obviously, the double return in the case of theft could evoke an accusation of the person who deposited the money or the tools – that his neighbor was a thief. This accusation was hard to prove in a local trial and this is why the

---

124. Schwienhorst-Schönberger, *Bundesbuch*, 198.

125. Schwienhorst-Schönberger, *Bundesbuch*, 205–208.

126. The differences between depositing and borrowing an animal were not the main point in Old Babylonian Law, which rules the shepherd's liability for animals (CH 267) as it was also the case when animals were borrowed and then died (CH 245). Furthermore, the liability was higher in the case of a deposit (CH 266) than when animals were rented or borrowed respectively (CH 244). Yet, both differences could be also explained with a difference of the place of the loss of the animal: CH 244 in the field; CH 266 in the stable.

127. E. Otto, "Zur Methodologie der Interpretation Biblischer Rechtsüberlieferungen. Diachronie und Synchronie im Depositenrecht des ‚Bundesbuches'," in *Altorientalische und Biblische Rechtsgeschichte* (Wiesbaden: Harrassowitz, 2008), 486–95.

128. Otto, *Wandel*, 14–15.

cultic mediation of the deity's decision provides a model for how a variety of decisions could proceed for cases that could not be clarified. "All things of guilt" in v. 8 designates a general rule for treating conflicts about ownership.[129] I concur with Otto on a basic layer of these neighbor-laws which distinguishes three cases of the safekeeping of money, the deposit of livestock, and the borrowing of livestock. The law introduces the single cases with the terminology "a man and his neighbor" which is influenced by Deuteronomic law.

Table 2.2

I GENERAL CASE:		safekeeping of money/tools (v. 6aα): "If a man gives his neighbor…"
subcase 1	v. 6aβb:	if thief is found, double retribution
subcase 2	v. 7aα:	if thief is not found, retribution by owner of the house
II GENERAL CASE:		safekeeping of livestock (v. 9a): "If a man gives his neighbor…"
subcase 1	v. 11:	if stolen, retribution
subcase 2	v. 12:	if torn to pieces by animals, not retribution, requires remains as proof
III GENERAL CASE:		borrowing of livestock: "If a man borrows … from his neighbor…"
subcase 1	v. 13:	if owner is not present, retribution
subcase 2	v. 14a:	if owner is present, no retribution[130]

The outline of these deposit rules suggests that they originated as independent, written tradition.[131] As to the rules which are part of the oldest collection of legal sentences in the Covenant Code however, the introductory clauses with their typical deuteronomic formula suggest the character of these rules as purposeful additions. Similar to the use of רע in Exod 21:14, they introduce the social status between a person and his neighbor. In the context of the laws, by necessity they require a long-term relationship. This is the criterion for the arrangement of the basic layer in vv. 6, 7aα, 9a, 11-12, 13, 14a. All three general cases and the subcases make sense only in a closely knit community in which a member would know their neighbors for a long time: the first general case discusses the theft of things when safekeeping deposits. This case, by necessity, presupposes a prior relationship between the two parties. The general cases 2 and 3 relate to animals. Case 2 necessarily introduces the possibility of an animal being killed by a predator, which required a proof. Case 3 distinguishes injury or loss of the animal in the owner's presence from their absence.

---

129. Otto, *Wandel*, 17.
130. Cf. the outline in Otto, *Wandel*, 16.
131. Otto, *Wandel*, 16.

The law of deposit originally solely considered the restitution of the deposited goods. It had no aspects of penalty. The new interpretation in the secondary layer of the *yᵉshallem*-laws collection suggests double restitution in cases of theft. Verse 8, as its center, introduces a twofold distinction: first, it introduces the double restitution (and a penalty) in the case of theft once the judge has declared who was guilty.[132] Second, and connected with this, v. 8 also highlights the relationship between two individuals in a general case of property law.[133] This new focus on the deity's judgment refers to a conflict between two parties, one of which was deemed untrustworthy and is therefore punished to doubly restitute. This emphasis on a particular relationship is significant. Casuistic law had originally ruled conflicts between one kin and another. In a more complex society, the threat of sanctions would become more important than the actual dispute settlement.[134] The explanatory model of sanctions is thus not only a secondary aspect of the law. Rather, I suggest the relationship between the two parties involved is the paramount systemic change, and that the law namely seeks to secure the liaison between "the man and his neighbor," so as to ensure peaceful coexistence. The introduction of sanctions into the process of dispute settlement is a mechanism that seeks to solve a problem between community members and helps to mend their long-term relationship: a matter that evidently was at the heart of a local court.[135] The breaking of the confidence between the two neighbors that are involved is a significant shared point of all three cases. The penalty that requires the neighbor to give back the double retribution thus addresses the lack of trust between both as inherent problem.

The introduction "a man and his neighbor" in v. 6a suggests that both members of the society knew each other and would in general maintain a trustworthy relationship. Neighbors were members of the community and as such were generally assumed to be trustworthy, but this trust is undermined by the possibility of a neighbor stealing the deposited property. The intent that forms the backdrop of these laws is the preclusion of community members becoming mutually suspicious of each other. The mutual long-term trust would otherwise become threatened, turning into mistrust and long-term quarreling. The explicit exclusion of a long-term relationship between opponents demonstrates the extent to which these rules are indeed based on the relationship between two members of the community. The secondary layer in vv. 7b, 8b, which take up the terminology "(a man and) his neighbor," emphasizes this aspect.

If a community indeed held up the mutually trustworthy relationship between neighbors as a high value, this poses the question about the necessity of the rules of deposit and of borrowing as a way of banning long-term hate between neighbors. The answer can be sought on two levels. First, the relevance of preserving a neighborly relationship in these frequent, severe cases is found in

132. Otto, *Wandel*, 19.
133. Otto, *Wandel*, 19.
134. Otto, *Wandel*, 21.
135. Otto, *Wandel*, 22.

the legal tradition as the comparable laws of CH 244, 249 and 266 demonstrate. Analogous to these laws of CH, the collection in Exod 22:6-14 also addresses the challenges of an intact relationship between two entrusted neighbors. The addition of v. 8 highlights the potential misuse of trust in the center of vv. 6-14: whoever is found guilty of the two parties will be exposed to the sanction to pay back double restitution. Consequently, in three areas the legislation in CC sees the precarious and unstable situation between neighbors in a community at a potential risk: homicide (21:14), nocturnal theft (22:1-2a), deposit and borrowing (22:6-14). Redaction critically, 22:6-14 with the idiomatic expression "a man and his neighbor" is on the same level as Exod 21:14, which explicitly considers the legal category of long-term relationships. This idiomatic clause expresses the fear that someone would expose themselves to the creation of long-term enmity between both parties.

In conclusion, in all three areas a possible or a factual escalation of a conflict into a long-term enmity, a distinct category in legal thought, would make sense as backdrop of the laws. It is plausible that long-term enmity informs legal reasoning when determining liability in homicide law as well as property law, yet it remains hypothetical whether Exod 21:13-14 indeed presupposes long-term enmity. The caveat of the preceding observations is that this law does not unequivocally define the slayer–victim relationship it supposes. As already seen above, it is critical for the interpretation of CC whether evidence that long-term opponents are in a particular social status may be found in other areas of law. And beyond this, it is relevant if the construct of hateful behavior between opponents can also be found outside legal tradition. If patterns of feuding between individuals form the backdrop of other traditions beyond law proper, this suggests its relevance more broadly. A comprehensive assessment is beyond the scope of this study, yet among the broader literary contexts that presuppose private enmity are the book of Proverbs' reflections on the relationship between opponents acting out hatefully. The following probes two cases of typical enmity behavior in Exod 23:4-5, behavioral patterns according to Exod 23:1-3, 5-8, and the assumptions about antagonistic behavior that inform Prov 25:21-22.

8. *Enmity Legislation in Exodus 23:4-5 and Proverbs 25:21-22*

8.1. *Exodus 23:4-5 in Exodus 23:1-8*
A fundamental law on conflict settlement and private enmity between two opponents, Exod 23:1-8 refers to long-term hateful relationships. Indeed, the two case laws in vv. 4-5 are the most outspoken witnesses for the construct of personal enmity. The following first determines the outline and then the specific legal procedure in its background. The passage consists of three parts, with two symmetrically arranged sets of laws relating to what could be framed as legal procedure in vv. 1-3, 6-8. In the center, vv. 4-5 make up a third part, whose two case laws provide classical examples of confrontations between opponents, one an escaped herd animal and another a broken-down pack animal. Source-critically

complex, not as an entire unit on the same level as Exod 21:12, and possibly later than Exod 21:13-14, these laws in the center of the composition more explicitly describe the relationship between the opponents[136]

> When you come upon your enemy's ox or donkey going astray,
> you shall bring it back.
> When you see the donkey of one who hates you lying under his burden
> and you would hold back from leaving to him,
> – you surely must bring it in order with him.[137]

Cast in conditional sentences, with an introductory conjunction כִּי, vv. 4-5 address enemy confrontation. The enemy referenced in Exod 23:4-5 with a personal 2nd person masculine singular suffix is a community member. There is no indication that this law would not share the social status of an equal, typically a member of another social network or clan. Opponents in dispute settlement, be it in formal litigation or in a conflict, act out publicly in the dynamic of challenge and riposte, naturally availing themselves of verbal and physical means.[138] Exodus 23:4-5

---

136. Exodus 23:4-5 is mostly seen as addition with the reason for its position here being enigmatic; cf. B. Jacobs, *Das Buch Exodus* (Stuttgart: Calwer, 1997), 720. Schwienghorst-Schönberger, *Bundesbuch*, 378–88, understands vv. 1a, 2a and 6* as older version ("Du sollst nicht auf das Gerücht hören, du sollst nicht nach den Vielen dem Bösen nachlaufen, du sollst den Fall des Armen in seinem Rechtsstreit nicht verdrehen") with additions in vv. 1b, 2b, 3-5 and "in seinem Rechtsstreit" in vv. 6, 7abα as pre-dtr conclusion; vv. 7bβ, 8-9 as dtr additions. Otto, *Wandel*, 8, 47-49, 53: vv. 1-3, 6-8 as basic layer; v. 7bβ as addition in first pers. sing. divine speech; vv. 4-5 as pre-dtr additions. J. W. McKay, "Exodus XXIII1-3, 6-8: A Decalogue for the Administration of Justice in the City Gate," *VT* 21 (1971), 311–25, 321 suggests a ten-partite unit (Decalogue) as the origin, with vv. 4-5 as additions. On the relations to Mesopotamian law, see Wright, *Inventing*, 314–18. Acknowledging the diversity of the material, for formal reasons of the chiastic structure Wright reads Exod 23:1-8 as one unit, including vv. 4-5, which he sees in analogy to the exhortatory block in CH 48:59–49:17. Verses 4-5 having possibly oral precursors could be loosely based on a law similar to Laws of Eshnunna 50.

137. A lexicographic conundrum are the three forms of עזב, "leave, forsake, loose," used in MT. LXX paraphrases freely with οὐ παρελεύσῃ αὐτό, ἀλλὰ συνεγερεῖς αὐτὸ μετ' αὐτοῦ. The last phrase עזב תעזב may be corrupt, and as the meaning "to help" for the root is not ascribed, a misspelling of an original עזר תעזר ("you shall surely help") could be assumed. Alternatively, as translated here, one assumes a word play with the first meaning in the first line and a root עזב II (cf. South Arabic *'db*) with the meaning "to renew, repair, put in order"; cf. G. Barbiero, *L'asino del nemico. Rinuncia alla vendetta e amore del nemico nella legislation dell'Antico Testamento (Es 23:4-5; Dt 22:1-4; Lv 19:17-18)* (Rome: Pontificio Istituto Biblico, 1991), 86. The return of the animal would be referred to as putting in order.

138. J. L. Ska, *Introduction to Reading the Pentateuch*, trans. Sr. Pascale Dominique (Winona Lake, IN: Eisenbrauns, 2006), 47.

refer to this status of enmity in the context of a set of laws, Exod 23:1-8,[139] that list further aspects of dispute settlement.

The formal differences between the two parts, vv. 1-3, 6-8 and 4-5, have often been described. Verses 4-5 differ in the context of Exod 23:1-8 in five ways from the remainder of the passage. First, formally, the conditional conjunction כִּי introduces the two cases, interrupting the flow of the other introductions. Second, the content of these verses refers to an enemy-constellation in conflict settlement in the general sense of any conflict, while the framing parts refer to trial procedure in what could be understood in a more technical-judicial sense.[140] Third, the terminology in vv. 4-5 differs from the framing parts. The terms directly address an "enemy" and a "hater" as opponents in the typical "If-You" style.[141]

Fourth, the form of the sentences in vv. 1-3, 6-8 is similar: a principal incitement with a vetitive that follows a prohibitive: "You shall not spread a false report – and you shall not join hands with the wicked to act as false witness" (v. 1).[142] Finally, fifth, vv. 3 and 6 (and possibly also v. 2) show concern for justice for systemically disadvantaged members of the community for which they use terminology of the *personae miserae*. They are typically the victims in unfair trial structures (vv. 1, 3, 7, 8). Verses 1-2, 7-8 ban the spreading of false rumor, joining a group of false witnesses and raising false charges (vv. 1-2, 7-8 with the parallels "the evildoer," רשׁע), including warnings not to follow the seduction "of the many," for evil (לרעת), nor to bend the law (v. 2b). Pivotal is the lexicography of the groups of the *personae miserae*, that are in need of protection, such as "the weak" (דל),[143] "your poor" (אביֹנך, vv. 3, 6) whose justice should not be bent, no false charges (שׁקר) be raised to kill the innocent (נקי) and the righteous

---

139. Barbiero, *L'asino*, 18–21, suggests v. 9 is part of the concentric composition. Formally, the three-partite outline of the sentence, like vv. 7 and 8, as well as the larger symmetry of a concentric passage, vv. 1-3, 4-6, 7-9, are main reasons to assume a literary unit.

140. See already M. Noth, *Exodus: A Commentary* (London: SCM Press, 1962), 188; Otto, *Wandel*, 47–48.

141. The formal difference between vv. 4-5 and the framing verses does not refer to a late date of origin. The form has been suggested to be both old or more recent; see the discussion in Barbiero, *L'asino*, 72, including the parallels in Exod 22:20-26. Mostly, the form relates to wisdom literature. Most importantly, the form occurs in rules that address specific status of groups, in particular the *personae miserae*. It has also been called "didactic" literature; see H. W. Gilmer, *The If-You Form in Israelite Law* (Missoula, MT: Scholars Press, 1975), 56. It has no parallel in any of the casuistic laws of CC. See Barbiero, *L'asino*, 72.

142. As a consequence, many redactional analyses see vv. 4-5 as a later addition; cf. Wright, *Inventing*, 317; Wellhausen, *Die Composition des Hexateuch* (Berlin: G. Reimer, 1899), 90; McKay, "Exodus XIII," 321; J. Marshall, *Israel and the Book of the Covenant: An Anthropological Approach to Biblical Law* (Atlanta: Scholars Press, 1993), 154; Schwienhorst-Schönberger, *Bundesbuch*, 378–88.

143. Cf. the contrast גדל-דל in Lev 19:15.

(צדיק, v. 7). The term ריב designates dispute settlement in vv. 3 and 6.[144] In the symmetric outline, vv. 4-5 are at the center of this composition, which is bookended by parts A/A' and B/B'.[145] Unlike the surrounding passages, the case laws in the center are not concerned about any imbalance between two opponents but rather address two personal enemies.

Table 2.3

  A Do not follow the false witness; fundamental command / vetitive / prohibitive (vv. 1-2)
     B Do not honor dispute settlement of the poor; prohibitive (v. 3)
        C Help to find the enemy's ox/donkey; help the donkey lying under his burden "if – then" (2×, vv. 4-5)
     B' Do not bend dispute settlement of the poor; prohibitive (v. 6)
  A' Keep away from lie [do not kill the just and innocent]; take no bribe (vv. 7-8) fundamental command / vetitive + motivation / prohibitive + motivation

8.2. *Legal Procedure between Opponents in Exodus 23:1-8*

The focus on imbalance in conflict settlement of the prohibitive rows (vv. 1-3, 7, and the vetitives vv. 1b, 7b) demonstrates that the passage represents ethics with a long-standing tradition reflected in sapiential literature, rather than law in a more strict sense.[146] This is relevant, as this form of literature acknowledges the distinct social status of individuals and points to the treatment of particular groups according to their specific social status. As vv. 1-3 and 6-8 perceive the *personae miserae* as distinct groups, they acknowledge their essential difference from members of equal social status, pointing specifically to the mechanisms that determine the fate of the *personae miserae*. This rather precise acknowledgment of the social status has a long-standing tradition in wisdom literature. In the context here, vv. 1-3, 6-8 indirectly affirm the social status of two enemies in vv. 4-5 as a distinct social construct.

Notably, in its bias of challenging typical values of the honor–shame society, the framing parts and the center piece both ascertain and question these social constructs of a preset enmity between parties and the behavioral norms that

---

144. These notions of the "evildoer/wicked" and the "just" in vv. 1 and 7 obviously are opposite pairs on different levels than the poor and the "enemy"; see Barbiero, *L'asino*, 41.

145. See this structure in Barbiero, *L'asino*, 40. Exodus 23:4-5 is suggested to be a later addition in this composition. It alludes to legal texts in Prov 24:17-18; 25:21-22; see Barbiero, *L'asino*, 92–101.

146. On the relation to sayings of Amenemope, see esp. S. Herrmann, "Weisheit im Bundesbuch. Eine Misszelle zu Ex 23,1-9," in *Alttestamentlicher Glaube und biblische Theologie. Festschrift für Horst Dietrich Preuß*, ed. J. Hausmann and H. J. Zobel (Stuttgart: Kohlhammer, 1992), 56–58, and Barbiero, *L'asino*, 81.

are associated with them. Exodus 23:1-3, 6-8 comment critically on the default techniques of harming enemies and, climactically arranged, vv. 4-5 admonish to actively overcome an enemy's default posture of standing by when an enemy encounters a defeat. A pivotal question for the concept of long-term enmity at large is whether Exod 23:1-3, 6-8 refer specifically to conflict settlement in centrally installed courts or whether they rather describe the asymmetries in settlement procedure in general. Can the contexts of their criticism be clarified? The following first discusses the criticism of Exod 23:1-3, 6-8 in relation to vv. 4-5, arguing that the framing parts relate to more common procedure between enemies, then ponders the social background of such rules and the relation of vv. 4-5 to wisdom tradition.

The framing passages A, B, A', B' consider legal procedure and trial mechanisms with the typically asymmetric constellations between parties. A, B, A', B' refer to unfair forms of trial. Hate against an opponent naturally would motivate false testimony. Beyond this, hateful interaction also includes generally biased allegations, to which 23:1-2, 7 refer. Such allegations, namely false testimony, were a prominent default device which enemies would use against their opponents. For instance, the idiomatic "violent witness" (עד חמס, v. 1b)[147] points to the seriousness of harming another community member.[148] These references to dispute settlement, a "precursor of a distinct Israelite procedural law,"[149] do not specifically allude to trial procedure practiced outside the local, kinship-based community, nor do they presuppose a centrally installed court operating beside the institutions that were rooted in the local, kinship-based community.[150] Indeed, Exod 23:1-3, 6-8 may best be seen against the backdrop of local conflict settlement and feuding mechanisms. They are part of the typical behavior between enemies and friends in local contexts, such as giving false witness for a friend (v. 1) and bribing participants in a lawsuit (v. 8). This theme is the frame of reference for the explicit case laws on opponents. "Your enemy" (v. 4) and "your hater" (v. 5) both relate to conflict settlement of the opponents in a judicially relevant relationship status. If vv. 1-3, 6-8 and 4-5 relate to each other in their content, a similar understanding of enmity and its opposite, friendship, informs both sets of verses. The practices mentioned in vv. 1-3, 6-8 would typically be used

---

147. Cf. this term in Deut 19:16; Ps 35:11.

148. See on witness law, in the Decalogues (Exod 20:16; Deut 5:20 and Deut 19:15-21), and specifically on this passage see B. Wells, *The Law of Testimony in the Pentateuchal Codes* (Wiesbaden: Harrassowitz, 2004), 137–38.

149. Otto, *Wandel*, 47.

150. Cf. Otto, *Wandel*, 47. Tellingly, the passage omits any institutions of conflict settlement in a centralized Judah, such as a judge. The closeness of 23:4 to tribal law is also recognized in Barbiero, *L'asino*, 82. The only potential reference to a title could be רבים (v. 2a). The use of the root רב II as a title is attested early on in Semitic, be it of a government official, a commander in Aramean, or representatives of cultic associations popular in Phoenician, Punic, Nabatean, Palmyrean contexts; cf. H. Fabry, E. Blum, and H. Ringgren, נבה *TDOT*, vol. 13 (Grand Rapids: Eerdmans, 2004), 272–98, here 294–95.

by friends against their enemies and Exod 23 points to their effects specifically when applied to particular groups of the society. The more explicit terminology of "opponent" and of "hater" also precisely addresses a specific social construct of private enmity as it points out unwritten rules[151] of conducting enmity. Urging abstinence from hateful behavior, vv. 1-3, 6-8 intend to actively curb conflicts and they also raise ethical concerns about unfair trials for the poor and for other disadvantaged groups.[152] Beyond calling for the exercise of restraint when engaging with enemies, vv. 4-5 urge opponents toward actively foregoing default behavioral patterns and reversing enmity into amity. This poses the question of the motivation for this unusual behavior.

When determining the reason why Exod 23:1-8 would ban typical behavior for opponents, a pivotal question is whether refraining from hateful behavior might have been an expected, default pattern or whether such behavior was rather conceived as counter-cultural. The escape of a herd animal or the collapse of a pack animal in Exod 23:4-5 are everyday situations in an agricultural community with serious socio-economic consequences. Mediterranean societies would normally face animal scarcity[153] and the loss or a potential death of a large animal would be substantial for the owner, in particular in Judah's small-scale agriculture. Solidarity, even with neutral neighbors, would naturally be expected in order to help each other as a form of locality-induced amity in neighborly relations that would follow suit in patterns of axiomatic amity among kin.[154] The legal history of tradition testifies to the expectation that a found good would be returned and the king would determine its rightful owner or, in the countryside, the elders respectively, as the legal tradition illustrates.[155] The return of stray animals to their rightful owner in 23:4 was an important custom in tribal societies that is deeply rooted in the respect for the property rights of others, an

---

151. Barbiero, *L'asino*, 46 with n. 106 for bibliography.

152. Hence, the redaction of 22:28–23:12 is suggested to be done by rural priestly or Levite circles; cf. Otto, *Wandel*, 49, 51.

153. On animal scarcity in the Mediterranean in both nomadic and sedentary societies that practice feuding, see J. Black-Michaud, *Cohesive Force. Feud in the Mediterranean and the Middle East* (New York: St. Martin's, 1975), 163, 165–66.

154. On the solidarity as the result of "a fusion of kinship and locality in neighborhood relations," see Fortes, *Kinship*, 242–49. For typical cases from the Hittite laws, to contemporary Bedouins in Moab and the Masai, see Barbiero, *L'asino*, 77–82, and below.

155. Cf. Hittite Laws §45: in general utensils would be brought back to their owner, otherwise the finder is considered a thief; Hittite Laws §71 refers to the finding of an ox, horse or a mule that the finder was required to take them "to the King's gate," when found in the country, to present it to the elders to determine its rightful owner, otherwise the finder is considered a thief; see further R. Haase, "Zur Anzeigepflicht des Finders nach hethitischem Recht," *WO* 12 (1957): 378–81; cf. also Barbiero, *L'asino*, 77. Cf. also H. B. Huffmon, "Ex 23:4-5: A Comparative Study," in *A Light Unto My Path: Old Testament Studies in Honor of J. M. Myers*, ed. H. N. Bream, R. D. Heim, and C. A. Moore (Philadelphia: Temple University, 1974), 271–78.

integral part of the self-identity of a community of equals in tribal societies and was treated as such. Amity in kinship-based societies has two roots. It is either grounded in an (extended) shared blood lineage, or it is of a contractual nature between befriended tribes.[156]

The formal distinction between Exod 23:1-3, 6-8 and the case laws vv. 4-5 poses the question whether the case laws in a climactic move now ban private enemy constellations altogether. Already Exod 23:1-3, 6-8 criticize the unfair hateful behavior of individuals in conflict in patriarchal, kinship-based societies. But beyond this, vv. 4-5 explicitly prohibit opponents acting out an agonistic ethos. Does the reference to "your enemy" and "your hater" reject the public excesses of hateful behavior at a particular point in time? The insertion of Exod 23:4-5 with the explicit terminology of "hater" and "enemy" targets the typical hateful patterns of behavior, urging the active overcoming of default passivity when experiencing an enemy's defeat. In contrast, the surrounding rules (vv. 1-3, 6-8) merely call for a change of behavior in legal practice.[157]

Exodus 23:4-5 is one of the clearest acknowledgments of the social construct of private enmity in biblical law, because it explicitly names this status in a row with the other social constructs of *personae miserae* in vv. 1-3, 6-8. Naming the status of enemies and haters points to specific contexts in which such behavior became detrimental for the community's wellbeing at large. By way of singling out two opponents, the law would question this form of a personalized conflict between two individuals. Its character as an addition to a pre-existing composition can either be interpreted as a more explicit description of the status of private enmity in light of its well-known nature or in light of the absence of explicit descriptions of the mechanisms of private enmity.

8.3. *Proverbs 25:21-22*

The above parallel for Exod 22:1-2 in Drakon's law already illustrated that the relationship between opponents in the case of homicide played a critical role in the legal thought of cultures outside of Israel too. Quintessential biblical texts beyond the legal sphere also presuppose constellations between private opponents. Besides, they provide a tradition-historical root of acknowledging and of bringing into question the status of enmity. In particular, sapiential traditions, such as Egyptian wisdom tradition in Amenemope 21.17-20 refer to similar lines of thought as Exod 23:4-5.[158] These wisdom texts and passages from Proverbs such as Prov 17:5; 24:17-18 and 25:21-22 equally urge the overcoming of extreme agonistic patterns, indicating a tension with traditional expectations of kinship solidarity.[159] This demonstrates that private enmity constellations posed pivotal ethical questions outside of laws, too. In particular, Prov 25:21-22 shares

---

156. Cf. Fortes, *Kinship*, 247, and Barbiero, *L'asino*, 92.
157. Rightly Barbiero, *L'asino*, 83.
158. See the references in Barbiero, *L'asino*, 79–81, including Amenemope.
159. See on the further roots and parallels Barbiero, *L'asino*, 94–97.

the hallmark criticism of hateful behavior with Exod 23:4-5. The sayings urge the provision of food and water to enemies, a synecdoche that criticizes the challenge and riposte pattern essential to private enmity, and a counter-intuitive act that is tantamount to undoing the fabric of hateful interaction:

> [21] If your enemies are hungry, give them bread to eat;
> and if they are thirsty, give them water to drink.
> [22] For you will heap coals of fire on their heads,
> and Yahweh will reward (שלם *pi.*) you.

The context of this passage refers to conflict settlement at large.[160] Verses 21-22 add two conditional warnings with two consecutive sentences. Analogous to the preceding vv. 18-20, the initial situation refers to a relation to an opponent, with v. 21 using the explicit terminology of "hate." In this case, unlike in the preceding verses, rather than a speech of the false witness (v. 18), v. 21 refers to a particular reaction in a situation of enmity. The person is called to act in line with reverse expectations, namely to feed a hungry and thirsty enemy. Both situations threaten one's life in existential ways, as does the false testimony of a witness. Interestingly, the motivation to reverse the hateful relationship is Yahweh's retributive justice in the future that will repay such action. Why would Proverbs emphasize the deity's retributive justice? It stands to reason that such reassurance would be needed as motivation in a situation of private enmity with the expectation of ultimate justice that would be established beyond the situation of the two enemies.

A need for motivation is all the more plausible in light of the command in vv. 21-22 to actively engage in interpersonal communication by helping an enemy. As in Exod 23:4-5, rather than the passivity of only refraining from glee in light of an enemy's defeat, the proverb urges active help for an enemy.

---

160. Verses 21-22 follow as a reflection on enmity against a neighbor (vv. 18-20) consisting of one pair (vv. 18-19) alluding to conflict settlement between neighbors and another reflection on inappropriate behavior (v. 20); cf. Meinhold, *Sprüche* (Zurich: Theologischer Verlag, 1991), 428. Verse 18 compares the warrior hammer, sword and arrows as analogues to a lying witness stepping up against his neighbor. This verse refers to an individual that is acquainted with details of a person's life and steps up as a witness against an acquaintance. Verse 19 compares a broken tooth (the root for "tooth" picks up חֵץ שָׁנוּן, v. 18) and an ailing foot to the unreliable confidence and trust in a friend at a point in time of affliction when trust would have been necessary. Verse 20 criticizes victorious songs sung for someone with a heavy heart. The point of the comparisons is to highlight the strength of essential parts of the human body and compare them to the essential function of the relationship with humans. The reason for the enmity between both parties remains open. The concluding v. 20 points to comparably absurd combinations, such as undressing on a cold day or as pouring vinegar (cf. pouring vinegar on a wound Prov 10:26) on an alkaline, as it would neutralize it and absorb its cleansing power. A song at the wrong time has a similar destructive effect; cf. Meinhold, *Sprüche*, 429.

Doing so would reverse a behavioral pattern between two private opponents and, consequently, expose oneself to imminent danger. The invigorated enemy could afterwards decide to continue the fight. As in Exod 23:4-5, the strong rejection of enmity patterns confirms the default behavioral patterns between enemies.[161] The parallels between Exod 23:4-5 and Prov 25:21-22 support that the reversal of mutual enmity patterns responds to an aggressive acting out of enemy patterns.

Proverbs' questioning of the dynamics of a hateful relationship has a complex background. In particular, Prov 25:21-22 see this reversal grounded in the deity's sanction.[162] Proverbs 25:21-22 refers to the deity's impending vindication,

---

161. The redaction-historical considerations of the saying in Proverbs are beyond the scope of this study but a few references are in order. This saying stands at the end of a composition in 25:11-22 that highlights the hope for divine retribution in a positive sense. A redaction-historical analysis points to exactly this function of Yahweh-sayings, referring to these sayings as "religious." R. Whybray, *The Concept of Wisdom in Proverbs 1–9* (London: SCM Press, 1965), originally developed his differentiation between Yahweh-sayings and wisdom; cf. further, Whybray, "Thoughts on the Composition of Prov 10–29," in *Priests, Prophets and Scribes: Essays on the Formation and Heritage of Second Temple Judaism, Festschrift for Joseph Blenkinsopp*, ed. E. Ulrich et al. (Sheffield: Sheffield Academic Press, 1992), 102–14. See also R. Whybray, *The Composition of Proverbs* (Sheffield: Academic Press, 1994), and idem, *Proverbs: New Century Bible Commentary* (London/Grand Rapids: Eerdmans, 1994). Originally focusing on Prov 1–9, Whybray assumes Prov 1–9 and 10–22:16 both "have been finally edited in the same spirit"; Whybray, *Proverbs*, 322. Beyond this passage, redaction-historically, the Yahweh-sayings are not only relevant in Prov 25:11-12. On a compositional level, Yahweh-sayings play a critical role in Prov 10:1–22:16. Proverbs 1–15 has 20 Yahweh-sayings, and Prov 10:1–22:16 has 55 Yahweh sayings out of a total of 86 for the entire book of Proverbs. Cf. A. Scherer, "'Sprich zur Weisheit: Meine Schwester bist du!' (Spr 7,4a) Weisheit in den Sprüchen Salomos," in *Die theologische Bedeutung der alttestamentlichen Weisheitsliteratur*, ed. M. Saur (Neukirchen-Vluyn: Neukirchener Verlag, 2012), 1–31, here 27. Proverbs 25–27 feature a relatively high number of admonitions and, for the most part, lack antithetical parallelisms as well as Yahweh-sayings, with the exception of Prov 25:22. The fundamental contribution of the Yahweh-sayings is their reflection on retributive justice in hateful relations as ultimately vindicated by the deity as agency. This seems to be more relevant than considering in general whether the isolated nature of the Yahweh-sayings in Prov 25–27 allows us to assume a "secular" context of the Proverbs. In fact, Prov 25:22 comments critically on the mechanisms of hateful conflict settlement when it, in the form of an admonition, points to the deity's sanction. In the context of the collection Prov 25–27, the Yahweh-sayings frame this as a motivation of their call to overcome hateful interaction. This function becomes even more apparent when juxtaposing the composition Prov 15:33–16:9 to 25:21-22.

162. A comparable passage is Prov 24:15-18. Verse 15 is a just–wicked proverb with an appeal to the wicked in a vocative, not to intrude into the private sphere ("dwelling," "resting place") of the just. Using the rare root "to lie in wait" (cf. Deut 19:12), v. 15 refers to ambushing of an opponent as what is seen as unfair behavior. The term ארב serves as

offering what may be called a theological substantiation.[163] Among the evidence for a deed-destiny-inclusion, the uniqueness of 25:22 is apparent in light of the singular function of Yahweh as a logical subject of the fulfilling or, as K. Koch more adequately asserts, as someone who "completed" an action. An explanation of Yahweh's completion of the good deed of the agent may thus refer to the legal understanding that informs such "completion" of an action in the *yeshallem*-laws in Exod 21:34; 22:1, 10-15.[164]

9. *Conclusion: Intentionality and Long-term Enmity*

Exodus 21:18-19; 22:1-2; 23:4-5 were adduced as laws and Prov 25:21-22 as sapiential text that possibly also substantiate the relevance of long-term relationship between enemies in Exod 21:13-14. Laws do not explicitly define the slayer–victim relationship, and its presupposition can thus only be substantiated indirectly. There is good reason to assume that already in Exod 21:13-14 not only the criterion of "intentionality" plays a role, but that a long-term private enmity between two opponents as a distinct social status also informs these laws.

This poses the question of how the slayer's intentionality as the classical criterion of distinction between the cases in Exod 21:13-14 relates to the status of private opponents in a feuding conflict settlement. Can the category

---

epitome for any clandestine attempt to hurt and potentially kill another individual. The imagery is set in an agrarian context, but at the same time, refers to a typical conflict between two opponents. Verse 15 combines this typical conflict situation the "wicked"–just contrast. Verse 17 urges against rejoicing over an opponent and v. 18 refers to the deity as judge and agent of retributive justice. The arrangement follows a clear pattern. The passage points to the serious nature of the threats against an individual's life. Verses 17-18 explicitly criticize from the perspective of a Yahwistic ethos.

163. For good reason Prov 25:21-22 have played a pivotal role in understanding the doctrine of divine retribution in the Hebrew Bible. Klaus Koch suggested the Hebrew Bible highlights the inclusion of consequences within one's actions. He supports this interpretation specifically with passages from sayings in the collections of Prov 25–29, namely, 25:19; 26:27-28; 28:1, 10, 16b, 17-18, 25b; 29:6, 23, 25; K. Koch, "Gibt es ein Vergeltungsdogma im Alten Testament?" *EvTheol* 52 (1955), 1–42, here 2–3.

164. Cf. Koch, "Vergeltungsdogma," 5. By doing so Koch seeks to demonstrate the intrinsic connection between a deed and its consequences, suggesting that in this case, Yahweh would not actually act independently from the preceding human agent but, instead, would simply ensure the completion of the wicked action as a form of closure. He compares Yahweh's function with a birthmother who merely completes and fulfills the task that humans have begun. On the other hand, in order to reject any notion of Yahweh in the role of judge, Koch highlights the use of the root in Hebrew and the fact that it never designates the act of the judge and, as a consequence, is not a term from the realm of institutional trial. It refers simply to the task of fulfilling what had already been part of the original deed.

of "intentionality" and its use in biblical law be clarified further? Generally speaking, assumptions about intentionality are typical for humans. Prone to intent, humans by default assign intentionality to other humans and the heuristic propensity of the human mind, an "intentional stance" played out even beyond human subjects, for instance, with regard to animals and in the perception of the divine that informs such statements as "the gods must be angry."[165] The present chapter attempted to reconstruct intentionality primarily on the basis of homicide law as a quintessential and grave case of hateful intent. Yet it makes the case that the final form of Exod 21:12-14 may have decided homicide cases neither solely on the basis of strict liability (Exod 21:12) nor strict intentionality or fault-based liability respectively. Rather, it pointed to the possibility that the determination of fault-based liability may in many cases have included a continuous influx of intentionality as apparent in the slayer–victim relationship. Intentionality as a criterion must thus be seen in the social context of the slayer–victim relationship. This result is important, not least because it questions any unilinear evolutionary trajectory from strict liability to fault-based liability. While for methodological reasons the relevance of the slayer–victim relationship in Exod 21:13-14 must remain hypothetical, there is good reason to assume that for homicide cases such a foregoing interactive pattern was relevant rather than assuming abstract "intentionality" as solely decisive criterion. De facto intentionality would have been apparent in a series of actions against a specific individual. Beyond the legal evaluation of homicide cases this is particularly plausible in light of the intrinsically public nature of private enmity in kinship-based societies, as legal anthropology points out. Because in such societies any enmity between individuals was lived out in public, an ongoing intentionality would manifest itself in a long-term hateful relationship and in ongoing hateful activities, such as the pursuit of one's opponent. This result allows for a provisional conclusion and it calls for a comparative view of intentionality and long-term enmity in ancient Near Eastern laws.

The further course of this study considers Deuteronomic and Priestly homicide legislation. As will become apparent, Deuteronomic law, building on previous tradition of legal thought, unequivocally specifies the long-term character of enmity and of priestly homicide law, taking into consideration very different aspects besides the binary of "intentional" and "accidental." Before detailing the concepts of Deuteronomic and of Priestly law, a brief summary overviews this intermediary result, pointing to other laws that reflect on the intentionality of a long-term opponent. The following sketches out how the various legal concepts gradually replace strict liability in homicide law as they specify the role of the construct of long-term enmity. First, a semantic clarification on "intent" in

---

165. See B. Strawn, "Intention," in Strawn, ed., *The Oxford Encyclopedia of the Bible and Law*, 1:433–46, here 434, as an example of a religiously framed assignation of intent, with reference to the theory that humans assume intent when predicting or explaining the behavior of a specific agent, as developed by D. Dennett, *The Intentional Stance* (Cambridge MA: MIT Press, 1987).

property law in the Decalogues demonstrates how the semantics of the verb, when seen against the backdrop of a long-term relationship, point to the notion of a continuous influx of intentionality in Exod 20:17 and Deut 5:21. Second, early Judaism's discussion of the category of enmity illustrates the relevance of it, shifts the discourse towards pure "intentionality" and towards intentionality when acting out an agonistic ethos.

9.1. *Intentionality in Ancient Near Eastern Law*

Intentionality is a prominent and pivotal category in ancient Near Eastern, Athenian and in biblical law. In particular, the distinction between intentionality and negligence as "culpable carelessness"[166] demonstrates its relevance in legal thought. Intentionality in ancient Near Eastern law is a complex field that is beyond the scope of this study, yet a few remarks are in order.

Specifically in homicide legislation, CH 206-207 consider intentionality as the main criterion when judging a slayer. This isolated category of intentionality clearly had an impact on biblical law, as can be seen in the fact that the formula "I did not strike him intentionally" has a parallel in Deut 4:42. At the same time, CH 206-207 is also impressively similar to Exod 21:18-19, yet different in that it does not require an oath. The case of the pregnant woman in Exod 22:22-25, in which intentionality is relevant, is found in the Sumerian Law Exercise Tablet §§1'-2' and the laws of Lipit-Ishtar §d, and so are laws on the goring ox (Exod 21:28-32).[167]

One attempt to synthesize the discourse on intentionality in ancient Near Eastern law is to distinguish between two areas of its relevance, as Strawn suggests. First, in most cases, these laws apply the principle of strict liability,[168] yet they allow in individual cases for mitigation in the punishment. More importantly, given the fact that some of the laws explicitly mention the criterion of intentionality, assumedly, therefore, intentionality needs to be inferred in other cases too, even though such laws may not explicitly mention it.[169] Second, the reason why laws refer to intention defies an easy explanation. The reflection on intention seems to develop over time and later law collections include this aspect more fully. Consider Westbrook's perception of "ample evidence in the sources of distinctions between deliberate and accidental acts, and even of nuances in between, such as foreseeability of consequences," while at the same time, law collections do not contain a systematic reflection on this matter.[170] In light of

---

166. Definition of B. Garner, ed., *Black's Law Dictionary*, 8th ed. (Saint Paul, MN: Thomson/West, 2004), 1061.

167. J. J. Finkelstein, *The Ox that Gored* (Philadelphia: American Philosophical Society, 1981), 1–89.

168. R. Westbrook and C. Wilcke, "The Liability of an Innocent Purchaser of Stolen Goods in Early Mesopotamian Law," *AfO* 25 (1974–77): 111–21.

169. Strawn, "Intention," 442.

170. R. Westbrook, *A History of Ancient Near Eastern Law*, 2 vols. (Leiden: Brill, 2003), 1:73.

these attempts to consider the role of intentionality, its evolutionary trajectory in law evidently requires further consideration in the more general developmental models of legal thought.[171] Given the lack of evidence of explicit discourses on intentionality in law, it is plausible to assume with Westbrook that the fact that intentionality was not explicitly mentioned most likely is grounded in the implicit nature of such mental aspects and in the casuistic character of the law collections at large that would not invite theoretical reflections on intentionality as a mental state.[172]

A sideways look at the category of negligence is helpful. Distinct from intentionality, negligence as "culpable carelessness" corroborates the relevance of legal reasoning on intentionality. Negligence may vary gradually[173] and the distinction between negligence and intent naturally is gradual and thus can be blurry. Consequently, laws explore various investigative strategies. Consider the relevance of negligence in construction law. Deuteronomy 22:8 requires securing the parapet wall so that it prevents fatal falls and, in this case, the negligence of the owner would acquire blood guilt, that is, the owner would be guilty as if he committed (intentional) homicide. The *Laws of Eshnunna* 58 likewise point to the liability of an owner whose wall has been declared unsafe but who did not secure it. He would, consequently, be punished were someone killed, and a similar constellation appears in CH 229-230 with the collapse of a house that causes the death of the homeowner then falling back to the builder. The comparability of the cases with the goring ox Exod 21:28-32 and its parallels (CH 250, 251; and LE 54,56) point to the relevance of negligence in legal reasoning. The variety of punishments in the various cases reflects degrees of liability. For instance, an inanimate object, such as a house, was entirely under the control of the builder, while an animal was less strictly controllable by an owner, thus leaving room to consider intentionality.[174]

Methodologically, this study has retrieved the category of long-term enmity as a social status of opponents based on its alleged context in a kinship-based society. The short references above on negligence and intentionality have further hinted at the complexity and the nuanced ascertainment of liability in ancient Near Eastern

---

171. For biblical law, the shift from strict liability to fault-based liability in Exod 21:12-14 reflects a literary development with v. 12 functioning as heading, rather than a legal historical development; see above, 4.2.

172. Cf. also Strawn, "Intention," 443.

173. See on the definition of negligence, Garner, *Black's Law*, 1061: "The failure to exercise the standard of care that a reasonably prudent person would have exercised in a similar situation; any conduct that falls below the legal standard established to protect others against unreasonable risk of harm, except for conduct that is intentionally, wantonly, or willfully disregardful of others' rights." Consequently, Strawn, "Intention," 443, points to the necessity to evaluate the implication of negligence throughout the biblical collections.

174. Cf. Westbrook, *A History of Ancient Near Eastern Law*, 1:416; cf. Strawn, "Intention," 444.

law. Altogether the analysis suggests biblical law leads an equally complex discourse that is embedded in its own larger contexts. In particular, the reconstruction of laws in which intentionality plays a role in both homicide and injury law demonstrates the relevance of a slayer–victim relationship in the additions 21:13-14 and the hypothetical reworking of 21:18-19. Methodologically, the essentially public notion of enmity in such contexts guided the analysis of both homicide and injury law: in the case of injury law, the fact that the victim could be seen in public served as evidence for their convalescence that was plainly visible to any community member. Any request for injury-reward would end at this point. In homicide law, public knowledge of long-term enmity between the parties and the long-term intent of killing a victim would *per se* serve as exclusion from asylum. The systemic exclusion of continuous intent essentially takes consideration of a long-term enmity between both opponents. The reference in Exod 21:14 to the intended victim as "his neighbor/companion," while not unequivocal, may especially when considered in the laws' present form, its semantics and the case/counter-case arrangement reveal the presupposition of a form of long-term homicide.

9.2. חמד: *Intentionality and Long-term Enmity in the Decalogues*

Semantic notions of the relationship between slayer and victim are decisive, as the pivotal role of the semantics in Exod 21:14 for the interpretation demonstrates. This poses the question whether besides the prominent case/counter-case outline in other laws semantic nuances in the language consider rather than sheer intent the status of continuous long-term enmity as a pivotal legal criterion. A prominent example for the semantic nuance of an ongoing intent is the use of חמד ("coveting") in the Decalogues to designate the ongoing attempt of seeking another's possessions. In this case the semantics of the verb imply a notion of a long-term relationship between two neighbors, at least from the active party's perspective. As this initial consideration on חמד ("coveting") illustrates, intentionality and long-term enmity may be interrelated already on the level of language. In order to further map the semantics of חמד ("coveting") in biblical Hebrew, suffice it to point to the plethora of devices Hebrew can use to express aspects of intentionality. Beyond narratives or laws they may also consist of a single term. Consider the metaphor of the "heart" (לב) as one among many possible conceptualizations of an individual's voluntary center. This stock metaphor in the Hebrew language can express both the intention of devising and conceiving evil, as well as positive intent. Prose and poetry alike employ the testing, probing and the knowing of the heart to evoke phenomena of intent.[175]

---

175. See the overview in Botica, *Intention*, 118–19. For negative intentions see, for instance, Gen 6:5; 8:21; Pss 28:3; 58:2; 66:18; Prov 23:7; 26:25; Isa 29:13; for positive intentions, 1 Kgs 8:17-18; 1 Sam 16:7; 1 Chr 29:19; Ps 24:4; and the object of divine testing in poetic texts, Jer 11:20; 12:3; 17:9; 20:12; Pss 7:10 (cf. Pss 17:3; 26:2; 139:1, 23); 44:22; Prov 21:2 (cf. Prov 15:11; 16:2; 17:3; 20:27); cf. Job 7:17-18.

Characteristic is the Holiness Code's association of hate, with the heart as the center of intentionality; as, for instance, in Lev 19:17: "Not shall you hate your brother in your heart."[176] Obviously, legal thought does not limit the expression of intentionality to the "heart," and a comprehensive systematic overview on the lexicography of intentionality would reveal a plethora of notions of long-term enmity that in itself informs the reading of law.[177] A complementary aspect to human intent is the deity's examination of intent, thoughts, and, more generally, of mind and heart.[178]

Heavily dependent on their context, semantic fields for intentionality often connect it with a relationship between two individuals. Consequently, the semantic notions of such relationships are pivotal for biblical law, as the use of the term רע ("neighbor/companion") for a personally known individual demonstrates.[179] These contexts of a private relationship demonstrate the depth of legal thought and, in the case of intentionality, provide examples for one of the semantic concepts. In Exod 20:17, the Decalogue uses חמד as a term for intentionality vis-à-vis a neighbor. A description of intentionality at the interface

---

176. Strawn, "Intention," 434, namely in narrative contexts, with reference to Gen 24:45; 1 Sam 1:13; 27:1; 1 Chr 15:29; Isa 14:13; cf. Eccl 3:17-18. See on intentionality also in Chapter 5, 3.4.2; 3.4.3.

177. Comprehensively grasping the theme through semantic studies is beyond the scope of this study. Suffice it to point to the enormous diversity of contexts and context-related terms for intentionality that vary in the diverse in legal, religious, cultic or specifically ethical literature (cf. Botica, *Intention*, 133–61); consequently, lists of terms vary depending on the respective textual field. For instance, lexicographic approaches list frequent designations for intentionality, including body metaphors and abstract terms, such as לב, מחשבה, יצר, קרב, כליה, מזימה, ערמה, צדיה; cf. Botica, *Intention*, 109. Alternatively, they describe the concept of hate or enmity with the nouns איבה and שנאה. Verbs that designate intentionality to commit a crime include: בקש (*pi.*); esp. used for the homicide attempts of Saul: 1 Sam 19:2, 10; 20:1; 22:23; 23:14 (2×), 25; 24:2; 9 (with object רעה); 26:2, 20; 27:4; see also 1 Sam 25:26, 29; 2 Sam 4:8, and others. Homicide legislation can specifically express the intrinsic, mental or emotive notion of intent with terms such as צדה, זיד, ארב, while on the other hand idioms like בלי דעת, בשגגה exclude intentionality; cf. Botica, *Intention*, 49.

178. Verbs of perception describe the deity's knowledge in a variety of activities: "to see," ראה, 1 Sam 16:7; Jer 20:12; cf. 12:3; Gen 6:5; "to know, discern," בין, 1 Chr 28:9; Pss 24:12; 139:2; "to know, recognize," ידע, Deut 31:21; 1 Kgs 8:39; 2 Chr 6:30; 32:31; Pss 44:22; 94:11. Another group of verbs describes the deity's active testing, for instance, בחן (Jer 20:12), תכן, חפש, פקד, חקר, צרף. Further, metaphors for organs that are the object of the deity's probing, such as בטן, כליה, קרב, לב as well as terms at the interface between physiological and emotive processes, such as רוח, נפש, and terms for cognitive, spiritual and emotive processes, such as יצר ("form, shape, create"), חשב, זמם, דמה, חרש, הרה; Botica, *Intention*, 124–33.

179. See above 4.4.

between intent and the actual attempt at property theft illustrates its relevance.[180] The prohibitive lists potential objects of theft, beginning with "the house of your neighbor," "the wife of your neighbor," "the servants, ox, donkey and any other property of your neighbor," and the repeated prohibitive form "you shall not covet" (Exod 20:17) identifies the relationship to the targeted individual as "your neighbor" or "your companion" (רעך).[181] The syntactical form of construct chains in Exod 20:17 draws attention to the meaning of חמד as an attempt at bringing belongings into one's possession in an intentional, repetitive act of one individual. In this context, as may possibly be the case in Exod 21:14, the term רע ("neighbor, companion") signifies programmatically the long-term status of the intent of hurting a particular, known individual. With this the agent apparently engages in an attempt to deprive their neighbor. The interpretation of חמד must be sought at the interface between an interior state of mind and the attempt of gaining ownership.[182] The notion of "attempted misappropriation"[183] is supported by the basic meaning "to incorporate something into one's own belongings which is not actually used by its owner."[184] At the other end of the spectrum, the translation "coveting" airs on mere intent. This meaning may point to the legal relevance

---

180. Intention, independent from its execution, is a legally relevant act. B. S. Jackson, "Liability for Mere Intentions in Early Jewish Law," in *Essays in Jewish and Comparative Legal History* (Leiden: Brill, 1975), 202–34, 213, suggests it may have been irrelevant in practical law and trial. However, as Phillips (*Avengers*, 16) demonstrates based on the case of Lysias 1, On the murder of Eratosthenes, that in fifth/fourth-century Athenian law sheer intentionality was fundamentally relevant for any investigation into relationships of enmity.

181. The variation in the parallel passage Deut 5:21 alters both the wording and the order, mentioning first the wife, then, in the second place, the house. It also distinguishes between an attempt to bring into one's possession (חמד) your neighbor's or companion's wife, and it continues, nor to "desire" (אוה *hitp.*) the house, field, servants, ox, donkey, nor any other property of "your neighbor" or "your companion."

182. See Strawn, "Intention," 434; P. D. Miller, *The Ten Commandments* (Louisville: Westminster John Knox, 2009), 389–92.

183. Jackson, "Liability," 203. The act of taking is highlighted in some instances, such as Deut 7:25, followed by "take, seize"; but "to covet and to take" in Josh 7:21; "covet and seize" in Mic 2:2. Without reference to an act besides that of "coveting, desiring," see Gen 3:5; Exod 34:24; Ps 19:11.

184. B. Lang, "Du sollst nicht nach der Frau eines anderen verlangen. Eine neue Deutung des 9ten und 10ten Gebots," *ZAW* 93 (1981): 216–24. Similarly, J. J. Stamm, *The Ten Commandments in Recent Research* (London: SCM Press, 1967), 103–104, suggests the Decalogue did not prohibit the impulse of coveting but the Decalogue intends to protect the fundamental right of property ownership from actual stealing. Lang and Stamm suggest the Decalogue protects the possession, including of a wife, against actual robbing or stealing.

of mere intentionality.[185] Furthermore, the parallelism of חמד ("desiring") with אוה *hitp.*[186] also substantiates this meaning. The parallelism firstly refers to a personally known individual, "your neighbor/companion," and secondly it repeats the verb חמד[187] (Exod 20:17) or modifies it (אוה *hitp.*).[188] Any attempt of seizing any of the property would occur over a period of time. The prohibitives clearly convey the ongoing character of the attempt of seizing a neighbor's property and thus point to a hateful relationship against a neighbor. The prohibitives refrain from pointing out the legal relevance of an ongoing attempt. Yet they clearly demonstrate that this potentially unilateral ongoing intent of theft was a consistent pattern and this supports that the prohibitives ultimately consider the nature of these attempts in light of the social status of the agent.

Attempted misappropriation and coveting are both possible meanings and, generally speaking, the shift in meaning between an interior state and an actual attempt of stealing is characteristic. Consider, for instance, the parallel of Mic 2:2 with the use of the verb for "seizing" an opponent's property. This is indicative of the attempt of stealing another person's belongings. The two parallel verbs גזל ("tearing away") and עשק ("oppressing") designate an activity that is directed against another individual, with the initial חמד as the first step. Arguably, it designates the intentional search for occasion as a preparatory stage to tear away property: "And they covet fields, and snatch them away, and houses, and tear them away; they oppress a man and his house, (even) a man and his inheritance." The sequence of verbs in Mic 2:2 therefore asserts intentionality as a relevant act and its gradual character of a transition to acting out, and it supports the understanding of intentionality as legally relevant.[189]

The reception history of the prohibitive of coveting Exod 20:17 in Philo, next to the subsequent interiorizing of commands in the Sermon on the Mount and in Early Rabbinic literature, all corroborate the legal significance of coveting.[190] In particular, independent from attempts to attribute this to an evolutionary pattern of a late, reflected, internalized form of legal thought, the reference to an ongoing intention demonstrates the perception of a long-term relationship between the agent and his victim and thus substantiates the specific nature of long-term private enmity as a category in biblical law. The dating of Exod 20:17/Deut 5:21 are disputed, yet they both represent stages of the reception of earlier biblical law. The Decalogues' reference to intentionality demonstrates the relevance of

---

185. See, for instance, a summary of this interpretation in Jackson, "Liability," 203–205, namely based on the parallelism with "to take" in Deut 7:25; Mic 2:2; on which, see below.

186. The *hitp.* designates the social status of someone who is coveting.

187. See the overview in Botica, *Intention*, 453–56.

188. Cf. G. Mayer, אוה, *TDOT*, vol. 1 (Grand Rapids: Eerdmans, 1974), 134–37, suggests it to be mostly in synonymous parallelism with חמד.

189. Jackson, "Liability," 202–34; Botica, *Intention*, 453–56.

190. Cf. Strawn, "Intentionality," 435; Botica, *Intention*, 169–317.

this concept and points to its context in a long-term hateful relationship between two opponents.

The semantic range of חמד and its use for intentionality support the relevance that laws attribute to intentionality in assault and injury laws such as Exod 21:18-19. In a combat that both opponents started voluntarily, a shared agency would naturally lessen the punishment of the prevailing party for an intentional attack. If both act intentionally, they consequently share the risk of injury.[191] The example of חמד thus demonstrates a nuanced perception of facets of intentionality. Other laws confirm this shared responsibility in the case of spontaneous intentionality. Consider, for instance, Exod 22:22-25, the injury of the pregnant woman in the course of a fight, and Deut 25:11-12, the wife of one of two quarreling men seizing the other man's genitals, evidently an intentional act. Besides taking action, forbearing protest can also be indicative of the intention of committing an act. The laws about a betrothed woman engaging in extramarital intercourse in Deut 22:23-27 declare her guilty if she was complacent and forbore crying for help if it happened in a place where she would have been heard.

9.3. Early Judaism

The preceding sections 9.1 and 9.2 have considered the relevance of intentionality in ancient Near Eastern law and substantiated how the semantics of חמד express intentionality in a one-sided hateful relationship to a neighbor. At the same time, they have challenged the notion that intentionality was the sole legal criterion in homicide legislation. They have pointed to the perception of long-term hateful relationships as indicative of a social, publicly visible status of the opponents involved. This raises the question whether the focus on sheer intent became increasingly relevant in the reception history of laws, such as the reception of Exod 21:18-19 in Philo's reflection. Following this line of thought, the distinction between action law and non-action law in Hellenistic Judaism helps to more precisely describe the increasing relevance of intentionality.[192] As became apparent, the terminology of חמד in Exod 20:17 and Deut 5:21 proposes a gradual transition between pure (non-action) intent and active execution. The later reception history recognizes the categories of intentionality and negligence, and, for instance, Philo, highlights it in the areas of criminal, cultic law and of religious and ethical law. Philo's emphasis on the internal life in general should be taken into account as it demonstrates how the increase of the category of intention as motivation for a particular criminal offense becomes evident. Multiple idioms in Philo's writings point to intentionality as a criterion in law.

---

191. Strawn, "Intentionality," 439; see also R. Haase, "The Hittite Kingdom," in *A History of Ancient Near Eastern Law*, vol. 1, ed. R. Westbrook (Leiden: Brill, 2003), 619–56, here 646.

192. Criminal law, suggests B. S. Jackson, typically distinguishes two types of cases: action law and non-action laws. See Jackson, "Liability," 202–206, particularly with reference to חמד (Exod 20:16; Deut 5:21).

The categories he uses are influenced by categories that are known from Greek law. Lexicographically, intention is associated with a number of idioms: ἑκούσιος vs. ἀκούσιος and their equivalent οὐκ/μὴ ἐκ προνοίας vs. ἐκ προνοίας. These distinctions substantiate Philo's grounding in the categories of Greek homicide law:[193] γνώμη, βούλευσις/βουλεύω, ἐπιτίθημι ktl., ἐπανίστημι ktl., δόλος/δολερῶς, διάνοια.[194] "Non-action" cases, which Philo references, partly in the tradition of biblical law,[195] are another category. For the development of legal thought, it is interesting that the relevance of the category of intentionality leads to Philo's assertion of and attention to the inward aspects of life, including the cult, which naturally highlight voluntary aspects of an individual such as intention.[196] This reception history in Philo attests to the wide relevance of intentionality in general and, more specifically, besides external influences. Philo draws to a large extent on intentionality in biblical law-building in Exod 21:12-14. As he points to the passage in light of default categories of biblical criminal law, construction law, laws of testimony, and property law that reflect intentionality, the more complex category of long-term relationship to an opponent is implied when such actions occur over a long period of time. For the interpretation of Exod 21:12-14 this raises the question of whether the isolated notion of intentionality was indeed the only criterion of homicide law or if this perception is shaped through the subsequent reception history.

9.4. *Summary and Outlook*

Regarding the overall scope of the present study, the analysis has yielded insights in legal thought in CC in which Exod 23:4-5 reflects a status of private enmity. Injury law (Exod 21:18-19), depository law (Exod 22:6-14), self-defense law (Exod 22:1-2a) reflect an ethical code that would make sense if these laws presuppose long-term hateful relationships between opponents. The insertion of Exod 22:1-2a suggests the increasing importance of the slayer–victim relationship as a social status that is driven by the intention to exclude the special case of homicide from the behavioral code allowed in cases of private enmity. It is thus possible that the objective of the laws in Exod 22:1-2a is to reflect on private enmity as a publicly known status of two individuals in a community, something which legal anthropology suggests is typically found in kinship-based societies.[197] The relevance of this status of active mutual hostility is grounded in the high degree of collective identity of individuals in Ancient Israel. This may be comparable with community identities in contemporary forms of collectivism as described in sociology, in particular, if members of a collective would prioritize

---

193. Botica, *Intention*, 201 n. 92, 239, with reference to I. Heinemann, *Philons griechische und jüdische Bildung* (Breslau: M. & H. Marcus, 1932), 385, 400.
194. Cf. Botica, *Intention*, 201–13.
195. Cf. Lev 4; 5; see Botica, *Intention*, 240–315.
196. Cf. Botica, *Intention*, 247–48, 316.
197. The necessity for such regulation differs in historical situations.

the collective's goals[198] and typically would be emotionally and socially attached to in-groups. Such systems share with Ancient Israel characteristic hallmarks, namely the regulation by distinctive group standards, their emphasis on in-group harmony, the acceptance of in-group authority and, the perception of the group as homogenous body.[199] For homicide law in Exod 21:13-14, the presupposition appeared as an interpretive possibility mainly based on the interpretation of רע ("neighbor/companion") as an indicator of a relationship in v. 14.

The discussion of laws in CC raises questions about conflict settlement and adjudication practice, including the alleged backdrop of legal thought which CC represents. To what degree does CC outside of Exod 23:4-5 consider situations of private enmity? This question has a bearing on far-reaching historical contextualizations of CC, namely whether the alleged lack of central authority and law enforcement, typical for segmentary societies and often presupposed for CC, suggests that legal procedure and authorized institution in kinship-based societies would acknowledge enmity over a long-term period. Notably, the legal material of "apodictic" law was seen as being primarily embedded in Ancient Israel's kinship-based society and thus reflecting the practice of these laws in this context.[200] A critical substantiation for this understanding is the Hebrew lexicon of terms for an individual's inclusion into their kin, specifically their relation to other kin members.[201] The form-critical ascription of individual legal sentences to one specific social setting has long since been questioned, as it seems to induce legal-historical evolutionary models. Legal anthropological research warns against unilinear evolutionary schemes. It instead suggests models of the concurrent use of legal systems, for instance, "dual legislation" that allow for complex legal developments in which, in spite of an overimposed central legal system, in a local polity the kinship-based context of law would remain in place. Thus the absence of any central legal institution in the laws of CC may not be as

198. Cf. A. Hagedorn, *Between Moses and Plato: Individual and Society in Deuteronomy and Ancient Greek Law* (Göttingen: Vandenhoeck & Ruprecht, 2004), 89–99, with the interpretation of Old Testament law as based on ideas of corporate personalities. "Dyadic" personalities in societies in antiquity, as, for instance, Ancient Israel, depend to a high degree upon the evaluations of others, i.e., they depended on external not internal values; Hagedorn, *Moses*, 93, in discussion with H. C. Triandis et al., "An Etic–Emic Analysis of Individualism and Collectivism," *Journal of Cross-Cultural Psychology* 24 (1993): 366–83.

199. Hagedorn, *Moses*, 94.

200. See, in particular, Gerstenberger, *Wesen*, 110–17, with reference to Jer 35 and Lev 18. Cf. also K. Elliger, "Das Gesetz Leviticus 18," *ZAW* 67 (1955): 1–25, here 8. and also in *Leviticus* (Tübingen: Mohr Siebeck, 1966), 234. Elliger in his analysis of Lev 18 has pointed to the context of kinship as the core and backdrop of this law, in an original list the relationship specifically to females in a kinship group, the shared life in a clan, respectively.

201. Gerstenberger, *Wesen*, 115, with reference to brother, neighbor/companion, people.

helpful for their historical dating as is often understood. The current interpretation thus suggests that laws on conflict settlement in CC well support the relevance of kinship-based institutions.

This study has on several occasions referred to legal anthropology. Can the fundamental relevance of kinship-based structures as the background of the laws of CC and the nature of private enmity as a social status be more systematically demonstrated and further supported through a legal comparative perspective? Seen through the lens of legal anthropology, Classical Athens' offers itself as a comparable milieu that has been described as an agonistic, litigious social sphere, namely as a polity where kinship and institutional law would naturally overlap in multiple ways, with feuding mechanisms as the dominating conflict settlement pattern rather than the notion of an objective "rule of law."[202] Only in selected cases would central institutions have become involved in routine conflicts. The Athenian paradigm suggests considering two other aspects.

First, the slayer–victim relationship and, second, the discourse between kinship-based feuding practices in their relation to an "objective" rule law. In Athens, particularly in homicide cases, the constellation between opposed parties was critical in trial.[203] The above considerations, far from naively assuming biblical law as positive law, suggested that Exod 23:4-5 and 22:1-2a in CC presuppose typical conflict settlement and trial situations in a kinship-based society, while others such as 21:13-14 may possibly presuppose it as their hypothetical social background. Clearly, the nuanced Hebrew lexicography used to express continuous intent and the elaborate and widespread discourse in legal thought on intentionality and long-term relationship between private opponents as background of Exod 23:4-5 attest to this context of a kinship-based society. Altogether they made the case that the underlying mechanisms of conflict situations in biblical law may be much more critical for exactly determining what is meant with fault-based liability than has hitherto been recognized.

Second, the legal anthropological lens on the concept of private enmity in other areas of laws, especially in classical Athens, leads into a discourse on the relationship between kinship-based feuding versus any notions of an objective "rule of law." This legal anthropological comparative approach thus indirectly contributes to the question as to what extent biblical law has any relevance for conflict settlement practice by way of pointing to the relevance of kinship structures and feuding in local conflicts. The majority of scholars in Attic law agree that there is good evidence that in fifth/fourth-century Athens feuding practices drove the dynamics as conflicts and resulting law cases would naturally

---

202. See the interpretation of litigation in Athens as feud in Cohen, *Law*, 87–118, and the interpretation of Demosthenes' *On the Trierarchic Crown* in Cohen, *Law*, 75–82, pointing to the fight for public recognition within hierarchical and egalitarian impulses in Athenian public. The social values that participants brought to the judicial process were obviously relevant, while neither judges nor litigants had any formal legal training; Cohen, *Law*, 61.

203. Cf. Philipps, *Avengers*, 77.

be handled at the interface between kinship authority and a central authority. A full evaluation of Attic forensic orators is beyond the scope of this study, but it suffices to refer to trials, such as Demosthenes' suit against Meidias, that "can only be understood as one part of a much larger part of transactions, transactions shaped by the dynamic of feud."[204] Lawsuits in Athens were of an intrinsically public nature and so was the status of private enmity between two opponents in their striving for honor. These lawsuits took place in a framework in which ultimately the polis for the good of the community would claim a primacy over the individual. Consequently, the parties in a lawsuit often would not only defend themselves in a specific case, they would also demonstrate their own integrity to the polity and contrast it with their opponent's shortfall as public in order to win over the jury.[205] This strategy is one example of the public nature of private enmity that naturally would encourage an opponent to rally as many members of the polity on his or her own side as possible. This dynamic explains why the status of enmity was transitive in the sense that each of the opposing parties would typically include their kin, and, as the conflict escalated, as many allies as possible.

This study seeks to analyze concepts of private enmity in the collections of biblical law. The analysis of laws from CC could demonstrate that the specific constellation between two opponents played a role in many laws, even though their social status as private enemies could only be hypothetically assumed for homicide law in Exod 21:13-14. It will consequently be a task to further describe the interconnection between kinship-based institutions, their practices of feuding, and the bodies of the larger polity as the literary contexts of biblical law construe them.

The unabated relevance of kinship-based law, in spite of Deuteronomic law's alleged background in a centralized Judean legal system, is immediately apparent: for instance, homicide law in Deut 19 for the first time mentions the character of the avenger of blood as a central figure in kinship-based law and thus acknowledges the victim's kin's right of avenging a member. It will be critical to see how this law puts the focus on procedural practice and on the prevention of the conflict between two opponents spreading into a typical kinship feud.

---

204. Cohen, *Law*, 90.
205. See R. W. Wallace, "Private Lives and Public Enemies: Freedom of Thought in Classical Athens," in *Athenian Identity and Civic Ideology*, ed. A. L. Boegehold and A. C. Scafuro (Baltimore: Johns Hopkins University Press, 1994), 127–55, esp. 144, pointing by way of example to ostracism, if a winning party without having committed a crime still would have to leave the city.

Chapter 3

LONG-TERM ENMITY AND LEGAL PROCEDURE IN DEUTERONOMIC LAW

1. *Private Long-term Enmity: A Legal Construct and Its Implications*

In a kinship-based society of rural Israel or Judah, it is to be expected that the social status of quarreling community members would be legally relevant. Selected laws from the oldest collection CC in Exod 21:18-19 and 22:1-2a indeed presuppose long term hateful relationships as typical for enemies, while for methodological reasons this could not be established for Exod 21:13-14. In homicide law, modifications in its literary form apparently mirror the shift from strict to fault-based liability. This has many consequences for the hypothetic imagination of any practice of law that is guided by the frame of reference of analogous cases in kinship-based societies as legal anthropology reconstructs. If a slayer would have to bring evidence for the accidental nature of a homicide case, any form of ascertainment of facts in order to determine the exact extent of the slayer's accountability would require a form of evaluation. Again hypothetically, this factual assessment would clarify whether the slayer acted out of intent formed prior to the assault. There are good reasons to assume that such factual assessment would not only reflect on the slayer's intentionality, but it would also determine whether the slayer and victim had engaged in a long-term relationship. Along this vein of thought, in a kinship-based society where enmitic behavior was acted out publicly, if any long-term relationship existed and both opponents were enemies, this state of affairs would practically rule out accidental homicide. Thus, in a local community when claiming the accidental nature of a homicide, this would require an impeccable collective reputation of the slayer. Any indication of a pre-existing hateful relationship between slayer and victim would adversely influence the decision, in particular in a moment of heated emotions after a homicide. This hypothetical reflection illustrates the immediate relevance of long-term private enmity as a social status between opponents in the quintessential case of homicide law.

The fact that for methodological reasons the assumption of a long-term relationship status between slayer and victim remains hypothetical for Exod 21:12-14 poses the question if other biblical law collections more plainly conceive of the continuous relationship between slayer and victim as "hate," defined as the posture of malevolence against another community member. In a local kinship-based community, the social appearance of long-term private enmity would expectably have distinct features. Unlike an eruption in a single isolated spontaneous act, the malevolent intent between enemies would unload continuously over a period of time. Thus, in a trial, the public perception of the opponents' behavior would be decisive. For the evidence of the law collection of CC it proved helpful to consider other laws that would more clearly reflect this social construct and in which the public perception was decisive. Injury law in Exod 21:18-19 uses the public appearance of the injured victim in recovery as criterion for the limitation of sick money, thus pointing to the relevance of the function of the public to testify to the relationship. This criterion of the victim's public appearance hints at the by default public nature of hateful behavior, i.e., a form of publicly lived out, legal status between two opponents from different kin – indeed a legal stance that can also be described as a social construct amenable to legal norms. Property law and procedural laws of CC further substantiate the construct of mutual malevolence between long-term opponents as a publicly visible state of affairs. As the analysis of laws in CC in the previous chapter shows, the laws address the public nature of these long-term relationships approximately via the narrative images conveyed through the semantic profiles of the legal texts themselves. These examples of laws from CC point to the intrinsically public nature of private enmity in the feuding patterns of local communities. When evaluating an evolutionary development of biblical law from CC to Deuteronomy it is critical whether the public notion of enmity and of an alleged kinship-related background persists, and if so, it will be relevant to analyze whether it fundamentally challenges some of the current assumptions about biblical law. Does Deuteronomic law allow the reconstruction of an evolutionary development from legal institutions that are typical for kinship-based societies and programmatically replace them by institutions of a centralistic organized jurisdiction? A comprehensive answer to this question is beyond the scope of this study, yet a source-critically informed perspective on selected Deuteronomic laws can contribute, as it demonstrates how kinship-based law persists. It first clarifies the definition of private enmity, starting with the analysis of homicide law and then evaluates the legal-historical evolution of such status.

This chapter unfolds Deuteronomy's concept of hateful relationships through five perspectives: first, (1) it considers the construct of private enmity as it informs the arrangement of Deuteronomic law. Second, (2) it points out how Deut 19:1-12 develops further the construct of private enmity on a compositional and a semantic level in homicide law. Third, (3) it clarifies the native categories of "hate" in contrast to "love," as well as the kinship terms "brother" and "neighbor/companion" in Deuteronomic language. In selected laws Deuteronomy speaks to the status of hate between opponents, in particular, to general behavioral rules (22:1-4), themes of marriage, divorce (22:13-21), and inheritance law (21:15-17), all of which clarify the legal nature of the concept of private hate (4). Fifth and finally, the concept of "brotherhood" illustrates the legal implications of the status of being in a fictive kinship lineage in Deuteronomy (5). Overall, encompassing the implications of each of these laws, this chapter draws out a nuanced picture of the social construct of long-term enmity for legal thought in its particular historical and literary contexts.

In anticipation of the result, one fundamental innovation of Deut 19 which comes more closely into view, may be briefly summarized. This relatively elaborate legislation highlights procedure at a moment in time when a homicide could easily trigger a feud between different kin. The pacifying tendency clearly seeks to secure a peaceful outcome. This is one of the reasons why Deut 19 carefully evaluates if the homicide could possibly have been an accident and why it considers how to provide valuable shelter for a slayer in such case. Homicide law in Deuteronomy thus significantly shifts the legal discourse with the specification that the slayer, in order to be eligible for asylum, had had to act unwittingly ("without knowledge," v. 4b; cf. v. 11) and the killing happened "without hating him (his victim) ever since." Building on Exod 21:12-14, these specifications in Deuteronomy further define the publicly lived-out legal status of two long-term enemies in the framework of which the law perceives the agent's continuous intent.

2. Hate and Enmity as Themes of the Composition Deuteronomy 19 and 21

Many areas of law represent extensive occasions of conflict and insinuate the legal nature of the status of two private opponents. The previous chapter chose homicide law in CC for this analysis and the present chapter also reflects on homicide as a quintessential extreme of fatal injury. Considering homicide in a kinship-based society in the absence of law enforcement through the lens of legal anthropology clarifies how the death of a kin member naturally would trigger the dynamics of revenge that become most apparent in this scenario. How would a collection of biblical law reframe and represent this central theme of kinship law, and how would central institutions of law react to fatal injury? Deuteronomy seems to be particularly instructive when considering this case through the lens of legal anthropology, given its references to the king and to courts as centrally established institutions. One may thus expect kinship-based law to be less pronounced in Deuteronomy compared with CC. Yet, already the arrangement of the law on homicide in Deut 19–25 points to Deuteronomy's perception of revenge as a pivotal part of kinship-based institutions. This setting of conflict settlement in the social realm of a kinship-based society is evident in the arrangement of laws in Deut 19 and 21 with their shared theme of personal long-term malevolence and the resulting dynamics of feuding. This focus on a kinship-based society becomes even more relevant when it is source-critically and historically put in perspective, namely in its relation to what is mostly the composition[1] of a late seventh-century

1. Wellhausen's content-based arrangement of laws in chs. 12–26 (with 16:18–18:22 dealing with authorities of theocracy; 19:1–21:9 related to criminal justice; and 21:10–23:1 focused on family law) remains unsatisfactory and was therefore the subject of further reflection; cf., among others, Otto, *Deuteronomium 12,1–23,15*, 1088. See the overview of various outlines in G. Seitz, *Redaktionsgeschichtliche Studien zum Deuteronomium* (Stuttgart: Kohlhammer, 1971), 92–93, and comprehensively Otto, *Deuteronomium 12,1–23,15*, 1082–93. Another explanation was to conceive of the arrangement of the laws as a catena in which laws were associated through cues or catch-words. H. M. Wiener, "The Arrangement of Deuteronomy 12–26," *JPOS* 6 (1926): 185–95; see the principle of systematic redaction of catch-words in OB law by H. Petschow, "Zur Systematik und Gesetzestechnik im Codex Hammurabi," *ZA* 57 (1965): 146–72. A. Rofé suggests similar catch-word-related arrangements: A. Rofé, "The Arrangement of the Laws in Deuteronomy," *EThL* 64 (1988): 265–87, idem: *Deuteronomy: Issues and Interpretation* (Edinburgh/New York: T&T Clark, 2002), 55–77. Close-readings in comparison with narrative material in the Pentateuch refrain from delineating any historical dimension of the laws; cf. C. M. Carmichael, *The Laws of Deuteronomy* (Ithaca, NY: Cornell University Press, 1974); idem, *The Origins of Biblical Law*. J. H. Tigay, *Deuteronomy: The Traditional Hebrew Text with the New JPS Translation* (Philadelphia: Jewish Publication Society, 1996), 446–49, with reference to Carmichael, suggests a mixture of thematic and associative criteria of arrangement as well as assuming that laws were interspersed with mutually explanatory midrashic interpretations. Another attempt conceives of the arrangement as thematic and conceptual strands – for instance, the arrangement of a chain of commands along the term and concept of the place (מקום) in a Josianic composition by W. S. Morrow, *Scribing the Center: Organization and Redaction in Deuteronomy 14:1–17:13* (Atlanta: Scholars Press, 1995) – or it explains the arrangement in line with the order of the prohibitives and the commands in the Decalogues – F. W. Schultz, *Das Deuteronomium erklärt* (Berlin: Gustav Schlawitz, 1859), 13. This explanatory concept is widely adopted by H. Schultz, *Das Todesrecht im Alten Testament*, BZAW 114 (Berlin: de Gruyter, 1969), 65–67; cf. also the portrayal of the theory in H. D. Preuss, *Deuteronomium* (Darmstadt: Wissenschaftliche Buchgesellschaft, 1982), 110–12; S. A. Kaufman, "The Second Table of the Decalogue and the Implicit Categories of Ancient Near Eastern Law," in *Love and Death in the Ancient Near East: Essays in Honor of Marvin H. Pope*, ed. J. H. Mark and R. M. Good (Guilford, CT: Four Quarters, 1987), 111–16; Deut 24:1-4 is an exception, as it does not reflect the theme of possession of the eighth commandment. Restricted to a deuteronomistic Deuteronomy, G. Braulik confirms such structure suggesting that Deut 12–26 in general spell out the Decalogue of Exod 20. Deuteronomy 19–25 were only added as a late-dtr redactional addition, with the assumption that Deut 24:10-17 adopts Ezek 18:5-20. G. Braulik, *Die deuteronomischen Gesetze und der Dekalog. Studien zum Aufbau von Deuteronomium 12–26* (Stuttgart: Katholisches Bibelwerk, 1991). In general, exegetes suggest that Ezek 18 is adapting Deut 24. D. T. Olson, *Deuteronomy and the Death of Moses: A Theological Reading* (Minneapolis: Augsburg Fortress, 1994), 63–64, similarly suggests a structure of the laws of Deut 12–26 in accordance with the Decalogue. This is also the attempt of K. Finsterbusch, "Die Dekalog-Ausrichtung des

deuteronomic adaptation[2] of Deut 19–25 – thus, at a time when the Judean monarchy supposedly had gained strength as central authority. At this point in time Deuteronomic law would thus have expectably replaced institutions and mechanisms of kinship-based law.[3] It will be necessary to first clarify the outline and the thematic structure in particular of Deut 19–21. As becomes apparent in Deut 19, multiple phenotypes of malevolence or "hate" and its opposite, "mutual benevolence," in ordinary life situations inform the arrangement of the laws. At the outset, asylum law (Deut 19:1-13*) represents one piece of this discourse, as part of homicide law that is traditionally seen as based on Exod 21:12-14. The meticulous description of the long-term character of the slayer's relationship with the victim in Deut 19:4, 11 goes side by side with the compositional emphasis reflected in the opening position of Deut 19:1-13* at one of the seams of Deuteronomy after

deuteronomischen Gesetzes," in *Deuteronomium. Tora für eine neue Generation*, ed. G. Fischer et al. (Wiesbaden: Harrassowitz, 2011), 123–46, and idem, *Deuteronomium. Eine Einführung* (Göttingen: Vandenhoeck & Ruprecht, 2012), 106–107. T. Veijola, *Das 5. Buch Mose. Deuteronomium Kapitel 1,1–16,17* (Göttingen: Vandenhoeck & Ruprecht, 2004), 129, suggests that the Decalogue was not known when the original law Deut 12–26* was written but was a secondary literary device.

2. Including a subsequent dtr version; cf. for the redaction history, for instance, E. Otto on revision and adaptation of laws of CC in Deut 12–26. In this model, the process of rewriting the law of CC in Deut resumes the preceding redaction historical process that created CC based on small sub-collections that were combined, similar to CC's adaptation of cuneiform law; Otto, *Deuteronomium 12,1–23,15*, 1100–107. The order of Deuteronomic law combines pre-shaped units from CC that Deut rewrites. The main law of cult centralization (12:13-27*) serves as an introduction. This results in various levels of parallels that bracket or bookend older passages: the urge of loyalty to Yahweh in 13:2-12* finds a thematic parallel in the curses in 28:(15), 20-44*, on which a social privilege law follows in 14:22–15:23. This has a parallel in 26:2-13*. The subsequent three parts refer to the festival calendar (16:1-17) and to the orders of the court (16:18–18:5). Then follows an arrangement of material law which, broadly speaking, relates to both the public as well as the private sphere in Deut 19–25. The order and principles of arrangement of these laws are disputed; cf. Otto, *Das Gesetz des Mose*, 127. For the arrangement of the laws in a fan-concatenation as interweaving of social ethics, family law and legal procedure in Deut 19–25, see Morrow, "Arrangement," 201.

3. Methodologically, this extrapolation of the construct of hate and enmity and legal procedure in homicide law in Deuteronomy does not carry any notion of the function of biblical law as positive law, but conceives of law as the product of legal thought and as a reflection of ideal-typical legal procedure. The conceptual framework of laws is a relevant source for the hypothetical reconstruction of legal practice. For a methodological approach on the relationship between biblical law and legal practice, see, for instance, Jackson, *Wisdom-Laws*, 23–35; Wells, *The Law of Testimony*, 11–15, and, earlier, A. Fitzpatrick-McKinley, *The Transformation of Torah from Scribal Advice to Law* (Sheffield: Academic Press, 1999), 81–112, as well as R. Westbrook, "Cuneiform Law Codes and the Origins of Legislation," *ZA* 79 (1989): 201–22.

the installment of judges and courts 16:18–18:5*. This initial position in the sub-collection shows the fundamental significance of homicide legislation for a kinship-based society.

As a brief overview demonstrates, the relevance of kinship-based structures for legal institutions becomes even more relevant in light of the composition of Deut 19 as it arranges three areas of conflicts. Deuteronomy 19 begins with homicide as the extreme consequence of malevolent behavior and its effects on the community (רצח, v. 3). The law excludes the right of asylum once a community member (neighbor, רע, vv. 5, 11) had turned into an opponent (vv. 11-12). Formally, with the use of the characteristic "you" in vv. 1-3, 7, 13, this law directly addresses its audience.[4] The composition mirrors the importance of conflict settlement between long-term enemies in the following law of testimony of the false, violent witness (Deut 19:15-21, esp. v. 15). Referring to a typical behavioral pattern against a long-term opponent, Deuteronomy programmatically reverses this hateful relationship by way of addressing the community member as "brother" (v. 18b). The law highlights the use of physical violence in conflict rather than the abstract term "hate" (חמס, v. 16),[5] as it points to the legal means of "lie" or "false statement" (שקר, v. 18) and their relevance in the framework of kinship law. Deuteronomy 19 arranges laws with a decrease in intensity, beginning with the most serious effect of hatred, i.e., homicide, continuing with the depletion of inherited means of production through boundary shifting,[6] and ending with the personal opposition lived out in trial through the indirect use of violence through a "violent witness."[7]

In the reference framework of a kinship-based society, the laws of Deut 19 share a thematic coherence around everyday conflict scenarios driven by personal hatred and enmity. What on a surface reading of the chapter appear to

---

4. The reverberation of private enmity from laws in CC illustrates in its own way the relevance of this theme and so does its reception history (Deut 4:42; Exod 21:12-17, 18-32, 21:33–22:14, 22:15-16, 17-19a); cf. Otto, *Deuteronomium 12,1–23,15*, 1100–107.

5. This is a reference to CC's procedural laws with the term "violent witness" (v. 18) being mentioned only in Exod 23:1, on which it directly depends; Otto, *Deuteronomium 12,1–23,15*, 1526.

6. This order does not follow the CC that has no law on shifting boundaries.

7. A quintessential illustration of the way in which mechanisms of intentional physical harm against an opponent function as a thematic thread in Deut 19 is the case of the violent witness, Deut 19:16, which quotes from Exod 23:1, which offers the only other reference to the term עד־חמס; Otto, *Deuteronomium 12,1–23,15*, 1526. Beyond the terminological overlap, the procedural rule Exod 23:1 resonates with Deut 19:16. The social context and the mindset of the "violent witness" in Exod 23:1 and Deut 19:16 are as follows: the protasis of a sentence about a "violent witness" (עד־חמס) in Deut 19:16 aims at the description of an opponent who intends to hurt another party. On the source-critical and conceptual reconstruction, see further Gertz, *Gerichtsorganisation*, 109–13; for scholarship history of source criticism, see Otto, *Deuteronomium 12,1–23,15*, 1518–21, and his suggestion on 1521–24.

be the disparate themes of homicide (vv. 1-13), boundary shifting (v. 14), false testimony (vv. 15-21),[8] in fact represent variations of standard malevolent behavioral patterns[9] between private enemies.

Casting a wider net from Deut 19 to 21, these laws reflect on hateful relations in the public sphere that were essential to conflict settlement in a kinship society. One typical feature beyond the thematic connections in these chapters is how they are written with a "pacifying tendency,"[10] intended to reduce violence: Deut 19 and 21 weave laws on hateful behavior into regulations on legal procedure which intend to ameliorate interaction between community members. In the larger composition of Deut 16–25 those indeed function as a "procedural interpretation of the court law of local and central court in Deut 16:18–17:13."[11] Likewise, already for the Covenant Code, long-term hateful behavior was a construct relevant in legal procedure and thus the laws that CC comprises weave in procedural aspects. Consider, for instance, the reference to legal procedure in Exod 23:1-3, 6-8, which serves as a bookending frame of two case laws about love for the enemy in Exod 23:4-5. Exodus 23:1-8 is thus a perfect example for the natural intersection of hateful behavior as personal posture in what appears to be a law relating to trial procedure in 23:1-3, 6-8 with typical behavior in favor of friends in legal procedure, while the case laws in vv. 4-5 allude to typical behavior vis-à-vis enemies. Both sections of this law thus refer to typical behavior in the conflict settlement of feuding societies.[12] The intertwining of case law about enemies and legal procedure in Exod 23:1-8 was formative for later tradition. Deuteronomy inherited this juxtaposition of procedural law and laws on benevolence and malevolence toward a personal opponent. Indeed, a thematic

---

8. These themes resemble the Decalogue; see, for instance, R. D. Nelson, *Deuteronomy* (Louisville: Westminster John Knox, 2004), 241, who tentatively suggests the Decalogue may have pre-shaped the arrangement of laws in Deut 19, yet see the critical reflections, above.

9. The arrangement is not entirely satisfactory; it still needs to allow for later catchword associations in additions. For instance, 19:14 on boundary markers is lacking from the CC. Verse 14 has often been assumed to have a key-word link to 19:3 (גבול) and thus was source-critically understood to be a marginal gloss inserted in a key-word connection between 19:14 and boundary (גבול) in Deut 19:3, 8 and נחלה in 19:10; the latter immediately affecting kinship authority. On the scholarship, see Otto, *Deuteronomium 12,1–23,15*, 1519.

10. Otto, *Deuteronomium 12,1–23,15*, 1549. In his synchronic reading Otto suggests that the legal hermeneutical intention of the combination of blood and procedural law in 19:1-21 is violence reduction, referring also to the closure with the talion formula in v. 21. An overview of laws outside Deut 19 further buttresses the social construct of long-term enmity as a principle when arranging laws. For instance, the arrangement of property law and family law (in a late seventh-century deuteronomic Deuteronomy) in Deut 22:1-12; 23:16-26; 24:6-25:4 equally allows for this conclusion.

11. Otto, *Deuteronomium 12,1–23,15*, 1549, translation is mine.

12. Otto, *Deuteronomium 12,1–23,15*, 1098.

synthesis shows the alternation between blood law and procedural law in a seventh-century deuteronomic Deuteronomy.[13] Laws and trial procedure in Deut 19:1-21 arrange conflicts that are typical for a kinship-based society with the background of malevolence or hate as the reason for these conflicts. As a result, the macrostructure of Deut 19 and 21 appears as follows:

Table 3.1

A	Judicial order, incl. procedural law	16:18–18:5*	
B	Blood law	19:2-13*	hateful vs. accidental homicide
A	Procedural law	19:15-21	violent witness
B	Blood law	21:1-9*	unsolved death, likely violent
C	Family law	21:15-21*	hate between closest of kin
B	Blood law	21:22-23	"death-sentence"; cf. Deut 19:6; Jer 26:11, 16

Compositionally, Deut 19 and 21* juxtapose the case of solved (19:2-13*) and unsolved homicide (21:1-9). The first three cases relate to physical effects, the latter two, 21:15-17, 18-21, reflect on the effects of hate between closest of kin and both affect the inheritance (presumably also in 21:18-21). The blood law of Deut 19 and 25:11-12[14] on the (physical) fight[15] of a man against "his brother"[16] form another inclusion.

Deuteronomy 21:1-21 provides the wider compositional context of the collection of laws. It is bookended by the phrase "the land that Yahweh your God is going to give you" (vv. 1, 21). The position of this law may be explained as the outflow of an associative arrangement. First, vv. 1-9 take up the theme

---

13. Otto, *Deuteronomium 12,1–23,15*, 1526.

14. Otto, *Das Gesetz des Mose*, 127.

15. נצה *ni.*; cf. Exod 21:22. The case is connected with the preceding passage, Deut 25:5-10, through the key terms "together" and "brother." It quintessentially reflects on the case of an assault of a woman on a man's genitals. Nelson, *Deuteronomy*, 300.

16. Otto, *Deuteronomy 12,1–23,15*, 1526, 1786, understands this arrangement as a seventh-century Deuteronomy exegesis of the laws of CC in the form of a fan-concatenation. The theme of the "violent witness" (Deut 19:16) thematically alludes to procedural law of Exod 23:1-3, 6-8. More specifically, it designates the witness, here simultaneously also in the function of a plaintiff, as false witness in Deut 19:18. The vetitives in Exod 23:1 intend to secure the proof of the witness. Deuteronomy refers to this law of the witness with Deut 19:16-21; see Otto, *Deuteronomy 12,1–23,15*, 1526. This will be pointed out in more detail. The formula of talion in Deut 19:21b originates from Exod 21:23b-24. It provides the hermeneutical key of the juxtaposition of asylum law on the one hand and the law of the witness 19:2-21* on the other. Furthermore, Deut 19:2-13* and 19:15, 16-21* thematically exegete Exod 21:12-14 and 23:1-3, 6-8. From the thematic analysis on the surface, Deut 19:2-13* and the procedural law represent separate strands.

of homicide or "manslayer" (נכה, v. 1; cf. 19:4, 6, 11), and the subsequently impending theme of bloodguilt through intentional "bloodshed" (שפך דם, v. 7), which consequently does not fall under the category of "innocent blood" (נקי דם, v. 8). By presenting the case in this framework, as a reflection on either accidentally or intentionally shed blood, this passage refers to hatred between two opponents as the reason for such behavior. It thus alludes to the social construct of long-term enmity.

The law about the treatment of a captive wife of an "enemy" of the collective (v. 10) in 21:10-14 takes up the theme of mutual benevolence between two partners in a marriage by way of including the potential separation from a war bride as a result of displeasing (חפץ) her husband (v. 14). One connection between this law and family law is the aspect of the honor of the wife, also a topic expressed with "humbling."[17] Terminologically, the law's reference to the relation of the marriage of a former captive to the theme of mutual hate or love is indicated with the term "enemy/opponent" (איב, v. 10), which designates an enemy of the collective, rather than a personal opponent. Thus, 21:10-14 connects war law and family law[18] as it maps out the exact status of the war bride in her new kin.

The law about the firstborn son's inheritance in case of "hatred" (21:15-17) speaks to the posture of mutual malevolence among the closest of kin, as does the law about the stubborn (סרר) and rebellious (מרה) son (21:18-21).[19] The following verses, 21:22-23, thematically refer to the death penalty of the previous passage. The phrase "the land that Yahweh your God is going to give you" is a bookending bracket of Deut 21:1 (and Deut 19:2) and refers to regulations in the land as a space shared by the community.

Thus a number of standard patterns of hateful behavior build the thematic backbone of Deut 19 and 21. This compositional analysis establishes the relevance of kinship-based law in Deuteronomy, a surprising outcome, particularly when read in the context of the late seventh century at a point in time when the central authority of the king allegedly would have increased. The compositional analysis of Deut 19–21 serves as the context for a reading of Deut 19:1-12 that demonstrates in detail the dynamics of the character of the social construct of private enmity in homicide law. This law seeks to ensure the fair practice of kinship law by way of detailing how legal procedure could protect an accidental slayer from a blood avenger through the institution of city asylum outside their own polity.

---

17. ענה in 21:14; 22:24, 29.

18. Cf. Otto, *Deuteronomium 12,1–23,12*, 1650, this connection between the laws is located on the level of a deuteronomistic Deuteronomy.

19. Cf. Otto, *Deuteronomium, 12,1–23,12*, 1656. The exact socio-historical backdrop of Deut 21:18-21 remains unclear. It may be economic pressure against poor landowners, as Prov 22:28; 23:10; Isa 5:8; Mic 2:2; 1 Kgs 21 may suggest, and, as already Amenemope 6 (ANET 422) seems to indicate; see Nelson, *Deuteronomy*, 261.

3. Deuteronomy 19:1-12 (19:2a, 3b, 4, 5, 6, 11-12)

3.1. Translation, Source Criticism, Outline

Table 3.2

	INTRODUCTION: POSITIVE COMMAND
שָׁלוֹשׁ עָרִים תַּבְדִּיל לָךְ ²ᵃ	You shall separate three cities for yourself
וְהָיָה לָנוּס שָׁמָּה כָּל־רֹצֵחַ: ³ᵇ	And it shall be that each slayer can flee there.
	SUPERSCRIPTION: GENERAL CASE
וְזֶה דְּבַר הָרֹצֵחַ ⁴ᵃ	This is the case of the slayer,
אֲשֶׁר־יָנוּס שָׁמָּה וָחָי	-who flees there in order to survive
	SUBCASE I
אֲשֶׁר יַכֶּה אֶת־רֵעֵהוּ ⁴ᵇ	-who has killed his neighbor
בִּבְלִי־דַעַת	-without knowledge
וְהוּא לֹא־שֹׂנֵא לוֹ מִתְּמֹל שִׁלְשֹׁם:	-without hating him ever since.
	Exemplary case law
וַאֲשֶׁר יָבֹא אֶת־רֵעֵהוּ בַיַּעַר לַחְטֹב ⁵	Namely, one goes with his neighbor in the forest to cut wood,
עֵצִים	
וְנִדְּחָה יָדוֹ בַגַּרְזֶן לִכְרֹת הָעֵץ	-his hand swings the axe in order to cut the wood,
וְנָשַׁל הַבַּרְזֶל מִן־הָעֵץ	-and the iron jumps out of the wood (shaft)
וּמָצָא אֶת־רֵעֵהוּ	-and it hits his neighbor
וָמֵת	-so that he dies
	APODOSIS SUBCASE I
הוּא יָנוּס אֶל־אַחַת הֶעָרִים־הָאֵלֶּה וָחָי:	-he shall flee to one of these cities and shall live there.
	Plausibilization
פֶּן־יִרְדֹּף גֹּאֵל הַדָּם אַחֲרֵי הָרֹצֵחַ ⁶	So that the avenger of blood does not pursue behind the slayer,
כִּי־יֵחַם לְבָבוֹ וְהִשִּׂיגוֹ	-because his heart is hot after him to pursue him
כִּי־יִרְבֶּה הַדֶּרֶךְ וְהִכָּהוּ נָפֶשׁ	-because the way is long, he slays his throat,
וְלוֹ אֵין מִשְׁפַּט־מָוֶת	-even though he has no death sentence,
כִּי לֹא שֹׂנֵא הוּא לוֹ מִתְּמוֹל שִׁלְשׁוֹם:	-because he (the slayer) is not hating him ever since.
	SUBCASE II
וְכִי־יִהְיֶה אִישׁ שֹׂנֵא לְרֵעֵהוּ ¹¹	-If there is a person who is hating his neighbor
וְאָרַב לוֹ	-and he lies in wait for him
וְקָם עָלָיו	-and he overcomes him
וְהִכָּהוּ נֶפֶשׁ וָמֵת	-and he slays his throat and he dies
וְנָס אֶל־אַחַת הֶעָרִים הָאֵל:	-and he then flees into one of these cities,

3. Long-Term Enmity and Legal Procedure in Deuteronomic Law 95

	APODOSIS SUBCASE II
‏¹²וְשָׁלְחוּ זִקְנֵי עִירוֹ וְלָקְחוּ אֹתוֹ מִשָּׁם	-then the elders of his city shall send and shall take him from there,
וְנָתְנוּ אֹתוֹ בְּיַד גֹּאֵל הַדָּם	-and they shall give him into the hand of the avenger of blood
וָמֵת:	-so that he dies.

This source-critical reading establishes a hypothetical seventh-century layer, leaving out later modifications and additions of deuteronomistic origin that do not significantly affect the concept of long-term enmity.

An introductory clause opens this passage in 19:1aα with a literal parallel in Deut 12:29, "When Yahweh your God will blot out the nations."[20] This introduction puts asylum legislation into a perspective of the context of Israel's separation from the nations representing a continuous threat of Israel to secede from Yahweh.[21] Together with 19:1aα, the remainder of 19:1 alludes to this context of the conquest of the land and hence can be seen as a secondary insertion. The situation of the extinction of the enemies is to be separated from the legal fiction of an asylum city.[22] The sentence may have been used as an etiology to legitimize when a city claimed to have the status of a sanctuary for asylum.[23]

Verses 2b and 3a interrupt the flow of the law of asylum cities. Verse 2b alludes with "in the middle of the land that Yahweh your God will give you to inherit it" to the passage in v. 1aβb and has been added on this level. Verse 7 repeats v. 2a and it seems neither to have known an earlier version of v. 2a nor of v. 3aα. The separation of the land into three areas explains the designation of three cities that is secondary to an older form of the law.[24]

---

20. In Deuteronomy, the verb form כרת hi. is found only here and in 12:29; the relative pronoun relates to the nation that is to be conquered. A history-related introduction to the commands is also found in Deut 7:1 and in the dtr summary of the conquest of the land against the enemies in Josh 23:4 who represent an ongoing threat to secede from Yahweh; see Gertz, *Gerichtsorganisation*, 119.

21. Deuteronomy 12:29 mentions this context much more explicitly and it is of more relevance there. In 19:1aα the insertion of the phrase is much more obvious than in 12:29: the seduction through the other nations is not as outspoken in Deut 19 as it is in Deut 12.

22. Seitz, *Studien*, 227–28, counts 19:1 with the remainder of Deut 19 and parallel to 12:29-31; Gertz, *Gerichtsorganisation*, 118–19, takes this to be a later insertion.

23. See the parallels in the jussive forms in 16:18 ("you shall install judges for yourself"); 17:17 ("you shall install a king over you"); 18:15 ("a prophet you shall lift up for you"); 19:1 ("three cities you shall separate"); see Seitz, *Studien*, 227.

24. A comparable separation is found in Josh 20:7: Galilee, Samaria, and Judah. This verse is an explication of the separation of three cities; see J. Hempel, *Die Schichten des Deuteronomiums: Ein Beitrag zur israelitischen Literatur- und Rechtsgeschichte*, Beiträge zur Kultur- und Universalgeschichte 33 (Leipzig: R. Voigtländer, 1914), 219–20 (together

Verses 8 and 9b assume a later gain in territory besides west Jordan that forms the basis for the later Deut 4:41-43. Verse 8, with the territorial aspects in this context, also interrupts the actual flow of legal procedure. The undertone of v. 9 is parenetic, which again may be a later addition. Verse 9b may have been inserted in order to harmonize this text with Josh 20 and Num 35:9-34.[25] The entire passage (vv. 8-10) is likely an addition.[26]

Consequently, the outline of the asylum city law in Deut 19:1-12 features an introduction, a superscript with a general case, and a subcase I and II, each with a protasis and an apodosis. In detail, v. 2a functions as an introduction opening with a command to the elders as authorities of the kin to designate asylum cities. Verse 2 authorizes the people to hold the jurisdiction over homicide law. The main part of the law, 19:2-12, follows the outline of Exod 21:13-14. It first presents a general case. Unlike Exod 21:12-14, however, the law first adduces a general case of a manslayer fleeing to another city to plead for asylum. Deuteronomy 19 presents this in a typical case/counter-case scenario offering precise legal categories of homicide that can be gathered from the description and the superscript of the case. Verse 4a first summarizes the case of an exception to strict liability for a killer: "And this is the case דבר of the slayer, who flees in order to live there." In the outline of the case, this functions as an introduction of the general case. Subcase I and II follow in vv. 4, 11-12 in a casuistic form. Verse 5abα offers a case law as an illustrating example for the accidental homicide of a neighbor. The last sentence of v. 5bβ leads back to the concern of asylum, by way of repetition of the apodosis of subcase I, indicating that asylum is a consequence of this case: "He shall flee into one of these cities and he shall live there." Verse 6 substantiates the need for asylum cities in light of the practical concern about their distance for an asylum seeker on the run.

Verses 4-6* and vv. 11-12 introduce subcases I and II. This poses the question about their relationship to vv. 2a and 3b. Seitz[27] suggests that vv. 4-6 and 11-12 are part of an old casuistic rule about the asylum cities that was secondarily linked to vv. 2a, 3b(+7). The reason is that all these passages address the reader

with 8b-9). Seitz, *Studien*, 229, leaves v. 3a as part of the original asylum law and cuts vv. 8b and 9a as additions.

25. Gertz, *Gerichtsorganisation*, 121. A comparable case, Deut 12:20, adds an explanatory remark to allow for profane butchering of animals in 12:13-19 in order to legitimize it in light of Lev 17:1-7, as suggested by Rofé, "The History of the Cities of Refuge in Biblical Law," in *Deuteronomy: Issues and Interpretation: Old Testament Studies*, ed. A. Rofé (Edinburgh/New York: T&T Clark, 2002), 121–47, here 135.

26. It has a parallel in Josh 21:43-45, which currently stands in the context of notes about the conquest of the land and hence may be older in Josh 21 than in Deut 19:8-10. Verse 9a may represent an even later addition within vv. 8-10 that separates the following sentence (v. 9b) from the preceding sentence (v. 8). Now, obeying the (sing.) command of Yahweh became the condition for the conquest of the land; see Gertz, *Gerichtsorganisation*, 121.

27. Seitz, *Studien*, 230.

in direct speech, using the second person masculine singular (vv. 2, 3, 7, 10, 13); they also include impersonal passages (vv. 4-6, 11-12) and they call the victim "neighbor," not "brother." Gertz[28] instead suggests a basic layer of vv. 2a, 3b, 4, 5b, 6, 11-12[29] (similarly Otto supports vv. 2a, 3b-6, 11-13[30]), arguing that the address in the second person is not the decisive literary criterion. Verses 2a and 3b are presupposed in v. 6 and, hence, they belong to one source as the outline above displays it. If so, noticeably, the distinction between subcase I and subcase II follows different criteria than Exod 21:12-14.

In conclusion, the source-critical analysis shows that the case outline is based on v. 4b and v. 11. The relative clause (v. 4b) and the counter-case introduced with adversative *w-ki* (v. 11) mention the criteria of the subcases. How do the twofold specification in v. 4b (without knowledge, without hating him ever since) and the threefold specification in v. 11 (he lies in wait for him, he overcomes him, he slays his throat and he dies) provide a semantic profile that defines the long-term relationship status between slayer and victim as a social status?

3.2. *The Continuous Nature of the Slayer–Victim Relation*

The distinction of the state of affairs of intended homicide, v. 11, from accidental injury with fatal outcome, v. 4b, presupposes an ascertainment of facts in a trial including a hearing procedure of the witnesses. Already Exod 21:13-14 presupposes this procedure and Deut 19 envisions it specifically as taking place in local courts. This further presupposes the involvement of kinship in conflict settlement on the local level, which has a number of consequences for asylum procedure, two of which are relevant here:

First, local kin are in charge of the trial and its context[31] where local sanctuaries would serve as asylum places.[32] The actual historical references remain strikingly

---

28. Gertz, *Gerichtsorganisation*, 118–26.

29. Gertz, *Gerichtsorganisation*, 123, considering v. 5a potentially to be part of the basic layer.

30. Otto, *Deuteronomium 12,1–23,15*, 1521–24. Otto suggests v. 13 to be a hallmark of the deuteronomic Deuteronomy, as in 13:9; 19:21; 25:12.

31. Whether this refers to a time historically prior to the late seventh-century cult centralization (so, e.g., Wellhausen, *Composition*, 204–205; idem *Prolegomena zur Geschichte Israels* [Berlin: G. Reimer, 1883], 156; Seitz, *Studien*, 225; Gertz, *Gerichtsorganisation*, 130) may remain open. The relation of Deut 19:2a, 3b, 4, 5, 6, 11-12 to the regulation of court administration (16:18–17:13) cannot be evaluated in the present context.

32. This suggests a date for asylum law of Deut 19 around the centralization of the cult in a context in which Deuteronomy itself places it. The relation to the centralization needs further consideration given the fact that Deut 19 does not use "gates" but "city" (vv. 1, 2, 5, 7, 9, 11). The relationship between the three/six asylum cities to the one centralization place is unclear, especially given the fact that narratives mention only one place (1 Kgs 1:50-51; 2:28-35; Neh 6:10). The laws of centralization cover the profane slaughtering

vague in the reconstructed deuteronomic layer – Deut 19:2a, 3b, 4, 5, 6, 11-12. While revenge patterns in feuding are at its heart, such as typical problems of the practicability of asylum in light of far-distant asylum places for the accused,[33] a concern Deut 19:6 ponders in detail is the avenger's fervent intent to execute a fugitive slayer without this person being sentenced to death (וְלוֹ אֵין מִשְׁפַּט־מָוֶת). Besides, Deuteronomy also unfolds rules of relevance to procedure, such as the handling of asylum and institutional or forensic concerns of dispute settlement.[34]

Second, the legislation intends to strengthen kinship-based judiciary: the vagueness in details of legal procedure, for instance, the exact circumstances of asylum in v. 12 and v. 4 on the one hand corresponds with a clear rendition of the elders' authority in the matter on the other. The law therefore indicates the role of

---

but the effect of the asylum cities on the centralization is not spelled out in Deut 19. The law is stylistically different from the actual centralization laws; see, for instance, Seitz, *Studien*, 227–28.

33. The same idiom is used in relation to tithing Deut 14:24aα.

34. I bracket out the practice of asylum; but see Chapter 5. The designation of asylum cities is unparalleled in ancient Near Eastern law, with the exception of an interpretation of Exod 21:13-14 as a designation of city asylum; see, for instance, Gertz, *Gerichtsorganisation*, 131, and on the subject matter, Otto, *Deuteronomium 12,1–23,15*, 1532–33. M. Weinfeld, *Social Justice in Ancient Israel and in the Ancient Near East* (Minneapolis/Jerusalem: Fortress, 1995), 97–132, suggests the analogy of the *kiddinūtu*-edicts of the kings that grant detainees freedom for construction work on the temple or in the city, yet this does not mean that the king would grant them asylum. The earliest references to asylum are of western origin, potentially, in second-millennium BCE Cyprus, where Alashia had this function; cf. M. Heltzer, "Asylum on Alashia (Cyprus)," *ZAR* 7 (2001): 368–73. Greek tradition refers to institutionalized asylum at the sanctuary as *hiketeia* (ἱκεσία). See S. Gödde, "Hiketeia," in *Brill's New Pauly*, vol. 6 (Leiden: Brill, 2005), 323. In a *hiketeia*, a fleeing individual sought protection at the sanctuary. This form of religious protection in cases of innocence while being persecuted, in cases of bloodguilt or other crimes, is to be found in Homer, *Il.* 16:573-574; Homer, *Od.* 15:271-273; and, critically, in Euripides, *Ion* 1314-1316. *Hiketeia* at the sanctuary usually was followed by incorporation into the community by granting a state of personal asylum or the status of *metoikia*. Yet, different from *hiketeia*, asylum originally regulates the protection of citizens against particular repressive measures they found themselves exposed to outside of the jurisdiction of their own country. See B. Turner, *Asyl und Konflikt von der Antike bis heute: Rechtsethnologische Untersuchungen* (Berlin: Dietrich Reimer, 2004), 66; U. Sinn, "Greek Sanctuaries as Places of Refuge," in *Greek Sanctuaries: New Approaches*, ed. N. Marinatos and R. Hägg (New York: Routledge, 1993), 88–109, here 90–91. A. Chaniotis suggests the institution first designated the safety of an individual at a sacred site and, with secularization of law, gradually a distinction followed between the protection through a sanctuary in connection with cleansing rituals and, on the other hand, personally guaranteed asylum through a place or a state or through the right of legislation. See A. Chaniotis, "Asylon," in *Brill's New Pauly*, vol. 2 (Leiden: Brill, 2003), 215–17, here 215, with reference to Delphi, the Artemisium of Ephesus and the shrine of Poseidon in Taenarum.

the elders as a kinship-related institution that receives the judicial authorization of denying or of granting asylum and has the responsibility to subsequently hand over a manslayer to the avenger of blood.[35]

3.3. Subcase I (v. 4b)

What are the exact qualifications of Deut 19:4b, "without knowledge, without hating him ever since," that exclude a public, long-term relationship between slayer and victim, and how does Deut 19:11, "he lies in wait for him, he overcomes him, he slays his throat and he dies," describe that relationship?

Subcase I, v. 4b, grants the slayer asylum, listing in a relative clause three criteria for the eligibility for asylum. Notably, each of them not merely qualifies the slayer's intent but also specifies his or her relationship to the victim. The first clause after the introductory relative pronoun אשר specifies the relationship between the slayer and his victim: the slayer is called "the one who slays his *neighbor*," i.e., an individual with whom he has been living for a long period of time, pointing out that the homicide happened in a community and not among strangers.[36] Second, the killing happened inadvertently "without knowledge"[37] of the consequences. This excludes that the slayer acted willingly or viciously in a typical escalation to kill his neighbor. Thirdly, this has happened "without hating him ever since." This threefold distinction in the subcase is outlined in the three qualifications of v. 4b, "who has killed *his neighbor, without knowledge, without hating him ever since*." Notably, rather than highlighting the slayer's intent as such (Exod 21:13 and 14), the three qualifications classify the case by way of negation of his advertence. They qualify him through the idiom "without knowledge." In light of the case law as exemplified in v. 5, Deut 19 specifies in v. 4b the accidental nature of the killing, the effect of which the slayer could neither intend nor foresee. The case law refers to the particular ballistic trajectory that the iron blade took when it detached itself from the wooden shaft, causing the death of the neighbor. In the case law the explicit allusion to the actual intent of cutting wood indicates the slayer's inadvertence of the killing.

Coming back to the third sentence, v. 4bβ2, "without hating him ever since," explicitly excludes the longevity of the mutual relationship between both slayer and victim: "And he does not hate him ever since" points out that the manslayer had not personally known his victim for an extended period of time but instead happened to live in proximity. The law more fully determines the random, neutral nature of the relationship to the neighbor by highlighting an opposite type

---

35. Analogous to other elder-laws, Deut 19 thus presupposes a public or a semi-public concept of the circumstances in which the city elders played a crucial role (v. 12).

36. There is good reason to assume Deut 19 deliberately choses the category "neighbor"; alternatives would have been איש or אדם.

37. The notions of "without knowledge" are different in LXX and MT. The MT uses this same terminology "without knowledge" in Josh 20:3, 5; Job 35:16; 36:12; 38:12; 42:3. The LXX translates ἀκουσίως in parallel cases, including: Lev 4:2, 13, 22, 27; 5:15; Num 15:24, 27, 28, 29; 35:11, 15; Josh 20:3, 9; Job 31:33; Sir 25:18.

of relationship, namely enduring enmity. Two formal peculiarities distinguish this relationship further. First, the use of the participle *qal* שנא, "to hate." The participial form emphasizes endurance or an ongoing mode. The action mode of "hating" is a continuous activity, a pattern of ongoing actions.[38] Second, by use of the rare adjective מִתְּמוֹל שִׁלְשׁוֹם,[39] "ever since," the passage additionally highlights the continuous relevance of an individual hating his neighbor; that is, someone acting like an opponent or a private enemy toward his neighbor.

Considering still v. 4, the following now points out how Deut 19:1-12 develops further the construct of private enmity on a compositional and a semantic level, focusing on the continuous nature of the slayer–victim relationship. Deuteronomy 19:4, 11 highlight the continuous nature of the slayer–victim relation that is fully apparent in the adaptation of Exod 21:13-14.[40] Exodus 21:13 is structured in a typical protasis–apodosis sequel, while Deut 19 opens its case/counter-case outline with a positive command in vv. 2a and 3b. A superscription for the following legal content opens with a general case in v. 4a. One relative sentence, "who flees there in order to survive," explains the case. To this general case, v. 4b adds a subcase and a second relative sentence, "who has killed his neighbor," and two additional specifications, one a nominal expression, "without knowledge," and the second a complete noun sentence that is added with a conjunction, "and he was not hating him ever since":

Table 3.3

Positive command	v. 2a
Introductory sentence	v. 3b
Superscription: General case	v. 4a
Subcase I	v. 4b

38. On the function of the active participle, see W. Gesenius, E. Kautzsch and G. Bergsträsser, *Hebräische Grammatik*, 28th ed. (1909: repr. Wissenschaftliche Buchgesellschaft: Darmstadt, 1995), §116, p. 370: "a consistent, uninterrupted action" (my translation); cf. R. Bartelmus, *Einführung in das Biblische Hebräisch. Mit einem Anhang biblisches Aramäisch*, 2nd ed. (Zurich: TVZ, 2009), 64: with regard to the action mode or procedural mode, the active participle describes an ongoing action, a durative mode.

39. Gen 31:5; Exod 5:7-8, 14; 21:29, 36; 1 Sam 4:7; 10:11; 21:6; 2 Sam 3:17.

40. This dependence is the consensus; cf., among many others, Gertz, *Gerichtsorganisation*, 128–29; implicitly Rofé, "History of the Cities of Refuge," 207; Stackert, *Rewriting*, 32–57, Otto, *Deuteronomium 12,1–23,15*, 1528. The opposite view, that Deut 19 predates Exod 21:12-14, was suggested by J. Van Seters, *A Law Book for the Diaspora: Revision in the Study of the Covenant Code* (Oxford: Oxford University Press, 2003), 106–108; but see the critique of B. M. Levinson, "Is the Covenant Code an Exilic Composition? A Response to John Van Seters," in *In Search of Pre-exilic Israel: Proceedings of the Oxford Old Testament Seminar*, ed. J. Day (New York: T&T Clark, 2004), 272–325. For the unlikely suggestion that Deut 19 borrows from Num 35:9-34, see Greenberg, *Asylum*, 131–32; Barmash, *Homicide*, 102–104.

3. Long-Term Enmity and Legal Procedure in Deuteronomic Law

With this sequence, Deut 19 reverts the protasis–apodosis order of Exod 21:13. It first mentions the general case: "this is the case of the manslayer who flees in order to live there"; in Exod 21:13 the equivalent phrase is part of the apodosis. More importantly, instead of adding the specific circumstances in the protasis, Deut 19 significantly alters the classification of the case. Deuteronomy 19:4b presents different categories of the case than Exod 21:13. First, it replaces Exod 21:13, "if he has not intended it," with "not one who is hating him ever since."[41]

Table 3.4

Exod 21:13	*If he has not intended it, ...* וַאֲשֶׁר לֹא צָדָה	Then I will set a place for you to which the slayer may flee.
Deut 19:4	This is the case of a slayer, who flees there, in order to live,	[...] *and he is not one who is hating him ever since*. וְהוּא לֹא־שֹׂנֵא לוֹ מִתְּמֹל שִׁלְשֹׁם:

Second, Deut 19:11a also modifies Exod 21:14 when it replaces the technical terms "maliciously intended" and "deception" with the word "hating" and "to lie in wait." The first replacement in Deut 19:4b and 11, "but he has not intended it" with "someone who was hating him ever since," highlights the ongoing relationship between slayer and victim. This corresponds to the term "neighbor" (Exod 21:14), which implies this same notion of a continuous knowledge of both opponents of each other. Deuteronomy 19:4 and 11 emphasize this aspect through their semantic choices and their description of the mode of action. The *qal* participle שנא expresses a durative mode of action, i.e., an ongoing act, which could be expressed with "a continuously hating one." Likewise, the idiomatic "ever since" at the end of v. 4 emphasizes the long-term relation that precedes the slayer–victim. This redundant terminology that shifts the focus of Deut 19 is critical for its legal understanding. From a judicial perspective, homicide of a long-term enemy categorically differs from intentional injury as Exod 21:18-19 and 22-23 address it. Depending on whether or not the victim survives,[42] the slayer may or may not incur blood guilt and, as a consequence, in the latter case would only be liable for paying a fine. Deuteronomy 19:4b, 11 need to be seen in this context.

---

41. See the respective graph to demonstrate dependence and modification of Exod 21:13 in Deut 19:4 in Stackert, *Rewriting*, 46.

42. Gertz, *Gerichtsorganisation*, 129, suggests that the rules about intentional homicide in 19:11 develop the cases of injury in Exod 21:18-19 and 22-23 further. However, it seems as if two distinct problems are mentioned, one being the problem of intentional injury within an ongoing quarrel (21:18) which as an outcome is then to be clarified by the two enemies, the other being the intentional homicide (19:11) allowing the blood avenger to become active.

Subcase II in v. 11 refers to homicide in the context of ongoing enmity.[43] The criterion for granting or denying asylum is the extended slayer–victim relationship. The subcases distinguish a spontaneous homicide from a homicide in a long-term enmity relationship. By introducing the term "hate," Deuteronomy marks a significant shift in its understanding of the relationship between slayer and victim. Not primarily an emotional expression, here "hate" designates a continuous attitude that defines a lasting social status of the slayer and that therefore is of legal relevance, as will be clarified further through its use in subcase II.[44]

3.4. *The Case Law (v. 5)*

The case law in v. 5abα makes more fully apparent the bipartite specification of the hateful relationship between the two opponents in v. 4. This case law functions as illustration of the ways in which accidents may cause homicide, and it also demonstrates how law seeks to prevent revenge and triggering a feud. Verse 5abα substantiates why strict liability may not be applied in accidental homicide cases. The apodosis in v. 5bβ summarizes the preferable outcome of the case: "He shall flee to one of these cities and shall live there." The case law's form, terminology, and its legal reasoning adduce a rationale that the circumstances of an accident are exactly the opposite of an intended attack. The description of these circumstances takes into account the relationship between slayer and victim as a social structure that is critical for the legal evaluation and thus deserves careful attention.

First, the case law breaks down into five clauses beginning with a *yiqtol* form, adding *w-qatal* forms. In the *yiqtol* it describes a random everyday activity, assumedly suggesting an iterative mode of action, as cutting wood jointly would now and then occur. The protasis arranges these activities in clauses of declining length, placing the shortest of the sentences with the final consequence at the end of the chain: "Namely, one goes with his neighbor in the forest to cut wood, his hand swings the axe in order to cut the wood, and the iron jumps out of the wood [shaft], and it hits his neighbor, so that he dies." The sequel of four acts of the case law that lead to the homicide is critical for understanding the rationale. The first two, going to the woods and cutting trees, do not intend to hurt the neighbor or companion. The second clause describes the wood cutter's intention with "in order to cut the wood." By doing so, the case law determines homicide was not the killer's intention but was caused by a defect of the instrument for wood cutting. The iron blade of an axe jumped out of the shaft.

Second, the addition of a sequel of subsequent random actions in v. 5 to fulfill an everyday task that ended in an accident may not be misunderstood as the effect of a long-term relationship between the victim and the slayer, such as the attitude of hate.

---

43. The specification "ever since" (מִתְּמֹל שִׁלְשֹׁם) is limited to v. 4bβ.
44. And see below under 4 on "hate" as a legal status in marriage and divorce.

Thirdly, the terminology of the case emphasizes the random nature of the homicide. Beyond the cutting of wood as the task at hand, the case does not presuppose a personal interaction between the wood cutter and the other individual, to whom the case later on refers as a close companion or "neighbor." The "neighbor" is a category that is neither a kinship member nor a friend nor an enemy, but a neutral individual randomly settling in the vicinity. The arbitrary nature of the type of relationship between the slayer and his victim is a critical condition that must be met in order for a homicide to be judged accidental.

Fourth, the case law demonstrates the extenuating fact of such an accident happening without a witness and, by doing so, it anticipates a problem in the focus of homicide legislation (Deut 21:1-9), as well as with respect to the false witness (Deut 19:15-21).

Finally, fifth, the presentation of the law in Deut 19:5-6 demonstrates the need for such regulation by a vivid allusion that contributes to a precise narrative image of the urgency of the situation of a homicide with an expectation of impending revenge that would ensue when kinship law would be in place according to the principle of strict liability. Verse 6 presents a detailed rationale functioning as a plausibility check of the above regulation of the installment of asylum cities. Six clauses substantiate the need for these cities in order to provide for the possibility of interrupting the fast-paced response of a revenge killing. The first sentence mentions the next of kin of the victim that is entitled to take revenge as "avenger of blood." The passage introduces three of the clauses with the preposition for substantiation, *ki*. The first two substantiations explain the fast persecution of the slayer as reason for the necessity of an asylum place. A conditional sentence demonstrates the fact that the avenger of blood would lack authorization through a death sentence to pursue and kill the initial slayer, but would rather as expected act spontaneously and be fast to avenge. The final sentence in v. 6 repeats the two conditions of a long-term relationship of enmity between the slayer and the victim of v. 4b, using the participle and the idiom for the time span, "hating from ever since." The repetition of the peculiar idiom demonstrates its relevance as a legal category in the case. Private opponents who have been "hating each other" over a long span of time are excluded and may not claim exemption from liability for homicide. The final sentence's repetition of the conditions of v. 4 uses again the participle and the clumsy formula "not from ever since." The idiom does not explicitly refer to the intentionality of the slayer. Rather, intentionality is implied when he was a "hater," that is, an individual who was in a long-term relationship to an opponent and, for this reason, would slay his opponent. The fact that the law mentions the concept of mutual hate, not the criterion of intentionality, is indicative for its legal rationale. In brief, the semantic profile, including the notions of the time that these idioms indicate, point to an understanding of enmity as a social structure. Clearly, in a local community, in the absence of a witness a long-term relationship between the two opponents would be critical for the evaluation of the case.

3.5. *Subcase II (vv. 11-12)*

Subcase II, vv. 11-12, discusses exclusion from asylum. Modifications of v. 4 and 5 include first, "if there is someone who continuously hates his neighbor," a qualification of the connection between the slayer and his victim as an ongoing correlation between two neighbors, i.e., of "hate" or mutual malevolence. Second, more precisely, both v. 6 and v. 11 unfold the slayer's intentionality in clauses with conditions that build on v. 4: "He lies in wait, he rises upon him, he slays his throat, so that he dies." The flight (נוס) in the case description finds an equivalent in v. 11 and the passage concludes with a fourth, final clause. The following table lists selected parallels between vv. 4, 6 and 11, pointing to literal correspondences.

Table 3.5. *Key Terms and Parallels (vv. 4, 6, 11)*

v. 4	vv. 6, 11
	שֹׂנֵא לוֹ מִתְּמֹל שִׁלְשֹׁם
נוס	
נִכָה רֵעֵהוּ	לְרֵעֵהוּ שֹׂנֵא
בִּבְלִי־דַעַת	לוֹ אָרַב
לֹא־שֹׂנֵא לוֹ מִתְּמֹל שִׁלְשֹׁם	עָלָיו קָם
	וּמֵת נֶפֶשׁ נָכָה
	נוס

Verses 6 and 11 repeat classifications from v. 4 using the participle of the verb "hate," and the category of the neighbor. Three separate clauses in v. 11 indicate subsequent actions pointing to the longevity of the relationship against the neighbor: lying in wait, overcoming one's enemy, and, finally, fatally slaying the opponent. The final clause expresses the flight into a city of asylum, with v. 4a mentioning this in the superscript.

The description of the case precisely emphasizes the ongoing nature of the correlation of enmity as one typical aspect. The heading in v. 4 readily makes this point, "he is a hater of his neighbor ever since," which is an idiomatic clarification that v. 6 then repeats. First, the participial form expresses the continuous demeanor of hatred. Second, the adjective "ever since" highlights the ongoing character of hatred. Verse 11 comments in more detail: to lie in wait, ארב,[45] is an intentional long-term activity. The subsequent "he rises upon him" designates an actual physical assault rather than verbal dispute. The third of the

---

45. The parallels of this lead to the narrative of the conquest of Ai (Josh 8:2, 7, 12, 14, 19, 21); see also this noun in Jer 9:7. Twice it is used for animals of prey and their waiting in an ambush in Job 37:8; 38:40. The verb is also used in the Samson tradition in a classic situation of a personal ambush (Judg 16:9, 12). See also ambush stories in cases of pursuit between the Israelites and the Gibeonites in Judg 20:29, 33, 36-38; as well as in 1 Sam 22:8, 13; Ezra 8:31; Job 25:3; a typical military ambush is to be found in Jer 51:12.

three clauses provides in detail the physical assault, including its consequence: "He slays his throat so that he dies" (v. 11; cf. v. 6). The final clause describes the slayer's flight into one of the cities.

Verse 12 describes the result of the case of v. 11: the elders of his city shall send and take him from the altar and deliver him to the blood avenger so that he may die. It is not entirely clear whether this passage refers to the elders of "his", i.e., the slayer's city of origin, with all the actions mentioned, or to the elders of the slayer's city of asylum. The elders have the authority to deliver the slayer while they are restricted to an administrative executive role and are not allowed not judge on the case as such.[46] With this focus on the elders' role, the passage embeds the relevance of homicide in the context of the social structures in the local community, thus reflecting on its relevance strictly to life in the local community, without any references to central institutions.

3.6. Conclusion

Deuteronomy 19:2a, 3b, 4, 5, 6, 11-12 offers a more precise definition of the criteria for the eligibility of asylum than Exod 21:13-14. With the unwitting nature of the onslaught as a necessary condition beyond the absence of sheer intent, Deut 19:4, 6, 11 require the exclusion of any ongoing relationship between the opponents as sufficient condition for eligibility for asylum. The idiomatic "he was not hating him ever since" introduces the legal definition of hate as the ongoing malevolent relationship between two private opponents. The continuous character of this relationship is based, first, on the use of the participle "hate" and, second, on the concept of time conveyed through the idiomatic "ever since."

From a legal anthropological perspective, Deut 19–21 reveals the relevance of structures of a kinship-based society and its feuding mechanisms. At the core of kinship responsibility, homicide law in particular illustrates the interpretation of the concept at large of private "hate." It sheds light on hate understood as a personal emotionally driven reaction that law at the same time perceives as a legally relevant attitude. Hateful long-term relationships lived out in a kinship-based society along a feuding pattern provide the backdrop of Deut 19. The pivotal relevance of hate as a legal term in conflict settlement and its legal status both require further consideration in light of their use in other laws of Deuteronomy. Homicide law offers one reflection on hate, yet the legal implications of hate between enemies in Deut 19 can be more precisely determined through a look at the framework of the concept of hate in biblical marriage law.

4. *"Hate" as a Legal Category in Deuteronomy and Beyond*

Deuteronomy 19:1-12* presupposes the concept of long-term acquaintance between two opponents. Individuals that hated each other over an extended period

---

46. Gertz, *Gerichtsorganisation*, 139.

of time which exposed behavioral patterns are best described as feuding.[47] As a consequence, laws that presuppose hateful modes of conflict settlement would seek to counteract the dynamics of escalation through the weaving together of procedural rules in law collections. Such was already the case in the procedural laws of CC, for instance in Exod 23:1-3 for false testimony, which Deut 19:15, 16-21 also takes up.[48] The appeal to come to the rescue at an animal's escape or at the breakdown of a pack animal (Exod 23:4-5) makes sense in a context in which, rather than showing mutual support, two opponents as "enemies" or "haters" would rejoice about such misfortune.[49] Deuteronomy adapts this law and, as was the case in asylum law, adds its own undertone in response to long-term hateful relationships.

4.1. *Deuteronomy 22:1-4 as Interpretation of Exodus 23:4-5*
In the context of the programmatic emphasis on brotherly love in Deuteronomic law, Deut 22:1-4 is a fundamental source for the interpretation of hate and private enmity. Quoting in the foreground the quintessential cases of losses of livestock from Exod 23:4-5, it characteristically extends them to include loss of undefined other goods[50] and to include an appeal for mutual help for compatriots as general benevolent interaction between individuals. Kept in parenetic overtones, without mentioning consequences, and thus associated with "ethics," rather than with law in the narrower sense,[51] Deut 22:1-4 replace the technical terms "hate," "enemy," and their derivatives from Exod 23:4-5 with "brother."

---

47. A long-term relationship also becomes apparent in the procedural rules about nocturnal theft; cf. above Chapter 2, 6, and in the later adjustment of two community members (רעהו, Exod 21:35; 22:6 MT).

48. Notably, the talionic punishment for a false "violent" witness (Deut 19:16-21) follows the principle of adequacy of the reciprocity in the responses between two private enemies; cf. on the hallmarks of private enmity below, section 6, "Outlook." False testimony (and its variants of false accusation) is a typical form of inimical behavior; see the broad attestation of false witnessing in biblical law in the Decalogues (Exod 20:16; Deut 5:20); twice in each the CC (Exod 22:6-8; 23:1-3) and Deuteronomy (Deut 19:15, 16-21), and in priestly law (Lev 5:20-26); and M. Klopfenstein, *Die Lüge nach dem Alten Testament. Ihr Begriff, ihre Bedeutung und ihre Beurteilung* (Zurich: Gotthelf, 1964), 21–22; on the "mirroring punishment", i.e., talionic punishment for false witness, see Wells, *Testimony*, 135–47, and Frymer-Kensky, "Tit for Tat: The Principle of Equal Retribution in Near Eastern and Biblical Law," *The Biblical Archaeologist* 43.4 (1980): 230–34; for ancient Near Eastern parallels, see Otto, *Deuteronomium 12,1–23,15*, 1543–44.

49. See above Chapter 2.

50. This change may represent an alteration in livestock in Deuteronomy to now include sheepherders. Deuteronomy 22:1-4 also refer to Exod 22:8; cf. among others, Otto, *Deuteronomium 12,1–23,15*, 1685.

51. Otto, *Deuteronomium 12,1–23,15*, 1696.

3. Long-Term Enmity and Legal Procedure in Deuteronomic Law

Table 3.6. *Parallels and Modifications in Exodus 23:4-5 and Deuteronomy 22:1, 4*

Exod 23:4-5	Deut 22:1, 4
כִּי תִפְגַּע שׁוֹר אֹיִבְךָ אוֹ חֲמֹרוֹ תֹּעֶה הָשֵׁב תְּשִׁיבֶנּוּ לוֹ:	לֹא־תִרְאֶה אֶת־שׁוֹר אָחִיךָ אוֹ אֶת־שֵׂיוֹ נִדָּחִים וְהִתְעַלַּמְתָּ מֵהֶם הָשֵׁב תְּשִׁיבֵם לְאָחִיךָ:
כִּי־תִרְאֶה חֲמוֹר שֹׂנַאֲךָ רֹבֵץ תַּחַת מַשָּׂאוֹ וְחָדַלְתָּ מֵעֲזֹב לוֹ עָזֹב תַּעֲזֹב עִמּוֹ:	לֹא־תִרְאֶה אֶת־חֲמוֹר אָחִיךָ אוֹ שׁוֹרוֹ נֹפְלִים בַּדֶּרֶךְ וְהִתְעַלַּמְתָּ מֵהֶם הָקֵם תָּקִים עִמּוֹ:

Brief remarks will focus, first, on the social status of a kin member in its comparison to an opponent, second, on the rejection of feuding and, finally, third, on the style of law that this passage represents.

First, Deuteronomy's replacement of "enemy/hater" in general supports the legal nature of the category of enemy and hater. The parallel versions on enemy interaction, Exod 23:4-5 and Deut 22:1-4, represent a strand of law that exposes the hateful nature of behavior in a quarrel against enemies. Deuteronomy 22:1-4 refer on multiple levels to Exod 23:4-5[52] and to the implied context of "enmity" as a social construct of legal relevance.

Second, Deuteronomy rejects specifically behavioral patterns of personal enmity, i.e., feuding structures,[53] which it contrasts with an ideal ethos of mutual kinship-solidarity, literally "brotherhood." Deuteronomy's social ideal of a community of brothers drives its adaptation of Exod 23:4-5, which disapproves of any hateful attitude and intends alternatively to motivate mutual benevolence that would be expected among family members. These expected roles are described in interactions with opponents through a framework of social behavior in a brother ethos, and thus representing the context of Deut 22:1-4 in kinship-based law. The addition of the term "your brother" in the expansion of v. 2 (2×) and in v. 3 highlights Deuteronomy's programmatic intent to establish kinship legislation.[54]

---

52. For further details of the adaptation, see, among others, Barbiero, *L'asino*, 183–89; Otto, *Deuteronomium 12,1–25,12*, 1684–85. The arrangement in 22:1-4 has also been described as replenishing additions, different in style from the diverse material in ch. 21, but without any sensical arrangement by G. Hölscher, "Komposition und Ursprung des Deuteromiums," *ZAW* 40 (1922): 161–255, here 209: "keine sinnvolle Anordnung der Gesetze." E. Nielsen, *Deuteronomium* (Tübingen: J. C. B. Mohr/Siebeck, 1995), 211, understands vv. 5-12 as taboo-like rules. In that line of thought, Deut 22:1-4 may be read as criticism of default behavioral patterns between private opponents.

53. See in particular Barbiero, *L'asino*, 190–94, 197, with references to feuding behavior in the Deuteronomistic History (Judg 9:24-25; 2 Kgs 2:5-6), the Saul–David tradition, the Absalom narratives, and the traditions of the sons of Zeruia.

54. These middle verses, 22:2-3, elaborate in more detail on behavioral expectations of a brother. Spatial distance from a neighbor would require taking in animals, keeping

Deuteronomy's legally loaded term for a close kinship relation, brother, sets the stage for an ethos of mutual benevolence.[55] The immediate context of Deut 22:1-4[56] in vv. 1-12 discloses further the meaning of mutual hate and enmity as far as it can be summarized in the expansion to positive commands, namely the passage's parenetic undertone to engage in active benevolent engagement. The quintessential cases in Exod 23:4-5 and their amplification in Deut 22:1-4 illusatrate the discourse about a fundamental way of interaction between individuals in these laws. Deuteronomy 22:1-4 urges members of the community to interact with mutual benevolence. The amplification of the scope of the domain of the case in Exod 23:4-5 is quintessential. Deuteronomy 22:1-4 reject mutual malevolence altogether in order to instead promote a "brotherhood" ethos. The command to interact with an (unknown) community member's misfortune in their favor rather than rejoicing in malevolence about their defeat, exhibits the reversal of the typical characteristics of hate and of enmity in kinship-based societies. Clearly, malevolence, "hate", and benevolence, "love," as expectable patterns of interaction create reliable social structures. This supports the view that these continuous attitudes constitute the essence of a social status. In the case of hostility, members of different kin would typically live out a hateful relationship in public and would follow the rules of escalating hostility between opponents when they determine

them among one's own livestock and the willingness to return them to their owner upon inquiry. From this expected behavior in Deut 22:2 it can be extrapolated that temporarily gathering animals and returning them upon request if a "brother" so requested was atypical. Deuteronomy 22:3 expands the purview to the donkey, garment, and "all that is lost from your brother."

55. Also, Deut 22 widens the meaning of the command by including a variety of properties: "a donkey, a garment, all that is lost" (v. 3). With the motif of the "garment/coat" (שלמה) it refers to Exod 22:8, 25, with Exod 22:8 being a core sentence of the laws of deposit; its summary sentence, "all which is lost," in Deut 22:3, quotes Exod 22:8. The result is the dependence of Deut 22:3 on both Exod 23:4-5 and 22:8. As a consequence, Exod 22:1-4 is to be read on the basis of the earlier law in CC; cf. Otto, *Deuteronomium 12,1–23,15*, 1685.

56. The source-criticism of 22:1-4 remains open in detail. The reason for the fact that Deut 22:1-4 does not serve as the source of Lev 19:17-18 is unclear. This is even more relevant in light of the fact that the prohibition to prefer the weak over the strong and vice versa in Exod 23:3, 6 and Lev 19:15 may also suggest Deut 16:18-19 as their source. In Lev 19:17-18, in its rendering of the procedural rules, H adds a more fundamental undertone to the procedural rules of Lev 19:15. Conceptual aspects of 22:1-12 as a multilayered composition of laws of various content that grew with additions in vv. 5-12 are beyond the scope of the present study. Otto suggests a subsequent development of partly corresponding passages AB/BE with a middle part C/D, while 22:13-29 exposes an outline of case/counter-case; Otto, *Deuteronomium 12,1–23,15*, 1676: A, vv. 1-4, brother-ethos; B, v. 5, mixed issues – post-exilic extension; C, vv. 6-7, animal ethics; v. 7b, post-exilic; D, v. 8, blood law, post-exilic; B, vv. 9-11, prohibited mixtures, post-exilic; E, v. 12, tassels on the outer garment as bridge to family law, post-exilic.

3. Long-Term Enmity and Legal Procedure in Deuteronomic Law

the exact measures of response. The reversal of the relationship between the two adversaries is cast instead as a brotherly relationship between these opponents. As a consequence, Deut 22:1-4 demonstrate the legal nature of hate between two opponents as the frame of reference for the appeal of exercising brotherly love. It describes how ongoing intentional malevolence against an individual governs a particular behavioral pattern of mutual enmity that Deuteronomic law identifies as the opposite of kinship amity. Narrative sources of the Deuteronomistic History recognize this enmitic pattern in their description of the rampant feuds between representatives of Israel and Judah as inappropriate, pointing to their relationship as brothers of the same kin in 2 Sam 2:12-32; 3:22-28.[57]

Thirdly, the modifications also affect the style of legal deliberation in Deut 22 that alters the "casuistic" content of Exod 23:4-5 in order to modify the prohibitives "you shall not..." in Exod 23 into positive commands in the initial clauses 22:1, 4. Unequivocally, this form intends to instruct their audience through the form of fundamental rules applicable in a community rather than a legal reflection of particular law cases. The mindset informing the teaching as a posture of apodictic legislation is the intent to highlight and implement rules, leaving out exceptions. The extension of obligations towards a brother includes the return of property to the owner. In line with this extension is the replacement of the "encounter" in Exod 23:1 with "seeing," thus extending the responsibility to a distant, uninvolved spectator. These changes reflect the hermeneutics of law or, as the laws omit sanctions, legal ethics. A specific modification of Deuteronomy is the addition of the "summative" prohibitive (עלם, *hitp.*)[58] in Deut 22:1, 4, urging not to withdraw from a neighbor in cases of their misfortune. Deuteronomy 22 repeats the key term "you shall not conceal yourself/you shall not hide" (עלם, *hitp.*) three times in vv. 1a, 3b, 4a, and adds this term to the version of Exod 23:4. In Deut 22:4 it replaces Exod 23:5, "you shall refrain from leaving it to him." These changes underline an ideal of a "brotherhood" of citizens excluding personal hate that urges its members to act out mutual responsibility, namely for a neighbor-brother in the community. This emphasis on mutual responsibility is programmatic for the ideal of brotherhood in Deuteronomy, a community ethos of fictive kinship.[59] The corresponding phraseology is found in Exod 23:4 and Deut 22:1 with the infinitive construct

---

57. Cf. Barbiero, *L'asino*, 194–95.

58. The term is only attested here in Deuteronomy; the *hitpa'el* is only attested in Ps 55:2; Isa 58:7 and Job 6:16; the *qal* is used in Lev 4:13; 5:2-4 and Ezek 22:26 and other places.

59. Wisdom and late prophetic tradition both refer to the status or posture of personal withdrawal or inaccessibility with Prov 28:27 *hi.*, Sir 4:2, and Isa 58:7 motivating not withdrawing from giving to the poor, using the verb in the context of social responsibility. In distress, Ps 55:2 assumes Yahweh may have withdrawn. In the reception history, the term designates hiddenness (Lev 5:2, 3, 4 and other references).

of שׁוּב hi. By way of the replacement of the phrasing from "you shall refrain from leaving it to him" in Deut 22:4 and by way of two additions of the term in vv. 1, 3b, Deut 22 stirs up ethical reasoning in a context when it would be possible to withdraw oneself from responsibility. Together with the infinitive construction of "do not refrain," this internalizes the ethical conflict.[60] The appellative character of this ethos of fictive kinship is apparent. It establishes a law that underlies the social structures. The law exhorts the listener or reader to adopt behavioral pattern that are expected between kin.

In conclusion, in line with the expansion of ethical requirements beyond immediate help with animal loss, the expected care for escaped livestock in Deut 22 extends the urge toward anonymous fellow-Israelites by framing this responsibility as help for "brothers." Deuteronomic law uses the fictional kinship to exhort its audience to adopt a social structure of fictive kinship that they would now attribute to their neighbors. In contrast to the well-known identity of the enemy or the hater in Exod 23:4-5, the kinship terminology widens the ethical discourse to include anonymous members of one's society, thus demonstrating reference to a kinship-based society,[61] albeit, in this case, structures and relationships would persist in the evocation of a fictive kinship ethos, actualized in practice. Deuteronomy 22 is an example for how laws mirror a specific social status, including the expectable behavioral patterns that are essential for this particular social status.

4.2. Marriage Law in Deuteronomy 22:13-21a; 24:1-4

The permanence of long-term enmity as opposed to the inner-kin relationship to a brother poses the question about social constructs in other family laws. A pivotal question is whether they also substantiate the legal nature of hateful relationships. "Hate" indeed is a key term in Deuteronomic marriage law.[62]

---

60. Cf. Otto, *Deuteronomium 12,1–23,15*, 1694.

61. The specific historical context of the adaptations of Deut 22:1-4 cannot be addressed here, nor can the legal historical references to Hittite law 71; cf. H. A. Hoffner, *The Laws of the Hittites: A Critical Edition* (Leiden/New York: Brill, 1997), 79–80, on Hittite Law 71; see also above Chapter 2, 8.2, and cf. Otto, *Deuteronomium 12,1–23,15*, 1695.

62. See, for instance, E. Lipiński, שׂנא, *TDOT*, vol. 14 (Grand Rapids: Eerdmans, 2004), 164–74, here 168–69, with reference to Deut 22:13, 16; 24:3; Mal 2:16. This semantic analysis puts the focus on the term in marriage law. Cf. also the general assessment of the terminology of hate by A. Riley, *Divine and Human Hate in the Ancient Near East: A Lexical and Textual Analysis* (Piscataway, NJ: Gorgias, 2017). It describes the semantics of "hate" in a spectrum between non-emotive and metaphorical meanings, separating human and divine realms and including ancient Near Eastern sources. Earlier studies include A. Wagner, *Emotionen, Gefühle und Sprache im Alten Testament. Vier Studien*, 2nd ed. (Kamen: Hartmut Spenner, 2011).

3. Long-Term Enmity and Legal Procedure in Deuteronomic Law 111

Deuteronomy 22:13, 16; 24:3 use this term (with the same suffix), as does Mal 2:16 and the Aramaic papyri on wifehood from Elephantine in the context of marriage agreements. Whether שׂנא as a technical legal term signifies the beginning, the result of the process of spousal separation, or altogether another form of a relationship to a spouse depends on the interpretation of biblical and extra-biblical marriage law. Next to Deut 22:1-4, marriage law in Deut 22:13-21a; 24:1-4 contributes to describing the meaning of שׂנא ("hate"). The laws presuppose in various ways the legal status of women as a result of her husband's "hate" and thus reflect the term's designation of a legal status. The following first considers Deut 22:13-21a and 24:1-4. Partially paralleled, these two laws refer to hate as the attitude of the husband against his spouse. The outline of the case about the slandered bride (22:13-21a) arranges in vv. 13-17 a general case with a subcase I and II. In a superscript, the law first mentions a case with a protasis: a man marries a wife, sleeps with her, hates her, and subsequently raises charges against her. Verse 14 literally quotes these charges. In a case/counter-case arrangement, the law details two scenarios: an apodosis in vv. 18-19 in subcase I follows the husband's unsubstantiated dismissal of his wife. The apodosis for the counter-subcase II, vv. 20-21a,[63] is the substantiation of the husband's suspicion, in absence of "evidence of virginity with regard to the young woman."

Table 3.7

[13] If a man takes a wife and sleeps with her but then hates her	SUPERSCRIPT – PROTASIS
[14] and brings shameful charges[64] against her, and causes an evil name to come upon her, saying: I took this woman, But when I approached her, I did not find in her the signs of virginity.	

---

63. Gertz, *Gerichtsorganisation*, 211–13, assumes vv. 20-21 are part of the literary unit while others suggested that the passage may have grown in its counter-case in vv. 20-21; see Rofé, "Family and Sex Laws in Deuteronomy and the Book of Covenant," *Henoch* 9 (1987): 131–59, here 135–37; Phillips, *Criminal Law*, 115–16; Mayes, *Deuteronomy*, 309–11.

64. The idiom עֲלִילֹת דְּבָרִים, found only twice in vv. 14 and 17, is best understood as objections that would be relevant for the marriage agreement.

¹⁵ Then the father of the young woman and her mother shall take out the evidence of the young woman's virginity to the elders of the city at the gate. ¹⁶The father of the young woman shall say to the elders: "My daughter I gave as wife to this man, but he <u>hates her</u>. ¹⁷ And see, he has put forth shameful words, saying: I did not find your daughter to be a virgin. But here is (the evidence of) my daughter's virginity." Then they shall spread out the cloth before the city elders. ¹⁸ Then the elders of the city shall take hold of that man and chastise him. ¹⁹ They shall fine him one hundred [shekels] of silver and give it to the father of the young woman, because he caused an evil name to come over a virgin of Israel. She shall remain his wife; he may not divorce her as long as he lives.	*APODOSIS SUBCASE I*
²⁰ –but if this charge is true, evidence of virginity with regard to the young woman not being found, ²¹ then they shall bring out the young woman to the entrance of her father's house and the men of her city shall stone her to death with stones, because she has committed a disgrace(ful act) in Israel by prostituting herself in her father's house.	*APODOSIS SUBCASE II*

The legal nature of "hate" in this law is best described on the basis of the form and the semantic profile. In the outline of Deut 22:13-21a, the superscript "but then he hates her," serves as a heading that points out the legal perspective on the two subcases I and II. The elders' laws follow a tripartite outline, defining first the criminal offence (vv. 13-14; cf. 21:18; 25:5-7a), then providing a section with procedural law (vv. 19-20).[65] Finally, the sentence or degree of penalty serves as closure or bookending part (vv. 18-19; cf. 21:20; 25:9-10).

Bracketing out various interpretations of the law, the two cases in the first subcase I and in the second subcase II are as follows: the husband, according to the first subcase, believes his wife had intercourse with another man before she married him. His accusation is not explained in detail but, assumedly, the husband was entitled to marry a virgin and this could be proven through the bloodstains as a result of the wife's broken hymen. The signs of virginity that ensure the exclusivity of the husband as partner of his wife would be the bloodstain in the sheet. The parents are supposed to supply an unstained sheet ahead of the wedding, meaning that any staining arose as a result of the consummation.[66]

---

65. In casuistic law, this is only found in the elders' laws; cf. Deut 21:19; 25:7b.
66. Carolyn Pressler, *The View of Women found in the Deuteronomic Family Laws* (Berlin: de Gruyter, 1993), 26–28; broadly on virginity, see T. Frymer-Kensky, "Virginity in the Bible," in *Gender and Law in the Hebrew Bible and the Ancient Near East*, ed.

If the accusations of the man are false, the consequences of the indictment for the lying husband are threefold: corporal punishment, a fine, and the prohibition of ever divorcing the wife. In subcase II the provisions are the stoning of the bride in front of her father's house. Three points clarify the specifically legal meaning of hate.

First, the use of hate in marriage law demonstrates its context-specific legal meaning. In this case the accusation against the wife occurs at the beginning of the marriage. In the definition of the criminal offence, the protasis in vv. 13-14 refers to the husband's questioning of his wife's status as a virgin. From a legal perspective, this is the first step toward divorce from his recently wed spouse. If the woman is found guilty at this point immediately after the marriage agreement was made, she will be divorced and consequently her family will be dishonored. The exceptional measure of stoning her in front of the house of her kin (v. 21) rather than at the city gate clarifies this point. The accusation within the legal framework demonstrates the seriousness of this offense at this point in time. The criminal offense in this law is starting out with the description of the intercourse between the man and his newly married wife. The man then comes to "hate" her. This is a legally relevant posture toward his recently acquired spouse. It demonstrates in this particular case the man's intent to separate from the wife he just took.

Second, different from one particular action, the husband's hate triggers a set of consequences in public that affect the honor of the wife's kin. A twofold sentence describes the husband's concrete actions: "he raises charges" and takes action to publicly defame or slander his wife, which the law quotes literally in v. 14b. Evidently, "hate" in this context is legally relevant, yet is not conceived as an individual act separate from the husband's actual complaints, but more exactly, as a posture that triggers subsequent acts. Slandering a married wife and accusing her of the lack of virginity meant a substantial attack against her kin of origin as a consequence of the violation of the marriage contract. Such accusations are directed in equal parts against the wife and her kin of origin, but the parents are called to respond. Following this outline, during the procedure of the trial, hate triggers the rejection, including the husband's public slandering of his wife. Verse 13 mirrors the public nature of the act that follows the husband's "hate," that is, the raising of charges and the slandering. The meaning of the phrase in v. 13, "he takes a wife, sleeps with her, but *then hates her*," exhibits the legal nature of hate as a posture that triggers the accusation in public which then leads to the lawsuit against the bride's kin in the criminal offense. The initial position of the term "hate" in the protasis underlines its precise legal nature. "Hate" designates the frame of reference of the following lawsuit within the constellation of the father of the accused bride who now defends the family's honor by adducing evidence in trial.

V. H. Matthews, B. M. Levinson, and T. Frymer-Kensky (Sheffield: Sheffield Academic Press, 1998), 79–96; see also B. Wells, "Sex, Lies and Virginal Rape: The Slandered Bride and False Accusations in Deuteronomy," *JBL* 124 (2005): 41–72, here 42.

Thirdly, the legal quality of hate is its function to trigger specific public forms of confrontation between the kin of the woman on the one hand and the kin of the husband on the other.[67] The use of a public trial is equally indicative of public interest in this case. The public interest is primarily an interest of the two kin involved. Hate is thus a legally relevant status that requires a public consideration between the two kin involved.

The legal status can be further refined. Throughout Deut 22:13-21a the husband's hate immediately affects the wife's reputation and ultimately that of her kin. The procedure of Deut 22:13-21a emphasizes the social aspect of what may, from a contemporary perspective, appear as an individual's (typically a husband's) separation from his wife. Furthermore, the clear outline of Deut 22:13-21a with a three-verb sequel in v. 13 – "hate," "go," "take" (v. 14a) – describes the consequences of the case and points to the legal nature of hate with v. 14b. The first of these verbs, "hate," varies the second ("go" with "to draw near") and the third gives a reason for the hate:[68] "I have not found virginity in her." The husband's hate has a demonstrable evidence base that substantiates his attitude. Far from arbitrary, his hate is substantiated in the fact that his wife was not a virgin. This is, however, relevant for the kin, since the wife was turned over from one kin to another. In the kinship structure, the husband's public accusation of the wife, i.e., his slandering of the wife's kin, is of relevance. The social relevance of divorce within the kin is also obvious in Deut 24:1-3, while, notably, nowhere does 22:13-21 give voice to the wife herself. Instead, her father as the most relevant person in the kin's hierarchy besides her mother, takes up the case. Terminologically, the father takes up the aspect of the husband slandering the female and he repeats these accusations of "setting bad words" on a person in 22:14, 17. Second, the father points out that the husband is badmouthing the female – which falls back on her father and her entire kin. The fact that the father repeats the slandering of the husband as the cause of the dispute (v. 17) points to the relevance of the public behavior of the husband. This is a matter of honor between the kin that extends beyond the relation between two individuals. Since

---

67. The case presupposes its context in an honor–shame society in which it immediately affects the kin of origin; see, among other interpretations of this law, for instance, A. Kocher, "Sex or Power? The Crime of the Bride in Deuteronomy 22," *ZABR* 16 (2010): 279–96, esp. 282, with the suggestion following Frymer-Kensky, "Virginity," 95, that the law ultimately puts the parents, pressed to defend their daughter, in the position of vindicating their own honor and that of their daughter's and to shame the bridegroom, which they could easily do by producing the evidence that was needed. Cf. on this case also Wells, "Sex, Lies and Virginal Rape," 41–72; C. Edenburg, "Ideology and Social context of the Deuteronomic Women's Sex Laws (Deuteronomy 22:13-29)," *JBL* 128 (2009): 43–60; J. Fleischman, "The Delinquent Daughter and Legal Innovation in Deuteronomy XXII 20-21," *VT* 58 (2009): 191–210; C. Locher, *Die Ehre einer Frau in Israel. Exegetische und rechtsvergleichende Studien zu Deuteronomium 22,13-21* (Göttingen: Vandenhoeck & Ruprecht, 1986).

68. Seitz, *Studien*, 119.

this is a public matter between the two kin involved, the father as legal representative gives his narrative of his daughter's case in front of the elders in which he literally cites the husband's verbal attacks in first person: "I gave [her] to this man as wife and he hates her..." (vv. 16-17). The public character of the procedure is front and center: the words "he hates her" in front of the elders are a public display of a status between a husband and his wife as this status is relevant among two kin. The outcome of the cases in vv. 18-19 and 20-21 again highlight the corresponding relevance of the husband's accusation: if the husband's assumptions are correct, he is entitled to send his wife off (שלח *pi.*, v. 19).[69] This will likewise play out for the kin's reputation, as it is represented in the father as the responsible parent: the daughter will be stoned in front his house (v. 21). This place, uncommon for an execution by stoning,[70] substantiates the relevance of the wife's behavior for the entire kin's honor. Likewise, v. 21 relates to her adultery as a liability of "her father's house" (v. 21). If he is not correct, he has to pay a fine to his wife's father whose reputation has been damaged. The fact that the father receives the money is yet another hint that the kin is the primary focus of this law.

In conclusion, hate in Deut 22:13-21a is the legally relevant posture of a husband to his newly wed wife that is presented overtly in the public sphere in the presence of the elders as kin representatives with the intention of terminating the legal status of marriage.[71] In line with the public nature of hateful interaction in general, "hatred" is a publicly and legally relevant posture. Its setting explains its effects, namely here, "hatred" is the result of reasons leading to divorce.[72]

The second case of marriage law in Deut 24:1-4 is in many aspects a parallel to the first in 22:13-21a. The introductory sentence of the case, "if a man takes a wife," is a parallel to Deut 22:13-21a. Yet, 24:1-4 is about two husbands, the first of which divorces his wife for a reason. She remarries, but the husband either divorces her out of hate or, alternatively, the marriage ends through death of the second husband. She cannot re-marry the first husband. In Deut 24:1-4, an elaborate protasis describes the sequence of a divorce, a subsequent second marriage, and either another divorce or the death of the latter husband. The more concise apodosis prohibits the former husband's remarriage of the once dismissed

---

69. See also in 22:29; Jer 3:1; Mal 2:16. Other semantic expressions include כריתות (Deut 24:1, 3; Isa 50:1; Jer 3:8) and גרש (Lev 21:7, 14; 22:13; Num 30:9; Ezek 44:22).

70. Normally, the stoning takes place in front of the city gate (Deut 17:5). In 21:18-21 "in the gate of this place" refers to the city gate. See also Deut 22:24; 1 Kgs 21:13; cf. outside the camp (Lev 24:14; Num 15:35-36). See further Gertz, *Gerichtsorganisation*, 210.

71. "Hatred" may thus not be mistaken as "emotion."

72. The understanding of hate as rationally not emotionally driven attitude is also found in the elder laws (Deut 21:18-21; 25:5-10). Both cases demonstrate the relevance of hate (explicitly mentioned only in Deut 25) in the public and in the legal sphere, and in both cases the authority is with the elders in public trial; see this point also in Gertz, *Gerichtsorganisation*, 215.

wife. Verse 4b extends the law with an additional rationale; a cultic taboo causing impurity of the land. In this context, in vv. 1-2 and 3 the law twice repeats the tripartite sequence of acts that lead to a divorce: he writes a certificate of divorce, puts it into her hand, and sends her out from his house. The triad of actions is separate from the actual "hate" of the husband, and together as a sequence they legally describe divorce from the woman. As a consequence, her first husband may not re-marry her.[73]

Table 3.8. *Deuteronomy 24:1-4*

¹כִּי־יִקַּח אִישׁ אִשָּׁה וּבְעָלָהּ וְהָיָה אִם־לֹא תִמְצָא־חֵן בְּעֵינָיו	¹ If a man takes a wife and marries her and it happens that she does not find grace in his eyes
כִּי־מָצָא בָהּ עֶרְוַת דָּבָר וְכָתַב לָהּ סֵפֶר כְּרִיתֻת	because he finds a shameful thing in her, -and he writes her a certificate of divorce
וְנָתַן בְּיָדָהּ וְשִׁלְּחָהּ מִבֵּיתוֹ:	-and puts *it* in her hand and sends her from his house
²וְיָצְאָה מִבֵּיתוֹ וְהָלְכָה	²-and she exits from his house and she goes
וְהָיְתָה לְאִישׁ־אַחֵר:	and she becomes (the wife) for another man,
³וּשְׂנֵאָהּ הָאִישׁ הָאַחֲרוֹן וְכָתַב לָהּ סֵפֶר כְּרִיתֻת וְנָתַן בְּיָדָהּ וְשִׁלְּחָהּ מִבֵּיתוֹ אוֹ כִי יָמוּת הָאִישׁ הָאַחֲרוֹן אֲשֶׁר־לְקָחָהּ לוֹ לְאִשָּׁה:	³ᵃ and if her latter husband hates her -and writes her a certificate of divorce -and puts *it* in her hand -and sends her from his house, ³ᵇ or if the latter husband dies who took her to be his wife,
⁴לֹא־יוּכַל בַּעְלָהּ הָרִאשׁוֹן אֲשֶׁר־שִׁלְּחָהּ לָשׁוּב לְקַחְתָּהּ לִהְיוֹת לוֹ לְאִשָּׁה אַחֲרֵי אֲשֶׁר הֻטַּמָּאָה	⁴ᵃ Then her former husband, who sent her away, is not allowed to take her to be his wife, because of her being made unclean.

73. Three problems are evident but cannot be discussed here: first, the reason for the first husband's being barred from remarrying his former wife; second, the exact nature and relevance of the rationale for the first divorce as "a shameful thing (literally: a nakedness-thing)"; third, the reason why the second case omits this and the exact function of "hate" in comparison. See, on these problems, R. R. Yaron, "The Restoration of Marriage," *JJS* 17 (1966): 1–11; J. G. Wenham, "The Restoration of Marriage Reconsidered," *JJS* 30 (1979): 37–40; R. Westbrook, "The Prohibition of the Restoration of Marriage in Deuteronomy 24:1-4," in *Studies in Bible*, ed. S. Japhet (Jerusalem: Magnes, 1986), 387–405.

כִּי־תוֹעֵבָה הִוא לִפְנֵי יְהוָה	4bα For that is an abomination before Yahweh
וְלֹא תַחֲטִיא אֶת־הָאָרֶץ אֲשֶׁר יְהוָה אֱלֹהֶיךָ נֹתֵן לְךָ נַחֲלָה:	4bβ and not shall you defile the land which Yahweh your god is about to give you as inheritance.

The law specifies the situation once the woman remarried with two distinct subcases. Either the second husband came to hate her (v. 3a), or the second husband died (v. 3b). In the first case, when the second husband who married the divorced wife in spite of the fact that the first husband had dismissed her based on a shameful condition, hate is the reason for her being dismissed. Verse 3a first mentions hate as such, then a threefold sequence of acts: "and he writes her a certificate of divorce, puts *it* in her hand, and sends her out of his house." The acts that the protasis enumerates in the case of the second husband who sends the wife away in v. 3a echo the acts which the first case describes in v. 1b.

As a consequence, first, "hate" as such in v. 3 is not in itself an act but, similar to previously considered laws, rather a posture that causes the husband to file the divorce, to write the letter, hand it to her, and send the wife away. Hatred as used in the context of divorce does not imply the actual dismissal of the partner. The adjournment is a separate step that is expressed with שׁלח (*pi.*), for instance, in Deut 24:3 and Mal 2:16.[74] Likewise, the idiomatic "finding grace in one's eyes" in Deut 21:14 and 24:1 contrasts with hatred. The legal reasoning of the case is this: the divorce of the first marriage was legal. The husband was free to divorce his wife for an unspecified "shameful matter." Yet, as this reason for the divorce has been accepted, this rules out re-establishing the marriage with that same man. Besides, the case of the second marriage that has been also divorced, achieves two purposes: first, the passage comments on the husband's permanent right to decide over the wife once he divorced her and also limits that same right. He may not first dismiss the woman based on a "shameful thing," then dissolve the marriage for that reason and, subsequently, remarry her. Second, if a man officially dismisses his wife, in general, she is free to enter into another marriage.[75]

---

74. "For the one who hates and divorces" is the most plausible translation; see M. A. Shields, "Syncretism and Divorce in Malachi 2:10-16," *ZAW* 111 (1999): 68–86, here 83–84.

75. E. Otto, "Verbot der Wiederherstellung einer geschiedenen Ehe: Deuteronomium 24,1-4 im Kontext des israelitischen und judäischen Eherechts," *Ugarit-Forschungen* 24 (1992): 301–10, here 309. An earlier interpretation suggested that the wife had committed adultery through her marriage of the second husband and that the first husband should be kept from participating in the wife's guilt. This interpretation was rejected by Yaron, "Restoration." E. Otto, in a reconsideration of the case of Deut 22:13-22, interprets "hatred" not as revelation of the guilt of the woman. Rather, שׂנא/Babylonian *zêru*, may indeed be used in a long form of a divorce, besides *ezēbu*, "to leave," and besides the other verbs נקף, "to leave," or שׁלח (*pi.*), יצא, הלך. Nevertheless, Otto, "Verbot," 303, questions whether "hate"

"Hate" in the second case, Deut 24:3, is a legally relevant factor when dissolving a marriage. Here, this attitude stems from some reason in the wife's past of the wife which then triggers divorce. The consequences of hate that triggers divorce are unclear and Deut 24 leaves them open. The second marriage in the logic of the case is only relevant insofar as it ends and the woman could theoretically remarry another husband. The major intention of the case law is to secure the fact that the woman has been declared "impure" and therefore may no longer be seen as marriageable. The former husband may not rescind his decision about the wife that he had taken. The form of the law demonstrates this intention with two details: first, by using the first husband as the logical subject of the action. He is the one who now seeks to marry his divorced wife and, as a consequence, it is this action that the apodosis indicts: "he is not allowed (לא־יוכל) to remarry her." Second, the outline of the law substantiates with the form of the apodosis (v. 4) the intent of limiting the right of the husband as the grammatical subject of the sentence. He is not allowed to re-marry the wife he has dismissed. Based on these formal grounds it is clear that the law restrictively limits the power of disposition of the former husband.[76] This law gives one decisive reason for this: "she has been declared unclean (טמא, *hothpaʻel*)." The first husband's public accusation of his former wife of a "shameful thing," i.e., of a sexual or intimate activity, affects her honor and her marriageability and the husband may not reverse his former judgment. The difference in the terminology of the divorce in the first and the second case are also comprehensible: the reason for the divorce plays an important role in the first case while it is of no relevance in the second case. The law thus seeks to limit the husband's ability to remarry a woman he has not considered marriageable.[77]

---

is an expression of a divorce for "purely subjective reasons, and the financial penalties, whether by contract or under the general law, will apply"; cf. Westbrook, "Prohibitions," 402. Otto argues on multiple levels for a more complex situation involving a variety of scenarios. First, he suggests the cuneiform evidence and the evidence from Elephantine are diverse, allowing for multiple possibilities. Not in all cases of divorce was the guilt of the former wife relevant for the provisions of the settlement between the two spouses. Otto, "Verbot," 304, with reference to the Middle Assyrian Laws, mass. K.A. §37, which allows for the husband to decide whether he wants to pay the wife a sum or not. Equally, mass. K.A. §29 reflects not a divorce but the husband's removal or retraction of the dowry in order to give it to his sons. From the diverse societies in the Near East a plurality of practices seems to come into view which allows for a variety of settings of divorce or demotion. Thus, on methodological grounds, in light of the wide range of marriage and divorce law, Otto does not read Deut 24:1-4 against the backdrop of any particular legislation.

76. Otto, "Verbot," 308.

77. Otto, "Verbot," 309, suggests that besides restricting the right of the first husband to remarry her, the case also secures the right of the woman to remarry after having once been dismissed by a husband.

4.3. "Hate" in Biblical Marriage Law and in "Wifehood" Documents from Elephantine

The preceding considerations on hate in Deut 22 and in marriage law tacitly assumed its nature as a legal construct that triggers divorce. This essence of marriage as a legal construct is relevant in this study, as it demonstrates that marriage law uses the term "hate" with a specific underlying legal meaning, namely to express the termination of the marriage contract. Seen through the lens of legal anthropology this term would thus be interpreted as a marker of the social status of legal relevance and this use of "hate" as designation of a social status consequently substantiates the analogous use in Deut 19 for the continuous malevolent intention that constitutes the status of private enmity. This analogous use of "hate" in homicide and marriage law is apparent, since the construct's legal nature in marriage law is undisputed. Its specific meaning in divorce, however, allows for various interpretations, as the following considerations briefly clarify.

Strictly speaking, marriage law primarily addresses the separation of the spouses. Marriage documents from Elephantine substantiate the concept of "hate" as a posture of legal relevance which triggers either divorce or demotion. Yet in spite of the clarity of the documents that expose the legal nature of "hate," they allow for controversial interpretations of whether "hate" triggers a divorce from the spouse or rather their demotion. The initial edition of selected Elephantine papyri had interpreted "hate" (שנא) as "probably a technical term for divorce"[78] and the subsequent edition labeled it as a "legal term for divorce."[79] The evidence of the papyri supports this interpretation. For instance, TAD B2.4:8-9 is about a grant of a usufruct to a son-in-law and provides rules for the case: "If tomorrow or the next day that land you build (up and) afterwards my daughter hates you and go out from you, she does not have right to take it and give it to others…"[80] The term "hate you" was translated by Cowley[81] as "divorces you." H. Z. Szubin and B. Porten's interpretation of TAD B3.3:7-9 instead interpret "hate" as a technical term for a hitherto unknown institution also known in biblical law.[82] The

---

78. A. H. Sayce, *Aramaic Papyri Discovered at Assuan, with the Assistance of A. E. Cowley, and with Appendices by W. Spiegelberg an Seymour de Ricci* (London: A. Moring, 1906), 38 n. 8.

79. E. A. Cowley, *Aramaic Papyri of the Fifth Century B.C.* (Oxford: Clarendon, 1923), 28.

80. B. Porten, *The Elephantine Papyri in English: Three Millennia of Cross-Cultural Change*, 2nd ed. (Leiden: Brill, 2011), 175.

81. A. F. Botta, "Hated by the Gods and Your Spouse: Legal Use of שנא in Elephantine and its Ancient Near Eastern Context," in *Law and Religion in the Eastern Mediterranean: From Antiquity to Early Islam*, ed. A. Hagedorn and R. G. Kratz (Oxford: Oxford University Press, 2013), 105–28, here 106.

82. Porten, *Elephantine Papyri*, 182 n. 42, interprets "hate" as reference to the marital status of a secondary wife which demotes her to this status. He interprets "hate" not as an equivalent for divorce but as a negation of her status as primary wife.

phrase specifies the "demotion" of the spouse, that is, she is still in the status of marriage, but now as "demoted" wife.[83] Szubin and Porten review the Akkadian term *zêru* ("to hate") in cuneiform law, diplomacy and narrative along with Egyptian demotic marriage contracts and biblical use of the verb "to hate" with their range of meanings. They conclude that legal texts use "hate" as a technical term. It "signifies repudiation or rejection, the effect of which is tantamount to a breach of contract due to demotion of status within an existing relationship."[84] In other words, "hate" stands for an action taken in the context of a legally defined relationship that possesses legal substance and is legally demonstrable through an action that then constitutes a breach of contract.

Their suggestion is disputed. For instance, R. Westbrook accepts the meaning of divorce for Elephantine documents, while rejecting this meaning in biblical law.[85] Westbrook suggests "hate" may be at first sight also seen in the cuneiform documents of Old Babylonian marriage contracts, as well as in a contract from Ugarit. As a consequence, the reconstructed formula in its full length is "he hates and divorces," as in a marriage contract from Alalaḫ, in which the clause that penalizes the divorce begins "if W hates H and divorces him…"[86] Westbrook also refers to the scribal dictionary of legal formulae with the full reference "if a wife hates her husband and says 'you are not my husband'…" To Westbrook, the formula expresses unjustified divorce. Divorce would usually require a justification and as a consequence the verb "hate" in this context expresses the fact that the divorce in this case was "for purely subjective reasons."[87] Following Westbrook, B. Wells[88] suggests it designates the rejection of a wife from her primary status to take on the status of a secondary wife[89] and defines hate as a reflection of a subjective, unjustified move of the party who requests a divorce. Otto suggests the opposite, assuming Westbrook reflects on motivations of the husband that the text does not disclose.[90] Nutkowicz re-examined Szubin and

---

83. H. Z. Szubin and B. Porten, "The Status of a Repudiated Spouse: A New Interpreptation of Kraeling 7 (TAD B3.8)," *ILR* 35 (2001): 46–78.

84. Szubin and Porten, "The Status of a Repudiated Spouse," 56.

85. An idea proposed, among others, by J. J. Rabinowitz, in reference to Deut 21:15-17; see J. J. Rabinowitz, "Marriage Contracts in Ancient Egypt in Light of Jewish Sources," *HThR* 46 (1953): 91–97.

86. Cf. D. J. Wiseman, "Supplementary Copies of Alalakh Tablets," *JCS* 8 (1954): 1–30, here 7, No. 94, lines 17-19.

87. Westbrook, "Restoration," 402.

88. Wells, "Sex, Lies and Virginal Rape," 58.

89. B. Wells, "The Hated Wife in Deuteronomic Law," *VT* 60 (2010): 131–46, here 138–39. Hate in Gen 29:31, 33; Deut 21:15 obviously designates a wife's status and her marriage relation in respect to other wives of her husband; it is not connected to divorce.

90. E. Otto, "Gottes Recht als Menschenrecht," in *Rechts- und literaturhistorische Studien zum Deuteronomium*, ed. E. Otto (Wiesbaden: Harrassowitz, 2002), 1–29, here 25–26.

3. Long-Term Enmity and Legal Procedure in Deuteronomic Law   121

Porten's suggestion and interprets "hate" as more than a demotion in status and, while she assumes that it does not mean divorce, it will lead to divorce.[91]

A. F. Botta assumes the meaning of שׂנא as "divorce" as a result of a review of the ancient Near Eastern use of the verb "to hate," which includes the Old and Middle Kingdom of Egypt, yet the verb is absent in Egyptian marriage documents. In essence, the Mesopotamian evidence for *zêru* that Szubin and Porten read as "repudiation or rejection," with the consequence of a demotion of status, to Botta rather suggests the end of a relationship.[92] Botta points, for instance, to a Neo-Assyrian document that Szubin and Porten quote (ND 2307: 47-48) about a slave girl that should be bough[t] in case the spouse does not conceive and bear children: "If she loves the slave-girl, she shall keep [her], if she hates her, she shall sell her. If Ṣubētu hates Milki-ramu, she shall leave [him], if Milki-ramu hates his wife[?], he shall pay [back the dowry] to her two-fold."[93] Clearly in this case, Botta argues, the use of the verb "hate" indicates the end of the relationship. The sale of the slave-girl means the end of the relationship as she will be leaving the household. Botta's evaluation of the 168 references for the biblical verb supports his claim. Hate usually has an active dimension and is dynamic.[94] Botta suggests the documents from Elephantine – TAD B2.4, the wifehood documents TAD B3.3 (Kraeling 2); TAD B2. 6 (Cowley 15) and TAD B3.8 (Kraeling 7+15+18/1, 3, 8, 13, 19, 22, 26, 30) – refer to situations between two parties in which one of the two parties proceeds "to declare hate" for the other.

TAD B3.3:7-9 offers an instructive example for the hate between two spouses in a wifehood document:

> Tomorrow or [the] next day, should Anani stand up in an assembly and say: 'I hate Tamet, my wife,' silver of hatre[d] is on his head. He shall give Tamet silver, 7 shekels, 2 q(uarters) and all that she brought in in her hand she shall take out, from straw to string.

The same could be stated by the wife TAD B3.3:9-10:

> Tomorrow or [the] next day, should Tamet stand up and say: 'I hate my husband Anani,' silver of ha[t]red is on her head. She shall give to Anani silver, 7 shekels 2 q(uarters) and all that she brought in in her hand she shall take out from straw to string.[95]

A main argument of Botta for the meaning of divorce instead of demotion is the use of the term for both the husband and the wife; demotion would be only

---

91. H. Nutkowicz, "Concerning the Verb *śn'* in Judaeo-Aramaic Contracts from Elephantine," *JSSt* 52 (2007): 211–25, here 220.
92. Botta, "Hated," 110.
93. Cf. the reference to it in Botta, "Hated," 112.
94. Botta, "Hated," 116.
95. Quoted from Botta, "Hated," 119.

used of the wife, not for the husband,⁹⁶ while the exact consequences and spatial arrangements of divorced couples could still significantly vary. Notably, "hate" is not per se questioned as a negative attitude toward a spouse in general.⁹⁷ The biblical evidence for the use of שׂנא as a technical term for repudiation or demotion, as in Gen 29:31, 33 in the case of Lea,⁹⁸ would, as Botta concedes, de facto often mean a spatial distance from the hated spouse; especially when used in combination with שלח, "to send away or expel,"⁹⁹ or with the verb גרשׁ, "to expel, drive away,"¹⁰⁰ or עזובה אשה, "abandoned wife."¹⁰¹

In conclusion, the verb includes a facet of meanings that range from divorce to demotion, with the evidence predominantly suggesting divorce. In either case, hate designates the rejection of a spouse and thus indicates a change in status in the context of a legally defined long-term status between two partners.¹⁰²

4.4. Inheritance Law in Deuteronomy 21:15-17

Deuteronomy 21:15-17 highlights a point of conflict after a divorce. While this law reflects on the customary inheritance of the largest portion of the goods by the first son, it discusses the consequences of love and hatred in this case with a polemical undertone.¹⁰³ The law seems likely to be drafted in reference to actual legal practice when it describes how the "hated" wife will be dealt with in case of an inheritance:

> ¹⁵ If a man has two wives, one loved and the other hated, and the loved one and the hated one both bear him sons, with the firstborn son belonging to the hated one,
> ¹⁶ then it shall be on the day he wills his possessions to his sons he shall not be able to designate the son of the loved one as the firstborn rather than the son of the hated one, the [real] firstborn.
> ¹⁷ Instead, he shall acknowledge the son of the hated one as the firstborn in order to give him a double portion of all he possesses. For he is the first of his potency [i.e., virility]; the right of the firstborn belongs to him.

---

96. Botta, "Hated," 119.
97. The use of "hate" in Mal 2:16, while potentially negative with the translation "He has hated, divorced, ... and covered his garment in injustice" (Westbrook, "Restoration," 403), does not substantiate the injustice of divorce. It substantiates that divorce is an act separate from the attitude or posture of hatred.
98. The unloved wife in a polygamous marriage; see E. Lipiński, שׂנא, *TDOT*, vol. 14, 164–74, here 168.
99. Deut 22:19, 29; 24:1, 3, 4 and others.
100. For instance, גרושה אשה in the sense of "divorcee" (Lev 21:7, 14; 22:13).
101. Isa 54:6b; see Botta, "Hated," 117.
102. Cf. Wells, "Hated Wife," 136.
103. C. Pressler, *The View of Women*, 17.

The legal meaning of hate includes the change in the inheritance regulation. With Szubin and Porten, Wells concludes hatred leads not to divorce but to the demotion of the wife in both the Elephantine wifehood documents and Deut 21,[104] suggesting that the concept of "hate" and "hated" refer to a subsequent action of the husband, and furthermore that the hated wife was either demoted within the household or has been divorced and sent away. Less clear is the third point in Wells' argument, namely whether hate refers to arbitrarily chosen action. Subsequently his further assertion becomes less likely, that the husband by acting arbitrarily would forfeit his right to at the same time demote his wife and to transfer the status of a firstborn to another. Likewise, the interpretation that if a husband did not arbitrarily demote his wife he would thus still have his powers to give the birthright to a younger son, is questionable. The point of the argument is that the husband would be free to give the birthright to another son as long as he had not "hated" his wife. He could have done so, even if this would have implied favoritism toward his son.[105] The consequence of reading this law is its limitation of the possibilities of the former husband and his freedom to act as he pleases once he chose to reject his wife without reason. The rationale for this understanding of the law, namely, that a reason for the hatred should be mentioned, is an argumentum *e silentio*. The law gives no reason and it does not explicitly point to the fact that it is because of the "arbitrary" character of the husband's decision that he is not allowed to exercise his right of inheritance as before.

4.5. Conclusion

"Hate" in the marriage law of Deut 22:13-21a; 24:1-4; 21:15-17 functions as the legal term for the husband's intent to separate himself from his wife. An adequate translation of hate is "I withdraw from the marriage contract, as follows." At the point in time when the male partner uses the phrase, this affects the legal status between the two partners. The husband is, consequently, "in withdrawal from the marriage contract" and the couple is in divorce. Notwithstanding the implication of divorce between two partners, in some cases the "hated wife" would remain in a marriage with her husband; Gen 29:31, 33. Marriage law thus illustrates the social construct of hate as a posture toward another individual in biblical law. In marriage law this posture is of the essence in divorce procedure. "Hate" as a category plays out as an ongoing posture directed against a former spouse that triggers the separation procedure. Arguably, this comprises a spatial arrangement of the two former spouses – though that may not always be the case. Hateful intent also has bearings on the former husband's freedom to govern his inheritance, as 21:15-17 demonstrate. In 22:13-21a, the husband's hatred includes consequences for the woman's kin of origin and herself.

---

104. Wells, "Hated Wife," 138.
105. Wells, "Hated Wife," 146.

5. *Cultural and Literary Historical Contexts:*
Deuteronomy 19:4, 11 (אח, רע)

The categories of neighbor and brother in homicide law are decisive when retrieving the social background of Deuteronomic law. The implications of "hate" in the comparative assessment of homicide and marriage law have demonstrated that the extent to which the attitude of hate constitutes a social status of spouses in a marriage. They have also confirmed its legal relevance in all these cases. This is relevant for the attempt of this study to, in general, demonstrate that laws typically presuppose a precise social status of the agents and victims involved. In particular, the previous reading clarifies the status of long-term enmity between a slayer and their victim or between two spouses in a marriage that law presupposes. This exact result for a reading of Deuteronomy thus complements the previous chapter's reading of the laws of CC. A limiting factor in the interpretation of Exod 21 had been the lack of clarity of the social context to exactly determine the understanding of the social category of "neighbor/companion." The analysis of Deut 19 demonstrated the extent to which laws as source texts allow the determination of the social constructs they presuppose. The following looks back at homicide law in Exod 21 in order to more precisely retrieve the meaning of the action verbs "love" and "hate" in Deut 19 as they are now read against the background of their meaning in marriage law.

"Hate" in marriage law designates an enduring posture between the spouses and, in the case of divorce, has legal implications. Both the continuing character of hate and its meaning as a social construct in law marking the end of the marriage status support the analogous interpretation of hate as a long-term legal status between opponents. As is evident in Deut 19, the attitude of personal hate between two opponents entitles the victim's kin to revenge, signaling a new legal status between both kin. The opponents in the feud, analogous to spouses in a marriage contract, acquire a legal status, defined by continuous malevolent intent. This status is highly regulated. As a consequence, homicide law describes the specific patterns and mechanisms of their interaction in great detail. As is evident, the specific status of opponent interaction in Deut 19:1-12* may, in more detail, be defined against the backdrop of previous homicide legislation.

Table 3.9

Deuteronomy 19:11 seems to take up this hypothetical precursor of Exod. 21:14*:

וְכִי אִישׁ הָרַגְתָּ בְעָרְמָה מֵעִם מִזְבְּחִי תִּקָּחֶנּוּ לָמוּת:

Exod 21:14*	If a man killed in an ambush, from my altar you shall take him to kill him.
Deut 19:11a	If there is a man hating his neighbor to lie in wait against him… וְכִי־יִהְיֶה אִישׁ שֹׂנֵא לְרֵעֵהוּ וְאָרַב לוֹ

3. Long-Term Enmity and Legal Procedure in Deuteronomic Law

The second stage of the relationships between the two texts can be reconstructed as follows:

Exod 21:14a	וְכִי־יָזִד אִישׁ עַל־רֵעֵהוּ לְהָרְגוֹ בְעָרְמָה If a man (maliciously) lies in wait against his neighbor to kill him in an ambush…
Deut 19:11a	If there is a man hating his neighbor and he lies in wait against him… וְכִי־יִהְיֶה אִישׁ שֹׂנֵא לְרֵעֵהוּ וְאָרַב לוֹ

The use of רע instead of אח might be explained as an adjustment to the final form of Exod 21:14.[106] The main reason to assume this development is the relevance of רע in Deut 19:1-12* as long-term relationship with a neighbor, i.e., an individual known to the slayer. Deuteronomy 19:4, 11 emphasize this by way of using the typical additions. Their use of רע in quotes from the Covenant Code adapt it to its own contexts and substantiates the insertion of רע into Deuteronomic law. Deuteronomy 12–27 uses this noun in six areas: (1) homicide and asylum;[107] (2) false testimony;[108] (3) violations of property law including border shifting between neighbors,[109] coveting or stealing possession, also of the wife of the neighbor (5:21), eating the grapes in a neighbor's vineyard (Deut 23:25), and plucking and eating of grain in his field Deut 23:26; (4) loans from a neighbor;[110] (5) marriage laws about the violation of a neighbor's spouse (Deut 22:24, 26);[111]

---

106. If so, the term רע in Exod 21:14* was likely inserted either at the same time as in Deut 19 or briefly before Deut 19:1-12* was written. See, on the four uses of רע in H, below Chapter 5.

107. Deut 19:4, 5 (2×); Deut 19:11; 4:42; including the clandestine slaying of a "neighbor" (27:42).

108. Deut 5:20.

109. גבול רעך סוג; participle סוג hi. in Deut 27:17; yiqtol in Deut 19:14.

110. Deut 24:10. Loans are also the reason for debt slavery and inform the law on debt remission for the neighbor in a *shmittah* year Deut 15:2. This passage that parallels the "Hebrew" slave passage in Exod 21:1-11* in Deuteronomy uses "neighbor" in a parallelism with "brother."

111. Cf. Deut 5:18. Cf. the prevention of a potential development of long-term enmity (Deut 22:23-27), and the rape of a betrothed female by a "neighbor." The consequences in an urban community for both male and female are located in the community's context. The neighbor knew his neighbor's spouse and he also knew her betrothal to another husband. The same is to be presupposed for Deut 19: the relationship to the רע as an acquainted neighbor (Deut 22:24 and 26). The husband who is a neighbor violated his neighbor's rights, i.e., he violated the rules of conduct between generally trustworthy people settling next to each other. This would have significant consequences for marriage law. Deuteronomy mentions the "neighbor" specifically in the laws about rape because this term puts the emphasis on the most significant element of the transgression between two individuals who settle continuously next to each other: a person who has known a neighbor, i.e., this

finally, (6) the seduction of worshipping other gods (Deut 13:7). The latter uses both terms, "neighbor" and the more narrow term "brother," for a communal member of the same ethnic and religious-cultic context.

It thus is apparent that the technical term "neighbor" in Deuteronomy describes the personal acquaintance with an individual and, consequently, Deuteronomy uses "neighbor" in the same category as "long-term enemy" or "long-term friend." As is the case in CC, רֵעַ is a randomly known character in a community personally known over a particular span of time that may turn into an opponent or an opposed party in a dispute.[112] Some laws of CC use the term in contexts in which they warn against long-term enmity between neighbors, as, naturally, the sheer closeness would include mutual borrowing, safekeeping in deposit laws Exod 22:6-13.[113] While in CC the arrangement of these laws suggests a specific social context that is relevant for determining the setting of the law and thus specifies the legal anthropological context of a community in which members would live close enough to borrow and to safekeep animals. When considering "neighbor/companion" in Deuteronomy, it is plausible that the term would acquire a context-specific meaning and designate a specific social status that may vary from the status of a neighbor that CC presupposes. Not only the socio-historical contexts, but also the specific use of the term in the literary contexts of Deuteronomic law shapes the nuance in meaning. Likewise, social constructs of kinship that are of critical relevance in all law collections may differ. It is thus necessary to determine how exactly the laws of Deuteronomy construe the category "neighbor" itself and how it construes this category in relation to other categories of kinship. The extensive use of kinship language, namely of the category "brother" in Deuteronomy, immediately demonstrates the relevance of kinship structures and the "feuding" patterns that are associated with these categories and thus supports their relevance for biblical law at large. This relevance of kinship terminology for Deuteronomic law requires further attention.

---

person has been aware of his wife's status. In voluntary injuries that cause homicide, the status between the aggressor and his victim are equally specified as forms of a long-term relationship.

112. Cf. above Chapter 2, 4.4. For instance, in the dtr announcement that David will be given the kingdom of his "neighbor" (1 Sam 28:17b), or the announcement that David's wives will be taken from him and given to his "neighbor" or rival, Absalom (2 Sam 12:11). Proverbs 18:17 uses "neighbor" likewise in the meaning of an adversary in court pleading his case cogently until his opponent investigates and dismantles or challenges his argumentation. See F. Horst, *Hiob* (Neukirchen-Vluyn: Neukirchener Verlag, 1963), 253, on Job 16:21, as well as Kellermann, רֵעַ, 551.

113. H.-P. Mathys. *Liebe deinen Nächsten wie dich selbst: Untersuchungen zum alttestamentlichen Gebot der Nächstenliebe (Lev 19,18)* (Fribourg, Switz.: Universitätsverlag, Göttingen: Vandenhoeck & Ruprecht, 1986), 32–34.

5.1. Fictive Kinship

The fictive kinship relation between members in Deuteronomic law is a construct that unfolds its meaning in a context in which individuals act out a conflict with their opponents. The urge to kinship solidarity in settlement procedure in Deut 22 is a call to apply the principle of the fairness of returning good received from another community member. It intends to avoid conflicts around loss or theft of goods, a frequently encountered problem. The extension to "anything that your brother lost" (Deut 22:3a) demonstrates the increased responsibility for the belongings of a "brother." This expansion further suggests a general posture of mutual solidarity in everyday life. The lack of a sanction in Deut 22, among other formal aspects, demonstrates the ethical character of this law. Its intention is precautionary. The recourse to a brotherly ethos preemptively excludes conflict scenarios that strain the community. This intention also drives other parts of the legislation of Deuteronomy. With the same overtone of preventing conflicts in the community, Deuteronomy's laws also address other areas of conflict settlement typically affected by mutual malevolence and proposes preventive strategies for avoiding conflicts.

Terminology and conceptual backdrop of fictive kinship are complex. A brief summary assessment of the use of "brother" points out where the brother-ethos serves as a fundamental ethical substantiation. Deuteronomy uses "brother" 48 times,[114] concentrated in the laws Deut 15–25 with 19 singular and 10 plural references.[115] The fact that all of the remaining references have suffixes[116] suggests that throughout Deuteronomy "brother" designates a member of the community. Fifteen out of the 19 singular[117] references have a second person

---

114. Used 27 times in the singular and 21 times in the plural. Half of the plural references and three of the singular occurrences are found in the framing chapters. Three of the singular references are out of topic: Deut 28:54 alludes to the biological brother; 32:50 refers to Aaron the brother of Moses. Of the 21 plural references, nine refer to Israel as "brotherly organization" in the framework of Deuteronomy: 1:28 ("our brothers"); 2:4, 8 (for Edom); 3:18, 20; 10:9; 33:9, 16, 24. Deut 1:16 uses "brother" twice when it applies the law to the community. L. Perlitt, "'Ein einzig Volk von Brüdern': zur deuteronomischen Herkunft der biblischen Bezeichnung 'Bruder'," in L. Perlitt, *Deuteronomium-Studien* (Tübingen: Mohr Siebeck 1994), 50–73, here 57–58.

115. Not included are the references to the physical brother in the Levirate marriage 25:5, 6, 7, 9 (sing.); 25:5 (plur.).

116. Perlitt, "Brüder," 58.

117. The plural references are secondary, attached to and derived from the singular references. Deuteronomy 15:7; 17:15; 18:15; 24:15 have second pers. sing. suffixes; 17:20; 18:2; 20:8; 24:7 have third pers. sing. suffixes; 18:18 has third pers. plur. Their secondary character becomes apparent when considering them in detail. Deuteronomy 15:7 picks up on 15:2. Deuteronomy 24:14 reads the same, "your brothers," as 5:7: it explains שכיר with "the poor and the needy" (ואביון עני), as is the case in 15:7. Deuteronomy 17:15, with the contrast between "a foreign man – from amidst your brothers,"

singular suffix.[118] The precise meaning of the term in an ethical discourse has been pointed out. As a category of fictive kinship in an ethical discourse, in the laws of Deuteronomy, following Perlitt, the community of the people as brothers was gradually growing within the paradigm of a parenetic agenda that implicitly required a certain behavior from community members. An observation about the form of prohibitives demonstrates this. Perlitt suggests that the terminology of fictive kinship in the "*your-brother*"-idioms much more frequently adhere to the prohibitives if already kept in the form of the second person singular. For instance, 15:7b-8 addresses the warnings and the promises and leads over to the clear prohibition in v. 11b: "Therefore, I command you: You surely shall open your hand to your poor and to your afflicted in this land!" In a similar vein, the prohibitive "you shall not oppress a hired servant who is poor and needy…" in 24:14 is now clarified by "one of your brothers." On the other hand, "you shall not take interest from your brother" in 23:20a is a clear-cut prohibitive from the deuteronomic author himself. The author of Deuteronomy's laws refrains from comments ("brother," "neighbor"), as is the case in 15:1-2. And, similar to 15:3, the author adds vv. 20-21 with the contrast between "your brother" and "the foreigner."[119] Already this concentration of the use of the singular form with a suffix in prohibitives in Deut 19–25 demonstrates that the parenetic overtone of the "brother"-layer specifically protects economically weak members of the community, that is, the brother is a poor, oppressed individual. More specifically, 15[120] out of the 19 singular references for "your brother" with the attached second person singular suffix use it as a fictional kinship term in an ethical discourse on three fields of conflicts: first, fair trial procedure, challenged namely through false testimony; second, economic dependence between community members through loans and through contingently impending debt-slavery; and third, the limits of punishment in an honor–shame society demonstrated in the case of corporal punishment Deut 25.

---

points to the similar contrast made in 15:3. Deuteronomy 17:20 and 18:18 need to be seen in light of this reference. 18:2a is a repetitious reference to 18:1; see Nielsen, *Deuteronomium*, 174. Deuteronomy 20:8 is added to the war laws, as a comparison with Deut 1:28 and Judg 7:3 demonstrates. Deuteronomy 24:7 refers to the theft of humans and is most probably added to "from the sons of Israel." It seems plausible that these uses of "brother" were secondarily brought into Deuteronomy and reflect the gradual increase of a moral aspect to brotherhood within Deuteronomy; so Perlitt, "Brüder," 59 n. 33. Different from Deuteronomy, the basic forms used in the CC are impersonal.

118. Deut 15:3, 7, 9, 11, 12; 17:15; 22:1-4; 23:20, 21; 25:3. The four other references presuppose probably an earlier use: 1:16; 15:2 ("his brother"). The use of 19:18b is explanatory for a treacherous witness, and 19:19a refers back to this use in 19:18b and depends on 19:18b; Perlitt, "Brüder," 58 n. 31.

119. Perlitt, "Brüder," 60–61.

120. Deut 15:3, 7, 9, 11, 12; 17:15; 22:1-4; 23:20, 21; 25:3.

5.2. The Singular "Your Brother" in Witness Law

Deuteronomy uses "brother," referring to the category of a closely related member of a kin group, a social construct that in a trial procedure by default would exclude false testimony or false accusation (Deut 19:18-19). This law of the witness follows after a general rule of invocation of two witnesses in allegations in Deut 19:15-17. This sequence allows a more precise determination of the meaning of the intention of the brother-ethos in 19:18-19. With a twofold reference to "your brother" it calls for the punishment of a false witness in reciprocity with the intended consequence of this witness.

Deuteronomy 19 reinforces this juxtaposition of asylum law with laws about the false witness through a formal bracket: the two laws of asylum in Deut 19:13b, 19b refer to each other by way of the idiomatic command to purge innocent bloodshed from Israel (*bi'arta*). This idiomatic interlacement of the instance of a denial of asylum in the case of intentional homicide in 19:11 with the rejection of the false witness in Deuteronomy requires an explanation. In a reflection on the backdrop of judicial institutions, E. Otto suggests Deut 19 arranges laws in a case/counter-case pattern. Deuteronomy 19:4-7 describes the asylum situation on the level of the local judicial authorities, while 19:15-21 supposedly are held in front of a central court. Deuteronomy 19 combines the authorities of the local judicial institution with those of a central judicial court. In the case of homicide, a verdict against a slayer that would be required for the blood avenger to execute revenge, that is, משפט מות (Deut 19:6b), requires two witnesses to testify whether or not a relationship of consistent mutual malevolence between slayer and victim existed. A local court was authorized to take the verdict, as 19:4-7, 11-12 demonstrate. In absence of two witnesses, however, the case needs referral to the central court, as Deut 17:8 points out.[121]

In Deut 22:1-4 the adaptation of the rules for conflict settlement from Exod 23:4-5 reverses the behavior of an enemy, favoring instead a concept of *mutual brotherly love* which, as a consequence, demands mutual benevolence between an enemy and his brother. Deuteronomy 22:1, 4 illustrates this in the quintessential escape of livestock including also other variants of loss.

5.3. Kinship Ethos and Social Justice

Kinship ethos is essential for understanding Deuteronomy's programmatic emphasis on fair economic exchange. For instance, Deut 15:1-11 illustrate the handling of lending as necessary practice among community members during times of economic distress in seventh-century Judah.[122] Economic dependence between community members through loans could entail usury. Another contingence of defaulted loans was debt-slavery. The exclusion of usury follows the

---

121. Otto, *Deuteronomy 12,1–23,15*, 1517.

122. See, on the brother ethos, E. Otto, *Theologische Ethik des Alten Testaments* (Stuttgart: Kohlhammer, 1994), 187; idem, *Deuteronomium 12,1–23,15*, 1341–49.

typical idiomatic style of a prohibitive. In its form similar to Deut 22:3, it first adduces two variants of the case (money, food), adding subsequently the idiom that generally broadens the case "or anything…": "You shall not charge interest to your countrymen: interest on money, on food, *or* anything that (cf. Deut 22:3) may be loaned at interest."

5.4. *Private Enmity as a Result of Economic Injustice*

Can we in more detail describe the legal implications of the status of private enmity beyond homicide law and usury? To slavery law, the construct of private enmity is relevant in economic terms; namely it is relevant with regard to the rejection of usury. Generally speaking, Deuteronomy drives this discourse out of a concern for social injustice. It promotes a kinship ethos that frames themes of economic dependence. The intent is preemptive avoidance of the escalation of stock reasons for conflicts around economic dependence. From a legal-historical point of view, the ideal of social justice drives the regular remittance of debt and the release of slaves, as this would be expected between siblings. The law's cultural-historical contexts are remarkably evident. The regularity of the release of debt and debt-slaves every seventh year contrasts the irregularity of a corresponding Neo-Assyrian practice which may have been known in Judah. The outspoken connection of the release of slaves with the law of divine privilege is a reason for E. Otto to relate the regular release of debt slaves to the Neo-Assyrian edicts and to interpret the regular liberation of slaves in light of the more irregular practice in Neo-Assyria.[123]

It has been in general held that among the aspects of civil law beyond Deut 19:1–25:19, the "law of privilege" (Deut 12:1–18:22) can be assessed. The brother-ethos plays a role in 15:12-18; the fictive kinship category "brother" is introduced in Deut 15:1-11 in the humanitarian laws in order to specify what in general has been said about the "release"-year.[124] The release law in Deut 15:1-11 and the slavery law in Deut 15:12-18 adapt Exod 21:2-12. Deuteronomy 15 arguably exposes the first programmatic development of the category of "brother" in Deut. Its use in 17:14-20 and 18:15-22 is presumably secondary.

---

123. Otto, *Deuteronomium 12,1–23,15*, 1349. On the familiarity of Judeans with the practice of the *an-durāru* that served the Assyrian propaganda, see W. S. Morrow, "Tribute from Judah and the Transmission of Assyrian Propaganda," in *"My Spirit at Rest in the North Country" (Zechariah 6:8)*, ed. H. M. Niemann and M. Augustin (Frankfurt: Peter Lang, 2011), 183–92.

124. An older general sentence about the release functions as superscription in vv. 1-2; originally without "brother" in v. 2aβ, b which is added to explain "the neighbor" in this same verse, C. Steuernagel, *Deuteronomium*, 2nd ed. (Göttingen: Vandenhoeck & Ruprecht, 1923) 109; cf. G. Seitz, *Studien*, 168, note 234. Contra Perlitt, "Brüder," 55.

The replacement of neighbor through 'brother' programmatically adapts the term neighbor from the CC to Deuteronomic law.[125]

Table 3.10

vv. 1-11	Release law
v. 1	Heading general case: "At the end of every seventh year…"
vv. 2-3	Implementary regulations: "your neighbor – a foreigner – <u>your brother</u>"
vv. 4-5	Subcase I: "However, as <u>no poor</u> will be among you"
v. 6	Blessing
vv. 7-10	Subcase II: "For as there is anyone <u>poor</u> among you…" <u>your brother</u>
v. 11	Parenesis: the <u>poor</u>: "… I command you…" <u>your brother</u>
vv. 12-18	Slavery remission
v. 12aα	Protasis "If <u>your brother</u> is sold…"
v. 12aβb	Apodosis "he shall serve…but in the seventh year…"
vv. 13-15	Subcase I: "But if you send him free…"
vv. 16-18	Subcase II: "But if he says…"

Deuteronomy 15:1-11 unfolds its subject matter of release first in a general case (v. 1). A set of implementary regulations distinguishes first the category of "your neighbor" from "the foreigner" and in v. 13 refers to the category "your brother." Upon this follows an arrangement of a case/counter-case in vv. 4-5, 7-10. This sequence distinguishes the situation of living without the poor from the situation of living with the poor in the land. The use of "your brother" is found in a type of implementary style of regulations v. 3, and in the subcase II (v. 7). The parenetic v. 11 reflects on the ethical necessities in light of the presence of the poor.

In the second set of regulations on slavery remission, Deut 15:12-18 likewise first exposes a general case before subsequently presenting it in two subcases: first, the slave who is released; second, the slave choosing to permanently remain in slavery. Both cases are introduced with a כִּי. The terminology of "your brother" is found in the protasis of the general case in v. 12aα.

Deuteronomy 15 reflects on potential conflicts with a close community member ("your brother") in two closely related areas of economy, lending and debt-slavery. Source critically, the legal reflections on slavery and debt are not all on the same level.[126] The use of "your brother" in Deut 15:11 is a reference

---

125. Perlitt, "Brüder," 63–64.
126. Source-critically, v. 11 together with vv. 4-6, are probably post-exilic extensions reflecting fundamentally on social injustice. While vv. 1-3 consider a crisis in the kinship society that challenges a society built on functioning kin and thus requests an ethos of

urging in a parenetic undertone to lend and to give freely to the poor and it motivates such giving in the logic of the fictitious kinship relation by a reference to the category of "your brother." 15:1-3, 7-10 are part of the deuteronomic brother-ethos exemplified in 14:28–15:18, where the seven-year rhythm underlies tithing (14:28-29 deals with third-year tithing, and 15:1 the release-year). Four of the references to "your brother" thus originated in a pre-exilic tradition of Deuteronomy. The brother-ethos explicates the exact ethical sphere of interaction between community members. This is evident in the categorization. In the implementary regulations, v. 3 differentiates three categories relevant to an economic ethos: first, "your neighbor," second, the impersonal "a foreigner" and, finally, the personal category "your brother." This categorization is comparable to the categorization of three groups in Deut 19. Asylum legislation in Deut 19:4, 11 sets apart the "random neighbor", traditionally used in homicide legislation Exod 21:12-14, from the category of a long-term opponent. The following law of the witness (19:18) refers in 19:15-21 specifically to the ethos among brothers, the third category of community members.

Deuteronomy 15:9 in particular addresses the economic disparity that guides considerations of money lending in the seven-year cycle, independently of the point in time within the cycle at which the money was lent. Deuteronomy 15:12 is programmatic as it introduces slavery legislation with the term "your brother" which, as a consequence, limits the relevance of this legislation to community members.[127]

Deuteronomy 23:20-21, in many ways a parallel to the slavery laws, adapts the prohibition of taking usury from Exod 22:24. As is the case in Deut 22:1-4, and in Deut 15:1-11, Deuteronomy introduces the term "brother" in lieu of other terms in the preceding laws of CC.

---

solidarity from their members, vv. 4-6, 11 argue from the standpoint of a general alternative to a given state of affairs. Otto, *Deuteronomium 12,1–23,15*, 1353, compares this general reflection in response to, for instance, descriptions of the state of affairs of a lack of social justice in Neh 5:1-13. Deuteronomy 15:4-6, 11 are thus post-exilic/dtr extensions, following Otto, *Deuteronomium 12,1–23,15*, 1335–36; see for other suggestions there. The protasis in v. 4a of the more fictitious case "if there is no poor among you..." is well explained as counter-case to the deuteronomic v. 7a, "if there is a poor among you..." In vv. 4-6 the motif of lending to the nations anticipates the post-exilic extension of the blessing in Deut 28:12-13. Deuteronomy 15:6b, "and you will lend to many nations, but you will not borrow; and you will rule over many nations, but they will not rule over you," literally quotes and extends its source in Deut 28:12b, "and you shall lend to many nations, but you shall not borrow."

127. These four references to economic disparity and lending to "your brother" in the fictitious kinship of Deuteronomy presuppose a seventh-century background.

Table 3.11

Exod 22:24	Deut 23:20-21
²⁴אִם־כֶּסֶף תַּלְוֶה אֶת־עַמִּי אֶת־הֶעָנִי עִמָּךְ לֹא־תִהְיֶה לוֹ כְּנֹשֶׁה לֹא־תְשִׂימוּן עָלָיו נֶשֶׁךְ:	²⁰לֹא־תַשִּׁיךְ לְאָחִיךָ נֶשֶׁךְ כֶּסֶף נֶשֶׁךְ אֹכֶל נֶשֶׁךְ כָּל־דָּבָר אֲשֶׁר יִשָּׁךְ: ²¹לַנָּכְרִי תַשִּׁיךְ וּלְאָחִיךָ לֹא תַשִּׁיךְ לְמַעַן יְבָרֶכְךָ יְהוָה אֱלֹהֶיךָ בְּכֹל מִשְׁלַח יָדֶךָ עַל־הָאָרֶץ אֲשֶׁר־אַתָּה בָא־שָׁמָּה לְרִשְׁתָּהּ:

Concentrically arranged, the prohibition of usury Deut 23:20-21 mentions as addressees "your brother," "the stranger," and again "your brother."[128] As is the case with slavery law, the replacement of "my people" and of "the poor"[129] with "your brother" illustrates that the notion of fictive kinship in Deuteronomy excludes the possibility of taking usury. While Exod 22:24 specifically refers to the poor, Deuteronomy leaves open the social status in detail and it frames lending as an act in a kinship relation. The backdrop of the prohibitive of usury is best explained with a brotherly emergency and, consequently, Deuteronomy casts lending in its typical ethos of brotherly solidarity while it elsewhere appears as public virtue (Pss 15:5; 37:26; 112:5). Apart from the replacement of "my people/ the poor" with "your brother," the arrangement of this law is similar to other revisions of laws from Exodus. Besides two examples, here silver and food, and the donkey and garment in Deut 22:3 respectively, the law ensues the characteristic expansion to analogous cases with the phrase "anything which you lend."

5.5. Brother Ethos and Honor: Deuteronomy 25:1-3

Fictive kinship, expressed by addressing community members as "your brother," confers respect and honor for community members. The term's use in a discourse on punitive measures in Deut 25:1-3 demonstrates the urging of respectful interaction with a community member. The law implements the judicial order for corporal punishment in a casuistic compound sentence with a general case (v. 1) and a subcase of handling a wronged party in the case of a capital punishment (vv. 2-3). The current form of the law is, arguably, the result of a twofold development. Originally, a simple apodosis describes in v. 1aα any form of quarrel between two men: "if there is a quarrel between two men." The protasis designates the case as a general conflict between two men that would not necessarily be resolved in court. Rather, the protasis is comparable with and potentially inspired by Exod 21:18: "and if men quarrel." This is a general opening statement that the subsequent clause specifies through a more precise state of affairs: "and one man slays the other." The following apodosis suggests (v. 1aβb) that the two contending parties consult a court that would declare one guilty and the other

---

128. Cf. Nelson, *Deuteronomy*, 282.
129. Oddly postponed after "my people."

one just (v. 1b). While it remains an open question exactly which court would handle this case, the subsequent vv. 2-3 then limits the case to the punishment of the guilty party.[130] This may lead to the conclusion that v. 1 is an older case law on which vv. 2-3 elaborate.[131]

    v. 1:   General case: If there happens a quarrel…
    vv. 2-3:   Subcase: and if it happens…

Verse 3 uses the kinship-category of "brother" with the intention of motivating such conduct so that it would mitigate the degree of shaming and would not permanently infringe upon a community member's honor. Verse 3 limits the maximum penalty to 40 lashes.[132] Honor and shame are important values in and outside of the kin[133] and the limitation ensures the community member's honor as a "brother," who would literally otherwise be "cursed" ("burnt," קלה *ni.*), an expression for the loss of public respect.[134] Different from other laws, the law on corporal punishment refers to the ethical implications of the social status of a member of one's kin, demonstrating the necessity of balancing honor and shame of a permanent kin member in an inner-kin conflict.

5.6. *Conclusion*
In the current analysis the urge toward mutual benevolence and the systemic exclusion of personal long-term hateful relations have emerged as the main

---

130. The development in two stages is also substantiated through the difference of the nature of the court. Verse 1 does not mention a group of judges (plur.), but vv. 2-3 mentions a single judge.

131. See Gertz, *Gerichtsorganisation*, 100, with reference to Seitz, *Studien*, 126, and R. P. Merendino, *Das deuteronomische Gesetz. Eine literarkritische, gattungs- und überlieferungsgeschichtliche Untersuchung zu Dt 12–26* (Bonn: P. Hanstein, 1969), 317–18; Nelson, *Deuteronomy*, 296.

132. Limitation of the corporal punishment to forty lashes was not unusual. It is comparable to penalties in the Middle Assyrian Laws. One hundred lashes for removal of the boundary is mentioned MAL B 8 and MAL F 1 for theft. Theft is punished with payment in Exod 21:37–22:1. For other offenses, about 50 lashes are an adequate punishment, according to MAL A 19, 21; B 9, 15. See also R. Haase, "Körperliche Strafen in den altorientalischen Rechtssammlungen. Ein Beitrag zum altorientalischen Strafrecht," *RIDA* 3-10 (1963): 55–75.

133. Cf. the *hiphil* participle, "treat with contempt, dishonor," is used for dishonoring the parental generation in Deut 27:16.

134. The noun קלון specifically refers to public respect; see J. Marböck, קלה, *TDOT*, vol. 13 (Grand Rapids: Eerdmans, 2004), 31–37, 36. The finite (*ni.*) form of this verb is used two more times in Isa 16:14 for the impending shame of Moab and in the discussion on true and false honor for the disgracing of rulers in Sir 11:8. Cf. the participle to express (public) shaming in Isa 3:5; 1 Sam 18:23; Prov 12:9.

intentions behind Deuteronomy's concept of fictive kinship. Rhetorically, the fictive kinship category "brother," with the typical enclitic personal suffix, promotes an ethos of default mutual amity among community members. The use of the term expects community members to adopt a posture of benevolence and inspires a congruent ethos of amity of the parties involved, including adopting economic fairness when giving out loans or hiring a day laborer.[135] The ethical relevance of fictional kinship becomes more fully apparent when seen against the backdrop of the use of "neighbor," for instance, with regard to boundary shifting (Deut 27:17; 19:14a). Furthermore, the implications of "brother" become apparent in ten passages in which CC uses the impersonal designation "neighbor" in the Covenant Code in casuistic sentences[136] that Deuteronomy replaces with "brother." Deuteronomy uses the form "neighbor" with its typical second personal singular suffix four times in the context of false witnessing and with regard to unfair coveting of neighborly belongings in the Decalogue (Deut 5:20-21).[137] The responsibility for a neighbor excludes blatant offenses, such as boundary shifting, public lies or seeking another person's possessions. The fictive kinship ethos exceeds responsibilities toward these individuals and requires more responsibility from them.

5.7. Excursus: "Neighbor" in Proverbs

The fictive kinship terminology with the programmatic use of "your brother" in seventh-century Deuteronomy contexts would remain mostly idiosyncratic, yet the following outlines a number of tangible positive effects of kinship ethos and clarifies the reason for the exclusion of private enmity in the personal sphere. The characteristics of fictive kinship ethos in Deuteronomy and the notions that are connected with it become evident in particular when juxtaposing the categories "brother" and "neighbor" in Proverbs.

Volatility of neighborly relations. Proverbs advises avoidance of close personal interaction with a neighbor, a warning based on the fragile nature and the

---

135. The prohibitive that excludes taking interest from a brother in the case of granting a neighbor a loan for survival, found in Deut 23:20 (see Nelson, *Deuteronomy*, 282), differs formally from the "when–if" clauses in vv. 22-24, 25-26. Steuernagel, *Deuteronomium*, 137–38, suggests it to be part of the D2C-edition and sees v. 21 as a secondary addition. Hölscher, "Deuteronomium," 210–14, takes it as part of the original Deuterg onomy. For instance, Deut 24:14 distinguishes between a "foreigner" (גר) and "brother" as day laborers who both should not be oppressed. Hölscher, "Deuteronomium," 209–10, takes this to be an old part of Deuteronomy; Steuernagel, *Deuteronomium*, 138–41, sees it as a part of the D2C edition; Nielsen, *Deuteronomium*, 226, takes it to be redactional; cf. Lev 19:18-19, 25:26, 46.

136. Perlitt, "Brüder," 63.

137. Used four times. Arguably, the Decalogue is part of the reception history of Deuteronomic law if not an entirely independent compilation.

ambivalence of the relationship between neighbors. In a variety of contexts Proverbs reflect on this typical relationship among community members in close vicinity. Consider Prov 25:17, part of a set of parallel verses, vv. 16-17,[138] which urges the respecting of the limits of healthy food consumption and warns against the digestive disturbances of overeating honey. As an analogous case it ponders the limits of neighborly contact. The warning undertone of this reflection on the relationship to a neighbor demonstrates the exposure to the particular degree of vulnerability of both neighbors. Most of all, a neighborly relationship does not imply mutual benevolence; friendship, in contrast, would be explicitly defined through such benevolence. Proverbs thus distinguishes the social construct of a neighborly relationship from friendship as characterized through unreliability and potential instability.[139]

Spatial and social proximity of neighborly relationships. "Neighbor" in Proverbs refers to an individual dwelling and settling in the vicinity who by default entertains a mutually neutral relationship and who by nature is not part of one's own kin. Consequently, the relation to a neighbor was considered volatile and only to a very limited degree trustworthy. A neighbor, not bound by kinship authority, could easily become an entirely untrustworthy ally. Proverbs warns that a neighborly relationship could theoretically turn into bleak opposition in a number of ambivalent relationships. Pointing to the structural unreliability when engaging with a person outside one's own kin as a typical feature of neighborly relationships, consequently, Proverbs recommends mistrust of a neighbor or a person of social affinity one would refer to as "companion." Proverbs 14:20-21 illustrates how Proverbs conceptualizes the "neighbor" as social term, i.e., as a member of a particular social status, settling in immediate proximity to others of the same social class. The essential relevance of one's social status when forming a friendship bond is immediately evident.[140] Proverbs 18:24 is a case in point: "A companion [is] to break, but there is one more loving and closer than a brother." Second, the sheer social proximity of a רע makes conflict situations more likely; i.e., they occur regularly in neighborly contexts.

The neighbor as ideal-typical interaction partner. Proverbs typically reflects on the category of the "neighbor" as an individual with whom one interacts, namely as an individual who is acted upon rather than describing the neighbor as a (primary) agent. This perspective on the neighbor is also characteristic for

---

138. The two admonitions are connected and expose syntactical, semantic, and content parallels: the second lines in both verses use "lest...and," both use roots with the consonants שבע and both carry the associations of "rejection" physically through "vomiting" as well as emotionally through "hate." See Whybray, *Proverbs*, 365.

139. See, in various ways, Prov 17:18; 18:17; 21:10.

140. Hellenistic contexts, as Sir 13:21-23 demonstrates, elaborate on this. Companionships were forms of social interactions shaped by the way in which social status would enable or limit friendships.

the term's use in legal texts. The ten occurrences of רע in CC,[141] in addition to the four in the Decalogue,[142] and those in Deuteronomy[143] and the Holiness Code (H),[144] never designate the other person as an agent. The ideal of a neighborly relationship reflects on how to reach out to another member of a community and on how to actively engage in this relation.[145] The category serves as an external descriptor for another community member and is connected with the expectation of treating the רע in a certain way.[146] The term רע evokes the mode of acting upon someone in this category as a pragmatic act. Proverbs uses רע by and large analogously to CC as neighbor. In the majority of cases, it can be rendered as "companion" or "fellow," a use that is more prominent in H.[147] Both these terms denote the social rather than the spatial proximity to the רע. Among other passages, Prov 14:19-21 support this meaning by pointing out that having a "companion/fellow" associated with the same social class, namely in circles that v. 20 refers to as "rich." A similar relationship between neighbors as "equals" or as individuals who are appendant to similar social circles informs Prov 22:11: "Who loves a pure heart and gracious lips, his neighbor is the king."

As is the case with friendship (אהב), a neighborly status in stable settlements was hereditary from one generation to the next.[148] At the same time, the sheer command of benevolence toward a neighbor demonstrates the volatility and the flexibility when interacting with a רע: an individual could find himself in a position of potential disloyalty to another and therefore act in disloyalty. Verbal conflicts between neighbors were typically the first step of an emerging conflict. At the outset of a conflict, two neighbors could act out their enmity through deceit, for instance, through falsely flattering words (Prov 16:29; 26:18-19; 27:14; 29:5).[149]

The neighbor as hypothetical opponent. As has been pointed out above,[150] Proverbs focuses on the social construct of the neighbor in light of possibly impending conflicts between close residents.[151] They would habitually begin with

---

141. Exod 21:14, 18, 35; 22:6, 7, 8, 9, 10, 13, 25 and see on the term above Chapter 2, 4.4.
142. Exod 20:16, 17; Deut 5:20, 21.
143. Deut 13:7; 15:2; 19:4-5 (2×), 11, 14; 22:24, 26; 23:25, 26 (2×); 24:10; 27:17, 24.
144. Lev 19:13, 16, 18; 20:10.
145. Cf. D. Kellermann, רע, *TDOT*, vol. 8 (Grand Rapids: Eerdmans, 2004), 522–32, 527.
146. J. Fichtner, "Begriff," 36.
147. Cf. below, Chapter 5, 3.4.
148. Proverbs 27:10 refers to this hereditary character: "Do not forsake your "companion" or the "companion" of your father."
149. See also Prov 11:9; cf. the possibility to protect a neighbor in Prov 11:12.
150. Cf. above, Chapter 2, 4.4.
151. A caveat of the following references to Proverbs is that a historically nuanced approach to proverbial wisdom is beyond the scope of this study. Far from offering

a random situation or a verbal dispute, yet, as the nature of the relationship to the רע is volatile at best, Proverbs typically warns not to be on overly trusting terms with a neighbor. Consequently, Proverbs tackles the fragility of the relationship and its reversal into mistrust, conveying the viewpoint of general mistrust as appropriate and beneficial in neighborly relationships. A decisive moment in the relation between neighbors occurs in need of trustworthiness and credibility. Proverb 17:18 highlights the instability of a neighborly relationship in general: "A man lacking in understanding claps a hand, he takes on a pledge before his neighbor." The neighbor misused the confidence that a person put in him. Lawsuits mention a similarly problematic role of neighbors (Prov 18:17). Hastily quarreling (ריב *qal*) with a neighbor is detrimental for one's reputation (Prov 25:8, 9). When neighbors use slanderous speeches, especially when witnessing in court, this could threaten one's existence: "With his mouth the impious spoils (שחת *hi.*) his neighbor, but the righteous are extricated by knowledge" (Prov 11:9).

Proverbs rejects treacherous or slanderous speeches (11:12) and humiliating rhetoric (בוז *qal*) as signs of a mindless person. Proverbs warns against harming a neighbor through accusations in speech; such behavior is explicitly called "impious," i.e., it is labeled as a cultural technique that is foreign to the Israelite ethos. Neighborly relationships should not involve litigation.[152] The admonitions to refrain from litigation are grounded in the ideal of a good and balanced long-term neighborly relationship.[153] Legal aspects of the relationship to a neighbor are often found, for instance, in the case of witnessing falsely or of deceiving through speech: "Do not be a witness against your neighbor without

---

timeless, general rules, proverbial wisdom is informed by historical developments, as becomes particularly apparent in their attention to the contractual relationship to a neighbor in Prov 6:1-3, which is best explained in the historical context of the (late Persian or) Ptolemaic period; cf. B. Schipper, *Proverbs 1–15: A Commentary* (Minneapolis: Fortress, 2019), 220–21, noting the parallels for the practice of vouching, literally "to grasp the hand," specifically in the 26th Dynasty Demotic Papyrus Rylands 9:20, 17; cf. the overview of S. L. Lippert, *Einführung in die altägyptische Rechtsgeschichte*, 2nd ed. (Münster: LIT Verlag, 2012), 105, as well as the use of the Demotic term specifically in land leases from the Ptolemaic period. This practice, not mentioned otherwise in biblical law, builds the socio-historical context of enmity between neighbors in Prov 6:1-3.

152. Prov 24:19-20: "Do not show heat" (contra Fox, *Proverbs 10–31*, 751, suggesting "envy 'evil men'" with variants of this admonition in Prov 3:31; 23:17a; 24:1; Ps 37:1) against the neighbors (מרעים); see on this form as derivative from רעע, Kellermann, רע, 548: perhaps Gen 26:26; Judg 14:11, 20; 15:2, 6; 2 Sam 3:8; Prov 19:7; maybe also Prov 19:4; Job 6:14. For the derivation of the term's meaning, see S. Olyan, "A Suggestion Regarding the Derivation of the Hebrew Noun *MĒRĒA'*," *JSS* 56 (2011): 217–19.

153. The end of the wicked in v. 20 is a typical threat that is found several times (see Prov 13:9b; 20:20b; 23:18), and it is the opposite of what happens in a good neighborly relationship.

cause, and do not deceive/seduce[154] with your lips" (Prov 24:28). Likewise, metaphors of warfare describe the physically destructive effects of speeches directed as weapons, such as a club, a sword and a sharpened arrow, against neighbors.[155]

Proverbs urges prudence and savviness vis-à-vis neighbors (רע) and warn against the naïve trust in a "neighbor." This stance sheds light on the adaptation of laws from CC to a brother-ethos and also informs Deut 19:1-12. Long-term private enemies would trigger blood feuds in a very different way than spontaneously angry neighbors. The volatility and the unpredictability of neighborly relationships prove neighbors as unreliable allies in conflicts. When Proverbs warn that neighbors whom they in principle consider as "equal citizens,"[156] could easily turn into enemies, it provides the backdrop for Deuteronomy's urge to cultivate a kinship ethos that creates more stable and reliable relationships in a community.

5.8. *Deuteronomy 19:3b:* רצח – *"to kill in a community"*
Complementary to the social construct of "neighbor" and "companion/fellow," homicide terminology in Deut 19:1-12 requires some brief consideration. More specifically, what comes into focus is whether the term for slayer in Deut 19 supports a particular ethos that allowed for this form of enmity. Deuteronomy 19:3b uses the term prominently in its opening clause, "Every one who has killed (רצח)." This is a technical legal term for homicide that replaces the more general מות from Exod 21:12-14.[157] It is critical that the aggressor and his victim have

---

154. פתה *piel*; cf. Prov 1:10; 16:29; Exod 22:15; with words: Judg 14:15; 16:5; 2 Sam 3:25. פתה *pual*; Jer 20:10; Sir 42:10; Prov 25:15.

155. Prov 25:18. Proverbs 3:28 criticizes unfair social behavior. Elsewhere in Proverbs, criticism is extended to other forms of behavior, such as despising in 14:21; seducing in 16:29, and deceiving in 26:19. The "King's friend," mentioned in 1 Kgs 4:5 and 1 Chr 27:33, designates a special role at the court.

156. Cf. K. Berger, *Die Gesetzesauslegung Jesu: ihr historischer Hintergrund im Judentum und im Alten Testament. 1, 1* (Neukirchen-Vluyn: Neukirchener Verlag, 1972), 86.

157. Cf. particularly the use in the Decalogue for homicide of a community member; a typical case is a neighbor. F. L. Hossfeld, רצח, *TDOT*, vol. 13 (Grand Rapids: Eerdmans, 2004), 630–40, here 633. A. Deissler, *"Ich bin dein Gott, der dich befreit hat." Wege zur Meditation über das Zehngebot* (Freiburg: Herder, 1975), 102, suggests the private sphere to be the place where the killing takes place, and J. J. Stamm, "Sprachliche Erwägungen zum Gebot ‚Du sollst nicht töten'," *Theologische Zeitschrift* 1 (1945): 81–90, here 88, highlights the anti-communal aspect of such killing. The most challenging reference is Deut 5:17. Note the three uses of *qal* participles – Hos 4:2; Jer 7:9; Job 24:14 – in lists of crimes. The context does not disclose whether those are intentionally or unwittingly committed; a similar ambivalence may be assumed for Deut 19:3b. This superscript leaves open whether the killing was intentional or accidental, while clearly the slayer is in

known each other over a long time. The verb is not limited to unintended killing in 19:4-6. Rather, it designates any homicide in one's community, independent from its motivation.[158] רצח by itself would not suggest a long-term enmity as a criterion for eligibility for asylum, yet, in conjunction with the notion of ongoing hate "ever since" between slayer and victim, Deut 19 clarifies the longevity of the relationship. Additional adaptations of Deut 19:11 corroborate the long-term nature of the slayer–victim relationship, such as the replacement of ציד* and/or ערמה with the term ארב ("to ambush"), typically used for military strategies of catching an enemy off guard.[159] Other examples are unanticipated waylays, a context in which late Persian and Hellenistic wisdom literature used the term.[160] The idiom "he rises up against him," v. 11, may denote any violent interaction with the intent to overcome an opponent.[161]

5.9. Conclusion

The legal construct of long-term enmity has major implications in and for Deuteronomic law. Five laws, Deut 19:1-12; 21:15-17; 22:1-4, 13-21; 24:1-4, illustrate hallmark features of personal enmity and hate: the public nature of ongoing conflicts among community members, the principles of reciprocity and escalation, and the long-term nature that sets apart continuous hate from an isolated hateful act. In two ways Deut 19 clarifies this concept: first, through the use of the participle for "hate"; second, through the explicit notion of the enduring character of enmity with the attribute "ever since." Likewise, with its emphasis on fictive kinship, Deuteronomy intends to motivate citizens to continuously engage in mutual benevolence rather than giving in to long-term hateful interaction.

a communal relationship with the victim. רצח does not denote the deity's punishment but may refer to retaliatory killing in a community, as in Num 35:30: "If anyone kills another, so he shall be killed." In Num 35:27, רצח designates the retaliatory killing of the slayer, i.e., in the community where the homicide took place. The killing of a neighbor in order to inherit property (cf. 1 Kgs 21:19 רצח) also points to killing in the community.

    158. Gertz, *Gerichtsorganisation*, 135.

    159. Cf. King Saul's ambush (*hiphil*) of the city of Amalek 1 Sam 15:5; cf. Judg 21:20. A metaphor for private feud uses it for the relationship between an individual and Yahweh: "He is a bear lying in wait for me, a lion in hiding," Lam 3:10; cf. also Ezra 8:31 and in the context of war, ambush against a city Josh 8:2, 12, 14, 19, 21; Judg 20:33, 36, 37, 38. Samson accuses the Philistines of having ambushed him in Judg 16:9, 12.

    160. Prov 1:11, 18; Sir 11:32; cf. also Mic 7:20. Proverbs 12:6 may allude to the context of trial; cf. also Job 37:8; 38:40.

    161. See, for instance, Ps 54:5. In the context of rebellion, see Num 16:2. Job 30:12 (with textual problems) and 20:27 potentially refer to dispute settlement; the subject is "the earth, the land," and the *hitpolel* results in "the earth will rise up against them [the heavens]."

3. Long-Term Enmity and Legal Procedure in Deuteronomic Law

The legal implications of the construct of long-term hate are apparent in Deuteronomy's references to legal procedure. For homicide law, the eligibility for asylum depends on the nature of the slayer–victim relationship. Long-term hate rules out the slayer's eligibility for asylum. A planned homicide committed in such a relationship would be intolerable. Deuteronomy embeds the claim of jurisdiction in a homicide case as part of the judicial authority of the kinship-based institution of the elders.[162] Marriage law (Deut 22:13-21a; 24:1-4) and

---

162. The scope of the elders' laws in Deuteronomy and their analogies in ancient Near Eastern and modern societies is to secure proper legal mechanisms typical for segmentary societies. See T. Willis, *The Elders of the City: A Study of the Elders-Laws in Deuteronomy* (Atlanta, GA: Scholars Press, 2001), 50–82, in general, as well as the parallels listed for individual cases such as homicide, 100–109; purity after bloodshed, 146–49; on the case of the rebellious son, 163–69; on chastity, 188–206; on levirate marriage, 238–51. The elders' laws cover critical aspects of collective responsibility for homicide, by both known and anonymous slayers (19:1-13; 21:1-9), marriage contracts (22:13-21) and discourses on the responsibility of a kin for a widowed bride (25:5-10). In societies in which kinship ties to a considerable degree exercise influence upon judicial affairs on the local level, these laws are of utmost relevance. Their literary and source-critical context, as well as the fundamental procedural rules and their relevance for the concept of private "hate" in Deuteronomy are beyond the focus of the present study. The extent to which the elders' laws reflect legal practice is disputed; cf. Willis, *Elders*, 21. Dating the elders' laws remains tentative for a variety of reasons. One is that the partial legislation in favor of the elders' authority that pertains to a conflict between members of their own kinship group. They take up a tendency of Deuteronomic legislation of holding the kin accountable to standards of the community, as the rebellious son (Deut 21:18-21) readily demonstrates. One function of the elders' laws was to strengthen their leadership as a kinship-based institution where they mainly have the task of the custodianship and the proclamation of the law; see Gertz, *Gerichtsorganisation*, 223. Kinship-based understanding of the society informs the elders' laws and it subverts other influences of non-kinship-based structure. Marriage, inheritance law, and the representation of a community in a local case of anonymous homicide all represent severe matters of legal dispute in kinship-based societies. Impending feud as a potential consequence of homicide caused by an identified or an anonymous slayer in 21:1-9 and 19:1-13, accidental or intentional, was equally serious. As homicide legislation demonstrates, cases of the elders' laws focus on situations in which long-term hate between kin members of a community could erupt in violence and threaten an entire kinship-based society caused by a sudden emergence of violence in an accidental everyday scenario. Gertz, *Gerichtsorganisation*, 222–25, conceives of the elders' legislation being representative for an old, local stage of kinship-based law that became gradually obsolete with the installation of professional judges under Josiah, which is reflected in Deut 16:18*. At the same time, the elders' laws, to Gertz, best reflect local jurisdiction of the Second Temple period. Legal-anthropological studies substantiate forms of concurring dual legislation of overlapping local kinship-based and central legal authority and procedure. That is, homicide would not easily be handed over to centralized judicial institutions; see, among others, Willis, *Elders*, 19–27, and Chapter 4 below.

inheritance law (21:15-17) also conceive of hate as a continuous legal state of affairs between two partners. Once this state of affairs is reached, the spouses dissolve the marriage and separate. Seen through the lens of the husband, the wife remains the "hated" wife (21:15, 17).

6. Outlook: Deuteronomy 19 as Response to an Agonistic Society?

Was Deut 19 programmatically developed in response to a culture of challenge and riposte in Judean honor–shame society? Deuteronomy 19 indeed responds to the dynamics of hateful interaction between opponents with unprecedented depth in its reflection on the status between long-term opponents. It construes enmity as a status opposite to friendship in the public sphere between the kin of the opponents, conceiving of private enmity as a legal construct characterized by specific hallmarks. Deuteronomic law thus refines private long-term enmity as an active state of mutual hostility. A social construct that is typical for kinship law indeed is at the heart of this law. The envisioned practice of homicide and asylum law in Deut 19 reflects feuding dynamics. As such it is of legal anthropological relevance, as the biblical law collection operates on the basis of concepts of kinship law with centralistic elements, such as the cities of refuge with their function of an idealistic remedy that is administered by the elders as kinship authorities and that alleviates and mitigates the typical dynamics of feuding in a national context. This sheds new light on the analysis of conflict settlement mechanisms in urban and rural areas and, in a legal comparison, it fits together with reconstructions of Athenian legal practice as feuding rather than the "rule of law." Feuding principles are operative in the case of homicide, which sheds new light on Deuteronomic law as example of legislation for an urban context that attempts to rally a community through a fictive kinship ethos.

The analysis of injury law in CC in the previous chapter has clarified how the continuous intention over a span of time was situated within specific social structures in which the determination of long-term private enmity was of critical relevance. The examination of the laws of Deuteronomy has located "hate" and "love" likewise and, with more precision, demonstrated how they function as attitudes within long-term or continuing social constructs in marriage and private enmity. As part of biblical law, Deut 19 and the related laws mirror the discourse about private enmity in a society that is based on amity among kin and that allows us to distinguish two ideal-typical appearances in biblical law. The case of the nocturnal burglar in Exod 22:1-2a was seen to reflect on a beginning long-term enmity between a burglar and its victim and thus illustrates what I identified as the attention to the slayer–victim relationship that can be also seen in the case of Exod 21:18-19. The scenarios of the cases provide good reasons to assume that the conflict-settlement mechanisms of feuding long-term enemies formed the backdrop against which these laws must be seen. They seem not to reflect on intentionality as an isolated criterion but to preclude the notion of a slayer–victim relationship coupled with intentionality, as it becomes plainly visible in Exod 23:4-5.

3. Long-Term Enmity and Legal Procedure in Deuteronomic Law

While for methodological limitations the historical context of homicide law cannot be fully reconstructed, the dynamics of private enmity become more apparent in more detail in Deuteronomic law. It exhibits how the exclusion of intent, that is, accidental homicide, must have been treated as a special case of homicide, different from the behavioral code for private enmity. It is therefore essential that Deut 19:4, 11-12 clarify the legal category of long-term enmity, a development that results from the intention to regulate private enmity as a publicly known status between two opponents. This clarification is indicative of the increase of either the explicit need to clarify the enemy-relation or it is indicative of the relevance of an enemy-relation when two individuals that identify as members of the same collective engaged in mutual hateful conduct. Another tribute to classical kinship-based society in Deuteronomy is the elders' function in homicide laws as representative of the clans. Biblical law does not focus on the isolated category of pure intentionality. Instead, the law on fatal injury perceives it as embedded in the social contextual framework in which it occurs. Consequently, Deut 19 considers whether a fatal injury was part of an ongoing feuding pattern via consultation with the elders as clan representatives. It is thus of importance to the community whether the slayer and victim might have acted following their expected role profile of the well-defined social status of personal opponents in a feuding pattern.[163] Kinship-based institutions are thus key to ending feuding patterns and Deut 19 demonstrates how the established categories of friendship and enmity would typically function in kinship law with the elders as the established kinship-based institution responsible for conflict settlement.[164]

This result has far reaching consequences for the biblical narrative tradition as a reflection of legal thought and institutions. From the plethora of material, suffice it to mention how the constructs of biblical law in detail shape narrative tradition, namely biblical narrative when read against the backdrop of typical social constructs of enmity and friendship or love. Among others, the broad stream of biblical case narratives about Saul's attempt to injure his rival David, the Joab–Abner and the Tamar–Absalom threads, all unfold in plotlines about intentional injury and homicide of long-term opponents.[165] Their reflection of

---

163. Exactly at what point in time and why this emphasis of the elders as institution in conflict settlement became essential, and whether a vacuum of legal institutions for local conflict settlement was the cause for emphasizing their relevance in conflict settlement (see the note above) is beyond the scope of this study; yet, see the specific historical background addressed in Num 35 and in Lev 19 in Chapters 4 and 5.

164. Cf. the context of the kin in marriage law of Deut 22:21. Consequently, the elders' judicial function exceeds their administrative authority in other contexts.

165. The theme of long-term enmity in the narrative tradition is beyond the scope of this study. See, for instance, the treatment of the Joab–Abner and the Tamar–Amnon–Absalom threads in D. Daube, "Direct and Indirect Causation in Biblical Law," *VT* 11 (1961): 246–69. For additional bibliography on the hermeneutics of law collections, see Jackson, *Semiotics and Legal Theory*, esp. 167–90, and for an attempt to reflect on biblical narrative material, J. Burnside, "Flight of the Fugitives: Rethinking the Relationship

feuding patterns is immediately apparent, while their detailed source-critical analysis in conjunction with biblical law remains a task for further study. Likewise, while this analysis of Deuteronomic law demonstrates the relevance of kinship-based law and the legal procedure of a local kinship-based community, it sheds light on only a limited context of Deuteronomy. While this result warns against any unilinear evolutionary theories that reconstruct a centralized concept of jurisdiction that would supersede kinship-based legal institutions, it does not attempt to comprehensively present the legal-historical development in Judah.

As the analysis thus far has demonstrated, Deut 19 presupposes the longevity of the slayer–victim relationship. It will now be necessary to analyze the concept of the longevity of opponent relations related to the priestly realm. It will likewise be interesting to consider whether other hallmarks of private enmity, such as the requirement of an overt act between the two opponents, are also evident in other laws, in the same way that Deut 19 assumes a publicly visible relation between slayer and victim. Further aspects concern the adequacy of reciprocation of hateful acts that allow for flexibility and variation, as well as the transitivity and heritability of hateful relationships in one's kin.[166]

---

between Biblical Law (Exodus 21:12-14) and the Davidic Succession Narrative (1 Kings 1–2)," *JBL* 129, no. 3 (2010): 418–31.

166. On classical Athens, see, for instance, Phillips, *Avengers of Blood*, 26–29, and see Chapter 1, 4.

Chapter 4

ENMITY AND HATE IN PRIESTLY LAW:
NUMBERS 35 (DEUTERONOMY 4; JOSHUA 20)

1. *Source Criticism: Enmity in Priestly Law*

The threefold qualification of the notion of the killer's inadvertence in Deut 19:4b and the fivefold specification of intentionality in 19:11 each respectively distinguish spontaneous accidents from a long-term planned homicide. Both verses are therefore important for clarifying the continuing social status of private enmity, namely when reconstructing private enmity through the lens of legal history, in what has been identified as conflict-settlement modes of feuding. When attempting to reconstruct social reality of conflict settlement based on literary concepts of laws and of feuding legal-historically, any such attempt must be based on a careful analysis of the sources in order to answer two questions. First, it must determine the relevance of premeditation in conflict settlement. Subsequent homicide legislation indeed takes further the consideration of the slayer's premeditation. The following thus traces the development of the concept of long-term enmity in biblical law through homicide legislation in the realm of P. The law in Num 35 points to the increased attention to the validity claim of asylum, depending on whether the killing that had occurred was accidental or the slayer and victim had been long-term enemies.[1]

The second question that this reading of priestly law must consider is its increasing attention to matters of practice around asylum cities, including procedural details. From a legal-anthropological perspective, the continuation of this trend of inclusion of legal practice as already seen in Deut 19 is of interest, as it attests to the relevance of institutions of kinship-based societies to which Deuteronomy refers for an urban polity at a specific point in time in Judah. The present chapter presents what can be gleaned from the use of such institutions given the historical context of Num 35 in the late Persian or Hellenistic epoch. In anticipation of the result, the following reading suggests that Num 35 would

---

1. Referred to, for instance, as the slayer's premeditation, Jackson, *Wisdom-Laws*, 124, or intentionality Stackert, *Rewriting*, 71.

be misread as source for the existence of asylum cities in Judah. Rather, this law programmatically emphasizes the jurisdiction of institutions of kinship autonomy with the intent of strengthening Judah as a polity.

While remaining critical to any unilinear reconstructions based on evolutionary theories of biblical law, this study primarily considers how the social constructs that are relevant to homicide law possibly already in CC and clearly in Deuteronomy, would relate to Num 35. Numbers 35:9-34 as law in the priestly tradition continues elements of Deut 19, with the arrangement of the cities of refuge and the practical concern for the city's access to the slayer. However, Num 35:9-34 also significantly modify the concept of asylum as city asylum from Deuteronomy that replaces refuge at the altar or sanctuary in Exod 21:13-14. This shift is relevant not so much as a specifically legal-historical, but as a literary-context-related and historical fact.

Furthermore, the following analysis seeks to demonstrate how Num 35 as law in the priestly tradition conceives of the construct of private enmity in a much more elaborate way than Deut 19. This will primarily become apparent through the semantic form of the law in Num 35. Furthermore, beyond Num 35, other sources of priestly law seek to also define more clearly the status of enmity, namely in light of its opposite, mutual friendship. Casting the net wider, Chapter 5 outlines the development of another strand of priestly law on conflict settlement and on long-term enmity in the row of the prohibitives found in Lev 19:11-18 (H). A parallel, the prophetic oracle on the systemic intentional blood bath among urban leaders (Ezek 22:1-12) is a type of twin-text that equally contributes to the discourse on intentionality in homicide law of Deut 19 and Num 35 and also illustrates how fatal attacks in an urban realm were concerning to the prophet, given the lack of sanctions imposed by authorities of the kinship-based society (mother, father).

Two results from this and the subsequent chapter may be anticipated. First, Num 35 more precisely than its predecessors mirrors specific legal and cultural historical contexts. The law details various modes of slaying, offers direction on asylum practice, and specifies this historical collective's jurisdiction in the matter.[2] In particular, it becomes apparent that the nouns "hatred" and "enmity" conceive of the social status as abstract at a precise historical point in time.

Second, the interest in legal procedural aspects plays out in the refined ascertainment of particular facts as relevant to determine the slayer's premeditation or intentionality.[3] This procedure's inherent challenges led on the one hand to the requirement of a human court that determines homicide judgment, which further prompts elaborations on legal procedure. On the other hand, it led to

---

2. On the historical reconstruction of asylum practice, see below 5.5.

3. Any reconstruction of a historical asylum practice in Judah based on Num 35 would be responding to an ill-posed question. The law details more about the jurisdiction of the "assembly" over asylum practice from what has been called a "theocratic perspective," see below.

the development of the theological concept of the deity's examination of an individual.[4] Furthermore, the parallel reading of Num 35, Lev 19:11-18, and Ezek 22:1-12 allows the identification of three distinct areas with their respective distinct literary and socio-historical contexts where the destructive effects of private hate particularly reverberate: Ezek 22:1-12, where the ruling elite of an urban community cause a blood bath as it breaks with traditional kinship-based authority over conflict resolution; Num 35:9-34, where a polity's claim of jurisdiction on asylum contests against a colonizing power; and Lev 19:11-18, which exemplifies an anti-agonistic community ethos that aims at altogether overcoming the status of private enmity through its opposite, mutual benevolence. The juxtaposition of asylum laws in Num 35 with Ezek 22:1-12 and Lev 19:11-18 intends to bring to light the variety of literary and historical contexts in which the construct of private enmity (together with its opposite, mutual benevolence or friendship in Lev 19:11-18) is of relevance. Across each of these sets of an admittedly eclectic selection of priestly laws, the contours of the social construct of private enmity and friendship become more clearly apparent through the refined lexicographic distinctions. At the same time, the contextuality of long-term private enmity in the specific literary frameworks and their historical contexts becomes apparent.

This chapter initially assesses (1) the history of traditions and the source-critical origin of Num 35, (2) its outline, and (3) the major developments from Deut 19 to Num 35 and the underlying notion of asylum. It then traces (4) how this law specifically construes the newly generated abstract category of private enmity, namely the particular mode of tragic inadvertence, and the variety of modes of action and the abstract terminology for enmity. Finally, (5) Num 35 modifies legal procedure assigning the authority of a jury to the community at large. The conceptualization of asylum for an extended period of time in an urban setting with the proposition of cities of refuge points to the law's historical context.

Why would Num 35:9-34 take up homicide and asylum legislation? Source-critically the ambit of P provides the backdrop for the repetition of homicide and asylum law. More specifically, Num 25–36 (or 26–36) belong to a late

---

4. The tradition-historical backdrop has been seen in ancient Near Eastern texts, in particular solar deities as gods of justice, more specifically in the Egyptian background of solar deities associated with the "weighing of the heart" cf. K. van der Toorn, "Ordeal Procedures in the Psalms and the Passover Meal," *VT* 38 (1988): 427–45. Another root of the tradition history within the Hebrew Bible has pointed to a "gate ritual" at the temple (Ps 11:4-5, 7, 15, 24) with a prayer formula recited before the temple gate; cf. the discussion outlined in Botica, *Intention*, 110. On the parallels between temple introduction liturgies in Psalms and the Egyptian Book of the Dead, including related short forms of lists of a protestation of guiltlessness found in the portico of the Horus temple in Edfu, see, for instance, N. H. Sarna, *On the Book of Psalms. Exploring the Prayers of Ancient Israel* (New York: Schocken, 1993), 100–102.

priestly supplementary layer of an earlier priestly Pentateuch edition.[5] Inserted after a preceding intermediary Hexateuch redaction of Genesis–Joshua,[6] this Pentateuchal layer was added after the decision to close the foundational history with the conclusion of Moses' death in Deut 34.[7] Later than the Hexateuchal

    5. See R. Achenbach, "Numbers," in *The Oxford Encyclopedia of the Books of the Bible*, vol. 2, ed. M. D. Coogan (Oxford: Oxford University Press, 2011), 110–22, esp. 114–16. The majority of scholars assume a basic priestly layer – Num 10:11-12; 20:1-13*; 27:13-23(?); Deut 32:48-52*; 34:7-9* – was augmented as expansions to P, spanning from Num 25:6–36:13 (with the exception of Num 32*, the settlement in Jordan) as part of a core of Numbers. Additions took place either at a point in time of an independent scroll of P or as postexilic additions to the Hexateuch. I. Knohl, *The Sanctuary of Silence: The Priestly Torah and the Holiness School* (Minneapolis: Fortress Press, 1995), 99, J. Milgrom, *Leviticus 17–22: A New translation with Introduction and Commentary* (New York: Doubleday, 2000), 1344 (for 35:1–36:13), and Stackert, *Rewriting*, 68 (for Num 35:9-34), assign them to the Holiness School. See, however, the methodological caveat raised by C. Nihan, *Priestly Torah to Pentateuch* (Tübingen: Mohr Siebeck, 2007), 572. On methods of redaction technique, see E. Otto, *Das Deuteronomium im Pentateuch und Hexateuch* (Tübingen: Mohr Siebeck, 2000), with the suggestion to compare the redactional reworkings in Numbers to redactions in Deut 1–3. If the first stage of the postexilic composition of the book of Numbers was a Hexateuch-redactor's work, the separation of a Torah in the shape of a Pentateuch represents a later stage of the development. Alternative to the ascription to H is the proposal that subsequent to the addition of the Holiness Code in Leviticus, Numbers adds late priestly compositions with theocratic overtones with the High Priest representing the community's true leadership (Num 1–2), doing so by freely adopting and adapting language of H; for which see R. Achenbach, *Die Vollendung der Tora. Studien zur Redaktionsgeschichte des Numeribuches im Kontext von Hexateuch und Pentateuch* (Wiesbaden: Harrassowitz, 2003). R. Albertz, "A Pentateuchal Redaction in the Book of Numbers? The Late Priestly Layers of Numbers 25–36," *ZAW* 125 (2013): 220–33, esp. 226, suggested a Pentateuch redaction responsible for replacing Joshua through Num 25–36 in an effort to promote a Pentateuch rather than a Hexateuch. The relationship to H in detail is disputed, and as a working hypothesis Num 25–36 can be dealt with as a product of rewritings of the Second Temple period from the time of Ezra, continuing into the mid-fourth century BCE, pace Achenbach, *Vollendung*, 130–40.

    6. Seen as a redactional combination of the Pentateuch and of the Deuteronomistic History, Noth pointed to the retrospective nature of Num 35 as already anticipating the establishment of asylum cities which became necessary after Josh 20 had become a part of the Hexateuch. He then suggested Josh 20 preserved older material, e.g. in 20:9 ערי המועדה for the asylum cities, a technical term he renders "cities of meeting/of appointment," which he suggests to be older than ערי מקלט (Num 35:11, 12, 13, 15); M. Noth, *Das Buch Josua* (Tübingen: Mohr Siebeck, 1953), 122–23.

    7. The exclusion of Joshua made it necessary to introduce his role in Numbers with three functions relevant to the framework of the Pentateuch, in part correcting the book of Joshua: Num 27:12-23, his installment; 32:28-32, his co-leadership in a military cooperation with Transjordanian tribes; 34:16-19, in the commission for land allotment;

redaction, this priestly layer with theocratic overtones[8] thus counts among the latest texts in the Pentateuch.[9] This redaction-critical backdrop bears relevance for the interpretation of private enmity. In anticipation of the result, I point to the lens through which this layer in the larger realm of P in Num 35:9-34 perceives the legal status of private enmity between two opponents. This result does not establish any potential practice of homicide and asylum law, but it points to the understanding of procedural law as forms for securing the traditional governance of institutions of a kinship-based society. Rather, the law contributes to a discourse on the level of governance in a "theocratic" conception in Second Temple Judah, a discourse on the purity of the land and its protection from pollution, and, finally, a discourse on the polity's claim for its own jurisdiction.

First, the law in Num 35 addresses the level of governance from a priestly point of view. More specifically, the theocratic overtones of Num 35 shape the backdrop against which the intent to secure the jurisdiction over the regulation of

R. Albertz, "A Pentateuchal Redaction in the Book of Numbers? The Late Priestly Layers of Num 25–36," *ZAW* 125 (2013): 220–33, here 224–25.

8. Achenbach, *Vollendung*, 629, suggests three extensive "theocratic editions" in Numbers, referring not to a direct rule of Yahweh, but to an indirect theocratic form of the deity's rule through a designated deputy. R. Achenbach, "Numeri und Deuteronomium," in *Das Deuteronomium zwischen Pentateuch und Deuteronomistischem Geschichtswerk* ed. E. Otto and A. Achenbach (Göttingen: Vandenhoeck & Ruprecht, 2004), 123–34, here 134, understands Num 35 as the third set of additions to Numbers after the Hexateuch redaction and the Pentateuch redaction. This multilayered "theocratic reworking" suggests that instead of the central sanctuary being in charge of asylum tasks, the assembly must subordinate to operate under the High Priest. For the piece's inner structure, Rofé outlines four sections – vv. 9-15, 16-24, 25-29, 30-34, with vv. 9-15 as the earliest, priestly stratum, which reserves רצח for accidental manslayer (while Num 35:12, 24-25 do not subordinate the assembly to the High Priest), while later sections use it in a broader sense, including the execution of the slayer in v. 27, and have the cities offering refuge for the time until the trial, unlike in vv. 25-32, where the cities are a place for the manslayer to live. Rofé, "Cities," 140, 143–44. This older layer served as literary basis for Josh 20:1-9. For a post-priestly redaction in Numbers, see, for instance, Ulrich Fistill, *Israel und das Ostjordanland. Untersuchungen zur Komposition von Num 21,21–35,13 im Hinblick auf die Entstehung des Buches Numeri* (Frankfurt: Peter Lang, 2007), 147–56. Exceptions from the priestly influence are discussed for Num 25:1-5 and verses from Num 32; see the overview in Albertz, "Pentateuchal Redaction," 221.

9. Drafted as or with the use of priestly tradition, these chapters function in their specific Pentateuch context as supplementary layer. On the intermediary Hexateuchal redaction prior to the conclusion of the Pentateuch, see Erhard Blum, *Studien zur Komposition des Pentateuch* (Berlin: de Gruyter, 1990), 363–65; idem, "Der kompositionelle Knoten am Übergang von Josua zu Richter: Ein Entflechtungsvorschlag," in *Textgestalt und Komposition: Exegetische Beiträge zu Tora und Vordere Propheten*, ed. E. Blum (Tübingen: Mohr Siebeck, 2010), 249–80, esp. 262–74 and for the discussion see Albertz, "Pentateuchal Redaction," 220–21.

long-term enmity can be explained. The attempt to legitimize kinship authority (in the form of the assembly) thus informs this layer. Establishing jurisdiction over long-term disputes between members of two kin, especially when a society was subject to centrally imposed rules, entails a discourse on governance in an association of individuals in a polity. In particular, homicide and ensuing feud, typical for a kinship-based society, are the forms of long-term enmity chiefly in focus. Comparable legal themes under the jurisdiction of the representatives of the kin are found in inheritance law in Num 27 and 36, which is equally claimed as a pivotal legal theme in a kinship-based society.[10]

A second aspect, the concern for purity of the land, is also a consequence of the (theocratic) claim to rulership of this priestly layer. The statements about conquest and land distribution in Num 35–36 complete the composition with additional regulations. The focus on land distribution, pivotal in Num 35:9-34, is to protect the land from bloodshed, a metaphor for avoiding feud. The closing v. 34 substantiates the necessity for the protection of the land's purity with Yahweh's presence in the land.[11] Bloodshed and expiation are crucial; avoiding long-term feud and its regulation through priestly authority is naturally at the heart of the layer.

Third, deuteronomic language and concepts have been found influential in this Pentateuchal editor's layer more than in any prior priestly editor in the Pentateuch. In particular, the addition in Numbers reflects on the formation of Israel's identity against the backdrop of foreign influence, for instance, in the call for distinction from foreign influences and the condemnation of mixed marriages – an overlap with H.[12] For asylum legislation, the concern about the pollution of the land through bloodshed is pivotal; here, this priestly layer reflects on the institution of asylum as an institution in Israel, which is absent in Near Eastern contexts yet is known in Greek culture.[13] In detail, and read against the backdrop of Deut 19:1-12*, Num 35:9-25, 26-29, 30-34 frame homicide legislation with a different intention.[14] When they embed the installation of asylum cities in a Yahweh-speech, this rhetorical device serves to legitimize rulership and to claim the "congregation's" jurisdiction. The contours of the context of this legitimization effort are evident. First, there is the envisioned social setting of the Israelites of Num 35. The narrative introduction insinuates Israel's dwelling in the

---

10. See Albertz, "Pentateuchal Redaction," 225–26.

11. Cf. the "land of Canaan" and the framing with this phrase in Num 33:51; 34:29. See Albertz, "Pentateuchal Redaction," 226. Knohl, *Sanctuary*, 99, refers to conceptual parallels in H Lev 18:25-29 and for Yahweh's dwelling in the land to parallels in H in Exod 25:7; 29:45-46; Lev 15:31; 26:11; Num 5:3; 16:3.

12. Albertz, "Pentateuchal Redaction," 232. Priestly interests are clear where he subordinates Joshua to the authority of the High Priest and mentions him in the commission of priests and laymen to ensure fair land distribution; see further below on source critical assignments.

13. On its cultural-historical origin, see below.

14. The context of the settlement also differs from Deut 19, see below.

land of foreign nations (גוים) as a situation requiring rules for separation from the foreign nations, envisioning the community as an assembly of citizens. Second, historiographically, Num 35:9 embeds the installation of asylum cities in the storyline of settlement when Israel had crossed over Jordan – "When you cross the Jordan into the land of Canaan" – assuming a presence of non-Israelites with v. 15 suggesting a (subsequent) explicit integration of the "sojourner" settling among Israel. In stark contrast, the introduction in Deut 12:29 and 19:1 – "When Yahweh your God cuts off the nations…"[15] – suggests the ideal typical framework of a segregated yet fully autonomous community, neither threatened by culturally or ethnically foreign practices nor developing their identity predominantly in an alterity discourse from surrounding nations. Third, in the form of a Yahweh-speech addressed to Moses (Num 35:9-34), vv. 9-15 frame the directive of installing asylum cities in this historiographic context in analogy to Deut 19:1-13. Fourth, Num 35 generates a technical term for asylum cities as dwelling places, assigning legal authority to the community (עדה). To this layer, long-term conflict settlement resulting in feuding is a critical theme for which it becomes necessary to claim judicial authority over a matter typically decided by kinship authorities. Such jurisdiction would include all the community of the Israelites at a point in time in which Israel would include "sojourners."

The foregoing analysis has pointed to three levels to which the law in Num 35:9-34 contributes: the theme of governance in a theocratic concept, purity of the land and Judah's claim for its own jurisdiction. These aspects of Num 35 have helped to clarify the historical and conceptual framework of this law. In order to more fully analyze the concept of private enmity in Num 35 in detail, its tradition-historical background within the history of law requires further analysis. Numbers 35:9-34 is based on older homicide legislation[16] and source-critical analysis perceives Num 35:9-34 not as a literary unit[17] but rather as multilayered

---

15. Deuteronomy 19:1 is parallel to Deut 12:29 and separates as entry formula the two parts of Deuteronomy, as has long been recognized; cf., for instance, Otto, *Deuteronomium 12,1–23,15*, 1514.

16. This is generally accepted, though not by Barmash, *Homicide*, 121 n. 5. See also below.

17. For instance, L. Schmidt, "Leviten- und Asylstädte in Num XXXV und Jos. XX, XXI 1-42," *Vetus Testamentum* 52 (2002): 103–21, here 104–105; Knohl, *Sanctuary*, 99, attributes the whole of Num 35 to H identifying criteria that distinguish Num 35 as characteristically H; for instance, the inclusion of the foreigner (גר) in v. 15; the divine speech in first person in 35:34; the address of the High Priest in 35:25, and the phrase of "the High Priest who has been anointed with the holy oil" in v. 35 that seems to cite Lev 21:10; "the statute of justice for our generations in all your inhabitants" in Num 35:29 and a similar phrase in Exod 25:8 and Num 16:3 (but see Stackert, *Rewriting*, 63 n. 92); the blood pollution in the land in 35:34; the deity's "dwelling in their midst" (שכן) in 35:34, which has parallels in other H phrases like Exod 25:8; 29:45-46; Lev 15:31; 26:11; Num 5:3 and 16:3, while not describing the dwelling in the tent of meeting as in P and the alternative assignment to Achenbach's theocratic reworking.

composite.[18] Namely, textual analysis separates the command of the installation of the cities of refuge in vv. 9-15 as an early core unit from the subsequent homicide legislation proper in vv. 15-29 and its extensions in vv. 30-34. One way of synthesizing this is to detach the earliest stage of a hypothetical older version of Num 35:9, 10, 11aαb, 12b from its later stage:

18. A. Rofé, "The History of the Cities of Refuge in Biblical Law," in Japhet, ed., *Studies in Bible*, 205–39, here 234, presents a thematic rather than primarily source-critical outline in vv. 9-15, 15-24, 25-29, 30-34, reconstructing the passage's emergence in a trajectory of three major stages of asylum law from stage 1, Deut 19:1-7, asylum in cities of refuge in safety from the avenger for manslaughter, to stage 2, which is represented by the priestly law in a version of LXXB in Josh 20:1-2, 3, 6* ("until he can stand trial before the assembly"), 7–8 with the intention of ensuring the slayer stands trial before being killed by the avenger. The slayer remains in the city only until the trial. This stage equals Num 35:9-15. Stage 3 is represented by a series of additions in Num 35:16-24 that are necessary to clarify the criteria that were subsequently brought to the trial. Again later, Num 35:25-29 order the confinement of the manslayer in the city of refuge and vv. 30-34 establish the further rules for judgment, such as witnesses, and the legal principles for intentional homicide. This suggestion operates on the basis of a combination of the cities of refuge with homicide legislation as a subsequent addition. Barmash, *Homicide*, 81–82, suggests Num 35:9-14, 24-29 to be the oldest priestly asylum law, with vv. 16-19, 20-21, 22-23, and 30-33 as additions; vv. 15 and 34 are additions from the H editor; following Knohl, *Sanctuary*, 99.

Stackert, *Rewriting*, 68, suggests a composite of three layers in 35:9-34 to H: vv. 9-15 (= source of Josh 20 LXX[B]); a second redactional layer vv. 16-29; and vv. 30-34 as miscellaneous redactional additions. Barmash, *Homicide*, 121 n. 15, assumes vv. 9-14 and 24-29 as the core unit with the additions in vv. 16-19 giving the definition of homicide, and vv. 30-33 potentially belonging to the same layer; vv. 20-21 gives a second definition of capital homicide and a corresponding definition of noncapital homicide appears in vv. 22-23; vv. 34 and 15 are the work of H/an editor.

F. Cocco, *The Torah as a Place of Refuge: Biblical Criminal Law and the Book of Numbers* (Tübingen: Mohr Siebeck, 2016), 52, offers a largely synchronic reading with the following outline: vv. 9-10aa divine discourse containing the law; vv. 10b-15, an injunction to designate cities of refuge; vv. 16-29, a distinction of cases of homicide; vv. 30-33, procedural clarifications and theological-religious conclusion. Source-critically, Cocco, *Torah as Refuge*, 87–89, suggests 35:9-11* without רצח, with vv. 13-15 as basic layer; vv. 12, 16-29 a secondary interpretive layer. The basic layer adapts Deut 19:1-13 by way of extending the range of cases in vv. 11 and 15 to include the legal concept of inadvertent, yet conscious homicide (בשגגה) (p. 65). The critical change of the basic layer is a "reformulation" of v. 11 with two critical aspects: the insertion of רצח as a term for homicide in the community and the judicial authority of the עדה as collective to decide the case. With reference to Childs, Cocco furthermore suggests a shift in the meaning of רצח from a general sense of killing within the community to a later meaning of killing in enmity, i.e., the killer's motivation, such as deceit and hatred are decisive aspects that vv. 20-24 highlight.

Table 4.1

v. 9	Yahweh spoke to Moses as follows:
v. 10	Speak to the Israelites and say: "Once you have crossed the Jordan into the land of Canaan
v. 11aαb	You will find towns, ... where the killer flees, who in inadvertence killed,
v. 12b	so that the killer will not be put to death before standing trial before the community."

This stage was augmented by vv. 11aβ, 12a, 13-15.[19] The entire passage, vv. 9-15, is originally set as a reference to the settlement east of the Jordan (v. 10b) and consequently to the cities established there. Yet v. 14 switches back to a perspective from west of the Jordan when it refers to the three cities "on the other side of the Jordan," that is, east of the Jordan. Verse 13 and 15 are linked to v. 14 and should not be separated from this verse.[20] The reflection on the six cities is thus an extension of the older layer of vv. 9, 10, 11aαb, 12b. Verse 12a interrupts the connection between vv. 11b and 12b. It is therefore best explained as the result of a reworking,[21] together with vv. 13-15. This introductory passage, vv. 9-15, describes in general terms the conditions that ensured a killer's survival after homicide.

Of relevance for the construct of long-term private enmity are the subsequent outlines of the casuistic distinctions Num 35:15b, 16-21 which unfold the procedural concern of v. 12, namely of revenge without exclusion of the killer's inadvertence. The legal thought of this law and its organization in a two-partite case-sub-case arrangement is in line with the same two-partite structure of earlier homicide law. An introductory sentence functions as the superscript for

---

19. Following the reconstruction of Gertz, *Gerichtsorganisation*, 141–42; a third layer in vv. 16-24 offers a sequence of eight subcases introduced with אם or או and a fourth addition in vv. 25-29 in which in vv. 25-28 the killer is not guilty of intentional homicide but has been cleared from this accusation; a further, fifth addition is found in vv. 30-34.

20. A reason to separate v. 15 from vv. 9-14 is that it is kept in third person singular and therefore syntactically in tension with vv. 9-14; Barmash, *Homicide*, 121 n. 15, separates it from vv. 9-14. There are three reasons for keeping v. 15 source-critically with vv. 9-14: it repeats the syntactic combination of "cities are" (ערי תהיינה) in Num 35:11aβ, 13b; the change from second person singular must be seen in the larger narrative context in which this verse is an aside to Moses alone, not on the same level as the deity's speech to Moses that he is to deliver to the community of the Israelites; finally, it has analogues in an equally redundant comment on the cities of refuge in Lev 17:12; cf. Stackert, *Rewriting*, 66–67.

21. Verse 15b repeats v. 11b and could thus be seen as addition.

the case of a slayer who, after having unwittingly killed, now finds himself in flight. In a first case, vv. 16-21, the ascertainment of facts lists three types of tools used. The law introduces the clauses with both the conjunction וְאִם and אוֹ. Verses 20-21 list the killer's specific motivation with three nouns: hatred, intentionality, enmity. Verses 22-23 describe a second subcase of admittance to asylum. In cases of spontaneous, erroneous action, thus without the killer's intent to engage in a long-term enmity. The specifications are redundant: without any evil intent (v. 22); without being an enemy, without seeking his evil (v. 23). Verses 24-25a conclude with an extended apodosis II.

Table 4.2. *Numbers 35:15-25a**

לִבְנֵי יִשְׂרָאֵל וְלַגֵּר וְלַתּוֹשָׁב בְּתוֹכָם	SUPERSCRIPTION V. 15 To the Israelites, to the sojourner and who settle among them,
תִּהְיֶינָה שֵׁשׁ־הֶעָרִים הָאֵלֶּה לְמִקְלָט	these six towns shall be as a refuge,
לָנוּס שָׁמָּה כָּל־מַכֵּה־נֶפֶשׁ בִּשְׁגָגָה:	In order to flee there, everyone having slain a soul *in inadvertence*
	SUBCASE I: Protasis I: intentional, according to tool/material vv. 16-18:
וְאִם־בִּכְלִי בַרְזֶל הִכָּהוּ וַיָּמֹת	- if with an *iron utensil* he *slew* him dead
וְאִם בְּאֶבֶן יָד	- if with a *stone in his hand* (he slew him)
אֲשֶׁר־יָמוּת בָּהּ	so that he died from it
אוֹ בִּכְלִי עֵץ־יָד	- or if with a *wooden utensil* in his hand (he slew) him
אֲשֶׁר־יָמוּת בּוֹ	so that he died from it
	motivation, mode of action vv. 20-21a:
וְאִם־בְּשִׂנְאָה יֶהְדֳּפֶנּוּ	- if *in hatred* he *pushed* him
אוֹ־הִשְׁלִיךְ עָלָיו בִּצְדִיָּה וַיָּמֹת:	- or if he *throws something* at him with *pursuit* so that he dies
אוֹ בְאֵיבָה הִכָּהוּ בְיָדוֹ וַיָּמֹת	- or *in enmity* he *slays* him *with his fist,* so that he dies.
רֹצֵחַ הוּא	Apodosis I: exclusion from asylum v. 21b He is a killer (in the community).
גֹּאֵל הַדָּם יָמִית אֶת־הָרֹצֵחַ בְּפִגְעוֹ־בוֹ:	The avenger of blood will put the killer to death as he meets him.

	SUBCASE II: Protasis II: Right of asylum vv. 22-23
	spontaneous, erroneous, without intention/ long term enmity vv. 22-23
וְאִם־בְּפֶתַע בְּלֹא־אֵיבָה הֲדָפוֹ	- and if he *suddenly pushes* him, *without enmity*
אוֹ־הִשְׁלִיךְ עָלָיו כָּל־כְּלִי בְּלֹא צְדִיָּה׃	- or he *throws* any utensil at him, *without pursuit*
אוֹ בְכָל־אֶבֶן אֲשֶׁר־יָמוּת בָּהּ	- or by *any (sort of) stone* so that he dies through it
בְּלֹא רְאוֹת וַיַּפֵּל עָלָיו וַיָּמֹת	- *without seeing* it, he *lets it fall* on him so that he dies
וְהוּא לֹא־אוֹיֵב לוֹ	- but *without* him *being his enemy*
וְלֹא מְבַקֵּשׁ רָעָתוֹ׃	- and *without being* (someone) *seeking his evil*.
	Apodosis II: granting of asylum vv. 24-25a
וְשָׁפְטוּ הָעֵדָה בֵּין הַמַּכֶּה וּבֵין גֹּאֵל הַדָּם עַל הַמִּשְׁפָּטִים הָאֵלֶּה׃	- then the congregation will decide in accordance with these rules between the one who struck and the avenger of blood,
וְהִצִּילוּ הָעֵדָה אֶת־הָרֹצֵחַ מִיַּד גֹּאֵל הַדָּם וְהֵשִׁיבוּ אֹתוֹ הָעֵדָה אֶל־עִיר מִקְלָטוֹ	- and the congregation will save the killer from the hand of the avenger of blood and the congregation will send him back to his asylum city.

2. *Outline and Legal Thought*

Numbers 35 lists relatively wide-ranging cases and emphasizes legal procedure and thus illustrates the development of biblical law and, in particular, the emergence of the construct of long-term private enmity between two opponents. Numbers 35 presents a four-partite homicide and asylum legislation: an asylum city regulation in vv. 9-15 (1); a case/counter-case homicide law that fundamentally distinguishes between two types of homicide, spontaneous and intentional killing in vv. 16-24 (2). Continuing with a set of procedural laws in vv. 25-29 (3) that introduce a notion of the asylum city as a place of confinement or exile of the unintentional slayer, it closes with loosely attached set of laws in vv. 30-34 (4). Already this outline, with its focus on the killer's dwelling in the asylum city, demonstrates how legal reasoning presupposes long-term enmity and how this concept of long-term enmity between the two opponents is relevant when homicide occurs.

The case/counter-case arrangement in vv. 15-25a* reverses the order of Deut 19 and begins with intentional homicide and the denial of asylum in vv. 16-18, 20-22, moving then on to accidental homicide and subsequently to granting asylum. A superscript opens the law and connects it with the establishment of the six cities in v. 14. The law is two-partite, with v. 15a as a general introduction of a distinction between three categories of killers eligible for asylum: the Israelites, the sojourner, and aliens who settle among them.[22] Verse 15b serves as a superscript for the general case of "homicide" that is perceived in three categories, either as "inadvertent (but conscious)," "foolish," or "unfortunate" (בשגגה). Already, previously, v. 11b mentions this particular category which informs both subcases of homicide.

Subcase I in this case/counter-case arrangement presents an elaborate protasis with two separate subcategories. Verses 16-18 lists, first, three sets of tools for homicide, an "iron utensil," a "stone" and a "wooden utensil." The reflection in particular on the tool used as the instrument to kill an enemy has an equivalent in the case law of Deut 19:5, which describes the iron axe falling out of its wooden shaft. While the reference to the material of the instrument of slaying vv. 16-18 (cf. vv. 22-33) is comparable to the concise case law in Deut 19:5, Num 35:16-18 also differs from it through its expansion from one quintessential case into a list of three potential tools of homicide arranged in a row of sentences, each ending with the root "die."

The second set of distinctions in the protasis (vv. 20-21a) enhances the elaborate list of Num 35. It adds the motivation in the first subcase, "in hatred," "with intentionality," and "in enmity," and further by way of distinguishing three modes of action: to push, to throw, to slay. The last two of these clauses note the fatal consequence (מות). The brief apodosis in v. 21aβb in a noun sentence first establishes the state of affairs of the slayer's homicide in the community (רצח) and, as a consequence, it declines the slayer's protection from the avenger of blood.

Subcase II spans from a protasis (vv. 22-23) to an apodosis (vv. 24-25a) of comparable length, unlike subcase I. The protasis of subcase II lists five cases, and while subcase I itemizes materials separate from the slayer's motivation, it combines modes of action and motivations of conscious yet inadvertent and thus non-intentional homicide with each of these cases. Rather than rendering eligible cases, the protasis of subcase II lists motivations for homicide that exclude the killer from the protection of asylum. The two initial terms of this passage for the motivation are "enmity" and "intentionality," which in a chiastic arrangement take up two terms from subcase I (vv. 20b-21), "intentionality" and "enmity." The first term from the first subcase in v. 20a, "hatred," lacks an equivalent in subcase II. The protasis of subcase II mentions, third, visual perception, and, fourth, the status of "enmity" or continuous malicious intent ("seeking his evil"). Verses 24-25a add an apodosis with two *waw*-perfect clauses. The law grants the authority to judge over the case to the "congregation," which saves the

---

22. Gertz, *Gerichtsorganisation*, 146, based on an understanding of Num 35 and Deut 19:1-13 with different intentions, both as asylum legislation. Deuteronomy 19:1, especially when the introductory remarks are seen in correspondence with 29:12-31, polemicizes against the nations (גוים) in the land before Israel lived there. The tone of the extended version of Num 35 is less polemical against foreign nations and extends asylum to include the "sojourner" (גר, v. 15) and "settler" (תושב, v. 15).

inadvertent slayer. The congregation is granted the authority to judge between the "slayer" and the "avenger." As the law assumes unintentional homicide, in this case the slayer is to be saved (נצל *hi.*) from the avenger's persecution. The outcome in this second case suggests the killer will be saved and sent back to his asylum city.

What does the inclusion of wide-ranging cases and the law's emphasis on legal procedure mean for the development of biblical law, namely for the emergence of the construct of long-term private enmity between two opponents? A striking feature of relevance to long-term enmity in a kinship-based society is the assignment of jurisdiction over the long-term enmity relationship to the congregation's judicial authority and thus into the public square where the homicide happened. Unlike Deuteronomy, the passage devotes attention to the implementation of homicide law, assigning a major role to the congregation (עדה, 35:12, 24, 25) at large. This institution has the authority to decide the slayer's entitlement to asylum. This authority may be compared to other cases in the priestly tradition in which the assembly has executive function in judicial matters.[23] The continuing emphasis of this institution also holds true in the subsequent extensions in vv. 26-34* and demonstrates the relevance of this law in the public square in which the community would be affected by a long-term enmity.

The modifications of Num 35 mentioned so far hint at a specific socio-historical context for the law and at the development of the social construct of long-term enmity. Consider, for instance, the differences compared with Deut 19:5 as it refers to one tool, where Num 35 employs rather more abstract terminology. Furthermore, it is unclear whether subcase I and subcase II distinguish between two separate forms of homicide along two different sets of criteria. The apodosis, vv. 16-18 first lists tools as criterion to distinguish between various forms of homicide. Then, vv. 20-21, 22-23 put the motivation and specifically the relationship between slayer and victim to the foreground, combining tools and motivation. The law juxtaposes these two sets of criteria to each other, refining the assessment of facts in the case of long-term enmity.[24] This poses the question why it deliberately uses two different criteria to evaluate homicide in one law. The following considerations will clarify the origins of the criteria for the evaluation of homicide.

3. *Numbers 35 and Deuteronomy 19:1-12: Parallels, Modifications, Clarifications*

Numbers 35:9-34 is drafted with Deut 19:1-12 as its main source. Its modifications are evident: Num 35:14 adds three Transjordanian cities and generates a technical term for these cities. Numbers 35:11 urbanizes asylum with the slayer fleeing and taking actual residence there (v. 25), and extends the case descriptions through subcategories in vv. 15-21. It further extends the case descriptions

---

23. See below on the role of כל העדה in Lev 24:10-23 and Num 15:32-36.
24. This seems to be the interpretation of Barmash, *Homicide*, 121, 123.

through subcategories in vv. 15-21, and through more and different legal procedural aspects, such as the jurisdiction of a not city-specific (central) institution of the assembly עדה as jury (vv. 12, 24, 25) and the subcase of the killer's encounter of the avenger of blood outside the city (vv. 26-27). It furthermore coins abstract terminology for the social construct of enmity, שנאה in Num 35:20, 21, and איבה in Num 35:21, 22, and even further בצדיה ("with evil intent") in Num 35:20, 22.[25] Therefore, as indicated, Num 35 relates the institution of the assembly and the procedures for determining the status of enmity as it includes intent. A continuing element between Deut 19:1-12 and Num 35, as laid out above, is the core of Num 35:9-12 in vv. 9, 10, 11aαb, 12b that corresponds with Deut 19:1-12, i.e., the arrangement of the case in the pattern "heading - subcase 1 - subcase 2".[26] Another procedural aspect of Deut 19:15 that Num 35:30, 32 modify is the law of the witnesses.

4. Legal Categories

The parallels and modifications of Num 35 in relation to Deut 19 have been pointed out, yet the key legal categories for the classification of homicide that best describe the development of legal thought in Num 35 still need to be pointed out. Therefore, in what follows, a selective reading evaluates some of the most relevant criteria for homicide and it then traces the background of legal thought of Num 35, beginning with this law's newly generated category of "unawareness" (בשגגה), the choice of tools, the modes of action, and the newly minted nouns "hatred," "enmity," "malevolence" or "evil intent."

It is apparent that Num 35 construe homicide and asylum legislation in the realm of specific late Persian or Hellenistic literary-historical and the historical circumstances of Judah. In order to deconstruct homicide legislation and to determine the contexts of long-term private enmity, the integration of Num 35 into these contexts requires attention. Thus, part 5 reflects on legal procedure and on the social background of Num 35:15 that self-describes a mixture of Israelites,

---

25. See for a listing of the differences, for instance, Stackert, *Rewriting*, 69–70.

26. Other outlines reconstruct a linear, three-part sequel of cases, for instance, Whitekettle, *Life's Labor*, 334: intentional, killable inadvertent, releasable inadvertent killer. Jackson, *Wisdom-Laws*, 128, suggests a deliberate chiastic concentric arrangement as a result of the case/counter-case arrangement: A1, if he kills him with a stone in his hand, the stone being normally sufficient to cause death – he is not protected (v. 17); B1, if he killed him in an ambush by throwing something at him (v. 20); C1, if he killed him with his fists out of enmity he is not protected (v. 21); C2, if he stabbed him not from enmity but suddenly (v. 22); B2, if he threw something at him not in an ambush, he is to be protected (v. 22); A2, if he killed him with a stone, even with which one may normally cause death, but without seeing him, and without previous enmity or having sought him out, he is to be protected (v. 23).

sojourners, and settlers. In addition, the law adds other aspects of legal procedure in vv. 25-29.

4.1. בשגגה – *"Inadvertently" or "Tragically"?*

Based on preceding homicide law, in Num 35 the slayer's intent and his long-term hateful relationship have emerged as conditions that are sufficient to deny asylum to a slayer. The subcases in Num 35 ponder clearly the alternatives between hateful, intentional murder on the one hand, and spontaneous, accidental homicide on the other, thus following the tradition of Exod 21:12-14 and Deut 19:1-12. A critical development of homicide law in Num 35, is however, the extension of the subcase descriptions (Num 35:15-23*) beyond their precursors in Deut 19. The expansions relate to the theme of intentionality as a pivotal criterion of homicide law. These elaborations primarily focus on premeditated versus accidental, unintentional homicide.[27] Numbers 35 deepens this reflection on premeditation versus unintentionality through a reference to various states of affairs for intentional homicide. The selection of the tool used (iron, stone, wood) categorizes and clarifies the state of affairs when distinguishing intentional from unintentional killing; it thus helps the jury to determine the slayer's state of mind. Num 35 suggests that the slayer's tools allow for determining whether he maintained a long-term hateful relationship with his victim and planned his attack or followed a spontaneous impulse.[28]

Yet, Num 35:15b in the superscript references neither distinction already known from Deut 19. It adds a different, idiosyncratic category, בשגגה, that does not square with the logic of subcase I and II in the remainder of this law. Rather, this category introduces a third option besides the alternatives for the slayer's fault-based liability. The category seems to be closely related to the unintentional homicide of subcase II insofar as it denotes unwittingly committed, not intentional homicide. Verse 11b also features the rare abstract idiomatic בשגגה. Lexicography sees its meaning in the superscript verses, vv. 11b, 15, oscillating between acting "foolishly" and "subconsciously, or in inadvertence."[29] The problem remains that this category is not fully identical with accidental homicide. Rather, the term relates to a problematic outcome of an act, the consequences of which the slayer was unaware. Much more than the status of conscience, it refers to the dreadful consequences of such action for the agent. A number of late priestly laws carry this notion. Numbers 15:22-30 in v. 22 (שגה)[30] and

---

27. See, for instance, B. A. Levine, *Numbers 21–36* (New York/London: Doubleday, 2000), 565.

28. Barmash, *Homicide*, 122.

29. Cf. also Cocco, *Torah as Refuge*, 67. Alternatively, T. Seidl, שגג/שגה, *TDOT* 14, 397–405, 402, assumes in P the roots acquire a broad semantic range that include sinful acts in general together with unintentional errors in cultic law.

30. The dictionaries distinguish the roots שגג and שגה; cf. D. J. A. Clines (ed.), *The Dictionary of Classical Hebrew*, vol. 8 (Sheffield: Sheffield Phoenix Press, 2011), 262–63,

v. 27 (בשגגה) reference the possibility of salvaging such actions through specific offerings for cases of inadvertent transgression.[31] Leviticus 4:2, 13, 22, 27 list four different subjects: the individual (4:2), the congregation (4:13), and the ruler (4:22-23); as well as any individual (4:27-28, נפש מעם הארץ). In none of these instances does this idiosyncratic term specify the violated command nor the exact violating act. Rather, the term designates a different category in light of the consequences of a false action.[32] This category is of relevance in the context of the discourse on intentionality in P. Leviticus 5:15 and 22:14 use this term for accidentally acquired guilt or transgression (חטא).[33] Against the background of the discourse on intentionality and guilt in homicide legislation, P and connected sources reflect on the effect of such actions in the cultic sphere.[34] Practically, the priestly realm mirrors guilt incurred through intentionality by matching it with corresponding offering types.[35] The evaluation of the sphere of this inadvertent wrong in connection with the term אשם, either "becoming guilty," or "incurring guilt," reflects on how exactly an individual would acquire guilt.[36] בשגגה in the

and Gesenius, 18th ed., 1322–23, suggesting the closely related meanings "make an error, sin inadvertently" and "go astray, err."

31. Botica, *Intention*, 86–87, points to the lack of specificity. The opposite of an unconscious tragic act is the conscious wicked act, characterized, for instance, in Num 15:30: "with an elevated, outstretched right hand," i.e., in a boldly, intentional act. See Botica, *Intention*, p. 87, note 87.

32. More precise actions committed inadvertently, בשגגה, are found in Lev 5:15, 18 (2×), with Lev 5:2-4 mentioning specific cases not found elsewhere in 4:1–5:13. Also, the term אשם is new in this passage. The cases are, first, willful neglect of a witness to speak out (Lev 5:1); second, the contraction of impurity because of a contact with carcasses (5:2-3); third, thoughtlessly taking an oath (5:4-5). These three cases are relevant for the sin offering and are explicitly repeated in what is presumably an addition; cf. Elliger, *Leviticus* (Tübingen: Mohr Siebeck, 1966), 64. Typical is the use of ונעלם (Lev 5:2, 3, 4) as a form of conscience, a cognitive aspect that leads to know the wrongdoing; see Elliger, *Leviticus*, 64; Botica, *Intention*, 77.

33. Leviticus 5 reflects on unintentional sin in matters of purity (vv. 2-3), on oaths (v. 4), on holy items (vv. 14-16), on the problem of unintentional sin in general (vv. 17-19), and combines it with intentional sin and with references to sinful refraining from witnessing in lack of other witnesses, to which 5:20, 21-26 add further instances of guilt aggravated through committed perjury. The combination of intentional and unintentional sin raises its own questions, and it is critical that the passage refers to a context of long-term litigation.

34. On the dependence of these cultic laws from homicide law, see F. Crüsemann, *The Torah* (Minneapolis: Fortress, 1995), 319; Botica, *Intention*, 53.

35. In particular the purification or sin offering (חטאת), the guilt/blame offering (אשם), as well as in the idiomatic "commands that ought not to be done." See Lev 4:2, 13, 22, 27; cf. Botica, *Intention*, 62.

36. Cf. J. Milgrom, *Leviticus 1–16, A New Translation with introduction and commentary*, Anchor Bible 3 (New York: Doubleday, 1991), 345, suggests this to be "the self-punishment of conscience," i.e., "the torment of guilt" and psychologizes the term.

outline of Num 35 in the superscript is a separate category besides the strictly legal case/counter-case arrangement of homicide. Further use of the term supports this observation. The Greek equivalent of ἀκουσίως, "involuntarily," also used in Num 35:11, 15, is a legal technical term for accidental homicide.[37] Dating from late Persian or Hellenistic time, the collection of various sins of Psalm 19B features this derivative, which in this context is often suggested to designate "inadvertent sin."[38] In homicide law, the use of the adverbial idiom in the superscript Num 35:11, 15 thus presents a reference frame to embed the subsequently following case.

Could the incongruence between intentional and accidental homicide and בשגגה as a third distinctive category of homicide legislation be specific for Hebrew thought and relevant for the outline of this law? Inadvertently committed homicide could incur disastrous consequences for the slayer. A textbook example that casts an unwittingly committed act as tragic is Saul's "foolish" engagement in a divination through casting lots in which he ultimately risks the life of his son in 1 Sam 14:24-46. Influenced by a popular version of the Greek notion of tragedy, this narrative in the Deuteronomistic history understands בשגגה ("in foolishness") in relation to a popular version of tragic failure. The idiom's focus is on the hero of the story, casting him in an ambit of tragedy, while not emphasizing any specific type of guilt associated with this notion, but instead, mainly casting it as an individual's unconscious failure without malicious intent.[39] The term's meaning ranges in many instances from "unconsciousness, nescience, foolishness," to "foolish"

See further Botica, *Intention*, 63–65. The examples listed are intentional sins that are typical for a long-term relationship vis-à-vis a private opponent.

37. This refers to the distinction in Greek and Hellenistic law between intentional (ἑκούσιος/ἑκών) and unintentional (ἀκουσίως/ἄκων) homicide, while sources for homicide with premeditation use the phrase ἐκ προνοίας; cf. Botica, *Intention*, 170.

38. The supplicant asks to be spared from hidden sins (שְׁגִיאוֹת) in Ps 19:13a. Context-related, the meaning of the verb שגה is rendered "to go astray, to err, being conscious of one's act but not of its consequences"; cf. *The Dictionary of Classical Hebrew*, vol. 8, 263, which may include a tragic notion. For instance, Job 6:24 and 19:4 indicate erring that falls back on the subject themselves. Proverbs 5:23 speaks of others lost to "tragedy." The use in Prov 19:27 requires separate reflection.

39. The motifs of tragedy in the narrative tradition of the Deuteronomistic history are by nature blurry and so is their notion of a tragically failing hero. The root שגג is here used in a layer to describe King Saul's character as he fails without sinful intent by giving a rash oath. The term is found in the *Vorlage* of LXX of a more elaborate MT version that introduces the subsequent narrative about King Saul's tragic decision to put his own son, Jonathan, at risk through the casting lots in 1 Sam 14:24. On the notion of the term as a tragic failing of Saul, its use in 1 Sam 26:21, and further the notion in Prov 5:23, Job 6:24, and 19:4, see, among others, K.-P. Adam, "Saul as a Tragic Hero: Greek Drama and its Influence on Hebrew Scripture in 1 Samuel 14,24-46 (10,8; 13,7a-13A; 10:17-27)," in *For and Against David. Story and History in the Books of Samuel*, ed. A. G. Auld and E. Eynikel (Leuven: Peeters, 2010), 123–83.

or "inadvertent," including the effects beyond the act itself.[40] With regard to the logic of the subcases in Num 35, the notion of accidental, conscious homicide in Num 35 is indeed best explained in distinction from the two outcomes in the subcases I and II. בשגגה in the heading in 35:11, 15b is not in line with the distinction in the centerpiece of the law in legal thought between intent on one hand and involuntarily committed homicide on the other, to which other parts refer. Consider, for instance, Num 35:23: a slayer either had acted "without seeing," had not been "seeking his evil," nor committed a voluntary act against an enemy. This category of an unintentionally false and in a wider sense tragic and inadvertent act gained popularity in wisdom thought.[41] With the idiomatic "unconsciously/unwittingly בשגגה slaying" of (a life), Num 35:11b, 15b, this priestly law partakes in a discourse on the ethical theme of unconscious foolishness and unlawful behavior in both Lev 5 and in homicide law Num 35:9-34.[42]

In conclusion, the notion of the unwitting slayer who is not aware of the consequences of his action adds one category of inadvertence to the distinction

---

40. The narrative demonstrates this; cf. also Lev 5; 15; 18, שגג//לא־ידע and the expression for a voluntary act "with outstretched arm" (Num 15:30); Gertz, *Gerichtsorganisation*, 144–45. A question that cannot be pursued further here is whether this term and the perception of inadvertence in Num 35 are comparable to acting tragically, as Aristotle describes it: "Take, for example, wounding with an iron weapon of a certain size and type: You could spend your lifetime counting them. So if the term is undefined, and one must legislate, it is necessary to speak in simple terms, so that even if a man wearing a ring lifts his hand or strikes someone, according to the letter of the law he is liable and does wrong, but in truth he does no wrong; and this is equity." Aristotle, *Rhetoric*, 1374a32-b1. It is more likely that the law may have been familiar with a less specific, popular notion of tragedy as it would have been informed by the modes of transmission and dissemination of post-classical Greek drama excerpts in performances of anthologies. This would explain the vague notion of "tragic" in late Persian- and Hellenistic-period biblical tradition; see Adam, "Saul as a Tragic Hero," 168–71.

41. This category is extent in late Persian and Hellenistic traditions found in Prov 5:23 and Ps 119:21, 118. The fact that biblical texts adduce many reasons for inadvertence and that they connect it with non-conscious behavior caused, for instance, through drunkenness (Isa 28:7; Prov 5:19-20; 20:1) points to their characteristically vague notion of tragedy as personal erring. Along a similar vein, Deut 27:9 refers to the problematic consequences of "misleading" a blind person.

42. The term elsewhere carries the notion of a tragic failure, to which Lev 5:4-5 refers with an example of a rash oath, be it for a good or an evil purpose. Another example is unintentional trespassing (Lev 5:15), or, in general, unwittingly (שגג//לא־ידע) committed sin (Lev 5:18). Notably, from a redaction-critical perspective, Elliger (*Leviticus*, 64) suggests that Lev 5:1-6 is an addition to an older basic layer, Lev 4:22-35. These passages about inadvertent guilt insert four pre-formulated cases, the last three of which retrospectively seek atonement. Elliger understands the terminological overlap of Lev 4, esp. Lev 4:13a, "all the congregation עדה of Israel" (cf. עדה, Num 35:12, 24-25), to likewise be the product of accrual writing added to a basic layer 4:13-21* on the sin offering for

of subcase I and II in Num 35. Different from the strict principle of intentional versus accidental homicide of previous biblical law, this other category reflects on the slayer's erring in a vaguely tragic sense, venturing the effects of the killing on the slayer's personal destiny.

4.2. *Distinction of Tools and Modes of Action in* trauma ek pronoias
The combination of the criteria of the tools together with the dispositional character of the killer in relation to his victim were thought to be significant. To what extent is the tool used for killing relevant for the mindset of the slayer? And how does the central criterion of the accidental or spontaneous nature of homicide in Deut 19 inform the law? Numbers 35 suggests that the tool is critical in the ascertainment of facts of the slayer's intent when standing trial. Evidence that the slayer had spontaneously killed, while not having planned his attack, could be based on the tools he used. The protasis of subcase I in vv. 16-18 thus differentiates the wounding according to the material of the slayer's instrument of choice. It distinguishes between iron, stone, and wooden utensils; furthermore, the protasis (vv. 22-23) differentiates "any utensil" from stone utensils. This distinction between tools in Num 35 points to a procedural aspect in the ascertainment of facts. The slayer's choice of weapon when inflicting a wound could be indicative of his intent.

The material of the tool played a role for the distinction between intentional and unintentional homicide as a parallel of the particular triad of weapons in Num 35 demonstrates. Athenian cases of intentional wounding (*trauma ek pronoias*) distinguish along the same line, mentioning a knife,[43] a rock,[44] or a club[45] as "quasi-formulaic catalogue of (civilian) weaponry."[46] The discourse on the material of the weaponry used in an assault is of relevance in a number of

the assembly (קהל). If so, this list of inadvertent transgressions has its own background, independent from an older layer of inadvertent guilt.

Notably, the theme of the rash oath spoken unaware of its potential consequences has a narrative parallel in Judg 11:30-40 that unfolds as an Iphigeneia theme, thus reverberating a fragment from popular Greek mythology without a precursor in the biblical tradition and unrelated to the remainder of the Jephthah tradition, which echoes the major plot line of the Greek tradition; see, among others, T. Römer, "Why Would the Deuteronomist Tell About the Sacrifice of Jephthah's Daughter?" *JSOT* 77 (1998): 27–38, esp. 34, 36, and idem, "La fille de Jephté entre Jérusalem et Athènes – Réflexions à partir d'une triple intertextualité en Juges 11," in *Intertextualités. La Bible en échos*, ed. D. Marguerat and A. Curtis (Geneva: Labor et Fides, 2000), 30–42, esp. 38–39. Furthermore, the constellation puts the focus on the main character's Jephthah's failure and the burden of his tragic consequences.

43. Source references from Phillips, "*Trauma Ek Pronoias* in Athenian Law," 98: Lysias 4.6; cf. Demosthenes 40.32; Aeschines 2.93; 3.51, 212.
44. Demosthenes 54.18.
45. Potentially Isocrates 18.52; cf. Lysias 1.27.
46. Phillips, "Trauma," 98, with reference to the orators Antiphon 4β2; Demosthenes 23.76; Aeschines 3.244.

cases and it would indicate whether the attack was premeditated or spontaneous. Two defense speeches in lawsuits[47] refer to the manslayer's weapon as a sign of assault preparation. In reverse, in another defense speech, Lysias makes the case that the use of a potsherd as makeshift weapon could hardly be considered as indication of premeditated assault. The weapon and the extent of preparation that went into an assault was legally critical whenever an accused pleaded that an assault was not premeditated. Instances in which an assailant would use a weapon to inflict an injury to an opponent qualified the injury as trauma, rather than another type of injury, *aikeia*, in which the assailant used his body to inflict harm on his opponent.[48] Characteristically, lawsuits around trauma arose from head wounds,[49] yet any injury could result in the accusation of *trauma*.[50]

The above parallel in Athenian homicide law points back to intentionality in legal thought in Num 35. Besides the quality of the weapons, the distinction of premeditated from spontaneous wounding in Athenian legislation points to the slayer's intent as a prerequisite mental aspect of the offence of *trauma ek pronoias*. The statement of facts of *trauma ek pronoias* neither requires prior planning nor considers reflection (premeditation) or an explicit intent to kill an opponent. Rather, in such cases the assault was carried out with a relatively spontaneous intent of merely wounding an opponent and it is thus described as wounding with intent.[51] The criterion for the legal category of a *trauma ek pronoias* was the "actor's intent to commit the act in question at the time of its commission; neither premeditation nor intent as to result was required."[52] Legal procedure in such a case is relatively clear: a defendant was limited to only one legal action, the *graphe traumatos ek pronoias*, which was to be heard by the Council of the Areopagus.[53] The consequence of a verdict upon a slayer was their perpetual exile from the city state[54] and property confiscation.[55] The

---

47. Lysias 3.28, 41-42 and 4.6; cf., in detail, Phillips, "Trauma," 75–76.

48. The distinction is found in Demosthenes 54.18, 19.

49. Cf. Lysias 4.9; Demosthenes 40.32; Aeschines 2.93; 3.51, 212; cf. Lysias 3.18; Demosthenes 54.35.

50. Lysias 6.15.

51. In Athenian law the idiom *trauma ek pronoias* is synonymous with *hekousion trauma*, a term used in Plato's *Laws* 874e-879b.

52. Phillips, "Trauma," 99.

53. Phillips, "Trauma," 99: Lysias 3.1; 4.1. Cf. Lysias 6.14; Demosthenes 23.22, 24; 40.32; Aeschines 2.93, 3.51.

54. Lysias 3.38, 42; 4.13, 18. Cf. Lysias 6.15; Demosthenes 40.32.

55. Lysias 3.38; cf. 4.19; cf. Phillips, "Trauma," 99. In all instances of Attic oratory, all references of litigants to *trauma ek pronoias* refer to a form of "writing"; cf. γραφή, Demosthenes 54.18; Aeschines 2.93; 3.51, 212; and the verbal form γράφεσθαι, Aeschines 2.93; 3.51, 212; Demosthenes 54.18, as distinct from *dikai kakêgorias* and *aikeias*; the idiom *dikazein traumatos ek pronoias*, Demosthenes 23.22, 24, and *dikai traumatos ek pronoias*, Aristotle, *Constitution of the Athenians* 27.3, both refer back to the law on

complexity of intentionality in Athenian criminal law is beyond this study,[56] yet this Athenian parallel on the procedure of wounding shares with Num 35 the distinction between instruments that could be used for wounding, as well as the consequence of long-term dwelling in an asylum place as a consequence of wounding with intent. In these cases the result of killing an enemy was not at the essence of its application. Rather, from another perspective, Plato's *Laws*[57]

---

the jurisdiction of the Areopagus to which Demosthenes (23.22, 24) refers and they are not witnesses of a separate type of trial for wounding besides the *graphe traumatos ek pronoias*; Phillips, "Trauma," 99.

56. Criminal intent in Athenian law from the early stages to Drakon, the classical time to the Athenian orators undergoes a long development, with the classical phase using *ek pronoias* synonymously with intentional (*hekon, hekousios*); D. M. MacDowell, *The Law in Classical Athens* (London: Thames & Hudson, 1978), 115; idem, *Athenian Homicide Law in the age of the Orators* (Manchester: Manchester University Press, 1963), 46, 60–70. Similarly M. Gagarin, *Drakon and Early Athenian Homicide Law* (New Haven: Yale University Press, 1956), 140, observing three changes – "the designation of death as the penalty for intentional homicide, the transfer of cases of intentional homicide to the jurisdiction of the Areopagos, and the prohibition of pardon after conviction for intentional homicide" – that provide further nuances between intentional versus unintentional homicide. Cf. also the references to homicide in cities outside of Athens in which the distinction between intentional and unintentional homicide plays no role: Gagarin, *Drakon*, 143–44. Gagarin assumes a continuity after Drakon in Classical law with regards to intent, suggesting later changes at the time of the orators in the fourth century BCE. See also the overview in Botica, *Intention*, 170–78, here esp. 176–77. Philosophical approaches to criminal law from the perspective of the mental state of the actor to commit wrong discuss intentionality on a level different from the specific legal historical and procedural point of view; cf., on this approach, J. W. Jones, *Law and Legal Theory of the Greeks* (Oxford: Clarendon, 1956), 251–58. In detail, lexicographic distinctions (*pronoia, bouleusis*) are also of relevance; see Loomis, "The Nature of Premeditation," 86–95, and for Greco-Roman contexts, Botica, *Intention*, 201–13. For the exact relation of Num 35 and to determine influences from Greek law, further study of the history of law in the fourth and third century BCE is needed. See the distinction in Ptolemaic law between "inadvertent homicide" (*phonos agnoemata*) and "guilty deeds" (*hamartemata*), intentional, culpable disregard of criminal law, referred to by R. Taubenschlag, *The Law of Greco-Roman Egypt in the Light of the Papyri, 332 B.C.–640 A.D.*, 2nd ed. (Warsaw: Panstowe Wydawnictwo Nankowe, 1955), 421. Dating from the Ptolemaic period, Papyrus Rylands 9 refers to the intentional killing of priests (2.2.15-16), which was punished with death (2.2.18); cf. Lippert, *Einführung*, 131; Botica, *Intention*, 188–89. On Philo, see Botica, *Intention*, 213–40.

57. The concept of trauma legislation reflected in Plato's laws differs substantially from the situation as the defendants of Lysias 3 and 4 have found it. The references in Greek forensic oratory to trauma need therefore to be distinguished from the understanding in Plato's laws; Phillips, "Trauma," 101.

argue that the decisive aspect was the actor's intent, not the outcome: "Let our law concerning trauma be written as follows: If someone, having intended by an act of will to kill a friendly person (except one of those whom the law allows him to kill), wounds him but is unable to kill him, under such circumstances the one who conceived this intent and wounded does not deserve pity and should not be treated otherwise than if he had killed, but should be compelled to submit to trial for homicide..."[58] Different from the perception of the Attic orators, conceptually, *trauma ek pronoias* in Plato's view is an attempted homicide; this understanding is in line with Plato's categorization, which treats trauma as second (*Leg.* 876e6-877a1) only to homicide (*Leg.* 865-874e2) and divides the categories of *traumata* identical with those used for homicide.[59] Unintentional wounding and homicide in this law falls into one of the four categories of Plato's Laws[60] in *Leg.* 874e-979b, which distinguishes between wounding that was unintentional, in anger, in fear and, intentional (*ek pronoias*).[61]

In conclusion, without establishing any direct connection between both legal traditions, three parallels between Athenian Law on intentional wounding and Num 35 can be noted. First, the distinction of the slayer's utensils according to material: metal, stone, wood. Second, the intent's spontaneous or planned nature.

---

58. Plato, *Laws* 876e-877a2; translation from Phillips, "Trauma," 101. For a legal-anthropological comparison between Plato's *Laws* and the blood law in Deuteronomy, see E. Otto, "Strafrechtstheorie und Rechtsanthropologie in Platons NOMOI und in der biblischen Tora des Buches Deuteronomium. Zweiter Teil: Strafrechtstheorie und Rechtsanthropologie im Buch Deuteronomium," *ZABR* 26 (2020): 161–234, esp. 202–10.

59. Unintentional, resulting from anger, resulting from fear; intentional *ek pronoias* 874 e5-7.

60. The law is developed in the form of an imaginary dialogue on the legislation for a new colony in Magnesia on Crete. The participants are Cleinias of Crete, Megillus of Sparta, and an anonymous Athenian stranger; the latter is the dominant speaker in this passage.

61. The relevant passage can be outlined as follows: (1) introduction of the topic of "trauma" and its division into types (874e3-10), (a) unintentional wounding, (b) wounding in anger, (c) wounding in fear, (d) intentional wounding *ek pronoias*... (5) wounding with intent to kill (cf. 1 [d], 876e5-878b3): (a) definition, *trauma* as attempted homicide; (b) jurisdiction, the corresponding homicide court (877a1-2-b4); (c) general case and penalty (877a7-b3): (i) permanent exile to neighboring city; no confiscation of property; (ii) simple damages assessed by court, paid to victim... (6) Wounding in anger (cf. 1 [b], 878b4-879b1): (a) general case and penalty (878c1-d6); (b) special case I, kinsman wounds kinsman (879d6-879a2); (c) special case II, slave wounds free man (879a2-b1); (7) unintentional wounding (cf. 1 [a]: 879b1-5). This passage from Plato's *Laws* is of relevance, even though it is in tension with what other sources demonstrate to be the undisputed elements of Athenian law of the intent to hurt (*trauma ek pronoias*).

Finally, the congregation's jurisdiction over such case. Athenian rules for intentional wounding and Num 35 refer to a collective as the institution that has the jurisdiction: the Areopagus and the assembly (עדה), respectively.[62]

4.3. *Nominalizations and Modes of Action as Evolutions of Homicide Law*

Numbers 35 refines legal thought detailing complex procedural aspects with a number of agents such as, for instance, the assembly (עדה) holding the jurisdiction in vv. 24-28. The law also illustrates the development of homicide legislation and of its underlying concept of private enmity and hate. A formal analysis of the outline of the passage, namely of the two subcases, demonstrates the evolution of legal thought. Evidently, the first subcase's distinction between tools and their materials is separate from the motivation and from the mode of action that vv. 16-18, 20-21a describe. The subsequent vv. 22-23 repeat these distinctions yet without distinguishing between various modes of action and tools. They combine three modes of action that they associate with specific postures or acts: either pushing someone in hatred, v. 20; pushing in enmity, v. 22; throwing with intent, v. 21/v. 22; slaying in enmity, v. 20; or killing with any sort of stone, v. 23. Not only does the passage list specific actions, it also combines them with unambiguous nouns, such as "hatred," "intentionality," and "enmity," to which v. 15 adds "unfortunate inadvertence." These abstract nouns distinguish Num 35 from preceding law. How does the legal construct of private enmity and the subcase that is comparable to a *trauma ek pronoias* in Athenian law potentially inform the outline of the law? A brief examination of the protasis and its subcases seeks to clarify this.

4.4. *Modes of Action: To Push, to Throw and to Drop, to Slay*

The protasis of subcase I, vv. 16-18, first introduces three different tools and one general mode of intentional killing. "To slay" (נכה *hi.*) is the classical verb for homicide in Exod 21:12. Furthermore, Num 35:16 also specifies the effect of death (מות) as a consequence of the action, as does Exod 21:12. The protasis of subcase I of Num 35 thus takes up both critical terms from the brief homicide law in Exod 21, repeating them throughout the protasis and arranging them programmatically in Num 35:16, 20b in an *inclusio* of "to slay" and "to die."

---

62. Numbers 35 considers cases of spur-of-the-moment injuries that neither required prior planning nor reflection (premeditation), nor any explicit intent to kill an opponent that Athenian law would consider as wounding with intent. In a Hellenistic context, this could have provided the backdrop to Num 35 and could possibly explain the repetitive "and he dies" in vv. 16-18, which distinguishes the result of wounding with fatal outcome from wounding with a non-fatal injury, yet this is beyond the scope of this study.

Table 4.3

Exod 21:12	Whoever slays a man must be put to death.
Num 35:15 Num 35:16-18	Everyone who in inadvertence has slain a soul - if with an *iron utensil* he slew him dead - if with a *stone in his hand* (he slew) him so that he died from it - or if with a *wooden utensil* in his hand (he slew him) so that he died from it
Num 35:20b	- or in enmity he slays him with his fist so that he dies

Verses 20-21a, the protasis of subcase I, furthermore distinguishes the modes of aggressive action that an individual would take against an opponent. Verses 20-21a mention three specific modes of actions. First, "to push" or "shove aside" (הדף), a physical movement imposed to move another person away[63] which may also imply the notion of pushing away a group.[64] Numbers 35:22 in subcase II repeats the term for spontaneously pushing someone away. The second term, "to throw" (שלך *hi.*) an object against someone, uses a more common verb.[65] The last verb used in the protasis, v. 21a, is "to slay" (נכה *hi.*) "in enmity".

In general, the repetition of "to slay" and "to die" in the protasis illustrates the fatal consequence of the action. Besides the repetitive outcome, the passage also refers to the motivation or the intention of the slayer with a particular terminology that further refines the legal status of private long-term enmity. Beyond this, Num 35 also employs specific terminology to clarify this legal status.

4.5. איבה, שנאה

Deuteronomy 19:4, 11 highlight the permanence of the slayer–victim relationship with the idiomatic "from yesterday and the day before" and the use of the participle שנא *qal* for the slayer's ongoing mode of action.[66] The term designates the slayer's victim in the vicinity as a "neighbor" or as "companion" (רע). Numbers 35:20 use the abstract "hatred" (שנאה),[67] which also designates the collective in the priestly-prophetic judgment oracle in Ezek 23:29, including the destruction of Oholiba/Judah through her enemies as a consequence. Parallels further include

---

63. Cf. 2 Kgs 4:27.

64. Cf. the thrusting away of the wicked in Prov 10:3; the weak in Ezek 34:21; the enemy in Deut 6:19 (*BHS*).

65. Used with the preposition על and a person as direct object in Josh 10:11; Judg 9:53; 2 Sam 11:21; 20:12; Nah 3:6; Pss 55:23; 60:10.

66. On the meaning of hatred as legally binding intent to change the legal relationship between two spouses in marriage law, see above Chapter 3, section 4.

67. LXX ἔχθρα; cf. Deut 1:27; 9:28; 2 Sam 13:15; Ezek 23:29; 35:11; Pss 25:19 (LXX 24:19, ἔχθρα); 109:3, 5; 139:22 (138:22 LXX, ἔχθρα); Prov 10:12 (18 LXX ἔχθρα); 15:17 (LXX ἔχθρα); 26:26; Eccl 9:1, 6.

references to personal enmity between two opponents in Ps 109:3, 5. The nominal form designates the abstract construct of personal "hatred."

The noun איבה[68] is mainly attested in priestly texts. A juxtaposition of passages from Deut 19:6, 11 with subcase I in Num 35 showcases the development of the construct of enmity from Deuteronomy through Numbers. Conceiving of enmity as a social status of legal relevance, Num 35 reflects legal thought and uses an abstract term to designate this status. The replacements illustrate the development of legal thought. Instead of a participle, Num 35:20 uses "in hatred" and "in enmity" to point to the legal status of the two enemies with two abstract terms. The development from Deut 19:6, 11 puts the focus on the root שׂנא that Num 35:20 uses. Finally, v. 21a adds the noun איבה.

Table 4.4

Deut 19:6	כִּי לֹא שֹׂנֵא הוּא לוֹ מִתְּמוֹל שִׁלְשׁוֹם:
Deut 19:11	וְכִי־יִהְיֶה אִישׁ שֹׂנֵא לְרֵעֵהוּ וְאָרַב לוֹ וְקָם עָלָיו וְהִכָּהוּ נֶפֶשׁ וָמֵת
Num 35:20-21a	וְאִם־בְּשִׂנְאָה יֶהְדָּפֶנּוּ אוֹ־הִשְׁלִיךְ עָלָיו בִּצְדִיָּה וַיָּמֹת: אוֹ בְאֵיבָה הִכָּהוּ בְיָדוֹ וַיָּמֹת

Deuteronomy 19:4b arranges accidental homicide as subcase I in juxtaposition with intentional homicide between long-term enemies in subcase II. Here too, Num 35 renders the negation of hatred with the abstract noun for "enmity" and adds the clarification "but he was not an enemy to him" together with the participle construct chain, nor was he "seeking his evil."[69] This triple qualification of

---

68. MT parallels for the noun are in Gen 3:15 and Ezek 25:15; 35:5. LXX parallels for Greek ἔχθρα in Num 35:20, 22 are more numerous: Gen. 3:15; 1 Macc 11:40; 13:17; Prov 6:35; 10:18; 26:26; Sir 6:9; 37:2; Mic 2:8; Isa 63:10; Jer 9:7; Ezek 35:5, 11. Jackson, *Wisdom – Laws*, 12 n. 49, refers to S. H. Rosenbaum, "Israelite Homicide Law and the Term 'Enmity' in Gen 3:15," *Journal of Law and Religion* 2 (1984): 145–51, here 148, with a distinction between איבה and שׂנאה. Jackson notes that the latter is twice qualified by מתמול שלשום. Rosenbaum instead suggests איבה to be a state of permanent, ultimately mortal belligerence originating in the tribal law in which a leader may declare someone an enemy of the tribe, with the enmity between Saul and David (1 Sam 18:29; 24:20) serving as examples. He interprets those not as a personal relationship but as conflict between representatives of two parties; Rosenbaum, "Homicide Law," 150. The considerations about the formal state of enmity are coherent, yet the differentiation between איבה and שׂנאה is questionable, given the shared contexts of both terms, as Jackson, *Wisdom - Laws*, 129 n. 49, points out: the terms are best explained as synonyms, rejecting the idea of a (formal) declaration of "enmity" between the two parties in Num 35.

69. Cf. the use of this construct in the personal enmity of Saul and David (1 Sam 24:10); cf. the participle מבקש, which, context-related, refers to the intention of homicide in 1 Sam 19:2; 20:1; 23:10; 2 Sam 16:11; Jer 44:30; cf. as intent to kill, 2 Sam 20:19; Ps 37:32.

Num 35 shows a refined understanding of long-term enmity as a social status. The further clarification of the case adds the notion of the slayer's "intent" (צדיה).

Table 4.5

| Deut 19:4b | אֲשֶׁר יַכֶּה אֶת־רֵעֵהוּ בִּבְלִי־דַעַת וְהוּא לֹא־שֹׂנֵא לוֹ מִתְּמֹל שִׁלְשֹׁם׃ |
| Num 35:22, 23 | וְאִם־בְּפֶתַע בְּלֹא־אֵיבָה הֲדָפוֹ אוֹ־הִשְׁלִיךְ עָלָיו כָּל־כְּלִי בְּלֹא צְדִיָּה׃ וְהוּא לֹא־אוֹיֵב לוֹ וְלֹא מְבַקֵּשׁ רָעָתוֹ׃ |

4.6. צדיה

The terminology for "intent" covers a wide semantic range.[70] The root of the abstract term for "pursuit" (צדיה) in Num 35:20, 22[71] is absent from Deut 19:1-12. Here, Num 35 draws on its only parallel in a negation of the participle in homicide law in Exod 21:13 (ואשר לא צדה).[72]

What is the relevance of צדיה? The exclusion of a pursuit of the victim would require as a necessary condition a determination that the slayer had not been attempting to kill his opponent in pursuit. Only spontaneous homicide would entitle the slayer to asylum. The term צדיה as abstract is critical for the legal discourse. The metaphor of the chase features prominently in a description of the relationship of private enmity between Saul and David in the narrative tradition 1 Sam 24:12. The discourse between Saul and David insinuates a court situation in which David in the role of a plaintiff in a declaration of innocence addresses his opponent Saul, pointing to his ongoing pursuit. The participle singular צֹדֶה accuses the defendant of an ongoing pursuit, self-describing as a victim that refuses to engage in a private conflict: "I will not raise my hand against you… but you, you pursue (ואתה צדה) my life in order to take it."[73] Lexicographers

---

70. See, for instance, the review of non-legal material that points to mere intent without acting out; Botica, *Intention*, 109, 117–32. Botica takes a semantic approach to define intentionality as "state of mind," which Hebrew expresses with such terms as לב, מזימה, כליה, קרב, יצר, מחשבה; and see further the overview Botica gives on p. 132.

71. This is attested in Num 35:20, 22, and is used in the description of the lampstand branches of Exod 25:32; 37:18. The Greek translation ἔνεδρα has parallels in Josh 8:2, 12, 14, 18-19, 21; Judg 9:25; 16:12; 20:29, 38; 1 Kgs 21:40; 1 Macc 9:40; 11:69; Ps 9:29; Job 25:3; Sir 11:29; Obad 7.

72. See above, Chapter 2.

73. The judicial character of this passage, namely the protagonists' short speeches, has long been acknowledged; see, for instance, H. J. Boecker, *Redeformen des Rechts-slebens im Alten Testament* (Neukirchen-Vluyn: Neukirchener Verlag, 1964), 32, 48–50: 1 Sam 24:13, 16, appeal; 24:18, non-guilty plea; cf. 1 Sam 26:18, formula of appeasement. T. Frymer-Kensky, "Israel," in *A History of Ancient Near Eastern Law*, vol. 2, ed. R. Westbrook (Leiden, Brill, 2003), 976–1046, notes David's oath in 1 Sam 24:21-22. Westbrook and Wells, *Everyday Law*, 40–42, do not refer to forms of forensic speech in either 1 Sam 24 or 26.

determine the meaning of צדיה as "pursuit, chase"⁷⁴ with reference to this narrative and the participle as a quintessential term for the pursuit of a personal opponent 1 Sam 24:12, besides its use in Lam 4:18.⁷⁵ Semantically more broadly attested, the related root צוד⁷⁶ denotes chase,⁷⁷ thus presupposing the intent of the hunter. Since the association with hunting animals of prey is more precisely attested for the root,⁷⁸ it is plausible to derive the abstract term from this root with two aspects that buttress this particular understanding. The rendering in the LXX supports this meaning and the other cognates also refer to a context of pursuit, using a chase as metaphor for intent. Often the constellation between the players clarifies the meaning of these cognates through the context.⁷⁹ Compared with this, other meanings are not far to seek, for instance, the nouns צַיִד ("hunting, prey, game")⁸⁰ and מָצוֹד ("prey").⁸¹

74. A verbal noun, cf. Gesenius, 18th ed., 1101, derives from the independent, etymologically unclear root I צדה, while not ruling out the noun to be a cognate of צוד, "to ambush." The Saul–David narratives use the noun for "refuge, hideaway, asylum" (מצד, 1 Sam 23:14, 19; 24:1; cf. further Jer 51:30; 1 Chr 11:7; 12:9, 17; Ezek 33:27; Isa 33:16; Jer 48:41).
75. In the original reading of Lam 4:18, "they pursued our steps".
76. This verb occurs 14 times including 11 times in the *qal*, 3 times in the *polel*. The derivatives include nouns, such as מצד/מצודה, but the derivation of the meaning "mountain fortress," "refuge, hideaway, shelter," respectively, is unclear as the shift from "prey, catch, net" to "shelter" is hard to explain. M. Oeming, צוד; ציד, *TDOT* 12 (Grand Rapids: Eerdmans, 2003), 270–75, esp. 271. Given the critical core of intentional pursuit it makes sense to associate the noun with the root for "chase."
77. This is also the sense of the rendering of MT צדו as ἐθηρεύσαμεν in the LXX's version of Lam 4:18.
78. Cf. on the image of enmity between God as lion chasing (צוד) Job in Job 10:13-16; see P. Riede, *Im Netz des Jägers. Studien zur Feindmetaphorik in den Individualpsalmen* (Neukirchen-Vluyn: Neukirchener Verlag, 2000), 187–88.
79. The derivation of the meaning from the root remains, however, uncertain. For instance, "fortress" in selected contexts specifically denotes "mountain fortress" for the participial forms and for the nouns מָצָד and מְצוֹדָה, while it takes a circuitous route and, presumably, it includes a synecdoche. The two nouns often rendered as "fortress" occur 38 times in the meaning of mountain fortress. See Oeming, צוד; ציד, 271. E. König, *Hebräisches und Aramäisches Wörterbuch zum AT* (Leipzig: Dieterich'sche Verlagsbuchhandlung Theodor Weicher, 1910), 6th, 7th ed. 1937, p. 240, first suggested a use of "hunting lodge" and then its use as synecdoche, i.e., as reference to shelter in a wider meaning. See the reference to what is translated as "siege work," מָצוֹד, in Qoh 9:14; Job 19:6 (uncertain); Ps 116:3 (conjecture).
80. See Gen 10:9; 25:27, 28; 27:3, 5, 7, 19, 25, 30, 31, 33; Lev 17:13; Prov 12:27; Jer 30:17 (conjecture). This unequivocal meaning of the term is limited to a few respective contexts, most prominently, Gen 27.
81. Cf. Prov 12:12; Qoh 7:26.

In conclusion, the semantic range of the noun צדיה in Num 35:20, 22 has emerged from a literal meaning "chase" that includes the notion of overcoming a spatial distance toward an opponent, into a technical term for "intent" in the respective contexts of legal thought.[82] Methodologically, in this case the narrative contexts of this abstract term contribute to its meaning in the context of personal enmity.[83]

4.7. Conclusion

The analysis of selected terms of homicide law in Num 35 has yielded results on various levels. On the one hand, it illustrates the law's distinct literary traditions and suggests its historical backdrop most likely in Hellenism through the use of distinct categories, for instance, the addition of the idiomatic בשגגה and its tragic notion. On the other hand, it revealed substantial development of legal thought, a precision in naming the status of enemies with abstract terms that hitherto went unnoticed. Three nouns in particular,[84] איבה, שנאה, צדיה, two of them derived from verbal roots, capture the essence of the social construct of "hatred" and "enmity" in Num 35 in abstract terms, with their meaning best determined against the backdrop of Exod 21:13. The complex theocratic layer of Num 35 thus presents two forms of legal reasoning. First, it generates the abstract terminology for private enmity as a distinct social construct. Second, closely connected with the layer in Num 35, case narratives in Num 27 and 36 function as examples for legal reasoning in the form of case law on central legal aspects of inheritance law. The lexicography of the law in Num 35 refines the interplay between narratives and law. The participle צדה is prominently used in a plaintiff's speech in a case narrative about Saul presenting it in a tragic notion, while raising the underlying legal question of intentional pursuit.[85] The constellation of fugitive and persecutor in narratives outside the actual law of Num 35 are examples of typical case narratives that include rhetorical discourses about the underlying intent of the slayer to kill their victim and they thus present such intent in its legal relevance. The intention of persecuting and of killing an individual, associated with "pursuit"

---

82. The diverse renderings of the cognates of צוד/ציד with 18 different terms in the LXX present a more complex picture of the meaning of the pursuit. The rendering in Num 35:20, 22 is ἐξ ἐνέδρου, "an ambush." Renderings of the root may deviate from the proper sense of "hunt" and render as "twisting" or "corrupting" of a soul; e.g. in LXX Ezek 13:18, 20, לְצוֹדֵד נְפָשׁוֹת, τοῦ διαστρέφειν ψυχάς; cf. 13:20: συστρέφειν; ἐκστρέφειν (τὰς) ψυχάς. See Oeming, צוד; ציד, 275.

83. This demonstrates a "narrative" approach to this term in legal thought as opposed to a "literal" or purely semantic; cf. Jackson, *Wisdom-Laws*, 24–29.

84. Cf. also the participle form, מבקש רעה.

85. Jackson, *Wisdom-Laws*, 24–25, argues that the cognitive structures going into the hermeneutics of biblical law are not narrowly semantic, but narrative. The root "pursuit" (צדיה) plays a pivotal role, but the reference is not literal but, in a wider sense, narrative. In this sense, the law covers an array of typical cases.

(צדיה), may best be clarified against the backdrop of the narrative contexts and constellations that illustrate this relationship. 1 Samuel 24:12 uses "pursuit," assuming a cognate of the root צוד ("chase"), as synecdoche and illustrates the mode of narrative logic of legal reasoning.[86]

The abstract nouns of Num 35 illustrate the "narrative" logic of legal thought. Absent from the preceding traditions of homicide law and emerging in the accrual of priestly law, these terms function as legal meta-categories that attract a number of other associated terms for long-term enmity. The abstract denominative איבה is derived from the frequently used "enemy," a form with which Num 35 refers to the construct of "enmity" as an abstract principle that likely was more commonly known at a point in time when Num 35 used this term. Numbers 35 highlights the legal meaning of the relationship between slayer and victim[87] and elaborates on this long-term relationship.

The particular focus on the relationship highlights the extension of private enmity over time, attracting other idioms, such as "seeking one's evil" (מבקש רעה).[88] Unparalleled in Deuteronomy, this idiom is distinct for a late or post-priestly layer in Num 35:23bβ. This participial idiom conveys the consistent effort of seeking an opponent's evil, i.e., the essence of long-term enmity as opposed to engaging in one isolated, more spontaneously erupting conflict.

In addition to Deut 19, Num 35 emphasizes the immediacy and the unprecedented nature of this assault in v. 22 with the idiomatic terms "suddenly" (בפתע) and "without ruse" (בלא צדיה). When Num 35:20-23 uses the distinctive terminology for premeditation it replaces the designation of the phrase "without intent" (בבלי־דעת, Deut 19) with the idiomatic בשגגה. The development of specific terminology to convey the long-term nature of enmity was thus a decisive feature in particular of Num 35.

---

86. The same applies to a number of parallel cognates of the identical root צוד/ציד. Conceptually, these cognates conceive of rescue in spatial metaphors. By way of spatial imagination, they construe Yahweh as materialization of an ultimate rescue from pursuit. These spatial metaphors express the surpassing or the overcoming of an ongoing accusation or aggression of an opponent as an action in the foreground. Notably, in the narrative context of 1 Sam 24 the image ascribes a passive role to the supplicant as ultimately seeking refuge in the deity's justice (1 Sam 24:12, 15), rather than acting out in a hopeless conflict constellation that is hard to overcome. Seeking refuge can thus refer to a counter concept to acting out enmity.

87. See also Barmash, *Homicide*, 121.

88. This idiom has two parallels in 1 Sam 24:10 and 1 Kgs 20:7. The *piel* participle is found in Gen 37:16; Exod 33:7; Judg 4:22; 14:4; 18:1; 1 Sam 19:2; 20:1; 23:10; 24:10; 2 Sam 16:11; 17:3; 20:19; 1 Kgs 11:22; 20:7; Neh 2:4; Ps 37:25; Prov 17:9, 19; Jer 5:1; Ezek 34:6; Mal 2:15.

5. Legal Procedure and Social Background

The abstract terms for hate and enmity in Num 35 substantiate the legal nature of long-term hateful relationships. Beyond its contribution to the theoretical assessment of enmity, this late priestly layer highlights legal procedure with the legislation that includes the sojourner and the settler. This hints at a historical context in the late Persian or early Hellenistic period at a point in time when Israelites would claim jurisdiction over their community's metics and settlers in a typical case of kinship law. The following considers whether Num 35 uses the idiosyncratic term "asylum cities" (ערי מקלט) as a token of a polity's claim for autonomous jurisdiction over homicide trial. The function of these cities is best considered in the legal-historical context of Num 35. The jurisdiction of the "congregation," the concept of the cities of refuge in vv. 11-12, 24, and the statutory regulations vv. 25-29 all are relatively late developments in biblical law. This first invites clarification in reference to early Greek, classical Athenian, and Hellenistic law.

5.1. *Israelite, Metic, Settler*

Numbers 35 adds a characteristic distinction between three categories of residents: the Israelite (בני ישראל, אזרח), the גר (cf. Josh 20:9) and the תושב (v. 15a). These categories speak to the social space that Num 35 presupposes. The classification is typical for a polity or a "citizen state" understood as an association of individuals that assigns a social status to its members.[89] Set over all the categories is the assembly (עדה) with jurisdiction in the (non-cultic) matter of homicide which implies long-term feuding. Jurisdiction of these cases would typically be with the leaders of the kin. In Num 35, while it presupposes a heterogeneous community, in homicide cases between any category or residents, those self-identifying as full citizens or Israelites in the assembly, this assembly would claim jurisdiction over all residents. For the construct of private enmity this suggests that a resident alien (גר) could enter the status of private enmity with a citizen. Conflict settlement would now occur between an (ethnically and culturally undefined) גר who could achieve comparable social prestige as an Israelite citizen. Exposure to revenge patterns and feud was thus not limited to Israelites in the narrow sense but rather included an array of individuals that were part of the polity. Consequently, homicide law would address this status of long-term opponents.

The following clarifies the nature of the status of the גר and the תוֹשָׁב in Num 35 in the realm of P, and of H. The category of גר as residents may best be rendered as metic (MT גר)[90] who dwelt in Israel, yet lacked the privilege of a biological affiliation with a clan represented in the government of the polity. In a kinship-based community, the lack of a wide-ranging lineage would put a גר at

---

89. Cf. on this terminology and its notion of a state constituted by the assembly of its citizens, W. Oswald, "Foreign Marriages and Citizenship in Persian Period Judah," *Journal of Hebrew Scriptures* 12 (2012): 1–17, here 6, 15, and see below.

90. LXX's rendering, προσήλυτος, adds a different notion; see further below.

a systemic disadvantage, vulnerable to assault and homicide, without an avenger who could deter potential assailants from attacking. To Deuteronomy, the social status of the גר was comparable to an orphan's or a widow's.[91] For organizational reasons the metic is joined with these others in the Sabbath rest.[92] Prominent in H (20×) and P (15×), גר designates the cultural alterity of a member of an Israelite polity.[93] Leviticus 17:8-9 consider him a protected member of the polity to whom the threat of the death penalty applies in case of illegitimate offering. The גר here is not an individual outside his kin, but instead a foreigner who is cast away from his original place for an unspecified reason, consequently seeking acceptance in his social environment.[94] The social and legal status of the גר was in flux, and the group was gaining influence and relevance during the time period reflected in H and in the tradition of Ezekiel. To H, at some point by and large the same laws for citizens would apply also to the גר[95] and their social status was of relevance in Lev 25:47-54, 55 with respect to the institutions of redemption and *yobel* in the

91. Cf. Deut 14:29; 16:11, 14; 24:17, 19, 20, 21; 26:13; 27:19, or a day-laborer, to which Deut 24:14 compares him: he is in need of the forgotten sheaf (24:19) and in need of gleanings of the olive trees and vine (24:20, 21) that are also reserved for the widow and the orphan. The command for fair treatment in judgment in Deut 1:16; 24:17; 27:19, and the Sabbath command in 5:14, which mentions him explicitly, as well as the laws on the Feast of Weeks in 16:11 and the Feast of Booths in 16:14 (unlike Lev 23:42 H), demonstrate his distinct status in Deuteronomy's perception. A sojourner's actual status was subordinate and as a consequence their advancement could be perceived as a sign of overturning of the social order (28:15-46; esp. 43-44). The command in 28:43; 31:12 to love the גר also demonstrates his distinct status with the historical reference to Israel's dwelling in Egypt (10:19). Deuteronomy 31:12 demands the presence of the sojourner for the reading of the law, which identifies his status as distinct from a brother's (24:14) and below that of a full citizen in the community, as a part of which he was expected to obey the law.
92. See Exod 20:10/Deut 5:14; at the same time, dietary laws were not applicable to him (Deut 14:21, τῷ παροίκῳ τῷ ἐν ταῖς πόλεσίν σου).
93. Elliger, *Leviticus*, 227 n. 29. See following D. Kellermann, גר, *TDOT* vol. 2 (Grand Rapids: Eerdmans, 1977), 445. Meanwhile, the historical contexts and their specific cultural identity remains to be clarified, which is beyond the focus here. Cf., for instance, M. Cohen, "Le 'ger' biblique et son statut socio-religieux," *Revue de l'histoire des religions* 207 (1990): 131–58, 156, who suggests associating them historically with northerners (Ephraim), esp. in Chronicles, i.e., coming from Samaria after the destruction and thus having no ethnic or exclusively religious connotation other than as a reference to a northerner living under Judean domination.
94. See Elliger, *Leviticus*, 227, on Lev 17:8-9.
95. Cf. the principle of having *one* law in particular in cases of injury and homicide for metics (גר) and the citizen (אזרח) in Lev 24:22, and note their explicit inclusion in the talion in 24:20. This corresponds to the parallels in rights and duties in Athenian legislation; see, for instance, D. D. Phillips, *The Law of Ancient Athens* (Ann Arbor: University of Michigan, 2013), 23–25.

case of a Judahite native who sold himself to a wealthy גר.⁹⁶ Independent from their social status a גר could seek access to Judaism in a religious sense. The Holiness School in some passages includes the גר in the cultic community – for instance, in Exod 12:49⁹⁷ – yet the record in H does not allow drawing a straight line toward full cultic integration.⁹⁸ The גר would be circumcised upon entering the cultic community as a full member. Once circumcised, the גר practically becomes a proselyte⁹⁹ and part of a house and subordinate to it.

Does the category of the metic/*metoikos* in Athens provide a comparable category to the גר and his legal status in P and related layers in Persian-period

---

96. See, on Lev 25:39-46, 47-55, G. Barbiero, "Der Fremde im Bundesbuch und im Heiligkeitsgesetz zwischen Absonderung und Annahme," in *RStB* 81–2 (1996): 41–69, quoted from G. Barbiero, *Studien zu alttestamentlichen Texten* (Stuttgart: Katholisches Bibelwerk, 2002), 221–54, here 249. While the גר was perceived on the same economic level as a "brother" (vv. 39a, 47b), the passage seeks to unite the brothers against the metics with the intention of protecting the community of brothers from him. He is economically free, thus not following the religious rules relevant to slavery; see C. Bultmann, *Der Fremde im antiken Juda. Eine Untersuchung zum sozialen Typenbegriff 'ger' und seinem Bedeutungswandel in der alttestamentlichen Gesetzgebung* (Göttingen: Vandenhoeck & Ruprecht, 1992), 187–88. The economically successful sojourner is a character from whom the Israelites distance themselves and who himself refrains from gaining access to the community. Bultmann, *Der Fremde*, 188, 190, with reference to Neh 5:1-8, which suggests a fifth-century BCE date.

97. Exodus 12:43-49 is either seen as late addition (so B. Baentsch, *Exodus*, 107–108; M. Noth, *Das zweite Buch Moses, Exodus* [Göttingen: Vandenhoeck & Ruprecht, 1959], 72), or is ascribed to H (see Knohl, *Sanctuary*, 21, with reference to Num 9:14; also in the minimalist view of H of Nihan, *From Priestly Torah*, 566).

98. At the same time, the lines of the socio-cultural distinction of this group from Yahwism differ from those Deuteronomy draws. For instance, Ezekiel and H can associate the sojourner with foreign non-Yahwistic cultic practice. Ezekiel 14:7 recalls the casuistic laws from Lev 17:3, 8, 10, 13; 20:2; 22:18, and, while the sojourner is supposed to have equal rights as the Israelites and therefore to be a part of the cult, Ezekiel considers him as the gateway for foreign cultic practice, specifically of the *gillûlim*. Cultic distance from the sojourner is evident in his exclusion from the Festival of Booths in Lev 23:43, while Deut 16:14 explicitly invites his participation. Leviticus 17:12 demands his protection as a citizen. In the realm of P, land ownership was not always possible for "strangers," as Ezek 47:22 requests to ultimately grant such privilege.

99. In general, in some contexts of H, the sojourner becomes a typical proselyte to whom the family laws in Lev 18:6-17 apply, as do rules of chastity (18:18-23) and the laws and commandments in general (18:26), including the prohibition of offerings to Molech (20:2) and social laws (19:10; 23:22; 25:6); cf. Kellermann, גור, 446, cf. J. E. Ramirez-Kidd, *Alterity and Identity in Israel: The* גר *in the Old Testament* (Berlin: de Gruyter, 1999), 64–67.

Judah?[100] After the reforms of Cleisthenes, 508/07, foreigners in Athens would remain foreigners and could merely hope to gain some privileges, not the citizenship status.[101] Free foreigners living in Attica, the *metoikoi*[102] were in general not full citizens. Broadly speaking, in Athens, their commensurability in the political arena was a denial of the rights of citizenship, which forced them into an inferior status in the polity than citizens.[103] Historically, in the fifth century the dividing line between *metoikoi* and visitors from abroad (*xenoi*) was fluid.[104] While *metoikoi* could hold the position of raising a complaint before an Athenian court, the *polemarch* (the *war archon*) had the authority of private proceedings (*dikai idiai*) in regards to *metoikoi* or *proxenoi*.[105] Their status was more routinely handled as their numbers increased in the fourth century B.C.[106] In Athens around

100. See the suggestion of R. Martin-Achard, גור *gûr* to sojourn, *Theological Lexicon of the Old Testament* vol. 1, ed. E. Jenni and C. Westermann (Peabody, MA: Hendrickson, 1997), 307–10, here 308; Kellermann, גור, 443.

101. Citizenship was contingent on an Athenian father and the formal acceptance in the deme; cf. U. Walter, *An der Polis teilhaben. Bürgerstaat und Zugehörigkeit im archaischen Griechenland* (Stuttgart: Franz Steiner, 1993), 208. Modifications were made in 451/0; see A. L. Boegehold, "Perikles' Citizenship Law of 451/0 B.C.E.," in *Athenian Identity and Civic Ideology*, ed. A. L. Boegehold and A. Scafuro (Baltimore: Johns Hopkins, 1994), 57–66, here 57. From the era of the Persian wars, for the first time, citizens of other cities who lived in Athens (*proxenoi*) are attested; see Walter, *Polis*, 209.

102. This group of immigrant citizens was already known at the time of Cleisthenes' reforms of 508/507 BCE. For the origin at that time, see D. Whitehead, *The Demes of Attica 508/7-Ca. 250 B.C. A Political and Social Study* (Princeton: Princeton University Press, 1986), 81. The term is first attested in the early fifth century; cf. Aeschylus, *Persians* 319, potentially in the late sixth century; Walter, *Polis*, 209.

103. Aristotle, *Politeia* 1275a 14-16, compared the *metoikoi* to children or seniors who either were not yet or no longer enrolled in the list of citizens. When setting up the *phyla* and creating Athenian democracy, the exclusion of the *metoikoi* from full citizenship and registration was grounded in their lack of family origin and permanent residency; see Herodotus 6.131, and cf. P. A. Cartledge, "Metoikos," in *Brill's New Pauly*, vol. 8 (Leiden: Brill, 2006), 810–14.

104. Cartledge, "Metoikos," 811.

105. Aristotle, *Ath. Pol.* 58.2. They were also required to pay a monthly poll-tax and to perform military service; Cartledge, "Metoikos," 811.

106. The foreigners had to register after four weeks in a demos (in Athens often Piraeus) and an Athenian full citizen needed to stand as legal representative (*prostates*); Cartledge, "Metoikos," 811. In Athens, the status of *metoikos* was also granted to freed slaves, some of whom were known for their wealth. While they were excluded from land acquisition, *metoikos* status permitted association with full citizens, and the women with this status were seen as potential marriage partners; Cartledge, "Metoikos," 812. Notably, the individual deme could devise rights or duties for the immigrant residents. On their tax status, see Whitehead, *Demes*, 81–82, and on the evidence of *metoikoi* in specific demes as known from epigraphic sources, see pp. 83–84.

313 B.C. virtually half of the population were *metoikoi*.[107] Legal regulation for this group was therefore essential[108] and indeed a small number of law cases involving *metoikoi*[109] are known.

This poses the question of the relevance of the metics' legal status in Athens, particularly with regard to homicide legislation in Num 35. It may be relevant for two reasons. First, questions of the jurisdiction of homicide when metics were involved are explicitly mentioned.[110] Second, in homicide cases outside the city the status of a metic was relevant on a practical level for claims for homicide cases between two cities.[111] Both cases demonstrate the impact of the legal status of a metic. The concern of the asylum city regulation found in Num 35:15 thus appears plausible in analogy to these distinctions in Athenian law that would explicitly include the metic in the asylum legislation in homicide law.

It seems plausible that the technical use of the term גר as metic in the narrower sense in biblical law co-develops with the more precise understanding of this legal category in many cases in comparison with the "full citizen." Numbers 35:15 juxtaposes the metic with the more common term for the Israelites (בְּנֵי יִשְׂרָאֵל). The use of the two terms for "full citizen," אזרח, always together with the root גור suggests the co-development of both terms.[112]

The third category of slayers in Num 35:15a is the תּוֹשָׁב (πάροικος) "settling among them." An exceptional *t-prefix* form,[113] mainly used in priestly texts,[114] it carries the aspect of taking residence of the verb ישב, "to settle"; the term is

---

107. Cartledge, "Metoikos," 812.

108. Cf. Aristotle's description of the responsibility of the polemarch to perform for the metics the same duties that the Archon performs for citizens (Aristotle, *Ath. Pol.* 58), cf. C. Patterson, "The Hospitality of Athenian Justice: The Metic in Court," in *Law and Social Status in Classical Athens*, ed. V. Hunter and J. Edmondson (Oxford: Oxford University Press, 2000), 93–112, 97.

109. Patterson, "Metic," 101.

110. The status was relevant in Athens, as Aristotle clarifies: "charges of unintentional homicide, conspiracy to kill and the killing of a slave, *metic* or foreigner, are heard by the Court of the Palladion." Aristotle. *Ath. Pol.* 57.3.

111. When an Athenian was killed in an allied city, a fine of five talents could be imposed; C. Patterson, *Pericles' Citizenship Law of 451/0* (New York: Arno Press, 1981; reprint: Salem, NH: Ayer, 1987), 104. A statute from 510/9 B.C.E. from the archonship of Skamandrios protects Athenian citizens against torture; Boegehold, "Perikles' Citizenship Law," 58, with reference to C. Hignett, *A History of the Athenian Constitution to the End of the Fifth-Century B.C.* (Oxford: Clarendon, 1952), 345.

112. Cf. in H, Lev 17:15; 18:26; 19:29, 34; 23:42; 24:16, 22; Exod 12:19, 48; Num 9:14; 15:13, 29; Josh 8:33; Ezek 47:22; cf. Ps 37:35 in a metaphoric sense. See also Martin-Achard, "גור *gûr* to sojourn," 309.

113. Cf. וְתוֹלָלֵינוּ in Ps 137:3.

114. Eight times in H, two more times besides Num 35 in other priestly texts (Gen 23:4; Exod 12:45).

seemingly close to גר.[115] It is used in construct with the person with whom the תּוֹשָׁב is staying (Lev 22:10; 25:6) and, as a consequence, it seems to designate a settler in a subordinate status, potentially an objective social condition of a "sojourner," rather than the social construct of the term גר, a free man who left his place of origin.[116] The תּוֹשָׁב had only a temporary right to settle, with limited rights of property acquisition (Gen 23:4). While he seemingly is excluded from participation in rituals of the kin, unlike the metic (Exod 12:45), in Lev 25:47b the distinction between the metic/גר and the תּוֹשָׁב was not always clear cut. The combination of the תּוֹשָׁב and the day laborer (שָׂכִיר) is found in Lev 25:6, 40; Exod 12:45; and Lev 22:10. The frequent use of this term in H (Lev 22:10; 25:6, 35, 40, 45, 47) suggests the dependence of Num 35 on these passages. When used for Israel as a collective, the term characterizes Israel's subordinate position comparable to the position of a "metic" vis-à-vis Yahweh, that is, as someone relying in his social status on a more influential and on a more established individual.[117]

In conclusion, the list of the distinct categories of citizen, metic, and settler as residents in Num 35:15 requires an explanation. Three reasons are extant. First, opponents in any conflict-settlement procedure belonged to the same socio-economic stratum. A party would by default engage in conflict with residents of a comparable social reputation and comparable status[118] with reciprocity and escalation as the fundamental principles of constellations of private enmity. While Num 35 does not explicitly mention Israelites in conflict with metics, it is likely that they could acquire a similar socio-economic status as Israelites and thus belong to the same social layer and this is the reason why the distinct groups are mentioned. Second, beyond the general requirement of socio-economic equality, Num 35 also demonstrates that the legal institutions of which individuals of various social ranks could avail themselves differed, and it declares

---

115. Cf. J. Joosten, *People and Land in the Holiness Code: An Exegetical Study of the Ideational Framework of the Law in Leviticus 17–26* (Leiden: Brill, 1996), 73.

116. Joosten, *People and Land*, 74.

117. It is also used in 1 Chr 29:19; 1 Kgs 17:1. The vulnerability to illegal action is expressed in Ezek 22:7; the term עשק ("oppress") appears in Exod 22:20; 23:9; cf. v. 12; gleaning of the vineyard is mentioned in Lev 19:10//23:22. His exclusion from participation in the Passover in Exod 12:45, unlike the participation of the sojourner in Num 9:14 (if he has been circumcised Exod 12:48), would point to the understanding of a non-Israelite who was not a proselyte; Kellermann, גור, 448.

118. Cf. P. Bourdieu, "The Sense of Honour," in idem, *Algeria 1960: The Disenchantment of the World* (Cambridge: Cambridge University Press, 1979), 85–109, here 101; for Athens, see Phillips, *Avengers*, 24; Cohen, *Law, Violence*, 114. The opponents in the trial in Lysias 4 both claim to own the slave; Archippus and Teisis, in the law case ascribed to Lysias "Against Teisis," belong to the same wrestling school; the case in Demosthenes 47 supposes that the speaker and his opponent served as trierarchs in subsequent years.

the availability of the cities of refuge to all of them.[119] As the *metoikoi* in Athens, metics in Judah would probably be locally assigned to the tribes and naturally many aspects of their status – for instance, the relevance and role of their own kinship relations would depend on this specific context. Given the far less refined description of legal procedure in homicide cases of Num 35, its clarification of the legislation for the metic/גר supports a reading of the law specifically oriented toward its local relevance. Notably, the clarification of the legal status of the metic is relatively broadly attested in H. The nuanced view on the metic in Ancient Judah's social structure demonstrates the complexity of the mechanisms of conflict settlement and feud. Third and finally, the specifics of homicide legislation for the metic may seem surprising, yet when seen against the backdrop of the glimpses into homicide legislation in Athens, here too, strikingly, the murder of a metic is not different from the murder of an Athenian and, at most, had the consequence of exile. The responsibility of the kin for revenge in homicide cases could make it particularly complicated for a metic to be vindicated.[120]

5.2. Jurisdiction of the עדה

The citizenship status of the manslayer, the role of the avenger of blood, and the congregation at large imply a nuanced perception of the legal status of enmity. Numbers 35 indeed specifies both, legal procedure and agents. The "congregation/assembly" (עדה) functions as the jury the killer would face in trial (Num 35:12). The law's attention to the male next of kin acting in the role of the avenger of blood becomes apparent when seen in the trajectory of homicide law. Exodus 21:12-14* does not mention him; Deut 19:1-12 refers to him twice (vv. 6, 12); and Num 35:19, 24, 25, 27 (2×) refers to him five times.[121] One reason that the elaborate law of Num 35 refers multiple times to the avenger of blood is its attention to the conflict's dramatic nature. The complex decision about

---

119. Cf. the responsibility of the polemarch in Aristotle's *Ath. Pol.* 58 for metics, tax-exempt metics, and *proxenoi*, with a detailed description for the procedure.

120. Comparable challenges in the case of a slave are known; cf. Demosthenes 47.68-73. The murder was neither punished nor prosecuted. Cf. Patterson, "Metic," 100. Thus, in Athens, while the metic's rights as a person and as a property owner fell within the responsibility of a public official, i.e., the *polemarch*, given the lack of tribe and *deme* and *anchisteia* in a judicial system that relied heavily on these social networks, the metic clearly was at a disadvantage; Patterson, "Metic," 101.

121. On the assumption that the blood avenger as an official charged with avenging homicide is a Deuteronomic innovation (M. Sulzberger, *The Ancient Hebrew Law of Homicide* [Philadelphia: Julius H. Greenstone, 1915], 53–54, 58), and on the assumption of him being the representative of the local elders (Phillips, *Criminal Law*, 103, see Barmash, *Homicide*, 51–52), as well on the continuity and relevance of blood feud as a relevant form of kinship-based conflict settlement from early time to the Second Temple period, see K. Koch, "Der Spruch „Sein Blut bleibe auf seinem Haupt" und die israelitische Auffassung vom vergossenen Blut," *VT* 12 (1962): 396–416, here 411.

whether homicide had occurred in a long-term hateful relationship could only be made through the congregation, i.e., the community in which the opponents had publicly lived out a hateful relationship. Numbers 35 thus naturally affirms the public nature of private enmity when it assigns jurisdiction to the עדה as jury and the subsequent procedural clarifications consequently reflect on aspects of the relationship between a slayer and the avenger of blood that would be noticeable in public. The rules of implementation or regulatory statutes (vv. 25-29) point to subcases in vv. 26-27 once the slayer left the asylum city, while v. 28 specifies the limitations on time an asylum seeker would spend in the city of refuge. Furthermore, the urbanization of asylum in Num 35 assumes the slayer's extended stay in an asylum city and consequently the possibility that the avenger of blood would take revenge over time.

Source-critically, the term does not originate before P and has been suggested to have been coined by a layer of P[122] that conceived of the עדה as a forum equipped with judicial authority.[123] עדה can also designate the ideal post-exilic Israel at large, and it typically oscillates between these two meanings. In Num 35, the context of this collective is the jurisdiction over asylum cases after homicide.[124] The term is (potentially) also known in Elephantine[125] as a designation for an institution that in Num 1:2-3 represents the assembly of the kin or clans (משפחת),

---

122. Different from Deuteronomy, using קהל; cf., for the post-exilic priestly layer, L. Rost, *Die Vorstufen von Kirche und Synagoge im Alten Testament. Eine wortgeschichtliche Untersuchung* (Stuttgart: Kohlhammer, 1938); cf. also Elliger, *Leviticus*, 70, with reference to Lev 4:13, 15; 8:3, 4, 5; 9:5; 10:6, 17; 16:5; 19:2; 24:14, 16. These substantiations mainly exclude the dating as pre-exilic in P and were later abandoned; see J. Milgrom, "Priestly Terminology and the Political and Social Structure of Pre-monarchic Israel," *JQR* 69 (1979): 65–81; A. Hurvitz, "Linguistic Observations on the Priestly Term *'edah* and the Language of P," *Immanuel* 1 (1972): 21–23.

123. Besides Num 35, cf. Lev 24:10-16; Num 15:32-36; 27:2, 12-27; 32:2; cf. Gertz, *Gerichtsorganisation*, 145; cf. J. Levy, J. Milgrom, H. Ringgren, and Heinz-Josef Fabry, עדה, *TDOT* vol. 10 (Grand Rapids: Eerdmans, 1999), 468–81, 472–73. On the concentration of the sacral and jurisdictional authority increasingly on the High Priest, the council of the twelve tribe leaders (נשיאם) and the "assembly" in the theocratic constitution of these late priestly layers, see Achenbach, *Vollendung*, 633. Barmash, *Homicide*, 88–89 with n. 62, however, suggests an early date of the term in Num 35.

124. עדה is typically used in priestly writings in Genesis–Numbers (129 out of 149 total references). Cocco, *Torah as Refuge*, 78, 113, associates the עדה with a secondary layer as he interprets their judicial authority as a supersession vis-à-vis earlier laws in that Num 35:12 requests any homicide to be judged by this assembly, rather than allowing the avenger of blood to potentially execute revenge. This institution as the representation of the local community under different circumstances naturally takes up the role of the elders in homicide law (Deut 19:1-12).

125. See Porten, *Elephantine Papyri*, 182–83 with n. 41, on Papyrus B 28:15, 26 (TAD B2.6; Cowley 15); in the case of a demotion of a spouse, this would be done in front of the congregation (בעדה), assuming a Hebrew loan word.

consisting of the בית אבות with their respective elders.¹²⁶ This collective body with a judicial function ("for judgment," למשפט, v. 12) differs from any comparable pre-exilic institution. In the priestly concept, it represents an authority that is comparable to the elders in other (earlier) contexts representing the community as a whole as an ideal-typical assembly around the אהל מועד under the leadership of the High Priest.¹²⁷ Practically, עדה primarily refers to the local assembly and their jurisdiction over kinship law¹²⁸ and when used with regard to the polity, it typically oscillates between a representation of the entire nation and the more tangible sense of a local congregation with judicial authority.¹²⁹

A classical element of kinship jurisdiction, this aligns with functions of the עדה in other matters. For instance, the oracular novella about the blasphemer, Lev 24:10-23, assigns agency for executing the stoning to "all the congregation" (vv. 13, 23). Likewise, the wood gatherer in Num 15:32-36 must be presented to the "entire congregation" (Num 15:33, 35, 36), which brings him into custody and sees the execution of the death sentence through stoning.¹³⁰ Earlier explanations have likened the entire congregation to an element of "primitive democracy," analogous to historical collectives that existed alongside Old Babylonian kingship,¹³¹ and Persian- or Hellenistic-period priestly law assigns the jurisdiction in

126. Gertz, *Gerichtsorganisation*, 146; J. P. Weinberg, "Das *beit 'ābōt* im 6.-4. Jh. v.u.Z.," *VT* 23 (1973): 400–414. Cocco, *Torah as Refuge*, 78, also points to the legislative and judicial functions. Numbers 1–2 creates a militaristic version of the עדה under the theocratic leadership of the High Priest, corresponding to the legal authority of this entity that Num 35 suggests. The houses of the fathers, a level below the עדה, are conceptualized as institutional entities holding important functions. See Est 4:2-3; 8:16-17, 29, with the modification שרי־האבות, 10:16; Neh 8:13; 10:15; cf. Num 36:1. See also Weinberg, "Das *beit 'abot*."

127. Whether this should be referred to as a "religious assembly" with a function beyond administrative duties of the elders, as described in the city of origin of the killer and in the cities of asylum (Deut 19:1-12), depends on the understanding of P at large.

128. See Levy, Milgrom, Ringgren, and Fabry, עדה, esp. 476; cf. also Barmash, *Homicide*, 89. Cf. the assumption of a local group made by Y. Kaufmann, with regards to Lev 24:10-13 and Num 15:32-36, as cases that needed to be decided locally and see on the evidence in Elephantine; Levy/Milgrom/Ringgren/Fabry, עדה, 469; R. Yaron, "Aramaic Marriage Contracts from Elephantine," *JSS* 3 (1958): 1–39, esp. 14-16. It is therefore hardly a programmatic element of a centralized adjudication of an asylum seeker's case as opposed to the elders of the slayer's local hometown (Deut 19:12); contra Stackert, *Rewriting*, 70.

129. This concept of jurisdiction under a High Priest (Num 17:16-26; cf. Achenbach, *Vollendung*, 126–28) is in tension with the concept of professional judges in Deuteronomy's ideal typical jurisdiction (Deut 16:18).

130. On the role of the assembly in Lev 24:10-23, see S. Chavel, *Oracular Law and Priestly Historiography in the Torah* (Tübingen: Mohr Siebeck, 2014), 65.

131. Cf. T. Jacobsen, "Primitive Democracy in Ancient Mesopotamia," *JNES* 2 (1943): 159–72. The discourse on the nature of the polity of Persian-period Yehud in comparison

homicide cases to the collective of Israelites.[132] In line with the theocratic notion of Num 25(26)–36, the collective's role in preventing a feud is an emancipatory act, arguably directed against a colonial power. If the slayer had entertained a long-term hateful relationship vis-à-vis his victim, persecuted him, and had publicly lived out this enmity, accordingly the congregation as a collective was qualified to decide about the slayer's relationship to his victim. The longevity and heritability of private enmity also suggest that such relationships were part of the collective memory and procedural details, such as the requirement for more than one witness in v. 30 further buttresses the congregation's forensic competence in the matter.

Joshua 20:6 and 9 offer the closest biblical parallels for an institutional role of the "congregation" in a homicide trial, with other cases referring to the congregation's judicial authority as executive organ pointing to the claim of ruling over matters of religious identity. These matters included the case of the stoning of a blasphemer in Lev 24:10-16, the transgression of Sabbath law in Num 15:32-36, as well as in the inheritance law of Num 27:2 and a typical conflict between the competing kin of the Reubenites and the Gadites about pasture land in Num 32:2. The latter two cases are classically covered by kinship jurisdiction. עדה as a term for congregation or for assembly may also refer to subdivisions of a general

---

with, for instance, Athenian democracy, is beyond the focus of this study. On popular participation for instance, see M. Van De Mieroop, "Popular Participation in the Political Life of the Ancient Near East," in *Der Alte Orient und die Entstehung der Athenischen Demokratie*, ed. C. Horst (Wiesbaden: Harrassowitz, 2020), 1–10. On the interpretation of Deuteronomy and its affinities to democracy, as well as Deuteronomy as the constitution of Persian-time Yehud, see, in the same volume, W. Oswald, "Die politischen Konzeptionen des Deuteronomiums als Teil des politischen Denkens der antiken Mittelmeerwelt," 55–68, here 57. Oswald's argument was inspired by the earlier discourses on the political concept of Deuteronomy by S. D. McBride, "Polity of the Covenant People: The Book of Deuteronomy," *Interpretation* 3 (1987): 229–244, then J. Berman, *Created Equal: How the Bible Broke with Ancient Political Thought* (Oxford: Oxford University Press, 2008), as well as B. M. Levinson's understanding of Deuteronomy as an "utopian model of community governance," anticipating the concept of a modern constitution in particular with the principle of an overarching rule of law and the separation of powers in distinct branches; B. M. Levinson, "The First Constitution: Rethinking the Origins of Rule of Law and Separation of Powers in Light of Deuteronomy," *Cardozo Law Review* 27 (2006): 1853–88, here 1857–58. Yet beyond Levinson's interpretation of Deuteronomy as a programmatic writing, Oswald, "Konzeptionen," 57, reads Deuteronomy as the constitution of Persian-period Yehud.

132. Other institutions of central leadership are beyond the scope of this study. For instance, Achenbach's first theocratic layer legitimizes the institution of Joshua as a much-needed military leader in Num 27:20, together with the High Priest Eleasar as a divinatory specialist in Num 27:12-23; that is, it legitimizes their leadership over the עדה and, ultimately, ensures Joshua's and the High Priest's leadership over the distribution of the land in Num 33:50-56; Achenbach, *Vollendung*, 557, 573.

assembly, and in the literary context it can designate the entirety of a polity while the literary source addresses only a fraction[133] rather than its entirety.

Casting a wider net and considering the asylum legislation of Num 35:9-34 in its larger legal historical contexts, its emphasis on the "assembly" is a claim of judicial authority over homicide cases that it relates to the local assembly of the individual cities.[134] The theocratic concept of Num 35 presents the local polity's claim of judicial authority in feuding as a genuinely kinship-related matter.[135] The context of the claim of the congregation's authority is particularly clear at a point in time when a centralized power would have limited its authority over areas of public life outside homicide legislation. Typically, a central empire's rule over kinship-based societies would not effectively claim to regulate conflict settlement between kin in cases of inheritance, marriage, and homicide law. Therefore, kinship-based mechanisms of conflict settlement and feud would assumedly have continued under Persian rule, alongside and in spite of the centralized forces of the Judean government.[136] Beyond the hypothetical historical development of asylum legislation in the late Persian[137] and Hellenistic periods, exile as a consequence of homicide in Num 35 is plausible.

133. See also the use of the rebellious followers of Korah in Num 16:5, 6, 11; Levy/Milgrom/Ringgren/Fabry, עדה, 476.

134. Whether Num 35, as it makes the case for the assembly's role as a judge and witness in homicide cases on the urban level, also mirrors an analogous scenario of contested judicial authority and of the administrative responsibility of asylum practice in seventh–fourth-century BCE Magna Graeca, requires further consideration. See, on the latter, J. Derlien, *Asyl. Die religiöse und rechtliche Begründung der Flucht zu sakralen Orten in der griechisch-römischen Antike* (Marburg: Tectum, 2003), 35. By nature, interm ests of individual *poleis* could collide with other hegemonial claims of, for instance, the Attic Maritime League, the Persian claim of territorial authority over Greek cities in Asia Minor, and the territorial claim of a Diadochi state in the mid-fourth century.

135. For the suggestion of a local character of the group, see Gertz, *Gerichtsorganisation*, 146.

136. Cf. Rofé, "Cities of Refuge," 219; D. A. Knight, *Law, Power, and Justice in Ancient Israel* (Louisville: Westminster John Knox, 2011), 71. For the conflicting claims of central governments to rule over kinship-based societies at other times, see, for instance, the ongoing feud in nineteenth-century Corsica among clans in a system that operated under a centralized colonial power. The parties would use the proceedings held in the courts of the French Republic as part of their feuding; see Wilson, *Feuding*. Wilson describes eight out of 57 places in Corsica based on documents on feuds from various geographical regions. Legal anthropology suggests that feuding societies throughout the ages would banish individuals during heated feuds that involved homicide so as to ensure social stability and to appease tension between the factions; see, for instance, Wilson, *Feuding*, 261–62, 292–93, 490 n. 73.

137. See, for instance, the reconstruction in Rofé, "Cities of Refuge," 236. He places a first stage (represented in Josh 20:1-3, 6*, 7-9; Num 35:9-15) at the beginning of the Judean monarchy and dates the second stage at the end of the sixth and in the fifth century.

5.3. The Local Congregation as Jury and עיר מקלט as "City of Refuge"

The programmatic claim of jurisdiction by the local "congregation" presents itself as part of the defense of the authority of a local kinship-based society against institutions of a centralized jurisdiction, and the legal-historical role of the עדה in this post-Hexateuchal redaction[138] becomes further apparent in the discourse on homicide jurisdiction of the local assembly in Num 35, namely in the idiosyncratic terminology "city of refuge."[139] The function of such cities is contextually clarified[140] with asylum cities in Num 35 offering temporary

The third stage, which assumes exile of the killer, he places at the end of the fifth or fourth century. Notably, examples for the exile of individuals from the city are found, for instance, in Ezra 7:26, with reference to banishment, confiscation of goods or imprisonment as punishment. These are not related to homicide, unlike 2 Sam 13:37-38 and 14:21, which speak to this asylum practice.

138. See above under section 1, and cf. Albertz, *Pentateuchal Redaction*, 221.

139. It has its only other derivative in the Hebrew Bible in Lev 22:23; here, קלוט has the meaning "withered, not fully developed"; W. Gesenius, 18th ed. Berlin: Springer 2013. More than half of the other 20 occurrences of the noun are found in Num 35; see Num 35:6, 11, 12, 13, 14, 15, 25, 26, 27, 28, 32; Josh 20:2, 3; 21:13 (2×), 21, 27, 32, 38; 1 Chr 6:42, 52. The LXX translates this term for asylum cities 14 times with φυγαδευτήριον; all instances in Num 35. Exceptions are 35:26 (verbal rendering); 35:27, 28: πόλεως καταφυγῆς; 25:32 εἰς πόλιν τῶν φυγαδευτηρίων. The use may deliberately avoid the Greek ἄσυλον, as is also the case in other authors in antiquity, such as Polybios; see K. J. Rigsby, *Asylia: Territorial Inviolability in the Hellenistic World* (Berkeley: University of California, 1996), 30. The LXX uses ἄσυλον twice only in Prov 22:23 with the meaning "to steal" and in 2 Macc 4:33 in the context of an asylum sanctuary in Daphne in Asia Minor. A third time the term ἀσυλία refers in 2 Macc 3:12 to the Jerusalem temple; cf. C. Dietrich, "Asylgesetzgebung in antiken Gesellschaften," in *Gesetzgebung in antiken Gesellschaften. Israel, Griechenland, Rom*, ed. L. Burckhardt, K. Seybold, and J. von Ungern-Sternberg (Berlin: de Gruyter, 2007), 193–219, here 195.

140. The term's etymology and its semantic core remain blurry. Derived from קלט I in Lev 22:23, it is translated with "to be too short, be stunted, underdeveloped," based on the occurrence in a merism with "too extended" (שׂרע). If related to the *hapax legomenon* קלט I, the meaning probably is "to be short, stunted, underdeveloped" (vs. to be long); on analogy, the noun would refer to a "short," i.e., a transitional place of refuge. Consequently, מקלט would denote "to provide short-term shelter." Yet the meaning in Lev 22:23 is uncertain due to lack of clear etymology; cf. Elliger, *Leviticus*, 291, 300. The first half of the LXX equivalent of Lev 22:23, κολοβόκερκον ("with a cut tail"), is phonetically remotely reminiscent of the Hebrew passive קלוט and poses the question whether the Hebrew term transliterates the Greek term; cf. H. R. Schmid, מקלט, *TDOT* 8 (Grand Rapids: Eerdmans, 1997), 552–56, here 552. Alternatively, L. Koehler and W. Baumgartner, *Hebräisches und aramäisches Lexikon zum Alten Testament*, vol. 3 (Leiden: Brill, 1983), 1030, derive from קלט II a meaning "to take up/in."

protection from the avenger of blood.[141] The writer of Num 35 may have coined מקלט for its use as a technical term in the judicial process of asylum in which the cities serve as long-term dwelling place for the asylum seeker.[142]

While the etymology remains unclear, parallels for a comparable conceptual level of refuge may be adduced. A close analogue to the asylum cities' function is the spatial terminology for refuge that the Psalms of the Individual prominently use when they refer to seeking refuge from accusation. The terms that these Psalms associate with Yahweh are "stronghold" (מעוז),[143] "safe heights" (משגב),[144] and "place of refuge" (מנוס/מחסה).[145] These metaphors have a spatial notion, yet arguably in their current context they denote virtual shelter associated with the deity.[146] The intrinsically passive protective notion is relevant for the interpretation of the spatial metaphors in Num 35 that *de facto* refer to situations of refuge in which a persecuted individual would refrain from taking further action against their opponent[147] and instead would seek shelter. In Num 35, beyond a

---

141. Num 35:12; cf. Josh 20:3; these same references, as well as 35:15, express the benefit offered by these cities in a situation of persecution (with the preposition ל); see, for instance, Clines, *The Dictionary of Classical Hebrew*, 467. The translation of LXX supports this meaning of πόλεις τῶν φυγαδευτηρίων (1 Chr 6:42, 52), a term used, among other passages, in Demosthenes 40.32, and *Against Boeotus* 2, for exile from the city.

142. Cf. also Cocco, *Torah*, 56.

143. The noun is used in a figurative "theological" sense; S. Wagner, עוז, *TDOT* 11 (Grand Rapids: Eerdmans, 2001), 1–11, here 10; on the interpretation of these references as metaphors for asylum, see, however, M. Löhr, *Das Asylwesen im Alten Testament* (Halle: Max Niemeyer, 1930), 209. Delekat subsequently offered an extensive interpretation which saw many Psalms being related to asylum; L. Delekat, *Asylie und Schutzorakel am Zionheiligtum: Eine Untersuchung zu den privaten Feindpsalmen* (Leiden: Brill, 1967), 11–39. However, see the criticism, for instance, of Barmash, *Homicide*, 81.

144. Used of Yahweh in a metaphorical sense; cf. H. Ringgren, שגב, *TDOT* 14 (Grand Rapids: Eerdmans, 2004), 34–36, here 36.

145. See the other lexicographic examples for rescue and shelter in, for instance, Dietrich, "Asylgesetzgebung," 195. For the figurative use of מחסה for god's protection, see J. Gamberoni, חסה, *TDOT* 5 (Grand Rapids: Eerdmans, 1986), 64–75, here 71.

146. The shelter metaphors have a particular notion to themselves. Psalms typically conceive of the hope for refuge as a form of ultimate justice associated with Yahweh, rather than with a triumph over an enemy as a result of an ongoing conflict. The supplicant's elusiveness that the spatial metaphors point out expresses practical shelter from opponents. The metaphors used for the fugitive are defensive and highlight the need for protection from accusation, rather than expressing intentional aggression against an opponent. They conceptualize the shelter as a space beyond and outside the reach of the atrocity individuals may endure from an opponent in a conflict and thus may suggest that the individuals seeking shelter foresee defeat in the near future.

147. Cf. the interpretation of Cocco, *Torah*, 57, 87; source-critically he limits its use to the secondary layer, 35:12, 16-29.

place, עיר מקלט refers to a social function in the polity. Cities of refuge are under the rule of the "assembly," including the decision on cases of homicide.[148]

5.4. Verses 25-29 as Regulatory Statutes

Numbers 35:25-29 function as regulatory statutes for the implementation of homicide legislation. After a brief description of the outline, the following limits itself to discussing the implications of these laws for the construct of long-term enmity with regard to first, their intention to dampen and to push back patterns of hot feud after the killer's return, and, second, to consider why these regulatory statutes envision in v. 28 that the matter be resolved and that the city of origin would allow for a return of the slayer to his place of origin.

Table 4.6

25 וְהִצִּילוּ הָעֵדָה אֶת־הָרֹצֵחַ מִיַּד גֹּאֵל הַדָּם וְהֵשִׁיבוּ אֹתוֹ הָעֵדָה אֶל־עִיר מִקְלָטוֹ אֲשֶׁר־נָס שָׁמָּה וְיָשַׁב בָּהּ עַד־מוֹת הַכֹּהֵן הַגָּדֹל אֲשֶׁר־מָשַׁח אֹתוֹ בְּשֶׁמֶן הַקֹּדֶשׁ:	25 and the assembly will save the killer from the hand of the avenger of blood. And they will send him back to the city of his refuge where he had fled to, and in her he will stay until the death of the High Priest who has been anointed with the holy oil.
26 וְאִם־יָצֹא יֵצֵא הָרֹצֵחַ אֶת־גְּבוּל עִיר מִקְלָטוֹ אֲשֶׁר יָנוּס שָׁמָּה:	26 Should the killer leave the bounds of the city of his refuge in which he has taken sanctuary
27 וּמָצָא אֹתוֹ גֹּאֵל הַדָּם מִחוּץ לִגְבוּל עִיר מִקְלָטוֹ וְרָצַח גֹּאֵל הַדָּם אֶת־הָרֹצֵחַ אֵין לוֹ דָּם:	27 and the avenger of blood encounter him outside the bounds of the city of his refuge, and the avenger of blood may kill without blood guilt,
28 כִּי בְעִיר מִקְלָטוֹ יֵשֵׁב עַד־מוֹת הַכֹּהֵן הַגָּדֹל וְאַחֲרֵי מוֹת הַכֹּהֵן הַגָּדֹל יָשׁוּב הָרֹצֵחַ אֶל־אֶרֶץ אֲחֻזָּתוֹ:	28 since the killer should stay in the city of his refuge until the death of the High Priest; only after the death of the High Priest is the killer free to go back to his own piece of property.
29 וְהָיוּ אֵלֶּה לָכֶם לְחֻקַּת מִשְׁפָּט לְדֹרֹתֵיכֶם בְּכֹל מוֹשְׁבֹתֵיכֶם:	29 Such will be the legal rule for you and your descendants, wherever you may live.

In this outline, v. 25 attaches the implementation rules with a consecutive perfect to the previous verse and presents them as a form of closure to vv. 16-24. Linking

---

148. Cf. also Cocco, *Torah*, 57.

v. 25 formally in this way demonstrates the legal effect of the preceding passage. Verses 25-28, 29 add a new aspect – the explicit reference to the space between the asylum city and the original dwelling place of the killer that were not a topic in the earlier law in which v. 29 functioned as closure.[149] The attached reflections (vv. 25b-28a) add another sub-case, namely the handling of the return of the killer to the city where he came from, after the death of the High Priest. Verse 26 reflects on the asylum seeker who leaves the town and his encounter with the avenger of blood (v. 27a) and his subsequent death (v. 27bα). The following declaration points out that this will not incur bloodguilt. Verse 28a adds as the rationale for this judgment the requirement for the killer to remain in the asylum city until the death of the high priest. The fact that the killer did not act accordingly is the underlying rationale for his bloodguilt. The historical backdrop of the title of the High Priest and the scarce use of this title suggest that in its current form, this verse did not originate before the time of the Diadochi.[150]

To what extent do these regulatory statutes of this priestly layer reflect the construct of long-term enmity? Clear evidence for the mechanisms of long-term enmity is to be found in the presupposed need for the expiation of the slayer, as it is grounded in the typical challenge and riposte requiring blood from the slayer's side. The regulatory statutes affirm the need for rectification and for pacification of a constellation of private long-term enmity. The implementation of these laws seeks to achieve reconciliation driven by their attempt to rectify hateful relationships in the community through the mechanism of the killer's asylum. Accordingly, true to their priestly categories, the laws respond to the blood guilt. Namely, in this priestly version of homicide law, the High Priest's death fulfills the need for blood in response to the killing in order to appease the clan of the victim.[151] The regulatory statutes affirm the need for blood in the sense that the death of the High Priest needed to be awaited in order to allow for the slayer's return. The High Priest's death functions as a vicarious life given for the slayer, and thus the priest's death would determine the point in time at which the release of the slayer would occur. This would allow the slayer to again live with his kin of origin.[152] This point in time would mark the end of the period for the slayer in

---

149. Cf. rightly Gertz, *Gerichtsorganisation*, 147.

150. Cf. Gertz, *Gerichtsorganisation*, 149, with the earliest datable references to the royal ointment of the High Priest in Sir 45:15; Dan 9:25-26; 2 Macc 1:10.

151. This is true even in cases of accidental homicide when asylum had been granted, in the line of thought of Gen 9:6. Rofé, "History of the Cities of Refuge," 144, also affirms the need for a sacrifice in response to the killing, suggesting, however, on the basis of Num 35:32, that in Deut 19 the clan of the slayer would, in his absence, arrange for a ransom to be paid to the clan of the victim in order to appease the situation.

152. This is the result of Whitekettle's examination of six classical explanations of the relevance of the priest's death: (1) the expiation explanation, which suggested that the priest died in expiation for the bloodguilt/impurity through the shedding of the killer's own blood, which would however be in tension with the evidence of Num 35:33 that the actual killer needed to be killed, and in tension with the fact that remedial procedures in case of

which the imbalance between the inadvertent killer and his victim ended.¹⁵³ The killer stays in confinement for the time period after the death of the victim until the death of the Priest, thus compensating for the death of the victim.

A second aspect, the heritability of enmity, illustrates how the construct of long-term enmity between slayer and victim informs this law.¹⁵⁴ Set in a kinship-based community, Num 35:25-29 envision that the matter be resolved at a certain point in time and suppose that this would allow for a return of the slayer to his place of origin, as v. 28 indicates. The phrase "to go back to his own piece of property" points to an ultimate reconciliation of the slayer with his opponent and the final return into the society whence the slayer came, leaving behind the pattern of long-term enmity between the two kin. This goal of an ultimate return into the community as a free citizen is analogous to the option for an indebted Israelite in Lev 25:40-41. His kinsman would redeem him in the Jubilee year from perpetual slavery so that, after the Jubilee year, he would become a free Israelite and fellow citizen. Both laws end with an almost literal parallel of the idea of a homecoming, framing it as "a return (שׁוּב) to his own (ancestral) property," an act that Num 35:25b announces to be initiated by the assembly (שׁוב hi.).¹⁵⁵ The ideal of a society of equally free citizens that live with each other in a peaceful society informs the notion of the killer's return after an accidental homicide without triggering the hateful aggression of a feud. Along the same line

---

impurity or offenses were *performed*, rather than being natural types of events, like death; (2) the time-period explanation, i.e., setting a time limit on the penalty duration; (3) the amnesty explanation of release of such things as debts, slavery, imprisonment, and exile that was granted by various ancient Near Eastern kings; (4) the pollutable local High Priest explanation; (5) a *paramone*-like relationship between High Priest and slayer, according to which one party would stay with the other for a specific period of time, potentially the remaining lifetime, and here the lifetime of the High Priest, to work for them and upon their death be sent home; (6) the Levitical bond explanation, based on the assumption that an inadvertent killer who by being granted asylum would then enter into a covenant with the tribe of Levi – the theory is that the High Priest's death would function as vicariously expiating for the bloodguilt of the slayer, who after this death had occurred, would return to his kin of origin; cf. R. Whitekettle, "Life's Labors Lost: Priestly Death and Returning Home from a City of Refuge in Ancient Israel," *HThR* 111 (2018): 333–56. See the interpretation in favor of the expiatory function of the High Priest's life to pay for the slayer's victim's life (in line with Gen 9:6; Num 35:33 as secondary insertion in H, as representative of the people before the Deity) in Stackert, *Rewriting*, 95, and in B. Schwartz, "Asylum," in *The Oxford Dictionary of Jewish Religion* ed. R. J. Z. Werblowsky and G. Wigoder (Oxford: Oxford University Press 1997), 77.

153. Whitekettle, "Life's Labors," 352.

154. On the principle of heritability and the call to vengeance as a dying injunction in Athens for instance, see Phillips, *Avengers*, 25–28, 65–68.

155. Cf. Lev 25:41: "he shall return to his own (ancestral) property." The correspondences between the Jubilee legislation in Lev 25 and Num 35 have been noted early on; see, for instance, Levine, *Numbers 21–36*, 565–71; see also Stackert, *Rewriting*, 89–90.

of thought, indentured slaves would eventually regain their freedom as citizens and free themselves from their economically caused hardship. The regulatory statutes thus envision a city inhabited by peacefully coexisting citizens that would overcome constellations of long-term enmity.[156]

Third and finally, Num 35:25-29 affirm the nature of long-term enmity because their complex regulation is only plausible if both clans subscribed to the principle of challenge and riposte beyond the life of the individuals immediately involved. The regulatory statutes of Num 35 specifically presuppose that the victim's kin share this understanding of the killer's expiation after the death of the High Priest.

5.5. *Asylum Cities as Places of Refuge in Classical Athens and in the Hellenistic Era*

Numbers 35 significantly varies the picture through both the use of abstract nouns for the slayer's motivation, and idiosyncratic terminology for asylum cities (ערי מקלט) as places of refuge. The terminology poses the question of whether it conceives of these cities of refuge upon analogy to other concepts of divine justice that are informed by a theocratic perspective. Did these cities claim local authority in a move to rebut other aspirations to power? And if so, does this suggest a dating of Num 35 in the late Persian or rather in the Hellenistic period? To answer the question whether the origin of Num 35 in the fourth or third century BCE as part of a long-standing biblical tradition on asylum is plausible, it may be helpful to clarify whether Num 35 must be seen in a discourse with legal concepts of Greek origin. Specifically, whether this priestly law may have been vaguely familiar with Hellenistic asylum practice, requires a brief consideration of Greek asylum law[157] and of the geographic extent of such practice.

---

156. The ideal of an ethical obligation to reconciliation in Num 35:25-29 comes close to what Joosten described for H and the implications of the holiness of the land, namely that the "entire territory settled by the Israelites…stands under the influence of the divine presence in the earthly sanctuary. Anyone established in the land, …must know that he lives in proximity to the sanctuary. He must therefore adapt his actions, his words and his thoughts to the holy presence of the God of Israel." Joosten, *People and Land*, 190.

157. Literary sources also provide evidence for asylum practices. Asylum forms the backdrop of such works of Attic drama as, for instance, Kassandra at the statue of Athena, the murder of Priamos, the Hiketides and the Oresteia; see the other examples offered by Dietrich, "Asylgesetzgebung," 200–202. Furthermore, evidence is also to be found in the scattered epigraphic acknowledgments from historians and epigraphic sources, from two main periods. First, the evidence for inviolability of a convicted unintentional killer suggests asylum for classical Greece in four cities, notwithstanding other questions, namely how the inviolability of a killer would be secured. In Elis, declared sacred after the Heracleidae returned to the Peloponnesus, the citizens could lead a sacred life as custodians of the Olympic games. The references are Ephorus, retold by Strabo; a different version by Diodorus; as well as general comments by Polybios; see Rigsby, *Asylia*, 41. Second, Delphi, with a sure *terminus ante quem* of 220 BCE for the Pythian Apollo's

First, several examples of refugees seeking asylum are extant, with one early example of a slave in a legal text from Gortyn.[158] Since the mid-fifth century BCE, cities could grant asylum.[159] References to asylum are found in homicide law from the time of Drakon; the killer would be guaranteed protection only as long as he did not leave the asylum place for walks along the border, to join the Panhellenic games, or to go to amphictyonic cities.[160] Exile is known as the punishment in a number of homicide cases. First, for unintentional homicide of

---

temple. The protected status of the temple is secured through Aeschines 3.109, with a reference to the oath of the cities of the Amphictyony to come to defend the temple should plunderers threaten it; see Rigsby, *Asylia*, 44. The access to the temple is acknowledged earlier in the Athenian–Spartan truce of 423 BCE from Thucydides 4.118.1. A similar unhindered access to the temple of Apollo and its "autonomy" was referred to in Thucydides 5.18.2 on occasion of the Peace of Nicias two years later; see Rigsby, *Asylia*, 45. While not granting "inviolability," the meaning of "autonomy" still remains opaque; a Roman letter from 189 BCE and a senatorial decree probably of 165 BCE refer explicitly to the inviolability ("asylum") of the temple; see Rigsby, *Asylia*, 46–47. The portraits of Delphi and Elis as cities that predominantly maintained their Panhellenic sanctuaries were, in the case of Delphi, already as early as 423 BCE, as the peace treaty suggests, associated with neutrality; Rigsby, *Asylia*, 48. Plataea's status is referred to in Thucydides 2.71, with the victorious Greeks promised the future security of the city that included "not to wage war unjustly or for enslavement"; their territory and city were autonomous and no one was to ever wage war against them; Rigsby, *Asylia*, 49. Delos' inviolability is attested through a promise of an agent of Xerxes not to harm the city in Herodotus 6.97, and it gains the aura of being the holiest of islands, without war, in Callimachos Hymns 4.275-280; Rigsby, *Asylia*, 51. Yet the evidence for the formal attestation of inviolability is scarce; only a law of 58 BCE by the Roman people includes a specific evocation of the cult of the Delian Apollo; Rigsby, *Asylia*, 52.

158. In a lawsuit on property right of a slave, from I Cret IV 41, IV, 6-VII, 19; cf. from I Cret IV 72 1,1 – II.2. XI, 24-25; see Dietrich, "Asylgesetzgebung," 197–99. Asylum in this case offers refuge and a safe space for a temple procedure. For asylum practice in Greece, see, among many others, Derlien, *Asyl*, 78–118. For potentially comparable cases of asylum seekers in the ancient Near East, including runaway slaves, artisans, military and civil detainees, see A. Altman, "On Some Basic Concepts in the Law of People Seeking Refuge and Sustenance in the Ancient Near East," *ZABR* 8 (2002): 323–42.

159. Another example that illustrates the variety of facets of this institution is the granting of asylum through the citizenship of a polis to foreigners, individuals and groups, as this is attested for tradesmen, merchants, athletes, academics, guests of the state (*proxenoi*) and in sister-city arrangements for mutual asylum of citizenship in particular in the Hellenistic period; Derlien, *Asyl*, 121.

160. Inscriptiones Graecae I² 115 = IG I³ 104, l. 26-29, 409/408 BCE; quoted from P. Sanchez, *L'amphictionie des Pyles et de Delphes. Recherches sur son rôle historique, des origines au IIe siècle de notre ère* (Stuttgart: Franz Steiner, 2001), 53. On homicide legislation in Athens after Drakon, see MacDowell, *Homicide*, 48–57, 117–25.

a citizen in Athenian law, judged at the Palladion, the penalty was exile,[161] but the victim's kin could pardon the killer if the killing was unintentional. Second, when the killer could demonstrate that he had killed lawfully,[162] in the trial (held at the Delphinion), the decision depended on two factors: the status of the victim, on the one hand, and the intent of the killer, on the other. Intentional killing of a non-citizen led to exile: unintentional homicide led to exile, with the possibility of pardon[163] and the subsequent need to provide for such conditions in asylum cities.

In the Hellenistic era, territorial inviolability applied to eight sanctuaries and cities in Boeotia,[164] as well as eight cases in Greece proper.[165] A wider geographic overview on territorially guaranteed inviolability for refugees in thirty-six other cities, along with places in Cilicia, Phoenicia and Syria, Palestine (Ashkelon, Gaza, Sepphoris, Caesarea-Panias, Joppa, Raphia, Jerusalem), the Decapolis (Gadara, Abila, Capitolias, Antioch by Hippus, Nysa-Scythopolis, Gerasa), Egypt and Rome.[166]

For the discourse on the distinction between temples and cities of refuge in biblical law, the epigraphic evidence from Hellenistic times may be relevant, namely the fact that epigraphic sources by and large do not distinguish between the inviolability of the temple proper as distinct from the entire city.[167] The main point was the slayer's inviolability, while the exact territorial extension of the

---

161. Phillips, *Avengers*, 59–60.

162. For instance, in an athletic contest, in self-defense of a highway-robber, by friendly fire, or in self-defense against a man caught with one's wife in bed.

163. Phillips, *Avengers*, 60. In the case of homicide committed while already in exile, the case was tried at the Phreatto in the Peiraeus from boats moored ashore; the criteria were the same as in the cases tried by the Delphinion.

164. The first decree of inviolability, extant on stone, was related to the temple of Athena Itonia in the 260s BCE by the amphictyony of Delphi; Rigsby, *Asylia*, 55; seven more cases include the temple of Apollo Ptoius in the territory of Acraephia, first attested in 220 BCE; Rigsby, *Asylia*, 59.

165. An uncertainty is that the majority of them are found in a list by Plutarch of inviolable temples attacked by pirates from Cicilia: Epidaurous, Calaureia, Taenarum, Hermione, Nicopolis, as well as Athens and Dodona, the temple of Artemis in Lusi; Rigsby, *Asylia*, 85.

166. Rigsby, *Asylia*, 95–574.

167. That both city and temple were considered inviolable is susbstantiated through the diplomatic procedures attested from certain Greek cities in the Aegean from 260–180 BCE, which seemingly sought through their sacred ambassadors to obtain the Panhellenic recognition of inviolability in honor of their main divinity. The procedure, the vocabulary and the envoys sent to make the petition in all these cases seem to be identical and the specific territory of the inviolability is seemingly irrelevant. See Rigsby, *Asylia*, 20.

protection was secondary. This sheds light on the discussion about the transition from altar to city asylum Num 35.[168]

For local asylum practice in Judah the epigraphic evidence of third-century BCE Egyptian material may be particularly relevant. While declaring a city as "inviolable" was generally understood to be a religious honor, it was considered the Ptolemaic state's privilege that it would, in an internal process, decide to grant the status of inviolability.[169]

The result of this digression into the dating of the origin of asylum law in Num 35 by nature remains tentative, as it is based on the isolated parallel discourse on asylum cities in the Hellenistic period that would not exclude an earlier date. Yet, when considering a tentative third-century BCE date of this (priestly) layer in Num 35[170] it makes sense to read it specifically against the backdrop of the colonial power's autonomy of declaring asylum places under Ptolemaic rule. The command of installing asylum cities would then have been an emancipatory, if not rebellious, act of Judah. The theocratic bias of this particular layer in Numbers lends itself to the interpretation of the declaration of asylum cities along the lines of an act of authority or as an openly declared resistance against the colonializing power of Ptolemaic Egypt.[171]

6. Reception History (Deuteronomy 4; Joshua 20)

The preceding analysis of homicide law in Num 35 has illustrated both a substantial development in legal thought proper on homicide and has also more precisely shown the historical context of this version of homicide law. The construct of long-term hate between two opponents continues to inform biblical

---

168. Notably, the actual practice of asylum may have been more diverse, since a standardized terminology of ἄσυλον or ἱερὸς καὶ ἄσυλος for the city and for its land is only attested in the third century BCE. See Rigsby, *Asylia*, 20. The first surviving declaration of a city rather than a temple (though the city was not yet independent from the temple) is known from Smyrna in the 240s BCE, while the formula "City and country sacred and inviolable" is first encountered about two decades later in 221 BCE Magnesia and potentially a little earlier at Miletus; see Rigsby, *Asylia*, 20. Cf. also Otto, *Deuteronomium 12:1–23:15*, referring to the grove of Phoibos Apollo (*Odyssey* 9.200-201), and Sinn, "Greek Sanctuaries."

169. Not, as in other cases, by Panhellenic recognition; the first Ptolemaic declaration dates from 96 BCE; Rigsby, *Asylia*, 21.

170. See on the source-criticism above in this chapter, section 1.

171. I. F. Baer and A. Rofé have both suggested an extended period of exile as punishment for a killer in Num 35 to be a result of the influence of the late Persian Empire's administrative law; see Rofé, "Cities of Refuge," 238, with reference to Greek influence on the ethics as suggested by I. F. Baer, "The Historical Foundations of the Halacha," *Zion* 7 (1952): 1–55, esp. 13–17.

law beyond Deut 19. In homicide cases an ongoing malevolence of the killer remains of major relevance as a reason for denial of asylum. Numbers 35:20-21 use the nouns "hatred" or "enmity." For the purpose of this study, the juxtaposition between Num 35, Deut 4, and Josh 20 demonstrates the distinctions in the use of the key term "hatred" throughout homicide law. Homicide regulation and asylum law in Deut 4 derive their criteria for categorizing homicide from Deut 19:4b. They reiterate the two criteria, "without knowledge" and "without having hated him ever since," which Josh 20:3, 5 also take up. The three asylum cities east of the Jordan are reported to have been installed by Moses. Deuteronomy 4 retrospectively remembers their installation, yet differently from Deut 19. This retrospective has redaction-historically been seen as a late addition to Deuteronomy. It testifies to the paramount relevance of asylum legislation in the Second Temple period and to the fundamental character of the concept of an enmity ethos.[172]

Table 4.7

Deut 4:41-42

| אָז יַבְדִּיל מֹשֶׁה שָׁלֹשׁ עָרִים בְּעֵבֶר הַיַּרְדֵּן מִזְרְחָה שָׁמֶשׁ: לָנֻס שָׁמָּה רוֹצֵחַ אֲשֶׁר יִרְצַח אֶת־רֵעֵהוּ בִּבְלִי־דַעַת וְהוּא לֹא־שֹׂנֵא לוֹ מִתְּמֹל שִׁלְשׁוֹם וְנָס אֶל־אַחַת מִן־הֶעָרִים הָאֵל וָחָי: | Then Moses set apart three cities across the Jordan to the east, that a manslayer might flee there, who unknowingly slew his neighbor: but he had not been hating him from ever since —and by fleeing to one of these cities, he might live. |

Deuteronomy 4:41-42[173] tangentially relates the establishment of a total of six cities of refuge in Josh 20 by Joshua and secures Moses' preeminence in

---

172. The verse is inserted into a larger context, introduced with the אז, "then," cf. late Dtr insertions in Josh 8:30; 22:1, after an instruction in the second person and placed before the laws and headings in 4:44-49 that also talk of Moses in the third person.

173. The passage in vv. 41-43 is found in the mainly parenetic material in chs. 4 and 5–11. Deuteronomy 4 is seen as an addition of the post-dtr Pentateuch editors; E. Otto, "Deuteronomy," in *RPP*, ed. Betz, Browning, Janowski, vol. 3 (Leiden: Brill, 2007), 786–88, esp. 788. Verses 41-43 precede in the current text two introductory formulas in 4:44 and 4:45, the latter with parallels in 6:1 and 12:1. The short passage exhibits a disjunctive grammar. The three verses are added with אז + imperfect, which indicates an unspecific chronological connection with a previous point in time; this form is indicative of later attachments; cf. Deut 22:1; Josh 8:30. The other reason to assume its genesis after 19:3-7 is the lack of reference in 19:3-7 to 4:41-43; for the late character, see Nelson, *Deuteronomy*, 71–72.

establishing cities of refuge. The references to the tribes' land east of the Jordan (Deut 3:12-20) triggered the reference to Moses' establishment of the cities of refuge. The secondary character of the passage and its condensed format demonstrate the key themes of asylum law. At its core is a homicide that occurred in the community (רצח) and the subsequent flight of the accidental manslayer. The flight of the slayer uses two criteria: on the one hand, the paramount criterion literally quotes 19:4, including the use of the participle. Furthermore, on the other hand, Deut 4:41 adds the negative clarification – "without knowledge" or "intent" – and Josh 20:5 uses the same idiom. This demonstrates the emphasis on the lack of intention with the same semantics as in Deut 19:1-13, namely the use of שנא, which is critical for the reception history. Deuteronomy 4 carries the notion that the manslayer would live in the asylum city, as the additions in Num 35:25-34 also suggest.

Joshua 20:1-9 begins with a Yahweh-speech with the command to Joshua to install asylum cities and with a reference to Moses (vv. 1-3). The asylum procedure follows in vv. 4-6. Verse 7 reports the execution of the selection of three cities west and east of the Jordan v. 8 and a summary concludes in v. 9. Source-critically, Joshua 20 appears to be a composite, depending on legal material from Num 35, and also picking up on elements from deuteronomic language. One way to synthesize the redactional process was to assume a basic layer in the tradition of Num 35:9-15 and 25-34 that was edited in deuteronomic language with a basic layer in Josh 20:1-3*, 6aαb, 7-9, and an addition of an editor in the style of Deuteronomy in vv. 4-5, 6aβγ.[174] The basic layer is virtually identical with the text of LXX[B].

For the tradition-historical roots of the legal construct of continuous private enmity in Josh 20 it is critical that one idiom is inspired by Deut 19, "without knowledge/unaware" (בבלי דעת), an idiosyncratic addition in v. 3, also used in v. 5, that counts as additions in Deuteronomy's style.[175] Meanwhile the idiom בשגגה in v. 3 is from Num 35:11b, 15b. As pointed out above, this noun designates a spectrum between the notion of "unwittingly," and in a vague sense "tragically," reflecting on the destiny of the slayer rather than the legal criteria for entitlement of asylum. Joshua 20 thus combines this notion of an "inadvertent" act with a focus on procedural aspects and the development of legal thought that defines enmity more clearly as a long-term legal construct.

---

174. For instance, "and he shall flee into one of these cities" in v. 4 is from Deut 19:5b, 11; v. 5aα's "and the avenger of blood pursues him" is inspired by Deut 19:6a. See Gertz, *Gerichtsorganisation*, 152, 154.

175. Gertz, *Gerichtsorganisation*, 154.

Table 4.8

Josh 20:3

לָנוּס שָׁמָּה רוֹצֵחַ מַכֵּה־נֶפֶשׁ בִּשְׁגָגָה בִּבְלִי־דָעַת וְהָיוּ לָכֶם לְמִקְלָט מִגֹּאֵל הַדָּם:	In order that the killer who in inadvertence, unknowingly slew a soul, that he would have shelter from the avenger of blood.

Josh 20:5

וְכִי יִרְדֹּף גֹּאֵל הַדָּם אַחֲרָיו וְלֹא־יַסְגִּרוּ אֶת־הָרֹצֵחַ בְּיָדוֹ כִּי בִבְלִי־דַעַת הִכָּה אֶת־רֵעֵהוּ וְלֹא־שֹׂנֵא הוּא לוֹ מִתְּמוֹל שִׁלְשׁוֹם:	Now if the avenger of blood pursues him, then they shall not deliver the killer into his hand, because he struck his neighbor unknowingly and he did not hate him from ever since.

These terms reflect the notion of an abstract, distinctly defined legal concept, namely the status of private enmity between two opponents. An opponent "in enmity" would be expected to act in a particular way.

The reception history of biblical law takes up the construct of long-term hatred and its relevance when it decides between intended homicide versus spontaneous killing, as Philo illustrates.[176] Philo's passage on the legal relevance of a spontaneously developing private enmity and an injury which caused a death refers to Exod 21:18-19. The concern for the escalation between both opponents is not so much for the enemy's harm, rather than a potential escalation into a blood feud. This is central to Deut 19:1-13 too, pointing from the perspective of Deuteronomy's cult centralization to the need for asylum cities close enough for a person to flee into exile after a homicide.

7. Conclusion

The analysis of homicide and asylum law in Num 35 has yielded results on different levels. On the one hand, it has revealed the development of legal thought through a plethora of new categories, in particular through the development of abstract terminology for the status of long-term private enmity. On the other hand, it was possible to illustrate in more detail than for CC and Deut 19 how the historical context of asylum cities in the Hellenistic era would shape the content of this law.

---

[176]. Philo, *De Specialibus Legibus* 3:104-107; cf. Jackson, *Wisdom-Laws*, 175, and see above, Chapter 2, sections 5.3; 9.3.

The core of the asylum regulation in Num 35:15-25a* largely follows Deut 19. Grounded in the tradition of priestly law, this legal collection generates its own lexicography that is remarkably independent from Deut 19 and from Exod 21:12-14. It does not use the idiomatic "from ever since," from Deut 19, but excludes long-term enmity of the slayer with phrases such as he "has not sought his evil." Verse 23b thus points out that the homicide happened unplanned, suddenly (v. 22a), or inadvertently, without seeing (v. 23a). It perceives "enmity" and "hate" as an abstract social status using these nouns and referring to the game of challenge and riposte between opponents as "pursuit." Located in its cultural context, Num 35 also introduces refined categories for the material of the tool known from laws on intentional wounding. The notion of unwittingly committed homicide with, in a vague sense, tragic consequences shifts the focus from a traditional strictly legal distinction to the slayer's destiny. Embedding homicide and asylum legislation in a theocratic concept of priestly Judaism, Num 35 points to the jurisdiction of the local community's assembly or congregation as עדה in matters of homicide law, establishing it as an institution that decides over blood guilt and cases of long-term enmity and intentional homicide in Judean cities under late Persian or Ptolemaic authority. In its claim of jurisdiction over homicide cases for the assembly, Num 35 includes metics and settlers, thus taking seriously the involvement of members of these groups in conflicts.

This study has set out to define the status of private enmity as a social construct in biblical law in CC, Deuteronomy, and in priestly law in Num 35. The laws on homicide and asylum hitherto analyzed have pointed toward an ongoing interest of biblical law in this status and they have also demonstrated how this status of personal enmity is an integral construct of kinship-based societies and shapes modes of conflict settlement. The analysis of Num 35 has in particular demonstrated the historical context of the legal category of private enmity and hate in late Persian and Hellenistic time Judah.

In light of the precise historical framework and the conceptual notions of priestly concepts, in what follows two more texts complement this study on different levels. First, with regard to the interpretation of the legal status of enmity as a social construct that relates to kinship-based law, it can be expected that it would be relevant beyond the selected laws this study so far has considered. The following chapter therefore includes a brief analysis of Ezek 22:6-12 as a side-text to the list of prohibitives in Lev 19:11-18. Second, the lexicography of the law in Num 35 demonstrates the extent to which this law defines the status of private enmity as a social construct as well as its relevance as a legal term. The reflection on private enmity in abstract terms, i.e., as a defined status in legal thought, poses the question of whether, by the same token, its opposite, the status of private friendship or love, likewise was understood as a social construct with well-defined legal implications. The analysis of marriage law in Deuteronomy has already shown the legal relevance of the two social constructs of "love" and "hate"; in addition, the former also designates the default attitude between members of a kin. A prominent law that also explicitly reflects on these two social constructs of "hate" and "love/friendship" is Lev 19:17-18. The following chapter will thus leave the framework of homicide law used in Chapters 2–4 and will more fundamentally reflect on the social status of enmity and friendship. It asks whether the social status of the latter can also be defined, and determines its particular historical and literary-historical background in H. The perspective on "hate" and "love/friendship" as complementary social constructs will demonstrate the legal relevance of the particular notions of mutual hate or benevolence and their legal implications in the context of a kinship-based society. As was the case in Num 35, the legal-historical and the historical contexts of this legal discourse (Lev 19:11-18) will prove to be a decisive factor for the specific composition of this prohibitive list.

Chapter 5

BROTHERLY LOVE IN LEVITICUS 19:11-18

1. *Brotherly Love*

In a plethora of laws that range from CC to Deuteronomy and to the priestly realm, the fundamental impact of feuding on a kinship-based society has become evident. Above all, Deuteronomic and priestly homicide law has demonstrated the impact of long-term private hate between opponents. The analysis of Deut 19 and of Num 35 could also trace the consistent elements and the development of the social construct of long-term private enmity. The comparative approach to homicide law in CC, Deuteronomy, and Numbers thus yielded a nuanced picture of the ways in which homicide legislation increasingly refines not only the legal ramifications of this social status but also affects its very essence. Deuteronomic law in particular highlights this status' longevity to which likely already the relational term רע (Exod 21:14) in CC hints. Numbers 35 rethink the status of two opponents with abstract terms for enmity, hate, and malicious intent in the corresponding asylum procedure. From a legal anthropological perspective, it is clear that in a kinship-based society, hateful interactions between individuals by nature would easily spiral out of control into a feud that would cause major social damage. Homicide legislation's pacifying tendency is best explained against the fear of such developments and thus makes plausible the fundamental relevance of private enmity in legal thought. In light of its longevity and its damage, the danger of the outbreak of a feud typically would peak in homicide cases and altogether it constitutes a prominent concern in kinship-based societies. The preceding analysis of homicide law shows these societies' increasing attention to clarifications of the state of affairs and their processes for refining the exact criteria for the eligibility of asylum. It has also revealed their attention to legal practice, including implementing regulations. Already Exod 21:18-19 carefully weigh the need for compensation for pain and injuries suffered and for medical treatment, so as to rule out that the hurt party would request excess of injury award. The law on nocturnal theft in Exod 22:1-2a is an example for the careful deliberation of the difference between spontaneous revenge with its exclusion of any time lapse that would allow for planned vengeful response on one hand and a delayed response that would be perceived as beyond sheer spontaneous self defense and thus bear in itself a typical pattern of long-term enmity on the other hand. Other aspects of distinction are the increasing attention to intentionality as the main criterion in injury law, for instance, in Num 35. Yet these laws focus not only on theoretical clarifications of criteria of homicide laws. Asylum laws in Deut 19 and Num 35 concentrate on implementation regulations, including details such as the accessibility of places of refuge as asylum cities. Deuteronomy 19 and Num 35 also conscientiously point to the blood avenger's significance as the kin's executive of revenge and the role of the elders as supervisors and trustees in the process of granting entitlement to asylum. Priestly tradition beyond Num 35 reflects in many ways on the long-term status of opponents in the public square as the present chapter will point out.

These analyses of Deut 19 and Num 35 specify not only the distinct versions of the concept of long-term enmity as pivotal to legal thought on conflict settlement, they also illustrate the interplay between the conceptual framework of the social constructs that inform law collections and, on the other hand, the execution of homicide legislation in specific historic contexts. A case in point, Deut 19:1-12 develops long-term "hate" as a category in a legal system rooted in a fictive kinship-ethos. The law defines private enmity on an ethical level as a mode of interaction that contrasts brotherly benevolence and shapes typical patterns of interaction in a kin group as mutual love. Deuteronomy 19 develops this conceptual background of mutual hate as a behavioral pattern in distinction from behavioral patterns of mutual love and as part of a strategy to re-constitute an urban community in Judah.

The analysis of the constructs of hate and friendship and their decisive modes of action at specific moments in the history of Judah is an essential result of this study. It demonstrates the interface between the historical context that informs Deut 19 and its intention of claiming authority for elders as kinship-based institution in conflict settlement, including homicide in a late seventh-century law and in its subsequent contexts.[1] Generally speaking, homicide law would strengthen genuine kinship institutions and it would assert the responsibility of established kinship-based modes of conflict settlement. At the same time, homicide law as legislation was deeply molded in a particular socio-historical context, as the analysis of Deut 19 and Num 35 has pointed out. Homicide and asylum laws in Num 35 systematically ascertain and strengthen kinship-based institutions such as the avenger of blood and the elders as established leaders of their kin. This includes in this historical context also the aim of priestly circles to claim jurisdiction over these cases under the Ptolemies as colonial suzerains. Subscribing to a theocratic ideal, Num 35 promotes the institutions of asylum cities and avengers of blood as key players in conflict settlement, emboldening the authority of

---

1. In this study, the source-critical and literary historical contexts of homicide law Deut 19 has followed the tradition's renewal of homicide legislation from Deut 19 to Deut 4:41-43 and Josh 20, which demonstrates the continuing interest in self-adjudication in multiple historical Second Temple Judah contexts.

Judean cities as polities in which homicide adjudication includes an anti-colonial move.² Homicide and asylum law in Num 35 illustrate the specific institutions of kinship-based law in their relevance in this law's socio-historical contexts. At the same time, Num 35 is grounded in priestly legal tradition. These results contribute to a complex picture of the development of legal institutions and legal thought in Judah beyond any unilinear assumption of a replacement of kinship-based law through centralistic institutions of jurisdiction.

The present chapter continues to focus on the interdependence between homicide legislation as part of the development of legal thought and as embedded in a specific historical context. It considers aspects of the motivation in the list of prohibitives in Lev 19:11-18, thus widening the scope to the most prominent source associated with love and hate in biblical ethics.

This chapter on Lev 19:11-18 argues on four levels. First, it carries on the historical contextualization of Num 35 as it unpacks the meaning of Lev 19:11-18

---

2. The socio-historical backdrop of the construct of private enmity as conceptually deeply embedded in kinship-based societies and in biblical law becomes more apparent in a comparative perspective. In particular, it may benefit from scholarship on private enmity as a construct in Athenian law. The recent discourses on Attic forensic oratory have demonstrated the relevance of private enmity as a construct for conflict settlement and trial procedure. The extent to which conflict-settlement procedure reflects feuding principles rather than "the rule of law" was clearly established by MacDowell's 1963 ground-breaking study on homicide: D. M. MacDowell, *Athenian Homicide Law in the Age of the Orators* (Manchester: Manchester University Press 1963), 141–50. This work suggests that the treatment of homicide in Attic law has emphasized three areas of its relevance: first, it sought to deter anti-social behavior; second, beyond mere compensation for other offences, murder additionally called for vengeance; finally, homicide had contaminating effects that law had to take into account. The role of the next of kin may not be underestimated. Homicide remained a private matter in Athens, which is evident in the ideal procedure, namely that the next of kin would ideally bring the *dikē phonou* on the dead man's behalf; cf. Todd, *The Shape of Athenian Law*, 272–73. In more detail, the private nature of the conflict after homicide has been pointed out in particular in Christ, *The Litigious Athenian*, 160–93, and Cohen, *Law*, 37 and passim.

For biblical law, a systematic examination of the record of the relevance of feuding as a mechanism of private enmity in kinship-based societies would be more complex. While it is clear that feuding patterns play a pivotal role, the specifics need to be historically distinguished for ancient Israel and Judah and Mesopotamia. Consider for instance, explicit references to challenges of oaths that illustrate that in Mesopotamian law evidence under oath would have been seen as partial. This seems to be the case in a re-evaluation of the proof of evidence and of the specific evaluation of judicial oaths in the Neo-Babylonian and Persian periods. Courts began to consider evidence that would contradict and would take precedence over statements given under oath. Analogous aspects of a rationalization of forensic thought has been applied to Deuteronomic law in Judah; cf. B. Wells, "The Cultic Versus the Forensic: Judahite and Mesopotamian Judicial Procedures in the First Millennium B.C.E.," *JAOS* 128 (2008): 205–32, here 213, 217.

as a prominent side piece of this late priestly law. In doing so, it seeks to deconstruct the status of mutual long-term hate between opponents as seen through the lens of priestly law of H in its manifestation in the long list of prohibitives in Lev 19:11-18.

Second, conceptually, it moves beyond the isolated consideration of the construct of private hate and enmity and points to the status of mutual benevolence as a complementary social construct. This heuristic approach has already been fruitful in Deuteronomic marriage law and when applied to Priestly law in Lev 19 it more fully unpacks the contrast between benevolent or hateful interaction between individuals.

Thirdly, rather than presenting an isolated analysis of Lev 19:11-18, this chapter considers the passage in its larger literary and conceptual contexts. Neighborly benevolence or love are pivotal categories that are best explained in their specific contexts in the history of the source-critical analysis in H. The present chapter on Lev 19 therefore casts wider the net, briefly considering this chapter within Lev 17–26 and, furthermore, it considers the internal development of the long prohibitive row that culminates in neighborly love. As will be seen, a number of side texts are essential, in particular, the Decalogue as a row of prohibitives that is formally closely related and also exhibits a pivotal thematic cross-reference (1.2), namely the verb חמד ("to covet") as an expression for the ongoing malevolent intent of begetting.[3] This offers additional perspectives and further substantiates the relevance of private hate in Lev 19:11-18. Besides these textual traditions a number of themes from the tradition-historical framework of Lev 19 require attention, namely the exodus, the perspective of small landownership, and H's pronounced alterity ethos (1.3.1) Second, a reflection on hate and conflict settlement in the context of patriarchal and communal authority briefly embeds Lev 19:11-17 thematically in H along these lines (1.3.2) and then unfolds the larger theme of brotherly benevolence in the contours of the polity that H envisions (1.3.3). The close analysis of 19:11-18 thirdly demonstrates in detail the understanding of this passage as a climactically arranged reflection on forms of mutual hate and benevolence.

Finally (4), this chapter clarifies the command to love your neighbor/companion in religious-historical, ethical and in historical contexts of the Second Temple period.

Leviticus 19:11-18 presupposes the legal ramifications of hate between community members when it refers to long-term enmity as the distinct status of mutual benevolence or friendship. The final verse pair of the prohibitive list in vv. 17-18 juxtaposes the behavioral opposites of enmity, "hate" and friendship, "love." The following seeks to determine the legal and social background of the command to adopt a posture of mutual benevolence toward fellow community members in Lev 19:11-18. It provides an introduction to the composition of Lev 19, to the context of H, and comments on the prohibitive row. An outlook

---

3. Cf. above Chapter 2, section 9.2.

assesses the posture of mutual friendship against the backdrop of rules for religious associations.

In anticipation of the results one main achievement of this study is its historical and religious-historical analysis, namely the community specific context for the passage Lev 19:11-18 (4.2). Second, the analysis and the backdrop of the side texts in the Decalogues and Ezek 22:6-12 demonstrate in more breadth and detail the relevance of private enmity for the ethos of biblical Judaism. This is particularly evident in the preferential form of prohibitives and in the thematic focus on private enmity, a result that sheds new light on the ubiquitous opponent as a theme in the Psalms of the Individual, which substantiates that this topic is at the heart of Jewish biblical ethics.

1.1. *The Composition of Leviticus 19:11-18*

Determining the meaning of the prohibitive rows with their culmination in universal benevolence requires reading them in the thematic contexts of H. Furthermore, the prohibitive row's compositional function in Lev 19 requires attention as it anchors this passage's meaning within its source-critical origin. These steps will contribute to clarifying this passage's current and its hypothetically retrieved previous religious-historical context.

When read in isolation, Lev 19:11-18 are a list of mostly prohibitives that, generally speaking, culminate in the command to urge a disposition of benevolence (love) rather than mutual malevolence (hate) among fellow community members (vv. 17-18). This culminating contrast between love and hate is how this passage is mostly referenced as a part of biblical ethics. This final command to exercise mutual benevolence is in line with the pacifying tendency found to be typical for injury and homicide law. Yet at the same time this final command of neighborly love supersedes preceding laws in its breadth and in its nearly unqualified universality of the "companion/neighbor" as object. The seemingly universal pacifying notion of this passage justifies an in-depth analysis of the backdrop of this prohibitive row's context in priestly law in the literary composition of H, namely it requires clarification about the specific context in which this law mirrors such a wholesale rejection of the destructive dynamic of the feuding patterns as the consequence of long-term enmity. The integration of this piece in its current literary context, namely already the outline and the form of vv. 11-18, corroborate the fundamental tone of this voice. Kept in the form of prohibitives like the Decalogues,[4] Lev 19:11-18 in its compositional context exhibits its function as a central apodictic passage and as a counterpart to the apodictic passage vv. 26-32. Leviticus 19 is a diptych composed of two symmetrically arranged panels. Each of these panels consists of an introductory, a general exhortation to holiness (vv. 2aβb, 19aα) and a sequel of three commands:

(a) fundamental prescriptions: Sabbath, idolatry (vv. 3-4); the prohibition of mixtures (vv. 19aβ, γ, b);

---

4. See below, sections 1.2 and 1.3.3.

(b) casuistic laws: sacrifice (vv. 5-8); gleaning of fields (vv. 9-10); sacrifice (vv. 20-22); harvesting of trees (vv. 23-25);

(c) other mixed prescriptions: the benevolence toward fellow community members (vv. 11-18); and corresponding prescriptions of cultural separation (vv. 26-32). A summary exhortation to keep and practice all statutes and ordinances in v. 37 concludes Lev 19.[5]

Table 5.1

Part I	Part II
general exhortation to holiness: *I am Yahweh your God (2×)* vv. 2aβ, b	transition to new exhortation: *Keep my statutes!* v. 19aα
(a) fundamental prescriptions: parents Sabbath prohibition of apostasy, idolatry vv. 3-4	(a′) fundamental prescription: prohibition of mixtures v. 19aβ, γ, b
(b) casuistic laws: sacrifice vv. 5-8 gleaning fields; leaving harvest vv. 9-10	(b′) casuistic laws: sacrifice vv. 20-22 gleaning trees; leaving harvest vv. 23-25
(c) other prescriptions: benevolence toward fellow-community members vv. 11-18	(c′) other prescriptions: cultural separation vv. 26-32 benevolence toward the metic vv. 33-34 benevolence/fairness in trade vv. 35-36a Exodus from Egypt v. 36b
Concluding exhortation: *keep and practice all my statutes and all my ordinances!* v. 37	

---

5. This outline was first proposed by E. Otto, "Das Heiligkeitsgesetz Leviticus 17–26 in der Pentateuchredaktion," in *Altes Testament. Forschung und Wirkung: Festschrift H. Graf Reventlow*, ed. P. Mommer and W. Thiel (Frankfurt am Main: Lang, 1994), 65–80, here 73, and again in Otto, *Ethik*, 245–46; cf. Nihan, *Priestly Torah*, 461–62. See the discussion of other outlines of Lev 19, in Mathys, *Liebe*, 71–77, and Barbiero, *L'asino*. Alternative proposals for an outline include: D. Luciani, "'Soyez saints car je suis saint.' Un commentaire de Lévitique 19," *Nouvelle Revue Théologique* 114 (1992): 212–46, here 222, which sees 19:2-37 as a concentric structure with a 2×3+1 center piece in vv. 19-22; J. Magonet, "The Structure and Meaning of Leviticus 19," *HAR* 7 (1983): 151–67, suggesting vv. 1-18 and vv. 30-37 as an *inclusio* framing vv. 19-29; cf. the chiastic arrangement – A, vv. 5-10, 11-18; B, vv. 20-26, 26-28; A', vv. 33-34, 35-36 in Barbiero, *L'asino*, 238–43.

Verses 11-18 describe behavioral patterns in relation to other community members and to Yahweh. Thematically, the passage resonates with the closure in vv. 33-36. Compositionally, the rules in vv. 11-18 address a circle that vv. 33-34, 35-36 gradually widen. The closure extends the rules for treating the metic.[6] Another indication that points to the social reality of the addressees of Lev 19 is the concept of the laws as a group-ethos, substantiating the alterity of others in combination with the terminology of holiness (v. 2b). As well, the demand of keeping the commandments in v. 19aα with the closing v. 37 in the function of a bookending parenesis reinforce that connection with holiness. The following first addresses the genre of the prohibitive rows and relates them to themes of H in the attempt to explain further the universal tendency of this passage.

1.2. *Prohibitive Rows and their Themes*
Four sets of apodictic laws in Lev 19:11-18, in the singular and in the plural, feature predominantly prohibitives that culminate in the command to community members to act out in mutual benevolence. This poses the question of the genre of this passage that has largely been seen in relation to the prohibitive rows[7] in the Decalogues, in particular the second half, with its concentration on conflict and dispute settlement in the eighth through tenth commandment[8] that overlap with prohibitives in Lev 19:3-4,[9] 11-18. At the same time, Lev 19:11-18, with their

---

6. The following brackets out an evaluation of the development of the theme of mutual benevolence in its relation to preceding law in Deut 24:17, 27:19, as well as parallels in H Lev 24:22, and other traditions, such as Zech 7:9-10.

7. Prohibitives as apodictic legal sentences are typically thought to express a group ethos that seeks to ensure order in a particular area of life; see W. Richter, *Recht und Ethos. Versuch einer Ortung des weisheitlichen Mahnspruches* (Munich: Kösel, 1966), 140, 117 n. 263; alternatively, they were suggested to express kinship-ethos; cf. Gerstenberger, *Apodiktisches Recht*, 110–17, based on Lev 18 and Jer 35.

8. Cf., for instance, Lev 19:12 and Exod 20:7/Deut 5:11 on the prohibition of swearing a false oath ("swear...to lie") in Yahweh's name. A comparison of Lev 19:11-18 with commands and prohibitives of the Decalogues would also demonstrate the differences. This can only briefly be addressed. Generally speaking, the Decalogues remain more vague in their exclusion of "misuse" of Yahweh's name. The alterity ethos of Lev 19 adds fear of "desecration" (חלל *pi.*) of Yahweh's name (v. 12); cf. Nihan, *Priestly Torah*, 473. Earlier source-critical reconstructions of an older Decalogue, such as Elliger, *Leviticus*, 252, 254, substantiate the focus on conflicts and on conflict settlement. They hypothesize a core of ten or twelve singular prohibitives in vv. 11-18 that approximately mirror the themes of an older Decalogue, summarizing its function to protect "property, law, honor, life of the neighbor, in brief, securing the social existence." Cf. also Nihan, *Priestly Torah*, 472.

9. The apparent differences between the Decalogues and Lev 19:11-18 are either explained as results of an adaptation of the Decalogues in Lev 19:3-4 (Milgrom, *Leviticus 17–22*, 1610; Nihan, *Priestly Torah*, 467) or as results of a concurrent development. Of

list of diverse examples of conflicts,[10] also roots in procedural law on fairness in conflict settlement.[11] Yet, reaching farther than the Decalogues, Lev 19:17-18 programmatically point to the underlying posture of individual acts with the opposite pair "hate" and "love."[12] The prohibitives as expression of a group ethos in Lev 18-20 with Lev 19 as their center[13] relate to themes that are typical for the community of H, as the following briefly unfolds.

In particular, the following clarifies the prohibitives' origin as an outflow of the identity of H that thematically roots in the self-placement in the narrative arch of the Exodus, in the perspective of small landowners and in H's signature alterity ethos. It then unfolds the conceptual backdrop of malevolence and of conflict settlement in the community that H envisions. It also points to the specific molding of brotherly benevolence as a prominent concept of H that is best seen in the tradition of Deuteronomy. This will provide a further framework to explain the prohibitive row's unconditional appeal to neighborly benevolence.

---

relevance in this context is their enhancement of the authority of the kin. Leviticus 19:3 increases the notion of parental respect through the use of "fear" (ירא), evidently with the intent of securing the authority of this kinship institute, while H otherwise restricts this term for the attitude toward "your God" and the sanctuary (Lev 19:14, 32, 25:17, 36, 43; for the sanctuary in 19:30 and 26:2, cf. Nihan, *Priestly Torah*, 468) and the Decalogues instead use "honor" (כבד, Exod 20:12; Deut 5:16). H considers the respect of kinship authority as fundamental and core to its version of Yahwism. ירא claims the ethical responsibility toward the kinship elders, including women. The command falls outside the area of the cult, cf. A. Cholewiński, *Heiligkeitsgesetz und Deuteronomium: eine vergleichende Studie* (Rome: Biblical Institute Press, 1976), 259. The respect of parental authority was widespread in the ancient Near East, according to Milgrom, *Leviticus 17–26*, 1610, and R. Albertz, "Hintergrund und Bedeutung des Elterngebots im Dekalog," in *Geschichte und Theologie. Studien zur Exegese des Alten Testaments und zur Religionsgeschichte Israels*, ed. R. Albertz (Berlin: de Gruyter, 2003), 157–85. The emphasis in Lev 19 on parental authority raises the question about whether at the time and in the context of H such authority needed to be secured, and, if so, who exactly would have been challenging it.

10. This may have contributed to the character of Lev 19 at large as a compilation of miscellaneous laws, seemingly lacking a thematic thread; see, for instance, Milgrom, *Leviticus 17–22*, 1596. Compositional analyses have challenged this notion and pointed to the compositional logic.

11. Namely Exod 23:1-8; Deut 22:1-4; see the evaluation of E. Otto, "Innerbiblische Exegese im Heiligkeitsgesetz Levitikus 17–26," in *Levitikus als Buch*, ed. H. Fabry and H.-W. Jüngling (Berlin: Philo, 1999), 125–96, here 141.

12. This is in line with Exod 23:4-5 and Deut 22:1-4. In comparison with Lev 19:17-18, in the Decalogues the final prohibitives in Exod 20:17-18 and Deut 5:21 (see also above Chapter 2, section 9.2 on the widespread attempts at property theft) may identify this as typical hostile behavior, yet the texts hardly provide closure on the comparable fundamental character as does Lev 19:17-18.

13. Nihan, *Priestly Torah*, 555.

1.3. Themes Relevant to the Community of H

1.3.1. The Exodus, Small Landowners, Priestly Identity in Alterity

Three underpinnings help determine the religious-historical contours of the community of H: their self-identity as a collective formed through the Exodus, their life as small landowners, and their general interest in priestly themes. First, the Exodus, rather than possession of the land, serves as exclusive marker of self-identification and as an essential foundation of the ethos of difference.[14] This self-placement informs the social and economic understanding of the laws of H and their relationship between law and the land. H develops the brotherly ethos of the Jubilee legislation in adaptation from Deuteronomy to support the validity of the land division between the Israelites (25:10, 13-15). Second, written from a perspective against the concentration of landownership of a small economic elite, this redistribution supports claims of small landowners, thus contributing to what has been labeled as a "provincial outlook"[15] of a priestly community represented in H, notably without references to central courts.[16] Finally, third, in line with their identification with the Exodus, H self-identifies in cultural distance from Egypt. Beyond the correspondences between Lev 19:11-18 and vv. 26-32, some of the cultic techniques to which vv. 26-28 allude have analogies to techniques H

---

14. It is subsequently seen as the product of Yahweh's separation from the nations, in which Yahweh consecrates himself (Lev 20:22-26; 22:33; 25:42, 55) and will entirely own the land (Lev 25:23), with the Israelites in the status of resident aliens sojourning in Yahweh's land as dependent workers; cf. F. Crüsemann, "Der Exodus als Heiligung. Zur rechtsgeschichtlichen Bedeutung des Heiligkeitsgesetzes," in *Die Hebräische Bibel und ihre zweifache Nachgeschichte: Festschrift für Rolf Rendtorff zum 65. Geburtstag*, ed. E. Blum, C. Machholz, and E. W. Stegemann (Neukirchen-Vluyn: Neukirchener Verlag, 1990), 117–29.

15. Joosten, *People*, 154–64. Markers that contribute to this picture are the attitude towards cities in some laws that refer to the countryside (Lev 25:31-34; 26:25); the relevance of agriculture (cf. Joosten, *People*, 157–58); the provisions for the poor at the time of harvest (19:9-10; 23:22); the prohibition against mixed breeding and sowing (19:19); the planting of fruit trees (19:23-25); the feasts in accordance with the agricultural activity (23:10, 29); potentially the references to animals (Lev 18:23; 20:15-16; 24:18, 21); and the presence of priests in the provinces rather than in the cultic center of Jerusalem – all of these relate to priestly themes; cf. Joosten, *People*, 158.

16. While the relationships between community members and kin feature in Lev 18:6-23 and 19, 20, central courts are remarkably absent. In contrast to Deut 17:8-13, cf. furthermore the absence of the king (Deut 17:14-20), military service (Deut 20:1-9), warfare (Deut 20:10-20; 23:9-14) and the theme of the captives of war (Deut 21:10-14) in H; see Joosten, *People*, 158. This may suggest that H was written from the perspective of a community (עם) of landowners with equal status, identifying foremost with the Torah as their organizing principle and their ethical center, bracketing out political and economic factors; cf. Nihan, *Priestly Torah*, 558.

associates with Egyptian culture.[17] As it defines cultural identity in alterity from Egypt, H motivates the commands that community members would distance themselves from practices labeled as "Egyptian," using the Exodus as a historiographic cypher to plausibilize Israel's cultural alterity.[18] The concerns of H in Lev 19 seem to reflect the mindset of a group of priestly scribes that clarifies its sacrificial cult in Lev 17 along with priestly responsibilities. Leviticus 21–22 interpret them as re-conceptualization of Israel as a community of sojourners selected by Yahweh, settling around their temple as Lev 25 suggests.[19] The centrality of the land in H is one reason for H to at some point include the גר into this concept, as he is dwelling for an extended time period around the group, in "your land" Lev 19:33. This intersettlement is the backdrop for H to remind the community of their status in Egypt as historiographic reference point

17. See, for instance, the cutting of the beard and the round cut of the hair in Lev 19:27; Herodotus reports of round haircuts of Arabs in *Histories* 3:8; cf. Milgrom, *Leviticus 1–16*, 1689. "Eating above the blood" in Lev 19:26 relates to the custom of offering blood on the ground and then eating above it. Cf. the parallel in 1 Sam 14:32-35 with the same idiom; here also, the refraining from blood consumption is a central point of Judean identity. Ezekiel 33:25 relates eating of the blood to "lifting eyes up to the (scarab shaped) amulets," that is, to cultic objects associated with Egypt, likely mediated through Phoenician city states. Three interpretations are brought forward. The preposition על may mean "with" the blood, thereby condemning blood consumption. Alternatively, it may mean "over" the blood, that is, while the blood is still in the sprinkling bowl (2 Sam 9:7). Finally, the prohibition may target meals "over" a ritual of ancestral spirits in a necromantic setting that it assumes. Such a cultural context may presuppose the veneration of ancestors and mantic activities in Near Eastern or Greek practices that are so much at the heart of H (see 17:7; 18:21; 19:31; 20:1-6, 27). This latter interpretation reads v. 26a in parallelism with v. 26b. Cf. the three alternatives in Milgrom, *Leviticus 17–22*, 1685–86, and the discourse on chthonic worship and ancestral cult found in other sections of H, as well as Milgrom's suggestion of a western influence.

18. The list of laws that cover the theme of loyalty to Yahweh in vv. 26-32 collects practices that H associates with foreign nations and cultures or that convey a cultural mindset that H rejects as non-Yahwistic or as superstitious; cf. the explanation of M. Noth, *Leviticus* (Philadelphia: Westminster SCM Press, 1965), 143; see also C. F. Keil, *Biblischer Commentar über die Bücher Moses. 2. Bd., Leviticus, Numeri und Deuteronomium*, 2nd ed. (Leipzig: Dörffling und Franke, 1870), 135. D. Hoffmann, *Das Buch Leviticus übersetzt und erklärt* (vol. 1, Berlin, 1905; vol. 2, Berlin: M. Poppelauer, 1906), 53; Elliger, *Leviticus*, 261–62. Verses 26-32 essentially set an Israelite ethos apart from foreign cultural practices. The diversity of the prohibitions and of their arrangement does not follow any particular theme, nor does the current arrangement follow any content-related order. Narrowing down the themes of laws in vv. 26-28 further to more specific commands about separation (thematically related to v. 19ab) seems to create an artificial umbrella theme, especially for the command not to soothsay in v. 26b, and the avoidance of incisions and tattoos in v. 28.

19. Nihan, *Priestly Torah*, 559.

(19:34). H gradually draws out its community ethos to include the resident alien or metic,[20] urging in vv. 33-34 to integrate them, to act fairly and not to "betray" him economically[21] as well as to recognize their vulnerability[22] and engage in mutual benevolence (אהב, 19:33).[23] There is thus good reason to connect the alterity ethos of Lev 19:11-18 with the socio-cultural environment of the group of H, in particular in light of the connection that H draws with Egypt and Israel's existence there.

1.3.2. Hate and Conflict Settlement

Leviticus 19:17-18 (H) reflect on conflict settlement in reference to the terms "hate" and "love," and the framework of vv. 3-4 refers to kinship authority, a context in which unconditional mutual benevolence makes sense. The larger

---

20. The status of the גר changed over time, see above Chapter 4, section 5.1. The reconstruction of the stages involved in the composition of Lev 19:33-36 is beyond the scope of this study; cf. for instance, Bultmann, *Der Fremde*, 177–79, suggesting 19:33 to be the result of three source-critical stages that presuppose two different concepts of גר. The גר is to keep the community's purity in respect to the most basic laws, such as not eating blood (Lev 17:8-9, 10-12, 13-14, 15-16) and not sacrificing to Molech (20:2-5); furthermore, the גר pledged oblations and freewill oblations (22:18-19); cf. Nihan, *Priestly Torah*, 560.

21. ינה *hi.* in Lev 19:33 designates verbal and physical aggression; cf. ינה in parallelism with חמס in Jer 22:3. Also, the notion of a physical attack is evident in the idiom "sword of violence" with the *qal* participle of Jer 46:16; 50:15; cf. "the wrath of violence" in Jer 25:15; six out of 20 references to the verb are in the *qal* – the remainder are in the *hi.* ינה relates to attacks that have an immediate impact on the honor and economic status. This notion is particularly clear in Ezek 46:18 with the confiscation of property; cf. the princes' oppression in Ezek 45:8; cf. on the notion of the oppression of the poor also 1QpPs 37:3, 7, and in the pesher on Ps 37:20; H. Ringgren, ינה, *TDOT* 6 (Grand Rapids: Eerdmans 1990), 104–106, here 106.

22. Unlike Exod 22:20-22 and Ezek 22:7, Lev 19:34 highlights vulnerability as it explicitly refers to the category of the אזרח ("native citizen") alongside the גר. The rules that apply to the interaction with the sojourner are less particular than those applicable to the narrow circle of "neighbors." A neighbor may not be oppressed fiscally (Lev 19:13), nor may he be the object of a life-threatening accusation or testimony (19:16aβ) – he is to be loved (19:18aβ). Similarly, the "compatriot" (19:17b) is the object of an extra-institutional form of dispute settlement by "indictment" or "reprimansion" in the community, parallel with the 'brother', i.e., a close of kin.

23. The positive notion in Lev 19:33 is evident also in the translation. J. W. Wevers, *Notes on the Greek Text of Leviticus* (Atlanta: Scholars Press, 1997), 309–10, notes that יגור is rendered by various words in Leviticus, but always by an attributive participle. The exception is Lev 19:33, where the translation is, uniquely, προσέρχομαι. The LXX translates plural. The apodosis "you may not afflict him" is rendered in a way corresponding to the Hebrew meaning. Cf. the uses of "oppression/affliction" otherwise referring a member of the people in Jer 22:3 and Lev 25:14, 17. Deuteronomy 23:16 uses it for the גר.

context embeds the passage in the framework of H, thematically different from the commands that establish social justice with regard to the land and its redistribution, and in Lev 18 and 20 with their focus on kinship relations as a form of communal rules. Kinship relations as the frame of reference is in the background when H is aiming at establishing identity in difference from surrounding cultures. H embeds this in the narrative and in its cultural-historical reference frame of a "sacral scheme: a god acquires a group of people – his 'slaves' – to serve him in his sanctuary; these servants are settled on a land surrounding the sanctuary and belonging to the god; since they are the god's personal possession, they may not be enslaved to any human master, and since the land they live on belongs to the god, it can never be sold."[24] The exclusivity of the Yahweh-covenant manifests itself in the parenetic undertone of an ethos of religiously motivated cultural alterity and in a kinship-based legislation. Based on alterity or "holiness" of the Israelites, Lev 19 frames the rules of 19:11-18 with the short formula of self-presentation "I am Yahweh," used to separate the sets of prohibitives vv. 12, 14, 16, 18. This framing of the ethical rules in 19:11-18 adds alterity in relation to its surrounding cultural communities.[25] This is indicative of the self-perception of the envisioned polity that Lev 19:2 addresses with the term עדה[26] that holds the judicial authority in the areas covered in Lev 19.

1.3.3. *"Brotherly benevolence" in Leviticus 17–26*

The demand of love and the implementation of conflict settlement in the polity of the עדה reflect a particular self-perception as different from surrounding cultures and to some extent in the line of Deuteronomy, as a community analogous to a kin group. The following assesses this religious-cultural profile of H, namely the community's ideal of brotherly benevolence in the context of Lev 17–26 as a form of reinterpretation of Persian-era Judaism around the second half of the fifth century[27] or after Nehemiah.[28] The ramifications of the literary and

---

24. Joosten, *People*, 135.

25. This evidence suggests that the other passages of the composition of Lev 19, with prohibitives and commands in the casuistic parts 1 and 2, together with the apodictic section of part 2, vv. 26-32, may also be best read against a particular cultural background from which H separates itself.

26. A concept best understood against the backdrop of the historical context in Persian or potentially early Hellenistic Judah; cf. Num 35:11-12, 24-25, which secure the self-adjudication of Judah under foreign rule. See also above, Chapter 4. Dating earlier, Milgrom, "Pre-Monarchic Israel," 69, points to the use of this term in constructs with various authorititative community leaders in Israel, thus marking an institution with authority in the polity at large.

27. Otto, "Das Heiligkeitsgesetz Leviticus 17–26 in der Pentateuchredaktion," in *Altes Testament. Forschung und Wirkung. Festschrift H. Graf Reventlow*, ed. P. Mommer and W. Thiel (Frankfurt am Main: Peter Lang, 1994), 65–80, and idem, "Innerbiblische Exegese," 125–96; Nihan, *Priestly Torah*, 548.

28. Nihan, *Priestly Torah*, 559.

cultural-historical contexts locate H in the history of biblical law after P and D[29] in a specific culture of conflict settlement.[30] H combines narrative and law along the lines of its historiographic self-perception, as Israel after the Exodus at the threshold of entering the land. Rhetorically, H expresses Yahwism's alterity with the idiosyncratic category of קדוש. The term functions as a cipher for the alterity of the Yahweh-community in distance from their surrounding cultures. Written from a priestly perspective, H presents itself as community law unfolding a concept of sanctity for sanctuary and priests that in Lev 19 unfolds the principles for the broad audience of "all the assembly of the Israelites" (Lev 19:2).[31] The conceptual framework of Lev 19 to construct holiness in alterity from the cultural surroundings reaches far beyond Israel's particular religious institutions of the sanctuary and of the priestly office as such (Exod 29; Lev 8) and address the community of Israel at large, especially in Lev 18–20. Israel is consecrated by Yahweh (Lev 20:8) and the community is consecrated to Yahweh (Lev 19:2; 20:7, 26), and thus the essence of Lev 19 develops along the paradigm of an inner-kin ethos in vv. 11-18 set in Israel's Exodus story in a move of a separation from Egypt.[32]

29. Four models of its literary origins can be distinguished. Either it was: an independent literary corpus prior to P and later integrated into P with the author of Lev 26 collecting and editing (Wellhausen); a supplementary extension of P, most comprehensively developed in Elliger's model of four ideal-typical strands PH 1-4, representing legislation as it gradually shifts its focus from notions of a priestly office toward the community of Israel at large in its center, and from the narrative of Israel toward the meaning of law for the larger community; the result of a reworking of Lev 1–16 (Milgrom, Knohl); or a late supplement to and part of the composition of P (Blum). Cf. the overviews on scholarship in M. Lyons. *From Law to Prophecy: Ezekiel's Use of the Holiness Code* (London: T&T Clark, 2019), 19–28; Nihan, *Priestly Torah*, 7–18; J. Stackert, "Holiness Code and Writings," in Strawn, ed., *The Oxford Encyclopedia of the Bible and Law*, 389–96.

30. Cf. below in section 4.1, on the reflections on conflict settlement and the comparison with Ezek 22:6-12 on urban feuding.

31. Leviticus 19:1, "all the congregation of the Israelites," is overloaded. On עדה in the wider context of the tradition of P to claim jurisdiction in certain areas of law, see above in Chapter 4, section 5.2. Leviticus 17 and 22:17-30 are a case in point for the priestly reality, as they present rules for the offering of sacrifices and for priests; cf. the relevance of the sanctuary in the rules for priests found in Lev 21:1–22:16.

32. Leviticus 18–20 refer on multiple levels to the framework of an inner-kin ethos that requires kinship authority, arguably, in contrast to foreign, "Egyptian" culture. The separation from Egyptian culture dovetails with the motif of the respect of parental authority in Lev 19:3. This may specifically be said in opposition to the Egyptian custom of not caring about mother and father if, Herodotus II 35, polemic aside, does indeed refer to a historical custom whereby sons had no obligation to provide parental care, which, in Greece seems to have been mandatory. D. Asheri, A. B. Lloyd, and A. Corcella, *A Commentary on Herodotus I–IV* (Oxford: Oxford University Press, 2007), 263, with

Can we further clarify the social, historical, and tradition-historical context of an inner-kin ethos? It became evident that fictive kinship ethos may best be understood against the backdrop of a disintegrated tendency in a newly constituted urban society, as the law of Deuteronomy suggests. In particular, do the prohibitives in 19:11-18 allow for a counter-statement against a culture shaped by (destructive) mechanisms of private enmity and revenge in Persian-period *Yehud*[33] that would motivate the urge to mutual benevolence? The four-fold terminological variety גר, בני עמך, רע, עמית used for community members in Lev 19:11-18 points to the passage's nuanced perception of the social context.

2. *Leviticus 19:11-18 in Leviticus 19*

Reading Lev 19:11-18 in the context of Lev 19 has brought to light the context of this row of prohibitives in the second half of a two-partite composition. As pointed out, the symmetric arrangement reveals a diptych[34] of vv. 3-18 on one side, and vv. 19aβb-36a on the other with two parallel halves, each built on a similar pattern, with both moving from a set of (a) laws on fundamental aspects to (b) casuistic laws and to (c) other mixed laws.[35] This outline assumes a combination of formal and content aspects as criteria for the arrangement of Lev 19 as diptych. The two parts of "mixed laws" pair laws on conflict settlement in vv. 11-18 with laws on cultural separation as their counterparts. Of the two central apodictic parts, vv. 11-18 and 26-32, a list of foreign cultic techniques[36] is part of the separatist ethos of H. The correspondence with vv. 11-18 suggests that this part also rejects non-Yahwistic behavior, namely in conflict settlement.

The arrangement of the diptych also reveals perspectives that the entire chapter shares. For the theme of conflict settlement between individuals in vv. 11-18,

---

reference to W. K. Lacey, *The Family in Classical Greece. Aspects of Greek and Roman Life* (Ithaca, NY: Cornell University Press, 1968), 116–17.

33. The alleged addressees vary, among other things depending on the source-critical model. Joosten, *People*, 92, 203–207, suggests, based on the assumption that rules on treatment of a sojourner require some degree of autonomy, the pre-exilic period; Knohl, *Sanctuary*, 190, also assumes the addressees represent the entire "nation" of Israel in a pre-exilic setting.

34. Following E. Otto, see above in section 1.1.

35. Further parallels between the two main passages corroborate this outline: with vv. 3-18 and 20-36a as corresponding parts, each of which can be broken down to a two-partite casuistic passages, vv. 5-8, 9-10 and 20-22, 23-25. The formula of self-announcement closes both (vv. 10bβ, 25b). The two passages with apodictic sentences follow: vv. 11-18 and 26-32. The first of these passages closes with the formula of self-presentation: v. 19aα. Verses 26-32 end more loosely, less distinct from vv. 33-36. The formula of self-presentation, "I am Yahweh," in v. 31b and the casuistic style of v. 33 are indicative of the separation of vv. 26-32 from 33-36.

36. See above, notes 12, 15.

two aspects of the compositional outline are critical. First, there is the reference to parental authority or kinship structure, an aspect that was seen as pivotal in conflict settlement as the emphasis of the role of the elders showed in Num 35, together with Sabbath and idolatry. As fundamental laws at the outset in v. 3 they inform the following, including the apodictic part on conflict settlement in the community vv. 11-18, as it develops its own model of conflict settlement: a pacifying plea to avoid long term hateful relations which is in the interest of the elders negotiating between different kin.[37]

Considering the prohibitive row in more depth yields the following result: Lev 19:11-18 breaks down into four sets or paragraphs[38] of prohibitions separated by the use of the formula of self-proclamation or self-assertion of Yahweh vv. 12b, 14b, 16b, 18b, of comparable length in verse pairs that end with a concluding self-introductory formula: "I am Yahweh." It considers four sub-themes:

1. Deception of a fellow countryman vv. 11-12;
2. Protection of individuals with low social prestige and with disabilities vv. 13-14;
3. Fair and just conflict settlement vv. 15-16;
4. Interaction with a brother in general vv. 17-18.

The thematic thread of vv. 11-18 is the relationship to a fellow community member in a potential, an emerging, or an ongoing conflict. Its intent is the exclusion of unfair forms of interaction.

---

37. The framing verses of Lev 19:3-4 are formally distinct from the two halves as they use long forms of the self-declaration that correspond to the formula used in vv. 33-36 (34b, 36bα). Once this correspondence between the introductory and the closing passage is established, the commands in vv. 3-4 come into view with their three themes that now feature so prominently in the chapter: the fear of and/or the authority of mother and father as elders in the kin; the keeping of the Sabbath; and, finally, the prohibition of אלילים and of "handmade gods" as symbols of foreign cultures. Verse 30 repeats the commands to keep the Sabbath and to honor the parents in a passage that goes on to rule one, the honoring of seniors (v. 32). In an analogous correspondence, the closing passage in 33-36 relates to the first apodictic passage in vv. 11-18: the command to love in v. 34 alludes to vv. 18aβ, and v. 35a reformulates the prohibition of doing evil in v. 15aα; see the outline above and, cf., among others, A. Ruwe, *"Heiligkeitsgesetz" und "Priesterschrift": Literaturgeschichtliche und Rechtssystematische Untersuchungen zu Leviticus 17,1–26,2* (Tübingen: Mohr Siebeck, 1999), 193. I bracket out the development of the chapter, yet see the attempts to reconstruct an older source of the prohibitive rows in vv. 11-18 that are now embedded in this context and framed through the command to honor parental authority.

38. Barbiero, *L'asino*, 245–96, sees things differently, suggesting two sections in Lev 19:11-18, with vv. 11-14 relating to the goods of the neighbor (and with the prohibition against stealing in v. 11a as its heading), and vv. 15-18 offering a "Dodecalogue" about justice (with v. 15aα's prohibition of injustice as its heading).

Table 5.2

11-18			Central Apodictic part I
11-12			Deception of a compatriot
11		a	Not shall you steal,
		bα	nor shall you deceive,
		bβ	nor shall you lie, a man against his compatriot.
12		a	And not shall you swear by my name to lie
		bα	in order to desecrate the name of your God,
		bβ	I (am) Yahweh.
13-14			Day laborer, deaf, blind
13		aα	Not shall you oppress your neighbor,
		aβ	nor shall you tear away,
		b	nor shall remain with you the wage of the day laborer over night until morning.
14		aα	Not shall you curse a deaf,
		aβ	nor shall you place before the blind an obstacle,
		bα	in order that you may fear (things) from your God.
		bβ	I (am) Yahweh.
15-16			Legal procedure
15		aα	Not shall you commit evil in trial.
		aβ	Neither shall you favor the face of the lowly.
		aβ	Nor shall you (overly) honor the face of the grand.
		b	In justice shall you judge your compatriot.
16		aα	Not shall you go round as (profitable) slanderer among your people.
		aβ	Nor shall you stand up against the blood of your neighbor.
		b	I am Yahweh.
17-18			Hate and love of a brother/compatriot/son of your people/ neighbor
17		a	Not shall you hate your brother in your heart.
		bα	Surely shall you reprimand your compatriot,
		bβ	in order that you will not lift up guilt on his behalf.
18		aα	Not shall you retaliate,
		aα	nor shall you bear a grudge against the sons of your people,
		aβ	so that you show love for your neighbor, as he (shows love toward) you.
		b	I (am) Yahweh.

The four slightly varying sets address common forms of hateful interaction. The first and the second set tie hateful communal relations between community members to the entire community's relationship with Yahwism as its distinct identity marker. Set 1 (vv. 11-12) ends after a reference to stealing and lying with falsely swearing by the divine name as a form of "defiling/desecrating the name of your God."[39]

Each set bans four (or four plus one) unacceptable interaction modes, vv. 11-12; 13-14; 15-16; 17-18 with three exceptions of positive commands: v. 15b, "you shall judge your compatriot in righteousness"; v. 17bα, "surely shall you reprimand your compatriot"; and v. 18b, "you shall love your neighbor," pointing toward an ethos of justice that, broadly spoken, excludes acting out mutual hate. When the hermeneutics of the prohibitives of vv. 11-18 at large are read against the background of these positive commands, their intention to avoid typical constellations and mechanisms of conflict settlement becomes apparent. Verse 17bα encourages members of the community to instead claim authority of conflict settlement, even when facing hateful members.

Leviticus 19:11-18 apparently address the community at large: fair judgment (v. 15b), authoritative "reprimanding" (v. 17bα) of a compatriot, and mutual benevolence, all point to a particular understanding of judicial authority in a community addressed as brothers, sons of your people, compatriots, companions. The following considers modes of interaction banned in the prohibitives and encouraged in the positive commands of vv. 17b, 18aβ, with the intention of clarifying how the notion of long-term personal enmity relationships shapes Lev 19:11-18. A subsequent outlook synthesizes the community model that informs this passage.

3. Conflict Settlement, Patriarchal and Communal Authority

3.1. Verses 11-12

Verses 11-12 consist of a row of four prohibitives, a negated consecutive clause (v. 12a), and a short formula of self-declaration (v. 12bβ). In the logic of this passage, the consecutive clause "in order to desecrate the name of your God" sums up the consequence in the case of a violation of the prohibitions using a metaphor for the perversion of the communal principle, for which the deity in Lev 19:11-18 is seen as a token of unity.

---

39. This may be said against a backdrop of surrounding non-Yahwistic cultures and, in light of vv. 26-32, in view of the prohibitives' tendency to proclaim an alterity ethos with Yahwism as an identity-marker. See also the profanation of the name of God among the nations in Ezra 20:9, 20, 22 and in Isa 48:11, even defiling God himself Ezra 22:16, 26. The judgment oracle in Ezek 20, however, points to the universal context of this profanization in face of the nations, that is, facing a non-Israelite audience or a cross-cultural context.

The prohibitives in vv. 11-12 list general behavior in disputes: theft, deceit, swearing a false oath have an introductory function for vv. 11-18.[40] More specifically, the first three prohibitives[41] are themed as general rules of default behavior between enemies. Theft (גנב), deceit (כחש) and swearing falsely are widespread manifestations of personal hate,[42] with כחש and שקר in v. 11bβ being used to secure control over a compatriot's (עמית) property. The parallels in the subject matter of stealing, lying and swearing falsely in the prohibitive rows of the Decalogues support further their character as default hateful interaction[43] and confirm that Lev 19:11-12 covers an array of transgressions of "basic ethical prohibitions."[44] Gradually, more specifically judicial procedure comes into view in Lev 19:11bβ, 12a, for instance, with swearing falsely (v. 12a)[45] as one act that can be part of property theft.[46]

The introductory prohibitives in vv. 11-12 thematically focus on conflict settlement in a community composed of equals. With the concluding consecutive clause, Lev 19:11-12 put a particular spin on hateful behavior when they point out that the active invention of lies under oath, a typical mechanism between opponents in feuding, would, beyond the level of individual justice or injustice, "desecrate" (חלל) Yahweh's name, i.e., would undermine and harm the communal identity.

40. They make consistent use of the plural and may potentially have replaced older singular forms. The beginning of this passage may be lost and vv. 11, 12a (in the plural now still found in the final clause v. 12bα and through v. 14), may have replaced an older introduction in the singular, that now is lacking; see already Elliger, *Leviticus*, 251. Otto, "Innerbiblische Exegese," 150, calls vv. 11-12 the "opening."

41. Cf. the background of lying in Ps 59:13 in a typical confrontation with enemies, and further Lev 5:20 and Gen 18:15; Deut 33:29; Josh 24:27; 1 Kgs 13:18; Isa 59:13; Jer 5:12; Job 8:18; 31:28. Lying (כחש) can specifically designate dishonesty vis-à-vis a more powerful and therefore a potentially more dangerous hostile interlocutor. Joshua 7:11 mentions both deception (כחש) and theft (גנב); cf. the three roots כחש, גזל, שקר in Lev 5:21-22 (MT, 6:2-3 ET); cf. J. E. Hartley, *Leviticus 1–27* (Dallas: Word, 1992), 315; Milgrom, *Leviticus 17–22*, 1630–31.

42. The first prohibitive, Lev 19:11a, evoking the Decalogue Exod 20:15/Deut 5:19 and underscoring the relevance of גנב ("stealing"). See Elliger, *Leviticus*, 256.

43. Cf., among others, גנב (Jer 7:9; Hos 4:2); in the context of Hos 4:1-3, v. 2 alludes to a lawsuit ultimately provoking divine judgment. Stealing in Exod 21:16 and Deut 24:7 possibly refer to human trafficking. Property theft is a theme of deposit law in Exod 21:37–22:3. Leviticus 5:21-26 uses גזל.

44. Milgrom, *Leviticus 17–22*, 1630.

45. Cf. the parallels for false oaths in Exod 20:7/Deut 5:11, namely "lifting" (נשא) the name of Yahweh to insubstantiality (שוא).

46. Cf. Lev 5:20-26; see Wells, *The Law of Testimony*, 139. Leviticus 5:20-26 mentions a false oath in a case of three misdeeds: lying about property of another that was not deposited, entrusted, or stolen (v. 21); extorting property from another; or finding a lost item and lying about it.

3.2. Verses 13-14

Verses 13-14 list five prohibitives, and contain a positive clause with a future sense (*w-qatal*) in v. 14aβ that concludes with the short self-introductory formula. This second set of prohibitives explicitly addresses the interaction among community members of uneven social rank. It urges fairness vis-à-vis community members who otherwise would easily fall prey to unfair treatment. Verse 13 puts the focus on economic aspects of the oppression and v. 14 reflects on unfair, harmful, and shame-inducing behavior toward impaired members of the community. Altogether, these five prohibitives point to the impact of uneven social statuses in a conflict constellation and thus present a counter-cultural model of an ideal society whose interactions would overcome those severe social differences. Verse 13 adds nuances to the theme of economic oppression. The first two prohibitives in v. 13a reject the exploitation of the neighbor/companion (רֵעַ),[47] the prohibitive v. 13b details in particular the payment of a day laborer's wage (שָׂכִיר).[48]

Oppression and theft are closely related to each other and as such are nuances of the more general modes of unrightful acquisition of property v. 11a. עשק names the oppression between two private enemies, semantically covering a facet of hateful behavior that harms an opponent economically or physically. The prohibition of oppression of the daylaborer has precursors in other laws, for instance, Deut 24:14-15a. The relation between both illustrates mechanisms of adopting legal tradition in Lev 19:13:

Table 5.3

Deut 24:14-15a	Lev 19:13
לֹא־תַעֲשֹׁק שָׂכִיר עָנִי וְאֶבְיוֹן מֵאַחֶיךָ אוֹ מִגֵּרְךָ אֲשֶׁר בְּאַרְצְךָ בִּשְׁעָרֶיךָ: בְּיוֹמוֹ תִתֵּן שְׂכָרוֹ וְלֹא־תָבוֹא עָלָיו הַשֶּׁמֶשׁ	לֹא־תַעֲשֹׁק אֶת־רֵעֲךָ וְלֹא תִגְזֹל לֹא־תָלִין פְּעֻלַּת שָׂכִיר אִתְּךָ עַד־בֹּקֶר:

Deuteronomy 24:14-15a limit the oppression of the day laborer as one example of the *personae miserae*, and H broadens this prohibition to "your neighbor" so as to indiscriminately include all community members.[49] The prohibition of oppression in Deut 24:14-15 is part of an alternating structure of legal traditions in Deut 24:6-7, 10-22; 25:1-4.[50] The logic of Lev 19 thus proceeds from a general prohibitive of the broad urge to not oppress the neighbor, to Lev 19:13b,

---

47. On רֵעַ, see above Chapter 2, section 4.4. on Exod 21:14.
48. The roots עשק and גזל, unfair "snatching away" (see also below), are used in parallelism elsewhere – for instance, in P, Lev 5:21, 23; also Deut 28:29; Jer 21:12; 22:3; Ezek 18:18; 22:29; Mic 2:2; Ps 62:11; Qoh 5:7. See besides oppression and stealing in Lev 19:11-18, also theft and swearing in P in Lev 5:21-23.
49. Nihan, *Priestly Torah*, 473.
50. Otto, "Innerbiblische Exegese," 150.

narrowing down the prohibition of retaining the day worker's loan over night,[51] in analogy to Deut 24:15.[52]

Fairness in interactions with impaired community members of lower social rank, such as a deaf or a blind person (v. 14), points to the tendency of Lev 19:13-14 to widen the horizon toward broadly including behavior detrimental to the community, such as unrightfully seizing property (גזל).[53] The illegitimate nature of "seizing, tearing away,"[54] as quick acquisition or robbery, affects in particular subordinate members of the society, the poor and oppressed.[55] Leviticus 19:13 excludes such typical unfair behavior[56] and thus criticizes these systemically unfair mechanisms in an honor–shame society. The ethical ideal of Lev 19:13 is a community of equal members that subscribe to an inner-kinship ethos. Habitually in inter-kin conflicts unfair treatment and injustice would be typical. The ethical ideal of Lev 19:13 extends the inner-kinship ethos to all

---

51. Malachi 3:5 also mentions oppression against the daylaborer. That the reference frame of oppression has socio-economic dimensions is evident namely in Prov 14:31; 22:16; 28:3, and potentially in Qoh 4:1. Oppression may also hit socially weak members of the society; cf. Amos 4:1; Deut 24:14; Jer 7:6; Ezek 22:29; Zech 7:10. It includes oppression through blood guilt (Prov 28:17). Yet, while a number of cases refer to physical violence (Job 40:23, of water; Isa 38:14; Ezek 22:29b) it may refer to violent speech in a dispute settlement.

52. Nihan, *Priestly Torah*, 473. Leviticus 19:13b modifies the wording of Deut 24:15a, using פעלה as a term for the payment.

53. This term is absent in Deut 24:14-15. The root designates typical illegitimate forms of property acquisition, i.e., "tearing/snatching away"; cf. Ezek 22:29 in parallelism with עשק as a behavior "without justice" (בלא משפט); and cf. also Lev 5:23; Ezek 18:7, 12, 16, 18. See also the noun, "robbed good" (Lev 5:21; Isa 61:8; Ps 62:11), in parallelism with the with verbal form in Ezek 22:29.

54. See, for instance, the case of the premature claim of inheritance referred to as sin (פשע) in Prov 28:24.

55. Psalm 35:10; cf. also Hartley, *Leviticus*, 315; Milgrom, *Leviticus 17–22*, 1638. Such acquirement of property could happen within situations of conflict, during which members of low social rank were at a disadvantage. During more peaceful time, kinship-based institutions would resolve property disputes "in the gate" (Amos 5:10; Isa 29:21), which was the local space of conflict negotiation (cf. Prov 22:22).

56. The reasons for Lev 19:14's banning of unfair constellations of enemies are complex and beyond the scope of this study. The tradition is found in wisdom literature – namely the examples of the deaf and the blind, not protected in any biblical law, are also found in Amenemope 478 and are thus not unique but rather reflect a typical constellation; cf. Otto, *Ethik*, 246. Beyond this cultural-historical background, in honor–shame societies conflicts take place between community members of one's own rank, as theories about private enmity and hate in kinship-based societies point out. See, for instance, the competing elites in classical Athens; cf. Phillips, *Avengers*, 24; Cohen, *Law, Violence*, 97, 187.

members of the community.⁵⁷ Syntactically, the last part of the sentence is kept as a consecutive with a *w-qatal* clause, thus again demonstrating the consequences "in order that you may fear (something) from your God,"⁵⁸ pointing to the vindication of the deity.⁵⁹

Oppression of the poor, stealing and the retaining of a day laborer's payment overnight, swearing in front of a deaf person, throwing a stumbling block before a blind person as indicative of a lack of "the fear from/of your God" find analogues in Proverbs⁶⁰ and thus ascertains a reflection on the theme of justice and divine retribution. Leviticus 19:13-14 convert this into a positive notion, rejecting long-term disputes between socially unequal members as opposed to Yahweh-fear, i.e., as damaging the community.

3.3. Verses 15-16

The concluding two sets of prohibitives vv. 15-16, 17-18, emphasize the ethos of conflict settlement and justice, as they point out how postures impact interactions between community members. Verse 15a lists three prohibitives and concludes with a positive command in v. 15b. Verse 16a adds two prohibitives, closing with a short introductory formula 16b. The general command of justice in judgment (v. 15b) is the first positive command in vv. 11-18 (cf. 17bα, 18aβ), highlighted through its form in the list of prohibitives. Less subtle than the previous set, the prohibitives of this passage straightforwardly address the posture and the behavioral aspects in legal procedure. They prohibit intentional, unfair plans in what may be referred to as trial and identify potential imbalances in conflict settlement of the poor and the respected (v. 15aβ). The reference to (indirectly or directly caused homicide ("blood") in v. 16b illustrates the seriousness of the outcome of a conflict.

This third set covers various forms of behavior toward a compatriot (עָמִית), including five selected aspects. First, a general prohibitive to refrain from committing evil; second, favoritism toward poor or influential community members; third, a positive command of just judgment of a compatriot; fourth, slandering v. 16a; and fifth, standing up as a false witness against a companion

---

57. See Chapter 1, section 4.

58. On elision of the object, see E. Gass, "'Heilige sollt ihr werden. Denn heilig bin ich, Jahwe, euer Gott.' Zur Begründungsstruktur in Lev 19," *MThZ* 64 (2013): 214–31, 221.

59. Fear from God here specifically points to the idiomatic "fear from your God," used four more times in H that is typical of one of the redactional layers of H outside 19:11-18 in Lev 19:32; 25:14, 17, 36, 43; cf. the close parallels for "fear from" in Persian- and Hellenistic-period prophetic and wisdom traditions alluding to this aspect, for instance, 1 Sam 12:18; 2 Sam 6:9 = 1 Chr 13:12; Isa 57:11; Jer 5:22; Jon 1:16; Job 9:35; 37:24. On the use of the idiom to "fear from" enemies, cf. the prophet's fear from enemies in Ezek 2:6 and Pss 3:7; 27:1, among others; for "fear from God," cf. Mic 7:17.

60. Cf., in a similar line of thought, Proverbs' criticism of oppressing or mocking the poor with the theological reference to their maker (עֹשֵׂהוּ); cf. Prov 14:31; 17:5.

(רע). These prohibitives and the positive command refer to consistent postures and behaviors in conflicts. This also applies to the prohibitive of not committing evil (עול) in judgment (משפט, v. 15aα).

The following limits itself to point out how this passage reflects on the status of long-term enmity as typical unfairness and on the behavioral roles (עול) as opposed to the ideal of "justice" (משפט). Furthermore, the subsequent study considers how the passage relates to its precursor for criticism of unfair conflict settlement in Exod 23:2-3, 6a and seeks to determine the contrast of the conflict settlement model in comparison with Deut 16:18-20 and to the character of the itinerant slanderer.

Verses 15-16 point to typical unfairness of behavioral roles. Two observations substantiate the reference of vv. 15-16 to a particular behavioral role in conflict settlement. First, עול designates the deliberately chosen posture of behaving treacherously as intentional systematic treachery or as deceit in trade,[61] and as a general expression of the unfair mindset in conflict settlement.[62] Second, עול designates unfair behavioral roles as a generic term for a variety of forms of intentional deceit and unfair actions.[63] עול designates unfair procedure and performance as the result of a general posture of an individual acting out various unfair deeds.[64] Deliberate or conscious injustice may be paired with it, and the term may also appear in parallelism with violent actions (חמס, Ps 58:3) and relate to works committed with an "unjust mind." This use is found in the literary compositions in which עול typically identifies a mindset, thus framing the posture of an individual availing themselves of a variety of unfair trial procedures. Characteristic for the traditions of Ezekiel,[65] עול designates the personal inclination toward systemic injustice or the exposure to such behavior at large.[66]

---

61. Notably the use of false weights Deut 25:13-16, echoed in Lev 19:35. Deuteronomy 25:16 in general rejects the use of false weight as a classical form of unfair behavior (Deut 25:13-15), and, consequently, as "repugnant" to Yahweh. It describes the objective deception causing systemic injustice. 25:15-16 may have been added as comment on vv. 13-14; see Nelson, *Deuteronomy*, 302. Alternatively, only the positive command in 25:15 may be a later insertion.

62. Cf. Pss 7:4; 82:2; cf. Ps 82:8; Prov 29:27.

63. Cf. J. Schreiner, עול, *TDOT* 10 (Grand Rapids: Eerdmans, 1999), 522–30, esp. 524, suggests that both the feminine and the masculine form of the term convey an evil mindset rather than an isolated action.

64. Cf. Ezek 18:8, 24, 26; 33:3, 15, 18 as close parallels of Lev 19:15; see also below.

65. Ten out of 21 occurrences are in Ezekiel. It is also used twice in Lev 19/H.

66. It is informed by an overall assessment of an individual's mindset and intent of acting wrongfully; cf. Ezek 18:15-18 (see also the parallel in Ezek 3:20; 18:24). Ezekiel 18:15-18 summarize various unfair ways of behavior, such as eating on the mountain, breaking a neighbor's marriage, oppressing in a pledge, stealing in robberies (Ezek 18:26 [2×]; 33:13 [2×], 15, 18); cf. also the use for the collective in the judgment oracle of Ezek 28:18. See furthermore the summarizing accusation using the plowing

"Doing justice toward a neighbor"[67] is the opposite of "doing evil" (עשׂה עול) in trial,[68] namely adopting a lasting enmitic posture.[69] In contrast, Lev 19:15 holds up the positive ideal of justice (משׁפט). The term "unfairness, injustice, deceit" thus provides the backdrop against which the individual behaviors in v. 15 unfold. Unfairness as posture is in a line of thought with other acts, such as lending for profit and charging interest. It also represents the opposite of honest judgment between one person and another (Ezek 18:8). The use of משׁפט in the sense of "trial, judgment" may refer to multiple aspects, either negotiations in the gate or more generally to trial or judgment as institution in kinship-based societies. This is the case in references to partiality in judgment or trial[70] and is in line with a directional sense that the preposition "to" (אל) takes in Deut 25:1.[71]

The social framework of this term in Lev 19:15-16 is the community or polity, twice explicitly mentioned as the members of your people (עמיתך, vv. 15, 16a). Throughout H, עמית applies to humans and it designates a member of the ethnic community or a fellow-countryman.[72] This allows to more precisely characterize the target group of Lev 19:11-18 as community or polity members among whom it bans relations of inherent malice in the negotiation process. H establishes an ethos for an inner-kin community that it highlights with the use of the term "your neighbor, companion" (v. 16b).

This ethos of mutual benevolence is grounded in preceding law, such as Exod 23:2-3, 6a,[73] and Lev 19:15 reflects along the legal tradition of their community ethos. The theme of favoritism toward the weak and the influential ("great") in v. 15b alludes to Exod 23:3, "You shall not honor the weak (דל) in his lawsuit," as well as to Exod 23:6, "You shall not bend justice due to your poor (אביון) in his lawsuit."[74]

(רשׁע)–harvesting (עולה) metaphor in Hos 10:13. It systematizes a behavioral pattern rather than individual acts.

67. Cf. the corresponding expression in Jer 7:5b, "to do justice between a man and his neighbor."

68. The use of עול in the DSS undergirds the term's references to a human disposition or behavior, as well as as an umbrella term for a number of actions; cf. Schreiner, עול, 529.

69. Schreiner, עול, 529. The doctrine of the two spirits in 1QS 3:13–4:26 lists a catalog of vices associated with the spirit of injustice in 4:9-11.

70. See the use of נכר פנים במשׁפט (hi.) in Deut 1:17; Prov 24:23.

71. B. Johnson, משׁפט, TDOT 9 (Grand Rapids: Eerdmans, 1998), 86–98, 89; see also the hall of justice in 1 Kgs 7:7; the place of justice in Qoh 3:16; and sitting in judgment in Isa 28:6.

72. Elliger, Leviticus, 241 n. 19; cf. Milgrom, Leviticus 17–22, 1643, "your fellow."

73. See already, for instance, Mathys, Liebe, 61–62; Barbiero, L'asino, 259–62.

74. A look at the details demonstrates that Exod 23:3, 6 are hardly literal precursors. Leviticus 19 uses only the term "weak" and v. 15aβ does not use the metaphor "honor," but instead the term "lifting the face." Exodus 23:3 and Lev 19:15aβ share the metaphor of "honor" (הדר pi.). The parallels of v. 15 (and vv. 15-18) to other, earlier legislation is evident. Verse 15 shares the terms משׁפט, הדר, דל with Exod 23:3.

Table 5.4

Exod 23:2-3, 6	Lev 19:15
² לֹא־תִהְיֶה אַחֲרֵי־רַבִּים לְרָעֹת וְלֹא־תַעֲנֶה עַל־רִב לִנְטֹת אַחֲרֵי רַבִּים לְהַטֹּת:	לֹא־תַעֲשׂוּ עָוֶל בַּמִּשְׁפָּט לֹא־תִשָּׂא פְנֵי־דָל וְלֹא תֶהְדַּר פְּנֵי גָדוֹל בְּצֶדֶק תִּשְׁפֹּט עֲמִיתֶךָ:
³ וְדָל לֹא תֶהְדַּר בְּרִיבוֹ:	
⁶ לֹא תַטֶּה מִשְׁפַּט אֶבְיֹנְךָ בְּרִיבוֹ:	

Besides these lexicographic parallels, both laws urge fair judgment of a community member. The epexegetical clause in Exod 23:2b rejects the bias of favoring the strong in a quarrel (ריב, vv. 2b, 3), as does Lev 19:15, urging not to unfairly "swell" ("honor") the weak in trial. The concerns about unfairness in the community were an important factor, with the calls for impartiality towards the rich and the poor in Exod 23:3 representing traditional values.[75] The demand of fair justice for poor and honorable alike in line with Exod 23:2-3 points to a community ideal that challenges the honor–shame categories as it defines justice beyond preset grades of honor.

The relationship of Lev 19 to Exod 23:1 reveals an existential dimension. The "violent/malicious witness" poses a physical threat. Leviticus 19:16aβ also refers to the violent aspects of dispute settlement as it chooses "blood" as a metaphor for life, thus highlighting the existential threat of these processes. Leviticus 19 thus echoes the concern of Exod 23:7, as both point toward the extreme of blood vengeance. Speaking more abstractly to the motivation for the typical challenge–riposte mechanisms in an honor–shame society, Lev 19:17-18 rejects those mechanisms, putting forward a critical perspective on social imbalances.[76]

19:15-16 address mechanisms of justice in fundamental ways as they envision a form of conflict settlement in the kin and consequently reflect on the effects of private enmity in the community in comparison with Deuteronomy. Leviticus 19:15-18, typical for H, conceives of trial arbitration as an activity for the community members and as executed by community members[77] and it nuances

---

75. The juxtaposition of the prohibition of favoring the honorable echoes Deut 1:17. It urges judges to listen to the poor and rich alike; Nihan, *Priestly Torah*, 473.

76. Deuteronomy 1:17 and 16:19 articulate the basis of the impartiality from a more neutral perspective but also point to the social imbalances.

77. H is not concerned with laws for local judges that would be centrally installed; cf. Deut 16:18-20; 25:1-3. Leviticus 19:15-18 and Deut 16:18-20 differ in their concerns, with Lev 19:18 envisioning conflict settlement among "the sons of your people" while Deut 16:18 presupposes to cover each city (gate) with a judge. Deuteronomy 16:19 remains more general in its prohibition not to deviate nor to bend the law (נכר פנים *hi.* / נטה משפט *hi.*). Both Deut 16 and Lev 19 use key terms for justice (צדק, שפט). At the same time, they demonstrate the differences in their understanding of legal authority. Leviticus

the effects according to the varying and unequal social status of the members of the community[78] while leaving out punitive sanctions.[79]

Leviticus 19:16a points to two behavioral patterns and characters that impact conflict settlement, the itinerant slanderer with economic interest (רכיל, v. 16aα) and a community member that "stands up against the blood" of their neighbor (v. 16aβ).

The רכיל (Lev 19:16aα) is a "slanderer" who stirs up conflict against another community member for his own economic benefit. Such behavior could have serious consequences, as the parallel with v. 16aβ indicates, that compares it with an accusation or a testimony against a companion with fatal outcome. The infrequency of the term and its concentration in the the post-biblical reception history are conspicuous. The contexts of some references of the participle *qal* point to the interpretation of רכיל as the agent of "itinerant oral commercial activity" from which the *hiphil* noun is derived.[80] "The semantic development is clear: it begins

---

19:15a refers to "judgment" (משפט), yet the following expects individual community members to take ownership of reprimanding each other. Deuteronomy 16:18-20, on the contrary, instructs judges as those responsible for resolving cases of conflict settlement; cf. Milgrom, *Leviticus 17–22*, 1643. Leviticus 19:15 (as does Exod 23:2-3) draws out the possibilities of imbalance of either favoring the poor or the "great" in trial. The final command in Lev 19:15 to judge your compatriot in fairness is comparable to the more general heading of Deut 16:18. On the relations between both texts, see also Cholewiński, *Heiligkeitsgesetz*, 293–94. Leviticus 19:17b, Deut 25:1, and Deut 16:18-20 reflect on procedural law, pointing to the same constellation of a personal conflict between two opponents.

78. Compositionally, the closing passage, Lev 19:35-36a, repeats the theme of procedural fairness "do not commit עול in justice," bundling it with fair measurement in trade in the society at large, specifically with metics vv. 33-34. In the current arrangement, fairness in justice and trade thus explain in detail the command of mutual benevolence pertaining also to the metic. In comparison, Lev 19:15-16 ban עול in general.

79. As H adopts and modifies older laws of CC and D, one striking difference between D and H is the lack of punitive measures throughout Lev 18, together with its cultic mindset based on the category of "purity and impurity." For an overview on legal revision and innovation in H, see Stackert, "Holiness Code," 392–93. This suggests a priestly circle as authors who were familiar with these categories; see Cholewiński, *Heiligkeitsgesetz*, 289, 296.

80. The meaning "itinerant merchant, a wandering peddler" (so E. Lipiński, רכל, *TDOT* 13 [Grand Rapids: Eerdmans, 2004], 498–99, here 498) is best attested through the list of merchants trading merchandise into Tyre; the list of trade products and trading places demonstrates that Lev. 19 is the source of Ezek 27:12-25a. See M. Saur, *Der Tyroszyklus des Ezechielbuches* (Berlin: de Gruyter, 2008), 235–43. A document from the circle of merchants dating no earlier than the seventh/sixth century was presumably the source. It specifically mentions "traders" or "retailers" of Tyre, i.e., entities that served as commercial intermediaries for the city of Tyre (27:3, 13, 15, 17, 20, 22-24), and, obviously, were biased. Merchants functioned as brokers and were thus typically itinerant,

with "'go from door to door' or 'peddle' and ends with 'swindle.'"[81] Such actions would by default be carried out clandestinely[82] and, as Jer 9:3 and Ezek 22:9 point out, had fatal consequences in a community.

In sum, itinerant slanderers and community members who would speak out against others with fatal consequences (Lev 19:16aαβ) are prototypical malevolent characters who would acquire information for economic gain in order to bring forward accusations.[83] Leviticus 19:16 thus interprets the peddling slanderer as a person that foregoes fairness.

Besides the theme of fairness in trial and in connection with it, v. 16 explicitly refers to death as a potential consequence of trial accusation[84] and the seriousness that could lead to death are apparent.[85] Leviticus 19:16 relates to earlier laws on conflict settlement, namely to Exod 23:2 prohibiting a biased "answer" (ענה) in a trial and the warnings against being a "violent witness" (עד חמס) are prominent.

The general urge of refraining from bias in judgment (v. 15), from slander and from putting a compatriot's life at risk[86] in trial illustrate the community ideal that informs Lev 19:16. The reference frame of the latter two is the community of "your people" and "your companion." The parallelism in v. 16aαβ thus refers to two behavioral patterns that forgo fairness in a community in which members of equal status and rank hold each other accountable.

---

i.e., peddlers. The representatives from the countries mentioned in the list usually traded with Tyre; typically, they took on the role of itinerant merchants; see Lipiński, רכל, 498.

81. See Lipiński, רכל, 499, with reference to Lev 19:16; Jer 6:28; 9:3; Prov 11:13 and Ezek 22:19 (plur.); cf. also 1QS 7:15-16; 1QH 5:25. Seen from a religious perspective, the commercial interest would lead to neglect of other commands; cf. Neh 13:20, which associates traders with a neglectful attitude toward the Sabbath command. This corresponds with the negative aspects of these traders or peddlers excluded from trade on the Sabbath. The LXX translation for the *qal* participle uses the equivalent ἐμπόριον, "marketplace/merchant," as well as ῥοποπῶλαι, "retailer" in Jerusalem Neh 3:31-32.

82. Proverbs highlight the secrecy of a plan that an itinerant merchant would reveal. Proverbs 11:13 relates to a specific economic reality, and Prov 20:18-19 allude to careful and wise plans, more specifically, to strategic plans for leading war, "thoughtfulness through advice" (בְּעֵצָה מַחֲשָׁבוֹת) and "guidance" (תַּחְבֻּלָה). Verse 19 points to the detrimental consequences of the disclosure of secret plans.

83. This is based on the term's notion in the prophetic tradition, namely on the frequently used *qal* participle in Ezekiel; the *hiphil* participle in Proverbs most likely is derived from there.

84. Cf. Isa 50:8, as an illustration of the judicial sense of "to stand up" (עמד) in a cohortative that announces a lawsuit.

85. A prominent case is, for instance, 1 Kgs 21. See recently A. M. Kitz, "Naboth's Vineyard after Mari and Amarna," *JBL* 134 (2015): 529–45.

86. On the meanings of עמד על דם, "standing idle," "arising against," "profit by" and "keeping far from a false charge," in parallelism with false slander, see Milgrom, *Leviticus 17–26*, 1645.

Why does Lev 19:16aα specifically exclude the slanderous accusation for economic gain and v. 16aβ proceed to the extreme of activities that lead to the death of a community member? This third set of apodictic prohibitives urges a sense of community and discourages legal pursuit against compatriots. This pacifying tendency is best seen in response to the quarrelsomeness of community members. In light of the litigiousness and cantankerousness also found in the reception history in the DSS,[87] these passages typically forego the consequences of such behavior and instead appeal to the group's self-identity rooted in Yahweh's idiomatic holiness. The following fourth set offers a more abstract answer pointing to the specific posture of the addressees as group members.

3.4. Verses 17-18

Verse 17abα juxtaposes a prohibitive with a positive command, and 17bβ adds a negative consecutive clause. Verse 18aα adduces two prohibitives and a positive consecutive sentence v. 18aβ. Verse 18b concludes with the self-introductory formula. With this juxtaposition of prohibitives and of positive commands, the verse pair differs from the preceding three. In v. 17 the arrangement of a prohibitive with a positive command and the conclusion with a consecutive (v. 17bβ) is unique in this passage. Verse 18 follows more closely the general pattern, pairing a series of prohibitives with a concluding consecutive clause that has parallels in vv. 11-12, 13-14 and v. 15. This unique form with the positive command "you shall surely reprimand your compatriot" introduced by the adversative "but you shall love" summarizes the fundamental expectations of behavior of the community members. The context of these positive commands of "reprimanding" and "love" are the opposites of (intentional) hate (v. 17aα), revenge and bearing a grudge (v. 18aα). This antithetic arrangement lists two specific behavioral modes between members of the community: not to enter the status of enmity against a "brother, kinsman" besides the positive command of reprimanding a countryman. "Hate" and "love" in the subsequent v. 18, as semantic and conceptual counterparts, are mutually explanatory, referring to the social status of private enmity and friendship, respectively. Yet, first the societal and legal backdrop against which "reprimanding" unfolds requires an explanation.

3.4.1. Verse 17bα: Reprimanding a Compatriot - חכי hi.
The antithetic parallelism of the prohibitive and the positive command in v. 17abα highlight the dialectic between the behavioral posture of "hate" in the first prohibitive, and, as its opposite, a more specific command to "surely reprimand your

---

87. On the reception history in Qumran 11Q19 (Temple Scroll) LXIV 6-13; 1QS VII 15-16, see J. Maier, "Verleumder oder Verräter: Zur jüdischen Auslegungsgeschichte von Lev 19:16," in *Altes Testament. Forschung und Wirkung, Festschrift für H. Graf Reventlow*, ed. P. Mommer and W. Thiel (Neukirchen-Vluyn: Neukirchener Verlag, 1994), 307–11. Maier distinguishes "treason" in the Temple Scroll from "going, walking" (as a false witness); see 1QS VII 15-16.

compatriot." "Hate" and "reprimanding" are not exact semantic opposites, yet the antithetic arrangement of v. 17b presents יכח (*hi.*) as the opposite of שנא v. 17a, as an expression of mutual benevolence. With the addition of the consecutive clause in v. 17bβ, v. 17 emphasizes the necessity of reprimanding a compatriot, pointing out that withholding a reproach would cause guilt. Likewise, in v. 18, the two prohibitives against retaliative behavior provide the backdrop for the urge to motivate an individual toward a general posture of mutual benevolence ("love") in the consecutive clause of v. 18aβ. The infinitive construction with יכח *hi.* serves as the opposite behavior of the reciprocal "hate" of a brother. The pairing of hate with its opposite, love, and reprimanding on the one hand in v. 17bα and the prohibitives against retaliation on the other in v. 18aβ, is telling. The meaning of the postures of love and hate toward community members unfolds against the backdrop of a particular community model. Specifically, what casting rebuke as an expression of love means, depends on the interpretation of "reprimanding" (יכח *hi.*, v. 17abα) and the addressee (עמית).

Used in P/H only here, יכח *hi.* denotes rebuke or reprimanding, namely to end a dispute. יכח *hi.* denotes "to decide, judge" (cf. Gen 31:42), but also "to reprimand"[88] and in Lev 19:17bα has legal overtones.[89] Rebuke or chiding would require jurisdiction.[90] Rather than being objective, since verdicts would typically be given in response to reasoning and to arguing between opposed parties,[91] rebuke could itself be driven by revenge and thus found to be unfair.[92] The absence of a "judge" in Lev 19:17b suggests community members would act in the unpopular role of judge or mediator, including negotiating complicated situations between

---

88. Especially when used with Yahweh as a subject of judgment; see Ps 141:5; Job 13:10; Isa 11:3-4. In Isa 2:4 and Mic 4:3 it is used with reference to the pilgrimage motif that takes up and counters Persian centralist ideology with Jerusalem as center, "to reproof, chide, to make right"; see cf. Hos 4:4, Ezek 3:26, Prov 24:25; 25:12. יכח *hi.* can include "to investigate in judicial hearing"; cf. H. Delkurt, *Ethische Einsichten in der alttestamentlichen Spruchweisheit* (Neukirchen-Vluyn: Neukirchener Verlag, 1993), 31–34. The noun, תכחת, can mean the forensic speech in favor of one of the two parties of a trial; see Hab 2:1; Ps 28:15; Job 13:6; 23:4, and cf. Mayer and Fabry, יכח, *TDOT*, vol. 6, 64–71, here 70. On the relevance of reproof for conflict settlement in Qumran, see for instance, 1QS 6:1; CD 9:2-8, cf. Schiffman, *Sectarian Law*, 94–95. The technical-legal denotation of the verb has been found pivotal for the reconstruction of trial procedure; cf. Boecker, *Redeformen*, 45–47; affirmed by Seeligmann, "Zur Terminologie des Gerichtsverfahrens im Wortschatz des biblischen Hebräisch," in *Hebräische Wortforschung* (Leiden: Brill, 1967), 251–8, here 254, suggesting a development from a technical legal notion to a more general meaning of rebuke, potentially assuming a too rigid difference between institutional trial and rebuke.

89. See, among others, Milgrom, *Leviticus 17–26*, 1647.

90. This is evident when the deity is the (implied) subject of rebuke (תּוֹכַחַת); cf. the parallelism of נקמה and יכח (*hi.*) in Ps 149:7.

91. See, for instance, the exhortation to engage in trial in Isa 1:18. See also Prov 9:7-8; 15:12; 19:25; 28:23, Jer 2:19; Job 40:2, with an undertone of instruction in Job 6:25.

92. Cf. Ps 39:12; Prov 29:15; Ezek 5:15; 25:17.

opponents. The loss of honor through rebuke is a theme throughout[93] and so is the lack of external institutional legitimization when terminating the dynamic of an ongoing quarrel.[94] The positive bias of יכח hi. is grounded in the pacifying effect of a judgment intended to end a feud.[95] Consequently, Lev 19:17bβ points out that bystanders enabling such a process would incur guilt, informed by understanding "reprimanding" as regulatory, instructional element[96] in the community.[97]

The lexicography of Lev 19:17-18 fits the pattern of dispute settlement between two enemies. In its frame of reference, this law ascertains that a continuous conflict between two litigants would damage the community more than a verdict or a judgment between "brothers." The contrast between the inclusion of v. 17a not to hate, with the concluding sentence in v. 18aβ, to practice mutual benevolence toward a brother, is key, thus referring to the need for mutual benevolence between kin members.

The relevance of the specific context and the addressee of the law indeed is pivotal when reconstructing the frame of reference. Next to יכח hi. for "reprimanding," the term compatriot (עמית) as addressee of a reproof also illustrates the nature of the community. Specifically used in Lev 19, עמית[98] appears always

---

93. See, for instance, the interpretation of the hurtful rebuke of the righteous (צדיק) as "grace" in Ps 141:5aα.

94. Consider, for instance, the insincere reconciliations of one of the opponents while de facto continuing the quarrel; cf. Absalom's feigned reconciliation with Amnon in 2 Sam 13:23-29, or Teisis feigning a reconciliation, and on the occasion of an invitation, intoxicating his opponent and subsequently flogging him almost to death in Lysias, *Against Teisis*, Lysias, fr. 75; see in Todd, *Lysias*, 347–51.

95. Cf. the function of the מוכיח as an individual that holds the jurisdiction in a verbal dispute or a litigation (Job 9:33). In detail, the verb conveys the notions of "reproaching" or "accusing" (Ps 50:21, arguably also in Ps 50:7). The relationship to the neighbor is the content of the reproach found in Ps 50:18-20. Psalm 50:16 is an example for the undertone of יכח ("instruction"). This includes the teaching of law which can happen in a dispute settlement. In this sense, the parallelism between תוכחת, as presumably an oral reproof, and מוסר refers to an overlap between rebuke and teaching; cf. also Prov 3:11; 5:12; 6:23; 10:17; 12:1; 13:18; 15:5, 10, 32; see Milgrom, *Leviticus 17–26*, 1647.

96. In line with the tradition in Prov 12:1; 15:5, 12.

97. יכח (hi.) in v. 17bα implies the overtone of "instruction" with the basic meaning to "put right" or "pointing out what is right"; see G. Mayer and H. Fabry, יכח, *TDOT*, vol. 6, 65. Cf. also Proverbs' framing of the function as an educative measure; see Prov 12:1; 13:18; 15:5, 10, 12, 31, 32, and, later, Prov 1:23, 25, 30; 3:11; 5:12. See too the notion of teaching commands or ethics in Prov 6:23 and 9:7b-8aβ that in particular illustrate the struggle of a mediating institution with a non-compliant לץ in the Persian and Hellenistic periods.

98. The etymology and the meaning of עמית ultimately cannot be retrieved with certainty, neither can it be derived from עם, "(the) people," or from a root *עמם/עמה ("to affiliate with") without other evidence; cf., among others, Noth, *Leviticus*, 49. Morphologically, the *–it* ending is used as affirmative and it serves the construction of an abstract

in the singular and with a suffix. In Lev 19 it primarily designates an abstract, fictive kinship affiliation.[99] A critical interpretive basis is the parallel with the less frequently used "the neighbor/companion" (Lev 19:13, 16, 18), known in homicide law as a designation of a personally known member of one's community.[100] The author of the Holiness Code has a preference for this technical term. It has been suggested that terms used in parallel (אח, Lev 19:17; 25:14; בני עמיך, Lev 19:18) point to its central aspect of shared identity to the same people of Israel. This presupposes that בני עמיך equals "brother" or is used in analogy to brother. The term may well designate the member of the same community in a certain time period. This shared identity as a member of the community of the same people[101] presupposes certain rules – for instance, refraining from evil (19:15a) and refraining also from unfair judgment (19:15b). The rules of the community in 1QS 6:24-27 penalize an offense against a member of one's own community with the exclusion of the offender.

The reception history[102] illustrates the necessity of immediate reconciliation. CD 9.6-8 describe the procedure, insisting on a companion's immediate repudiation to avoid ongoing long-term enmity: "If he keeps silent vis-à-vis him from day to day, and then speaks in his wrath against him, he has spoken in a matter of death against him, because he has not established God's command that he said to him: You shall surely reprimand your neighbor, so that you will not load guilt upon yourself." Also, CD 9:2-4 rule out that a member would raise a complaint against a companion in wrath or in the presence of the elders rather than with the companion. The conflict settlement strategy is clear: settlement must occur immediately, in a fair form and in the presence of the companion who is accused, for the community does not tolerate long-term enmity relationships.[103]

This strategy needs to be seen in the context of the behavioral expectation toward a compatriot in Lev 19:11, that in general forbids community members from stealing, denying, or betraying the compatriot and with the general request of fair judgment (Lev 19:15). Also, in the case of a conflict, Lev 19:17 urges a community member not to "hate" a compatriot but "to reprimand" (יכח *hi.*) him (v. 17).

---

term; see H. J. Zobel, עמית, *TDOT* 11 (Grand Rapids: Eerdmans, 2001), 192–96, here 193. The noun is attested 12 times, 11 times in Leviticus and Zech 13:7.

99. Used as an absolute with a concrete noun (גבר, Zech 13:7) that has elapsed.

100. See above, Chapter 2, section 4.4 on Exod 21:14. Used in H, outside of Lev 19:11-18, Lev 20:10 refers to the wife of his רע//Lev 18:20 the wife of your עמית.

101. Zobel, עמית, 194, with reference to Elliger, *Leviticus*, 258: "Glied der Volksgemeinschaft."

102. A comprehensive reception history is beyond the scope of this study. See, for instance, Sir 19:13-17; 20:2: "It is better to reproach than to be angry," and see J. L. Kugel, "On Hidden Hatred and Open Reproach: Early Exegesis of Leviticus 19:17," *HThR* 80 (1987): 43–61, esp. 48.

103. Cf. Mathys, *Liebe*, 122.

In conclusion, v. 17abα urges members to actively bring about conflict settlement in quarrels through the authoritative rebuke of community members. This preferred conflict settlement model gives jurisdiction to individual community members but also urges community members to refrain from revenge and resentment. In this line of thought v. 18aα further refines conflict settlement strategies and v. 18aβ points even beyond the prohibitives to the positive command of mutual benevolence.

3.4.2. *Verse 18aα: Refraining from revenge and retaliation*

Urging opponents from taking revenge (נקם), from acting out retaliation through "bearing a grudge" (נטר) in Lev 19:17-18 in effect is to encourage practices of interpersonal conflict settlement. Already v. 17abα urges restraint from hating a brother and instead exhorts the participants to reprimand each other and accept a verdict. This exhortation would de facto end enemy-conflicts as they by default would have been lived out in the public square. Not taking revenge when seen against the backdrop of default dispute settlement patterns between two private enemies is thus counter-intuitive. Preventing opponents from vengefully acting out against each other partakes in a discourse on typical conflict settlement mechanisms. Private law uses various terms for the mutual claims of parties besides נקם[104] with designations around vengeance and retribution. The subject noun is critical. It was suggested the term denotes "extralegal retribution… forbidden to men, …exacted by God."[105] Yet the three overlapping core areas[106] of the term in law, judgment prophecy, particularly in its later use in Hellenistic time and more broadly in private enmity, provide further context relevant to Lev 19:17.

First, in biblical law, the legitimate act of נקם for "revenge" with a human logical subject is limited to the treatment of slaves in Exod 21:20-21.[107] The

---

104. For instance, בקש *pi.*, with the object "soul/life" (Exod 4:19); for instance, "blood" (2 Sam 4:2; Ezek 3:18, 20; with elision of the object "to take revenge," Josh 22:23); the "avenger" (גאל, Num 35:12, 19; שוב *hi.*, 1 Sam 25:39); Yahweh as God of "recompense" (גמלות) and שוב *hi.* ("give back" with גמל, Pss 28:4; 94:2; Lam 3:64; Obad 15; Jon 4:7).

105. Milgrom, *Leviticus*, 1651.

106. The root occurs 79 times in the Old Testament, the verb 35 times, the masculine noun 17 times and the feminine noun 27 times; see the overviews in G. Sauer, נקם *nqm* to avenge, in E. Jenni and C. Westermann (eds.), *Theological Lexicon of the Old Testament*, vol. 2, translated from German by M. E. Biddle (Peabody, MA: Hendrickson, 1997), 767–69. Cf. E. Lipiński, נקם, *TDOT* vol. 10, 1–9. For an extensive treatment, see G. Chirichigno, *Debt Slavery in Israel and in the Ancient Near East* (Sheffield: Sheffield Academic, 1993), 155–69.

107. Three explanations have been adduced. First, interpreting the infinitive construct נקום ינקם as a reference to blood revenge has been doubted, since מות יומת would instead be expected in the context of slavery law. Consequently, some argued that the process

underlying understanding of the idiom to a large extent depends on the nature of the slavery.¹⁰⁸ Arguably, no capital liability would incur in the case of a foreign slave. Consequently, if this is a debt-slave,¹⁰⁹ normal rules of revenge would apply. This would mean that the kin of the dead slave would seek blood revenge. As is implied in Prov 6:34-35, a form of a כפר or a (large) bribe שחד could theoretically remain an option for appeasing a cuckolded husband as an alternative to executing נקם,¹¹⁰ with Prov 6 assuming that the cuckolded husband by default would take revenge and execute the adulterer.

Second, narrative contexts of the use of the root among humans are scarce,¹¹¹ while it generally assumes the relation of the term to revenge patterns in conflict settlement, it refrains from using this term for retaliation,¹¹² namely in the case of blood revenge. Notably, the proverbial announcement of retribution lacks a

in this passage deviates from the default procedure of blood revenge. Given the slave's distance from his relatives, another institutional body would take over the task of the closest of kin as avenger of blood. Westbrook assumes that in exchange for the slave a vicarious member of his master's family would have to die; R. Westbrook, *Studies in Biblical and Cuneiform Law* (Paris: Gabalda, 1988), 89–100; cf. Jackson, *Wisdom-Laws*, 246. The substantiation is, in part, based on vicarious punishment ordered in LH 116, and also on the widespread use of the נקם for establishment of divine justice vis-à-vis collective entities. Consequently, in continuation of Westbrook's thought, the idiom could be understood as a form of assurance of the execution of divine justice in the absence of a next of kin. A third explanation for the root in this context is that the idiom refers to a fine instead of a capital punishment; see among others, following Cazelles and Driver, Jackson, *Wisdom-Laws*, 247.

108. Schwienhorst-Schönberger, *Bundesbuch*, 71, suggests the idiom refers to revenge from the perspective of the victim, i.e., the slave in Exod 21:20; cf. Jackson, *Wisdom-Laws*, 248.

109. Jackson, *Wisdom-Laws*, 241, establishes an original set of laws on slavery in 21:20-21 and 21:26-27.

110. Jackson, *Wisdom-Laws*, 248.

111. In Gen 4:15, 24, נקם unequivocally refers to blood revenge, though it does so in a passive form of the *hophal*, avoiding a logical subject.

112. The source-critical consideration of the narrative, being largely built on a genealogy of P, highlights the context in a paradigmatic kinship-based society, and, consequently, understands revenge and retaliation in their relevance to this specific society. See, for instance, M. Arneth, *Durch Adams Fall ist ganz verderbt... Studien zur Entstehung der alttestamentlichen Urgeschichte* (Göttingen: Vandenhoeck & Ruprecht, 2007), 168–69, 233. Genesis 4:1-16, 25-26, with the exception of vv. 6-7, form a post-Priestly stratum, while the genealogy of P in vv. 17-24 contains older material, probably reworked; with the function of the demonstration of the display of a twofold humanity in Gen 4:17-24, is a genealogy known to P, while 4:1 and 25-26 are oriented toward the genealogy in P.

logical subject noun in Gen 4:15, 24, thus ultimately securing it as the deity's privilege[113] in a discourse on feuding mechanisms.[114]

Third, Second Temple prophetic tradition and Psalms reserve the motif of vengeance as a privilege of the deity to ultimately establish justice.[115] Isaiah 61:2 is an example of a type of (retrospective) prophetic announcement, specifically of the "day of revenge"[116] that this Persian-period prophetic tradition ultimately eschatologizes[117] and that, subsequently, in the Hellenistic-period prophetic

---

113. The noun is predominantly used for the execution of justice, with Yahweh as agent; a human agent appears in Jer 20:10; Ezek 25:15a; Lam 3:60; Ps 18:48/2 Sam 22:48. The narrative reflects on homicide law, with Yahweh taking up the role of the avenger in vv. 9-14, and on the talion law of blood vengeance within the kin. On the phrase the blood "cries out" (צעק), see K. Koch, "Der Spruch „Sein Blut bleibe auf seinem Haupt" und die israelitische Auffassung vom vergossenen Blut," in *Um das Prinzip der Vergeltung in Religion und Recht des Alten Testaments*, ed. K. Koch, *VT* 12 (1962): 396–416, here 407; cf. D. Daube, "Law in the Narratives," in *Studies in Biblical Law* (Cambridge: Cambridge University Press, 1969), 13–15. On the literary text as a genre that presupposes a narrative, see Barmash, *Homicide*, 18–19. The plural of the term was suggested to emphasize the guilt; cf. H. Christ, *Blutvergiessen im Alten Testament. Der gewaltsame Tod des Menschen untersucht am hebräischen Wort* dām (Basel: Friedrich Reinhardt, 1977), 63, yet more likely is a reference to the context of blood revenge; see H. G. L. Peels, *The Vengeance of God: The Meaning of the Root NQM and the Function of the NQM-Texts in the Context of Divine Revelation in the Old Testament* (Leiden: Brill, 1995), 67.

114. Cain's expectation of outstanding blood vengeance in v. 14 alludes to his status as a fugitive murderer exposed to revenge, and the assumption of the deity as avenger of blood in Gen 4:15 presupposes the death penalty in the case of homicide. This illustrates an individual's vulnerability in the absence of a next of kin that could function as deterrent; cf. the vicarious protection through the deity's agency and also the pattern of revenge in Gen 4:23-24.

115. Cf. Deut 32:35, 41, 43; Jer 46:10; 50:15, 28; 51:6, 11, 36; Ezek 25:12, 14, 15, 17; Mic 5:14; Nah 1:2. Cf. Peels, *Vengeance*, 132–208.

116. נקם replaces an original "day of salvation" upon analogy with Isa 49:8; the material in 61:1-11 dates mainly to the Persian era; cf. O. H. Steck, "Der Rachetag in Jesaja 61:2. Ein Kapitel redaktionskritischer Kleinarbeit," in *Studien zu Tritojesaja* (Berlin: de Gruyter, 1991) 106–18, with an overview table on p. 278.

117. The day of revenge in its current setting in Isaiah appears in 61:1-11. Steck, "Rachetag," 106–107, assumes one source-critical unit, yet originally this day of salvation for the broken-hearted and the afflicted is part of the larger concept of a "day of revenge" of an a Hellenistic-era overarching redaction of the entire book of Isa 1–66*; Steck, *Studien zu Tritojesaja*, 278. This layer includes three passages of נקם in Isa 34:8; 35:4 and 59:18 – each time an act of Yahweh against his enemies, to which Isa 61:2 refers back. At the same time, the day of revenge in Isa 61:2 anticipates the final day of wrath or revenge in one of the core passages of the Isaiah-book redaction, Isa 63:1-6, that also includes the garment metaphor. The focus, suggests Steck, is on an eschatological day of revenge against the enemies with a typical twofold outcome: on that day of revenge, the

context leads to the day of revenge with נקם understood as the day of final universal judgment. Leviticus 26:25 in H echoes this understanding of a final vindication with Yahweh taking revenge on those in aberration from the law, as Isa 1:24 likewise echoes.[118] This notion of an expected trial also forms the backdrop of Lev 19:18.[119] Various literary contexts critically evaluate individual revenge and ultimately conceive of it as a boundary transgression. Unlike the term פקד as reference to a legitimate type of claim as "the official investigation executed in one's own jurisdiction that holds those concerned responsible for failures and offenses and takes action against them," the concept of vengeance refers to the "typical private penalty that properly pertains to persons outside one's own jurisdiction and authority."[120]

Abstaining from revenge patterns is a complex topic that has roots in Exod 23:4-5 and Deut 22:1-4 that is prominent beyond instructions for inner-kin conflict resolution. In the wider area of biblical ethics, refraining from revenge is a topic that is extant in the Psalter. The Psalms of Revenge quote the oppressed individual's cry for justice to Yahweh. They thus partake of a strand of biblical thought that expresses the hope for ultimate justice in light of an opponent's threat.[121] These Psalms reflect on retaliative justice and on revenge patterns in the conceptual and in the formal framework of lament and plea. They pair their typical advice to refrain from taking revenge with the plea toward the deity, thus expressing the hope that the deity would rebuke opponents and establish justice. This context illustrates the backdrop of the use of נקם in Lev 19:18. Consider, for instance, Psalm 149:7 with the parallelism נקמה // תוכחת and as expression of injustice vis-à-vis the nations as opponents in a trial. The Psalm construes this in analogy to a lawsuit against a personal enemy.[122]

---

part of Israel that repents, including the unrepentant members of Israel (Isa 61:2aβ), will see ultimate salvation, while, on the other hand, the nations will see definite punishment in an ultimate act of vindication; see Steck, "Rachetag," 118. Notwithstanding the positive allusions to the salvation of the nations found elsewhere in Isaiah, Steck argues that the overriding perspective of the book of Isaiah as a whole is on the salvation of the people of Israel.

118. Further parallels for the use of this term in judgment oracles against Israel are found in Ezek 24:1-14 (esp. v. 8); Jer 5:9, 29; 9:8 (MT). See among others, the overview in Peels, *Vengeance*, 102–31.

119. Barbiero, *L'asino*, 282, sees "revenge" oscillating between both the judicial and the more internal way of interacting and conflict solution.

120. Cf. F. Horst, "Recht und Religion im Bereich des AT," *EvTh* 16 (1956): 49–75, esp. 73.

121. Cf. the overview by F. Hartenstein, "Ein zorniger und gewalttätiger Gott? Zorn Gottes, ‚Rachepsalmen' und ‚Opferung Isaaks' – neuere Forschungen," *VuF* 58 (2013): 110–26, esp. 121–23.

122. Cf. the same constellation of the nations as enemies (plur.) that in Ps 79:10 would confront the collective of "your servants." In compliance with a pattern of blood revenge that manifests itself in the procedure of a trial, Yahweh is called to vindicate his

In conclusion, the biblical tradition distinguishes the use with the deity as subject as an act of establishment of justice from its use in the human sphere. When seen through the lens of the texts that announce the deity's implementation of justice, they retrospectively reflect on the distance at particular historical points in time.[123] Still, by tendency just forms of "revenge" remain reserved for Yahweh, as human agency typically would blur or pervert intent of just retaliation. Examples point out how revenge seeks to hurt the offender's kin at large, not necessarily only one specific individual, with the exception of the case of an adulterer. Thus, revenge is acted out by a collective and directed toward another kin.[124] The explicit prohibition of revenge is a theme in narratives discussing the behavioral patterns of opponents,[125] in the Psalms of Revenge,[126] and in prophetic judgment oracles.[127] In conflicts, revenge patterns were the default legal mechanism in the dispute settlement process[128] to which נקם refers. It is prominent in

servants. This correlates to Ps 8:3, which refers to the general attitude of taking (blood) revenge in case of accusations, and Ps 44:17, where the individual prays for rescue from the avenger of blood as it is exposed to an opponent. Also, from this epoch or from late Persian time, Prov 6:34 presents revenge in the case of adultery seemingly in a neutral way: "For jealousy is the anger of a heroic (man); and no compassion does he show on the day of revenge." As a commentary on the legal procedures of taking a neighbor's wife in Prov 6:25-33, such anger and reaction have parallels in other legal passages. Cf. A. Loader, *Proverbs 1–9* (Peeters: Leuven, 2014), 271, 288; cf. the death penalty in Deut 22:22; Lev 18:20; 20:10, and the anger caused through adultery in Ezek 16:38-40; 23:45-46.

123. See, for instance, J. Jeremias, *Der Zorn Gottes im Alten Testament. Das biblische Israel zwischen Verwerfung und Erwählung* (Neukirchen-Vluyn: Neukirchener Verlag, 2009), 77, on the four modes of the Dtr see the reference to the deity's wrath on pp. 46–77.

124. Whether, in retrospect, the deity's act of "revenge" in biblical thought at large can fully be separated from a previous action as a form of retaliation in response to a previous offense remains debated. One important touchstone is whether the evidence in Proverbs allows us to assume a form of divine "retaliation" or presupposes a more immediate, implicit destiny-deed connection; cf., with regard to early wisdom in Prov 25–28 and prophetic traditions, cf. K. Koch, "Gibt es ein Vergeltungsdogma im Alten Testament," in *Um das Prinzip der Vergeltung in Religion und Recht des Alten Testaments*, ed. K Koch (Darmstadt: Wissenschaftliche Buchgesellschaft, 1972), 130–80, including the discussion in this volume and, among others, B. Janowski, *Ein Gott der straft und tötet? Zwölf Fragen zum Gottesbild des Alten Testaments* (Neukirchen-Vluyn: Neukirchener Verlag, 2013), 64–65, and the bibliographic references cited, 405–406.

125. See, for instance, 1 Sam 24:12; 25:22, 26-31; see also, without the verb, 26:8 ("enemy") and many others.

126. See, for instance, E. Zenger, *A God of Vengeance? Understanding the Psalms of Divine Wrath*, trans. L. M. Maloney (Louisville: Westminster John Knox, 1996).

127. E.g. Ps 109; cf. also Deut 32:35, 41; Isa 35:4; 59:17; 63:4; Nah 1:2; Ps 58:10.

128. Noth, *Leviticus*, 22, suggests this meaning; he seems, however, to assume a trial or some form of an institutional judgment in the more narrow sense. See H. Jagersma, „*Leviticus 19"*. *Identiteit. Bevrijding. Gemeenschap* (Assen: Van Gorcum, 1972), 98, with

the rebuttal of assaults against the foes of a group, directed against the nation in Yahweh's ultimate trial.[129] The use of the term in Psalms alludes to this universal context of the establishment of an ideal of justice in the execution of revenge to which the language of Lev 19:18 refers. The passage uses "revenge" without reference to a centrally regulated dispute settlement, such as an impartial institutional trial in front of a judge,[130] and, while fully aware of the need of revenge at the public–private interface,[131] as is typical of the skepticism of this term of revenge in the Persian era, it rejects such mechanisms of נקם/נטר, excluding any notion of revenge in hateful constellations between personal opponents.

The reception history echoes the ban on revenge that became a hallmark of Jewish communal ethics at large and in particular became a touchstone of ethics of the close-knit community represented in the Dead Sea Scrolls.[132] Leviticus 19:18aα excludes revenge, נקם, within the community as an expected default pattern, in, for instance, cases of blood guilt. This aligns with an overarching tendency to more broadly also reserve vengeful interaction between different kin for the deity.[133] The default meaning is to perform an act of revenge against an

---

reference to Exod 21:20-21 and Num 31:2. Mathys, *Liebe*, 66, rejects this, suggesting instead Exod 21:20-21 refers more generally to punishing, not to revenge.

129. Lipiński, נקם, 3–5, lists besides blood revenge rape or other serious transgressions; cf. the references to threats of serious physical injury in Judg 16:28-30 and in Jer 20:10; cf. 26:11.

130. See, for instance, E. Merz, *Die Blutrache bei den Israeliten* (Leipzig: Heinrichs, 1916), 9 n. 2, normally executed by an institution above the individual parties and executed in line with socially accepted norms. See, in contrast, F. Horst, "Recht und Religion im Bereich des Alten Testaments," *EvTh* 16 (1956): 49–75, with the suggestion that this designates the typical private retribution.

131. See above Chapter 1.

132. In the reception history, the DSS require a reproof to precede punishment. Only after an initial reproof could a transgression of the law be penalized. The intention was not to punish someone in anger but instead to reprove this individual, presumably based on a substantiation in the law; cf. the references to the DSS in Milgrom, *Leviticus 17–22*, 1652; L. H. Schiffman, *Sectarian Law in the Dead Sea Scrolls: Courts, Testimony and the Penal Code* (Chico: Scholars Press, 1983), 89–98. The command's reception history in the DSS, a cornerstone of this group's ethics, is discussed in Milgrom, *Leviticus 17–22*, 1649–53. Rather than belonging specifically to a minority opinion, legal anthropology suggests that the command represents the effort of a close-knit group to effectively pacify conflicts.

133. While in tension with traditional ethics, particularly with the talionic principle of Lev 24:17, clearly vengeance at this point in time was a legitimate, deadly punitive recourse taken by Yahweh in order to maintain the covenant according to Lev 26:25. It is as an act in the future detached from the tradition of blood revenge in homicide legislation (Exod 21:12; Deut 19, as well as Gen 9:6). To ensure a direct connection between the death of the victim and the retribution, the avenger must carry out blood revenge with his own hand (Ezek 25:14; 1QS 2:6). Leviticus 19:18aα uses "taking vengeance" intransitively,

opponent.¹³⁴ Instead of acts of revenge, Lev 19 suggests an ideal-typical model of mutual legal instruction within a community, thus implementing peaceful conflict settlement in a polity analogous to inner-kin community.¹³⁵ Refraining from revenge is further enhanced through the prohibition in v. 18aα which aims at discouraging any consistent posture of holding back the voicing anger (נטר) against a community member, in line with the subsequent urges to mutual benevolence (v. 18aβ).¹³⁶

comparable to the lack of an object in the following prohibitive, as is the case in some prohibitives of the Decalogues. Usually an object is mentioned. Taking revenge can be expressed in various ways; see the overview on grammar and syntax in Lipiński, נקם, *TDOT* 10, 1–9, 2–3, who argues that the idiomatic use of "revenge" usually has the preposition מן and then mentions as object the enemies, in 1 Sam 14:24; 24:13; Judg 16:28; 2 Kgs 9:7; Est 8:13; Isa 1:24; Jer 15:15; 46:10; cf. Jer 11:20; 20:10, 12. Other prepositions are מאת in Num 31:2; ב in Judg 15:7; 1 Sam 18:25; Jer 5:9, 29; 9:8; 50:15; Ezek 25:12 (cf. CD 8:11-12; 1QpHab 9:2); ל in Ezek 25:12; Nah 1:2; CD 8:5-6; 9:5. The subjective genitive designating the avenger usually refers to God in Num 31:3; Jer 11:20; 20:12; 50:15, 38; 51:11; Ezek 25:14, 17; 1QS 1:11; 1QM 4:12, and also his wrath in 1QM 3:6. In Lam 3:60; Sir 46:1 and 1QS 2:9, it refers to the adversaries taking vengeance.

134. The jurisdiction and the mode of an institutional or a personal handling remain open. Milgrom, *Leviticus 17–26*, 1651, suggests implicit extralegal retribution, but it seems rather to be the default reaction to an offense of, for instance, homicide.

135. Cf. Mathys, *Liebe*, 120–23, describes the ethos in H as inner-group ethos. On the developments of talion in ancient Near Eastern and biblical law, see further Chapter 1; cf. also A. Bartor, "Blood Guilt," in *The Oxford Encyclopedia of the Bible and Law*, vol 1, ed. B. Strawn (Oxford: Oxford University Press, 2015), 65–68, and T. W. Thompson, "Punishment and Restitution," vol 2, 183–93, esp. 183–88. See also the overview on revenge in W. Dietrich, "Rache, Erwägungen zu einem alttestamentlichen Thema," *EvT* 36 (1976): 450–72.

136. The legal aspects of such behavior are evident in the command "you shall not bear a grudge" against the "sons of your people" (v. 18aα; cf. the closest parallel for the construct chain "sons of your people" in Ezek 3:11; 33:2, 12, 17, 30; 37:18; cf. also Dan 12:1). This refers to the engagement in continuous feuding and its revenge patterns between private individuals; cf. the typical attitude of enduring, inheritable hate of an enemy, comparable to the everlasting brutal grudge of collectives as archenemies such as Edom; cf. Amos 1:11. The notion of this behavioral pattern is the same for Yahweh and human subjects. Yahweh as subject appears three times. In Ps 103:9 it serves in an epexegetical function of the formula of grace, explaining the term רב חסד with "but not forever will he bear a grudge." Jeremiah 3:5 poses the question "Will he bear a grudge forever?" which the (assumedly secondary) oracle 3:6-12 answers negatively. With the deity as subject, Yahweh's ongoing revenge in Nah 1:2 serves as a designation for impending punishment.

Leviticus 19:18 became formative for the behavior of community members and their relationship to each other in the reception history of the DSS.[137] As Milgrom points out, the intensity of rage and anger that this term implies can be seen in the serious intention to harm another member of the community. The repeated use of this prohibition in the DSS demonstrates this community's intent to avoid long term enmity among their members urging them to act out conflicts immediately. CD 9:2-8 is an example:

> And as to that which he (God) said, "you shall not take vengeance nor keep a grudge against the sons of your people" anyone of those who enter in the covenant who brings a charge against his neighbor without reproof before witnesses, but brings it in his burning wrath or tells it to his elders to put him to shame, is taking vengeance and bearing a grudge. It is written only "He takes vengeance against his adversaries and keeps a grudge against his enemies." If he was silent from day to day and in his burning wrath charged him with a capital offense, his iniquity is upon him, for he did not fulfill the ordinance of God which says to him: "You shall surely reprove your neighbor so that you do not bear sin because of him."[138]

In conclusion, the warning of Lev 19:18 to avoid long-term hateful relationships between members of the community is a concern the DSS amplify multiple times. The Damascus document points to the need of a close-knit community to immediately pacify nascent conflicts and the urging of community members to take responsibility for ending conflicts quickly rather than bearing a grudge.[139] This echoes the urge to refrain from revenge in Lev 19:18, suggesting a close-knit community as a frame of reference of this ethos.

3.4.3. Verses 17a, 18aβ: Love and Hate in Legal-Historical Perspective

Compared with the preceding sets of apodictic prohibitives, Lev 19 exhibits a programmatic undertone, namely with the bookending pair of "hate" and "love" in vv. 17a and 18aβ. Verses 17a and 17bα use hate in opposition to mutual reprimanding in a community and thus point to an understanding of the functions of

---

137. Cf. 1QS 7:8; CD 7:2; 8:5; 9:2, 3; 13:18; 19:18. As a rule for the members of the community, see CD 7:2; 9:2, 4; 13:18; 1QS 7:8. See H. Madl, נטר, *TDOT* 9 (Grand Rapids: Eerdmans, 1998), 404, and a similar list in Mathys, *Liebe*, 120–23.

138. Translation of J. M. Baumgarten and D. R. Schwartz in J. H. Charlesworth (ed.), *The Dead Sea Scrolls: Hebrew, Aramaic, and Greek Texts with English Translations*. Volume 2, *Damascus Document War Scroll and Related Documents* (Tübingen: Mohr Siebeck; Louisville: Westminster John Knox, 1995), 43; cf. also CD 7:8: "Whoever bears a grudge against his fellow unjustly, shall be punished (for) one year."

139. Milgrom, *Leviticus 17–26*, 1652; and see the quotes of Lev 19:17-18 from Qumran in Mathys, *Liebe*, 120–23, listed above. Unlike the multiple allusions to the prohibition of mutual hate, the combination with the positive command of neighborly love is found only once in CD 6:20–7:3, as Mathys, *Liebe*, 122 points out.

judicial authority each member of the community is charged with, and mutual benevolence as complementary. Read in conjunction with vv. 18a and 18aβ, "love" as mutual benevolence is cast as the opposite of the typical retaliative patterns of challenge and riposte in feuding honor–shame societies. Leviticus 19:17-18 associates mutual malevolence with those patterns instead of which it proposes an ethos of amity as typical for inner-kin relationships. Verses 17-18 thus present love and hate as opposite social constructs that are associated with precise conflict-settlement patterns. Namely, an inter-kin feud would imply that both parties find themselves as long-term opponents, while within the kin, mutual benevolence would be the default. This asserts that Lev 19:11-18 presuppose a community of shared jurisdiction of all members and refer to a social status in contrast to long-term reciprocal hate and retaliatory behavior, such as bearing a grudge or taking revenge.

The legal-historical tradition points to previous laws in Exod 23 and Deut 22. It also points out how Lev 19 systematizes the categories of members of the polity and focuses on the hater's intent. Determining the legal-historical roots of the opposite postures of hate and love and the status of long-term enmity would require further attention to previous legal traditions. Two selective contexts of preceding laws on mutual benevolence and malevolence, trial law in Exod 23:1-3, 6-8, including the case laws vv. 4-5, and Deut 22:1-4 are the thematic, literary and compositional[140] precursors[141] that inform Lev 19:17-18. Leviticus 19:17a takes up "hate" from Exod 23:5 and the kinship term "brother" from Deut 22:1-4. In light of these, Lev 19:17-18 also reflect on a pending quarrel or lawsuit between two individuals[142] as a matter analogous to inner-kin law.

Leviticus 19:17-18 systematizes the relationship between two individuals, a tendency that is apparent in the composition. The first half of the positive command (v. 17a) explicitly addresses private enmity and hate. Together with the closing command "love your neighbor (רע)" in v. 18aβ forms an inclusio. This inclusio is relevant in light of the use of all four terms for community members in vv. 17-18. The first sentence addresses a relationship between brothers (v. 17a), and subsequent sentences all use the other three terms "your compatriot," the "son of your people" and "your neighbor," thus highlighting the relevance of vv. 17-18 for the entire prohibitive list in vv. 11-18.

---

140. Cf., compositionally, the connection between Lev 19:17-18 and the prohibition against mixtures in Lev 19:19, and already in Deut 22:1-12, with vv. 1-4 referring to the enemy, and vv. 5, 9-11 to mixtures.

141. See, among many others, Otto, *Ethik*, 247. See also Nihan, *Priestly Torah*, 474, contra, for instance, G. Braulik, "Die dekalogische Redaktion der deuteronomischen Gesetze. Ihre Abhängigkeit von Levitikus 19 am Beispiel von Deuteronomium 22,1-12; 24,10-22 und 25,13-16," in *Bundesdokument und Gesetz. Studien zum Deuteronomium* ed. G. Braulik (Freiburg: Herder 1995), 160–61 with the unlikely suggestion Deut 22:1-4 depend on Lev 19:17-18.

142. See, for instance, Elliger, *Leviticus*, 259; Otto, *Ethik*, 247.

Finally, the systematizing tendency of the status of enemies or friends as a deliberately adopted posture toward a community member is also evident in the idiomatic use of hate as a long-term intentional aspect (לב, Lev 19:17). As is the case with long-term enmity, long-term love or benevolence refers to a legal status that entails specific expectations of mutual solidarity[143] and presupposes a particular intention. Thus, Lev 19:17-18 pairs friendly behavior toward an opponent in public with open support or, on the contrary, clandestinely committed vicious deeds that would hit an opponent worse than laid out plans.[144]

The meaning of "love your neighbor" is best described in the compositional context of the two prohibitives v. 18 after which this positive command follows in a *w-qatal* sentence with consecutive meaning "so that." All preceding acts of reprimanding a community member, of refraining from revenge patterns, would happen to ensure this last consequence, to make apparent the benevolence toward a neighbor or companion. The syntax of v. 18aβ is unusual, with its construction of אהב with the preposition ל, "toward."[145] It is thus best understood as a way to express a comparative in the object of the clause, along the lines of "type" and "emulation," namely as "precedence" and "repetition," more specifically as a short form of a comparison: "so that you show love to your neighbor, as (love is shown to) you."[146] The clause thus highlights the character of love and friendship as it would unfold as the result of ongoing friendship, as opposed to the posture of ongoing mutual enmity. Treating members of one's community as friends implies exercising mutual benevolence. Reading Lev 19:18aβ with a

---

143. See, for instance, the role expectations to a friend Ps 55:13-15 MT (12-14 ET).

144. Cf. the reference to the secret nature of evil plans Ps 28:3. Job 1:5 mentions sins that were committed "in the heart" without being carried out. See Mathys, *Liebe*, 63–64.

145. The unusual construction has been noticed, for instance, by P. Mendes-Flohr, *Love, Accusative and Dative: Reflections on Leviticus 19:18, The B.G. Rudolph Lectures in Judaic Studies* (Syracuse, NY: New York University Press, 2007), 13. Usually the verb is associated with the preposition את with humans or with the deity as object, for instance in Gen 25:28 (2×); 29:18, 30; 34:3; 37:3-4 and others. Few instances use the verb without preposition, Deut 10:18; Judg 16:4; 1 Kgs 11:1; Job 19:19; Ps 146:8; Prov 15:9; 16:13; Jer 2:25; Hos 3:1. The assessment of the unusual ל varies. Inserting an obliterated object – "You shall love the good for your neighbor, as you love the good for yourself" – is possible but not without difficulties; Gass, "Problem," 209. Alternatively, assuming Aramaic origin, it has been suggested that it corresponds an accusative note; Mathys, *Liebe*, 5; cf. Barbiero, *L'asino*, 284. Finally, it may be understood as *lamed applicationis* in transitive verbs that designates the object as affected by the action; cf. E. Jenni, *Die hebräischen Präpositionen. Band 3: Die Präposition Lamed* (Stuttgart: Kohlhammer, 2000), 122, and see on this below.

146. Cf. E. Jenni, "Zur Semantik der hebräischen Personen-, Tier- und Dingvergleiche," *ZAH* 3 (1990): 133–66, here 143–44. The verse follows the pattern of mentioning first a "precedence" that is then followed by a "repetition." The interpretation assumes that ל may drop out, while in comparison it would usually be expected to follow after the preposition כ; cf. the interpretation in Gass, "Problem," 208.

prepositional interpretation of כָּמוֹךָ supports benevolence being an *aspect* of the action, an expression of the active posture of love *for or toward* the neighbor or companion.[147]

In its setting in H, Lev 19 urges the adopting of mutual benevolence as a posture among community members, comparable to the posture vis-à-vis members of one's kin. Insisting on this posture and implementing it beyond the polity of equals in vv. 33-34, it prioritizes peace within this community over individual interests of gaining honor.[148]

This raises the question about how Lev 19:11-18 balances benevolent interactions with a neighbor/companion against the segregation from which it draws its self-identity through alterity from surrounding societies. While a comprehensive history of the reception of the prohibition of mutual hateful interaction is beyond the scope of this study, it is at first glance apparent that one textual corpus of Judaism refers multiple times to the prohibition of private hate from Lev 19:17-18. The inner-kinship ethos of mutual benevolence is specifically prominent in the DSS and its ethical ideals among community members. Notably, the DDS in a similar way pair cultural segregation from the surroundings with an ethos among community members as a move of alterity, i.e., as a form of distancing oneself from the patterns of an agonistic nature perceived in the surrounding cultures. The stipulation to immediately end nascent conflict engagement in favor of mutual benevolence in the DSS illustrates the seriousness of the continuing hateful interaction between community members.[149] Therefore, a comparison

---

147. The relation between the individual and the neighbor or companion for reasons of syntax does not carry a reflexive notion "as you love yourself." The prepositional כָּמוֹךָ is not to be read as adverbial reflexive. The parallel in Deut 13:7, "your neighbor who is like your life" (רעך אשר כנפשך), demonstrates this as it has no reflexive meaning. Consequently, as Gass notes, the command in Lev 19:18aβ does not understand self-love as prerequisite for the love of the neighbor, a notion that the Greek rendering with preposition supports: καὶ ἀγαπήσεις τὸν πλησίον σου ὡς σεαυτόν. The LXX interprets the Hebrew in a particular way; as is also evident in its translation of רע with πλησίος, a person "near or close to" oneself. The Hebrew term covers both facets "neighbor" and "companion"; cf. on this and on the reading of כָּמוֹךָ, Gass, "Problem," 204–206.

148. Determining the nuances of benevolence required in detail toward brother, companion, compatriot, sons of your people is beyond the scope of this study; cf. the use of "brother," בן: Lev 19:17; 25:14, 25, 35, 39; Deut 15:7; 22:1; "sons of Israel," בני ישראל: Lev 17:14; cf. Exod 27:21; Lev 22:32; and בני איש ישראל: Lev 17:13; cf. Exod 27:21; Lev 22:32 and others.

149. In addition to the quotes of Lev 19:17-18, implementation regulation points to the specifics of the conflict settlement, namely to reprimand each other "in truth, humbleness, and faithful love" (באמת וענוה ואהבת חסד, 1QS V, 25), and to refrain from bringing an accusation to the many (the full assembly) before reprimanding the person in the presence of witnesses (בתוכחת לפני עדים 1QS V, 1). Both opponents should explicitly refrain from the evil spirit (רוח רשע) and hate (שנא), and the rebuke must happen on the very day (ביום, 1QS V, 25), so that the conflict could be ended immediately. These implementation rules

juxtaposes internal conflict settlement in close-knit communities with the model of conflict resolution in the Dead Sea Scrolls (4.2). First, however, the following section compares and contrasts the ideal of long-term mutual benevolence in the social reality of H's[150] legislation with the priestly-prophetic view on the urban polity in the twin tradition in Ezekiel (4.1).

4. Outlook—Religious Historical Parallels

4.1. Hate and Urban Carnage

Leviticus 19:11-18 relates in many ways to the judgment oracle in Ezek 22:6-12,[151] which describes the effects of hateful conflict driven by the leadership elite of the "princes" or "rulers of Israel" in the framework of urban Jerusalem. Verses 6-7 specifically blame city authorities for the carnage. Verse 7 specifies the reason as it puts in perspective the rampant killing with the officials' disrespect for traditional kinship institutions (father and mother) and the resulting oppression of sojourners, orphans and widows. The bold rejection of kinship-based institutions

specify the need for immediate reconciliation urging to a "rebuke in love," i.e., as a form of mutual benevolence that would exclude hate. Similarly, compare the punishment of six months for reasonlessly bearing a grudge (נטר) or for taking revenge (נקם, 1QS VII, 8-9) and the prohibition of these behavioral patterns and of creating a hateful relationship to a community member (CD IX, 1-8; furthermore CD VI, 20–VII 3, and see the discussion in Mathys, Liebe, 120–23).

150. Such a treatment is outside the scope of the present work; see the discussion of H as a potential reflection of the transition from a polity to a "denominational association" in M. Weber, *Gesammelte Aufsätze zur Religionssoziologie, III, Das antike Judentum* (Tübingen: Mohr Siebeck, 1923) and briefly Mathys, *Liebe*, 125–27.

151. On the close relationship of Ezek 22:1-12 to Lev 19:11-18, and Ezek 22:9 to Lev 19:16 and generally, see M. A. Lyons, *From Law to Prophecy. Ezekiel's Use of the Holiness Code* (London: Bloomsbury T&T Clark, 2009), 115–17. Ezekiel 22 contains three units – vv. 1-16, 17-22, 23-29 – delineated through the idiomatic introduction "the word of Yahweh came…": vv. 1, 17, 23. See K. F. Pohlmann, *Der Prophet Hesekiel/Ezechiel Kapitel 20–48* (Göttingen: Vandenhoeck & Ruprecht, 2001), 329, with a source-critical suggestion. Hossfeld suggests vv. 6-12 represent the old core unit of this oracle, vv. 1-5 serve as an introduction without the classic sub-forms of prophetic "accusation" and "threat." The outline is as follows: introductory formula (vv. 1-2); command directed toward the prophet to act as judge, including a summons (vv. 3aβ-5); cf. on a basic exilic layer and later reworkings, Hossfeld, *Untersuchungen zur Komposition und Theologie des Ezechielbuches* (1977, here quoted after the 2nd ed.: Würzburg: Echter, 1983), 109, 148–52, 524–29. See also D. I. Block, *The Book of Ezekiel: Chapters 1–24* (Grand Rapids: Eerdmans, 1997), 708, and K.-P. Adam, "Bloodshed and Hate: The Judgment Oracle in Ezek 22:6–12 and the Legal Discourse in Lev 19:11–18," in *Second Wave Intertextuality and the Hebrew Bible*, ed. M. Grohmann and H. C. P. Kim (Atlanta: SBL Press, 2019), 91–112.

of conflict settlement (Ezek 22:7) enables the urban rulers' bloodshed. Ezekiel 22 demonstrates the detrimental effects of the ethos of conflict settlement in a city polity. The focus of Ezekiel's metropolitan perspective is revealing. It aligns the rampant carnage of contractual killings with a betrayal of the community's shared values, such as the holy day of Yahweh's Sabbaths, the default inter-kin care for members with a precarious loss of kinship affiliation (widow, orphan) presenting many parallels with Lev 19. The framework of Lev 19:11-18 in vv. 3-4 supports, similar to Ezek 22:6-12, a kinship-based jurisdiction that urges respect for parental authority in the hierarchy of the kin. The juxtaposition of Ezek 22:6-12 to Lev 19:3-4, 11-18 illustrates how two different socio-cultural contexts would reflect on private hate and enmity. Ezekiel holds accountable the leadership in the legal contexts addressing the situation in the Judean capital of Jerusalem, providing a metropolitan perspective as compared to the decentralized notion of the community that Lev 19 addresses.[152]

Leviticus 19:3-4, 11-18 and Ezek 22:6-12 both discuss kinship-based institutions of conflict settlement and their differing perspectives point to different addressees. The fact that Ezek 22:6-12, given all the parallels between both passages, does not draw the consequence of Lev 19:18 to call for mutual benevolence among citizens, points to the distinctiveness of the polity H addresses with the counter-cultural imperative "love your neighbor." The later extension of the command of mutual benevolence in Lev 19:33 beyond an originally close-knit community supports a development from an exclusive inner circle that represented the command's original audience. The analogous emphasis on hateful conflicts and on the Sabbath as a festival day, the rejection of paternal and maternal authority in both Lev 19:11-18 and Ezek 22:6-12, all suggest that Lev 19:11-18 addresses communities self-identifying in opposition to an agonistic ethos practiced among their surrounding communities. Their urge for refraining from litigiousness in general, as compared to Ezek 22's attack of blatant violence, and the call for compliance with established conflict settlement modes are best explained in their alleged historical setting of Persian- or Hellenistic-period Judah. A key theme of this ethos that Lev 19 puts to the fore is the expectation of mutual "reprimanding/teaching" of law through authorities of the kin that self-identify as "brothers." In a first step, one may best consider the focus on the loyalty between community members by comparing it with historical analogues, specifically the reception of vv. 17-18 in the 1QS 6:24-27 and CD 9:2-4, 6-8 in the DSS. Addressing the inner circle of a community, it

---

152. A comparison between Ezek 22 at large and Lev 19 is beyond the scope of the present study. Ezekiel 22, for instance, in vv. 23-29 arranges accusations according to "professional" groups: priests, princes, עם הארץ. Leviticus 19 does not differentiate between professional or social groups, but distinguishes social categories of "the companion," "sons of your people," "brother." With the latter it picks up on the laws of Deuteronomy, but especially the "compatriot",' which is a category typical for H.

represents a group ethos,[153] with the primary intention of these laws being to order communal behavior.

4.2. *Conflict Settlement and Enmity in Religious Associations*

The reception of Lev 19:17-18 in the DSS brings to our attention the use of these commands for a closely knit community. 1QS 6:24-27 and CD 9:2-4, 6-8 quote the ban of hateful conflicts from Lev 19:11-18. Different from the oracle in Ezek 22:6-12, the DSS do not address an urban polity. Comparative studies of ethical concepts have hitherto suggested rules of religious cultic associations that are closely related to the community represented in the DSS. Yet, the rules of religious associations significantly overlap with the prohibitive row of Lev 19:11-18. For one thing, they seem to be comparable: the rules of cultic associations address their members who have joined those communities voluntarily. The associations were essentially selective and required an active commitment. Subscription to their rules required members to adhere to certain forms of conflict settlement and to comply with commitments in collaborative activities.[154] The oldest example is a sixth-century BCE association of funerary

---

153. See for instance the interpretation of the command of mutual love as a group ethos in Mathys, *Liebe*, 119, 128.

154. See on the associations E. Lüddeckens, "Gottesdienstliche Gemeinschaften im pharaonischen, ptolemäischen und christlichen Ägypten," *Zeitschrift für Religions- und Geistesgeschichte* 20 (1968): 193–211; M. Muszynski, "Les 'associations religieuses' en Égypte d'après les sources hiéroglyphiques, démotiques et grecques," *OLP* 8 (1977): 145–63. On the rules, see also B. Muhs, "Membership in Private Associations in Ptolemaic Tebtunis," *JESHO* 44 (2001): 1–21. Biblical scholarship has frequently compared Hellenistic religious associations with community rules with the community at Qumran; for an overview see E. W. Larson, "Greco-Roman Guilds," in *Encyclopedia of the Dead Sea Scrolls*, vol 1, ed. L. Schiffman and J. C. VanderKam (Oxford: Oxford University Press, 2000), 321–23. See further Y. M. Gillihan, *Civic Ideology, Organization, and Law in the Rule Scrolls: A Comparative Study of the Covenanters' Sect and Contemporary Voluntary Associations in Political Context*, Studies on the Texts of the Desert of Judah 97 (Leiden: Brill, 2012), with the observation that the associations seek to imitate civic structures. The typology distinguishes "assimilative associations," with the intent of incorporation of small groups into civic bodies, and "alternate civic associations" that claim superiority to the state. The community at Qumran distinguishes between citizens and outsiders, full members, resident aliens, and the priestly hierarchies and it perceives itself as superior to the general Judean community. See R. Herrmann. "Die Gemeinderegel von Qumran und das antike Vereinswesen," in *Jewish Identity in the Greco-Roman World: Jüdische Identität in der griechisch-römischen Welt*, ed. J. Frey, D. R. Schwartz, and S. GripenG trog, Ancient Judaism and Early Christianity 71. (Leiden: Brill, 2007), 161–203. For a comparison of the communal bylaws; membership at large, including punishments; and fines with the Manual of Discipline (1QS), see M. Klinghardt, "The Manual of Discipline in the Light of Statutes of Hellenistic Associations," in *Methods of Investigation of the Dead Sea Scrolls and the Khirbet Qumran Site: Present Realities and Future Prospects*,

workers from Thebes that was still active in the fourth century BCE.¹⁵⁵ The majority of the rules of cultic associations come from the Fayyum and date to the Ptolemaic period. At this point in time, these rules for cultic associations were valid for one year and all members were required to abide by them, which also prompted an occasion for them to be rewritten annually. Excavations in Tebtunis have yielded the majority of the papyri that relate to religious associations. The most common Demotic term for "association" was "the house," a specific term referring to professional and religious associations.

The ethics and economics of these religious associations in Ptolemaic times may best be compared to those of trust networks that would provide their members with sufficient security by establishing their own rules. Four hallmarks characterize their institutional structure and demonstrate their essence as trust networks. First, members of a trust network were willing to put their financial resources at risk because they assumed other members will use the money responsibly and will also reciprocate and cooperate. Second, both the investment and the commitment to the rules of the association would signal to other members one's conformity with the association. Third, fines and cost for the association further underline the relevance of the association to one's own life and raise the level of trust. Fourth, the establishment of trust networks increases the divide between trust networks and ordinary social networks and it increases the value of trust networks in which the cooperation with each other could be handled with more efficiency and less cost.¹⁵⁶ In the case of the Ptolemaic-period associations in Tebtunis, the association protected their members from legal and economic hardship and secured the burial of family members. The members of these associations in Tebtunis supposedly were affluent by the standards of the village and provided relatively high value loans through the association.¹⁵⁷ Relevant for the firm rules to mutually exercise private benevolence and to exclude malevolence

---

ed. J. J. Collins, M. O. Wise, N. Golb, and D. Pardee, Annals of the New York Academy of Sciences 722 (New York: Academy of Sciences, 1994), 251–270. See also M. Weinfeld, *The Organizational Pattern and the Penal Code of the Qumran Sect: A Comparison with Guilds and Religious Associations of the Hellenistic-Roman Period* (Fribourg: Editions Universitaires; Göttingen: Vandenhoeck & Ruprecht, 1986), with a comparison of the Manual of Discipline (1QS) and the Damascus Covenant (CDC) with Greek, Roman, Egyptian groups. The associations have rarely been related to contexts in the Hebrew Bible, but see L. S. Fried, "A Religious Association in Second Temple Judah? A Comment on Neh 10," *Transeuphratene* 30 (2005): 77–96, with a reading of Neh 10 in light of religious associations.

155. Such associations did not exist before Saïtic Egypt; cf. F. de Cenival, *Les associations religieuses en Égypte d'après les documents démotiques* (Cairo: [Institut français d'archéologie orientale], 1972), 141; Muszynski, "Associations," 159.

156. A. Monson, "The Ethics and Economics of Ptolemaic Religious Associations," *Ancient Society* 36 (2006): 221–38, 237.

157. Monson, "Ethics," 237.

are the regulations pertaining to the relationship with a companion, namely the prohibitions against forms of unfair mutual interaction. Also, the procedure of handling conflict settlement in the association is of interest. The parallels to Lev 19 go beyond these legal aspects in detail, including on a wider-scale rules relating to the festival day and the commitment to the venerated deity and the rejection of other deities.

Religious associations are particularly relevant when it comes to the social construct of enmity. Their rules exclude enmity between members as they explicitly ban certain types of hateful behavior in conflicts and essentially rule out that members would enter into the status of mutual enmity. Seen through the lens of the sociological analysis that describes the religious associations as trust networks it is of the essence that they would determine the relevance of internal conflict management[158] with their rules excluding litigation through officials outside the association.

Understanding the religious associations in analogy to trust networks helps put in perspective the above comparison of Lev 19:11-18 with the closely related oracle in Ezek 22:6-12 that assumedly addresses a different social realm. While both Lev 19 and Ezek 22:6-12 refer to oppressive relationships, Ezekiel's view on urban Jerusalem specifically associates this behavior with the "people of the land" (עם הארץ, Ezek 22:29). The oracle rejects the urban society's oppression (עשק) of the poor and, in a move beyond the core community, also the oppression of the metic (v. 29b). In comparison, Lev 19:13 argues on a more immediate neighborly level, referring to forms of oppression, such as property theft (גזל). Closely related, the rules of cultic associations known from Demotic sources also harshly reject insults as typical conflict-inducing behavior,[159] including stealing and witnessing falsely against a "companion."[160] Most relevant for the context of private enmity, the rules would expect members to settle their disputes within the association without appealing to outside authorities. Members of the association would subscribe to a regulation against taking accusations outside the "house," that is, neither in a court of the "military," nor to any law enforcement agency,[161] and,

---

158. For corresponding assumptions about the priority of internal litigation and trial in Qumran, see Herrmann, "Gemeinderegel," 191–93. The sole responsibility of courts in the community is attested in 1QS VI 24–VII 25.

159. Superiors and co-members are not to be insulted; see Papyrus Lille 29.14. Papyrus démotique Caire 30605 l. 20-21 prohibits insults and in such cases administers a fine on a sliding scale for insults of a comrade, a chief, a "second," or an ordinary priest or of insults of something he commits himself of 25–90 *deben*. Papyrus démotique Caire 30605 l. 21, prohibits from physical battery. Papyri quoted from de Cenival, *Associations*.

160. Papyrus Lille 29:15; cf. Lev 19:11, גנב; 19:13, גזל; cf. Lev 19:12, false swearing; 19:16/Ezek 22:9, slanderer among your people/stand up against your neighbor's blood; Lev 19:17-18a, no hate, no revenge; Ezek 22:29, oppression.

161. Cf. "the police," Papyrus Lille 29, 23-24; cf. Papyrus démotique Caire 30605 l. 19, betrayal in the civil or the military authority; cf. Lev 19:17, "reprimand your companion" (הוֹכֵחַ תּוֹכִיחַ); Lev 19:18, love instead of hatred; Ezek 22:2-4, 12, 25, 27, bloodshed.

consequently, the rules penalize external dispute settlement between community members and prohibit the rebuttal of a verdict spoken in the community.[162] On many levels the rules expect full solidarity among the members, namely to testify positively on behalf of each other, to appeal for fellow members to free them, for instance, from prison,[163] and to witness in favor of fellow members in trial.[164] The rules further ban adultery with a companion's wife.[165] All of this amounts to them barring long-term enmity between any fellow member.

In comparison, Ezekiel's oracle calls out violent conflict settlement particularly with regard to the leading elites of the civic urban community, accusing them of bloodshed (Ezek 22:3), as well as bribery as a hostile (and possibly litigious) behavior (Ezek 22:12). Different in nuances, both the city community of Jerusalem and the community of Lev 19 in general assume the detrimental effects of the character of the itinerant accuser seeking a quarrel for their own economic gain (Lev 19:16; Ezek 22:9). Analogously, as a rule, the membership in religious associations excludes the seeking of economic advantage through claims against other members.

The appointment of the festival day in the rules of cultic associations is another aspect Ezek 22 and Lev 19 share. This cultic command stands out in the composition of Lev 19:3, 30 and Ezek 22:8, 26. The concern about missing out on the participation in "my Sabbaths," with the typical plural and the first person suffix, is a signature feature of Lev 19:3.[166] This relevance of the Sabbath corresponds to that of the festival day in religious associations. Their rules fine members that sow discord with regard to the day of "delivering" (P. Lille 29:11) and members failing to join a convocation (P. Lille 29:9) or a procession if they had pledged to walk behind the "head of the falcon" and the other "heads" of the "house."[167]

Similar to the commitment to one particular deity in the rules of the cultic associations is the urge to maintain holiness in H that instead presupposes the veneration of only one God. Both Ezekiel and H frame the commitment of community members to Yahweh as a behavior that reflects his "holiness,"

---

162. Papyrus démotique Caire 30605 l. 19-20: whoever enters into a dispute by appealing to the court without having first requested internal conflict settlement in the association has to pay a fine of 50 *deben*.

163. Papyrus Lille 29,16.

164. Otherwise he is fined 50 *deben*; Papyrus Prague 20. In the case of justified imprisonment, positive witness for the imprisoned is expected, Papyrus Prague 26.

165. Papyrus Lille 29, 10; Papyrus démotique Caire 31179, 22; the latter imposes a fine and expulsion from the association. Ezekiel 22:11 considered it an "abomination." While family law is not in the focus of Lev 19:11-18, v. 29 refers to issues of family law protecting daughters against what is seen as unfair patriarchal marriage politics, and Lev 18 and 20 cover family law.

166. In the Sabbath command, the object stands before the predicate, adding emphasis on the Sabbath; see Milgrom, *Leviticus 17–22*, 1611. In the rules of cultic associations, see, for instance, Papyrus démotique Caire 30605 5-6 and 31179 6.

167. Papyrus Lille 29:11-12.

including their behavior in conflict settlement. In comparison, religious associations would attach themselves to the tutelary god of the sanctuary. These were never national or dynastic gods, but rather local versions of a deity[168] or even of deities not represented in the official pantheon.[169] The engagement with other gods, the rules of the associations suggest, would imply different forms of conflict settlement. Along a similar line of thought, Ezek 22 juxtaposes violence ("blood shed") in the community of Jerusalem with "idols" (גלולים) it associates with Egypt. And passages such as Lev 19:4 presuppose a material representation of the deity, while leaving open its shape, whether anthropomorphic, theriomorphic or abstract or cult symbol. Such objects were assumedly venerated in processions. This verse also relates to deities that are culturally connected with Egypt, though it names them with terms used in Isaianic tradition. Leviticus 19:4 specifically excludes the veneration of אלילים, a term that is also used for cultic objects brought to their cultic niches after having been carried around in processions (Isa 2:20-21). Isaiah 19:1, 3; 31:3 explicitly relate them to Egypt.[170]

168. Muszynski mentions late second- and first-century BCE examples, for instance, the "Isis-of-Chemmis" stele of the glyptothèque Ny Carlsberg, Copenhagen, AEIN 826; 68 BCE; Muszynski, "Associations," 159.

169. One association in the Fayyum honors Prammares, the deified pharaoh Amenemhet III; see Muszynski, "Associations," 159 n. 59: Stela from the Egyptian Museum Berlin, 17683⁹, 104 BCE.

170. The allusion to אלילים in Lev 19:4 likely presupposes Isaianic polemics against foreign cultic figurines. In Isa 2:20-21 אלילים were potentially mummified gods, which matches the polemics of Lev 19:4 to call them "handmade gods." Ezekiel connects them with Egyptian culture; in H the אלילים are in a tradition with the polemics against foreign religions and cultures. אלילים is used 20 times in the Old Testament – 10 times in Isaiah: Isa 2:8, 18, 20 (2×); 10:10-11; 19:1, 3; 31:7 (2×); twice in Lev 19:4 and 26:1; and Ps 96:5 = 1 Chr 16:26; Ps 97:7; once each in Jer 14:14 Q; Ezek 30:13; Hab 2:18; Zech 11:17; Job 13:4; cf. also Sir 11:3; 1QM 14:1; cf. Isa 19:1; 1Q22 1:8. Textual emendations are suggested for Isa 10:10; Ezek 31:13; Zech 11:17. S. Schwertner, "אליל *ᵉlîl* nothingness," in E. Jenni and C. Westermann (eds.), *Theological Lexicon of the Old Testament*, vol. 1, trans. M. E. Biddle (Peabody, MA: Hendrickson, 1997), 126–27. Isaianic passages focus on the pilgrimage to Zion; cf. Isa 2:20-21 and 2:8 in a subsequent judgment oracle following 2:2-5. Verses 6-8 describe the land of the enemy as "full of god and silver," and full of horses (and numerous chariots), and full of "elilim." The objects are described as "handmade gods" that are adored. Verses 20-21 state that these objects are made from silver and gold are thrown away. The specific historical context of this oracle can only tentatively be suggested. The pilgrimage to Zion motif has been ascribed to Persian times. The judgment oracle in Isa 19 also mentions אלילים. It relates them more specifically to Egypt within the context of the sequel of judgment oracles from 14:28-31 the Philistines; 17 Damascus/Ephraim; Kush 18, Egypt 19, Jerusalem 20, 22. The final form of the composition is post-Babylonian, from the Persian era. See, for instance, U. Berges, *Das Buch Jesaja. Komposition und Endgestalt* (Freiburg: Herder, 1998), 150. Evidence for אלילים as material remains from an Egyptian cultural background is to be found in Ezek 30:13. The

The rejection of deviant cultic behavior may possibly be seen upon analogy to traditions and activities, for instance, processions, mentioned in the rules of cultic associations.[171]

Additional parallels between the religious associations first found in 26th Dynasty Egypt suggest they self-identifed as "brotherhoods." Another parallel between them and the hypothetical social realm of the community of H is their segregationist ideology. These religious associations were potentially used strategically as bulwarks the population built with the main purpose of affirming their own cultural identity against a more or less massive foreign influx into the Nile valley. They gained their popularity as a form of a response at a time of the loss of knowledge of an archaizing religion that no longer lived up to its aspirations.[172] Their function in this context may have been to enhance the knowledge about their religious tradition and to secure their alterity as associations against influences of a surrounding foreign community. This context offers yet another parallel between the rules of religious associations and the ethos of holiness as segregation from external influence in the laws of Lev 19.[173] While H addresses a nation as a whole,[174] the parallels between 19:11-18 and comparable rules for religious associations point to their understanding as an elite group that self-identified as distinct from the surrounding culture.

The rules in vv. 11-18 in Lev 19 thus in a wider sense represent a "priestly" ethos for a group's internal life. Whether the priestly group's behavior indeed reflects the way in which this group normally would act in the larger public is

---

handmade figurines are comparable with and juxtaposed to the גלולים that Ezekiel also associates with Egyptian culture and religion. The specific iconographic background of אלילים (for instance, to the Apis-bull) remains to be explored. In Ezek 30:13 these cultic objects, possibly figurines that may represent an Egyptian (or a non-Judean) influence, arguably refer to executions of these objects in the style of southern Palestine.

171. This is beyond the scope of this study, yet see above on Lev 19:26-32, potentially as reflections of foreign culture, in particular "eating above the blood" (Lev 19:26); cf. also "eating on the mountains" in Ezek 22:9.

172. Muszynski, "Associations," 161.

173. To Knohl (*Sanctuary*, 205), H was a response to "the incursion of idolatrous practices into Israel, especially the worship of Molech and soothsaying and conjuring of familiar spirits; the development of social polarization leading to the uprooting of farmers from their lands and their enslavement to the rich; and the detachment of morality from the cult."

174. See, for instance, Knohl, *Sanctuary*, 190: laws of H pertain to the entire community in 18:1–20:27 and are followed by restrictions specifically for the priests in Lev 21:1–22:9; cf. Gerstenberger, *Leviticus*, 18, who argues that the theology of holiness in H "also elsewhere includes the entire people of Israel". Joosten, *People*, 91, suggests that H refers to the "people of the land" as addressee; not understood as a political party. Alternatively, he suggests that it refers to "people" in the sense of a kinship group, as in the case of 2 Kgs 4:13.

another question. Rhetorically, Lev 19 addresses the community at large and the behavior among community members (vv. 11-18).[175]

The composition of rules for internal conduct of a community in Lev 19:11-18 leaves open the possibility of their external behavior outside the group. There are indications that their internal behavior within the priestly community was in stark contrast to conflict settlement outside their immediate community. Three reasons support this. First, Lev 19:11-18 limits itself to internal rules of a community, as the possessive pronouns indicate, "your brother" (אחיך), "neighbor/companion" (רעך), "son of your people" (בני עמיך) and "compatriot" (עמיתך). Second, besides the rules for general benevolence, Lev 19:34a and 19:35 detail fair conduct in judgment and trade interactions with the metic. They do not specify examples of Lev 19:11-18.

Finally, records from the period of the 26th Dynasty include a historical example of the behavior of a closely knit priestly group and their use of aggressive and harmful techniques against opponents. It puts into perspective the difference between internal benevolence of members of an association and their foes. At the time of the 26th Dynasty, under Dareios I (513 BCE), probably slightly before H was drafted, Papyrus Rylands 9[176] refers to a petition of an Egyptian priest, Peteese. The elaborate and long petition of this priest, a simple scribe of the Amun-Temple at *el-Hibe*, reports that Peteese was sent to a high official (*senti*) in the administration of Memphis. Over the course of his petition the priest recounts his family history from the time of Psammetichos I (664 BCE). Peteese hails from an influential family of harbormasters whose members held a number of relevant positions in the priesthood of *el-Hibe*. The family was, however, stripped of their positions with the help of priestly groups. In the petition, Peteese requests that his own family be reinstalled in those offices. Papyrus Rylands 9 offers a vivid insight into aggressive type of behavior of a priestly association at a local sanctuary in Egypt at the time of the Saitic Dynasty and beyond. The writer of the petition describes in detail how, after having affirmed their entitlement of priestly income, under torture, the priests of the sanctuary had forced him to make a statement, and further mistreated him with the intention of killing him.[177]

---

175. On a later level, adopted rules for fair trade and fair judgment would gradually widen the circle to include metics previously excluded from the ethos of neighborly benevolence vv. 33-36.

176. A demotic papyri found in el-Hibe.

177. G. Vittmann, *Der demotische Papyus Rylands 9, Teil 1, Text und Übersetzung* (Wiesbaden: Harrassowitz, 1998). In detail, the papyrus renders on 25 columns the history of a community of priests over multiple generations. The petition begins with the time of the ninth year of Dareios I, 513 BCE, in col 1. Column II reports the torture of the claimant's ancestor during transport on a ship to Herakleopolis. Furthermore, this ancestor's petitions to the official in Memphis, the minister of finances, were thwarted through bribes of the priestly association (Col. III). The income of the claimant's father is based on his office as a prophet of Amun and of sixteen other Gods, as he points out (col. III). The draft of a complaint that the plaintiff writes is the object of the mockery of the priests who, in

This example points to the possibility that such communities would pair a rather aggressive outside conduct with peacableness in internal conflict settlement.

4.3. Conclusion

The parallels between the prohibitive row in Lev 19:11-18 and the genre of community rules sheds new light on the ethics of H's envisioned conflict-settlement modes. The socio-historical analogue of religious associations as priestly communities with their separative ethos at a distance from their surroundings, in combination with a strong internal mutual support for group members, suggests a similar communal identity for H. On a conceptual level the behavioral rules for interactions between community members mirror the typical ethos of amity expected among kin. This ethos appears as the opposite of enmity and hatred, which imply a clear-cut social status of the opponents when quarreling outside one's kin. While the priestly communities represented in H would exclude internal mutual enmity, a historical analogue suggests that they would probably not shy away from harsh confrontation with exterior enemies.

This result adds in significant ways to the analysis of the social status of private hate and friendship and their modes of action at specific moments in Judah that the respective biblical law reflects. It demonstrates the interface between the historical context of the development of mutual benevolence as an element of Jewish biblical ethos in H. In the course of this study, the reflection on mutual benevolence as part of an inner-kin ethos has added an essential context of legal tradition and this has been mainly pointed out with regard to the status of private enmity. It has also demonstrated how private enmity as an essential construct of the social context of kinship-based societies continued to shape laws on conflict settlement. Homicide legislation in Deut 19 develops the construct of long-term private hate as part of a fictive kinship ethos in a late seventh-century BCE context. Numbers 35 reflects with refined abstract legal terminology the context of a claim of jurisdiction over homicide cases as part of a theocratic program to strengthen traditional kinship-based institutions of Judean polities. Leviticus 19:17-18 adds to the status of private enmity the complementary positive construct of mutual benevolence or friendship as the requirement for a group ethos in a close-knit community. The law is conceptually grounded in the

---

the course of the procedure, set his house on fire (col. IV). The petition includes a detailed report on the substantiations of the claims to the minister of finances (col. V). The claimant's father receives the right to be temporarily re-installed as priest of Amun (col. IX) and his successor can even retrieve the undivided official power (col. X). The aggressive and violent acts of the priests continue into the 31st year of Psammetichos I (634 BCE), with the killing of two brothers, grand children of the claimant, on the occasion of the distribution of grain (col. XI). Further conflicts between the priests and the harbormaster's family follow, including the bribing of judges (col. XV) and revenge measures of the priestly association including the rejection of the payment of the sinecure the plaintiff sees himself entitled to receive (col. XXI).

analogous model of Deuteronomy, molding the command of mutual love in the tradition of amity as the default posture vis-à-vis other members of one's kin. Yet already the uniquely diverse four-fold terminology of "compatriot, brother, neighbor/companion, son of my people" in 19:11-18 widens the application of mutual benevolence towards members of a specific group. Together with the form of mainly prohibitives, this suggests reading this law as analogous to rules of priestly communities at the time.

Conclusion

This study set out to describe the nature of private enmity as it informs kinship law in Israel. Legal anthropology's understanding of the nature of dispute settlement of feuding within kinship-based societies served as the basis of an analysis of the mechanisms that inform biblical law. More specifically, the examination of those mechanisms focused upon how biblical law presupposes a long-term private enmity between two opponents. Based on the reflection on conflict settlement in diverse kinship-based, honor–shame societies, including discourses about feuding as conflict settlement procedure in Athens, the study defined private enmity as a social construct that realizes itself in diverse ways in various segmentary societies. A socio-historical working definition first suggested enmity as the social status of an individual in conflict with an opponent. Its five hallmark signs define this status: (1) enmity is intrinsically public in nature, which includes an initial form of public declaration; (2) the opponents act out their hate with flexibility in various ways; (3) enemies would engage in a reciprocal process; (4) reciprocity between opponents typically escalated and could reach its climax in one party's attempt to kill their foe; (5) private enmity was also transitive, insofar as it would draw in members of one's kin and allied friends in expectance of their solidarity in conflict.[1] These hallmarks of the social status which inform its legal implications are analogous to the status of marriage, divorce, enslavement, to being guilty or innocent of a crime, or analogous to the status of a citizen neighbor. Critical towards any unilinear evolutionary arc in biblical law, four chapters traced how the social status of enmity in the kinship-based structure of society is typical as a constellation between opponents in feuding and how it shapes the tradition in Deuteronomic and (post-)priestly law.

Selected laws of CC demonstrate the presupposition of long-term enmity, with the slayer–victim relationship becoming possibly already of relevance in the final form of the homicide law in Exod 21:12-14 when seen against the backdrop of typical kinship-based conflict settlement. As part of a pattern of continuous intentionality, and a legal criterion separate from it, this social construct in a kinship-based society arguably informs Exod 21:14. Hateful relationships would by default escalate and lead to the prolonged quarreling between the

---

1. Besides kin members, friends were requested to join in the fight against a private opponent. As a consequence of this transitivity, private enmity bore the inherent threat of potentially splitting a community in two confrontational camps.

parties. The injury law in Exod 21:18-19 and self-defense against a burglar in Exod 22:1-2 more clearly indicate the relevance of the relationship aspect between an agent and their victim. Laws exhibit three techniques to more exactly designate long-term enmity hallmarks: first, semantic markers, such as the term "neighbor/companion" (רע, Exod 21:14) possibly, depending on their exact social background, hint at a continuous relation between two individuals that is distinct from the trustworthy status of a friend or of a clan member; secondly, expressions of intentionality through action verbs. For instance, the attempt of theft of neighborly property over time that is expressed through a verb (חמד, Exod 20:17; Deut 5:21), and that applied to a hateful relationship. Finally, the explicit enemy terminology of איב and שנא in two case laws (Exod 23:4-5) unequivocally marks a slayer–victim relationship. The injunction to overcome typical mechanisms of enmity in proverbial wisdom, for instance in the exemplary saying found in Prov 25:21-22, further demonstrates the relationship's relevance in everyday life and its detrimental effect.

More precisely, and in more detail than in Exod 21:13-14, homicide legislation in Deut 19:2a, 3b, 4, 5, 6, 11-12 defines the criteria for asylum eligibility. It envisions asylum cities that host slayers in cases of accidental homicide (vv. 11-12), in a concept that vv. 2a, 3a, 9-10 later extend. The law references the long-term neighbor (רע, vv. 4, 5) from Exod 21:14. Yet it generates idiomatic phraseology to characterize long-term enmity as a relationship in which opponents would hate each other from "ever since" (מתמול שלשם, vv. 4b, 6b), as opposed to cases of spontaneous, accidental, inadvertent (בבלי-דעת, v. 4b) homicide. The law embeds a further hallmark of the continuing nature of hateful interaction within its discourse through the participle form (שנא, vv. 4, 11a). With the slayer's typical unawareness as the necessary condition beyond mere absence of intent, Deut 19:4, 6, 11 also refine the characterization of the ongoing nature of private enmity between the opponents in a community (רצח, vv. 3, 4, 6). Deuteronomy 19 holds the constantly enacted hostile relationship as sufficient criterion for exclusion from asylum. Finally, the law refers to the avenger of blood (Deut 19:6, 12) as the next of kin in charge of executing revenge in feuding societies. Systematic references to fictive kinship in Deuteronomic law juxtapose the posture of amity as the default patterns of action opposed to relationships of long-term hate.

Homicide law in the late priestly layer found in Num 35 redefines enmity with the use of abstract terminology, such as the social status as איבה and with the denominatives שנאה, צדיה. The lexicography of Num 35 further refines the interplay between narratives and law, adding the notion of fateful inadvertence, בשגגה as a category foreign to the legal distinction that highlights the dreadful consequences homicide could bear for an unintentional slayer. Next to the discussion of homicide in the realm of legal texts, terms such as the participle צדה refer to a plaintiff's speech in the case narrative 1 Sam 24:12, which ponders the underlying legal question of intentional pursuit. Part of a theocratic post-Hexateuch layer, Num 35, partakes in a discourse on homicide jurisdiction. It potentially points to the historical context of a fourth-century BCE Persian or, more likely, to a third-century BCE Ptolemaic Judah. In this period, the polity, represented through their "assembly," עדה, reclaimed its function as the jury the killer would face in trial (Num 35:12). The regulatory statutes in Num 35:25-29 specifically assert the jurisdiction of the עדה over homicide cases as the institution representing the local polity; a move best interpreted as the defense of local kinship authority against Ptolemaic (or Persian) claims in this genuinely kinship-related matter.

Leviticus 19:11-18 mirrors the rejection of hateful interaction between enemies in close-knit communities in H as it insists on mutually benevolent, constructive ways of conflict settlement. The composition of four sets of prohibitive rows that narrowly resemble the Decalogues, offers rules for the behavior in a close-knit community. Analogous to rules of religious associations known since the sixth century BCE, the passage offers basic instructions for mutual engagement of members in a community. Its final verses ban any form of typical enemy relationship (שׂנא) in favor of the positive urge toward acting with mutual benevolence (אהב). Leviticus 19:11-18 thus effectively ban typical mechanisms of hateful interaction between private enemies, such as bearing a grudge (נטר) or revengefulness (נקם). The criticism of conflict-settlement dynamics in vv. 15-16 and the urge to mutual benevolence include important information about the social framework of the community H presupposes. Detailing typical patterns of enmity (stealing, deception, lying, false swearing, vv. 11-12a) and banning hateful neighborly interaction (oppression, property theft, withholding of wages v. 13), discrimination against socially vulnerable groups, such as the deaf and the blind (v. 14a), the passage highlights particularly unfair conflict-settlement procedures and forms of quarrelsomeness between community members (vv. 15-16). Leviticus 19:17 authorizes individual community members to engage in mutual conflict settlement (יכח *hi.*, v. 17bα) in ways that are mutually benevolent to companions in a community (v. 18a).

Beyond the results for biblical law, the emphasis of mutual benevolence in Lev 19:18 clarifies the meaning of neighborly "love" as the social status of private friendship, characterized by mutual benevolence as the opposite construct of private hate. An eminent emblem of Jewish law and ethos, H thus introduces a peaceable policy of community members aiming at internal constructive quarrel solving, an ideal of an inner-kinship ethos that it develops most likely against the backdrop of the destructive habitual hatred of an agonistic society.

As legal anthropology suggests, comparable to the status of marriage, divorce, enslavement or imprisonment, private enmity as a social construct is of tangible legal relevance far beyond its function as criterion for the eligibility of asylum in homicide cases. In detail subject to the historically changing contexts of kinship-based societies, this category informs biblical law and other areas that this study largely bracketed out, such as, for instance, the Psalms of the Individual, biblical narrative tradition, Proverbs and Ben Sira.

Bibliography

Achenbach, R. "Numbers." In *The Oxford Encyclopedia of the Books of the Bible*, edited by M. D. Coogan, vol. 2, 110–22. Oxford: Oxford University Press, 2011.
Achenbach, R. "Numeri und Deuteronomium." In *Das Deuteronomium zwischen Pentateuch und Deuteronomistischem Geschichtswerk*, edited by E. Otto and A. Achenbach, 123–34. Göttingen: Vandenhoeck & Ruprecht, 2004.
Achenbach, R. *Die Vollendung der Tora. Studien zur Redaktionsgeschichte des Numeribuches im Kontext von Hexateuch und Pentateuch*. Beihefte zur Zeitschrift für altorientalische und biblische Rechtsgeschichte 3. Wiesbaden: Harrassowitz, 2003.
Adam, K.-P. "Bloodshed and Hate: The Judgment Oracle in Ezek 22:6–12 and the Legal Discourse in Lev 19:11–18." In *Second Wave Intertextuality and the Hebrew Bible*, edited by M. Grohmann and H. C. P. Kim, 91–112. Atlanta: SBL Press, 2019.
Adam, K.-P. "Saul as a Tragic Hero: Greek Drama and its Influence on Hebrew Scripture in 1 Samuel 14,24–46 (10,8; 13,7–13A; 10:17–27)." In *For and Against David: Story and History in the Books of Samuel*, edited by A. G. Auld and E. Eynikel, 123–83. Leuven: Peeters, 2010.
Aeschines, *Aeschines with an English Translation by C. D. Adams*, Cambridge, MA: Harvard University Press/London: William Heinemann, 1919.
Aeschylus, *Persians and Oher Plays*, transl. C. Collard. Oxford/New York: Oxford University Press, 2008.
Albertz, R. "Hintergrund und Bedeutung des Elterngebots im Dekalog." *Zeitschrift für die Alttestamentliche Wissenschaft* 90, no. 3 (1978): 348–74. Repr. in *Geschichte und Theologie. Studien zur Exegese des Alten Testaments und zur Religionsgeschichte Israels*, edited by R. Albertz, G. Kern, I. Kottsieper, and J. Wöhrle, 157–85. Berlin: de Gruyter, 2003.
Albertz, R. "A Pentateuchal Redaction in the Book of Numbers? The Late Priestly Layers of Numbers 25–36." *Zeitschrift für die alttestamentliche Wissenschaft* 125 (2013): 220–33.
Altman, A. "On Some Basic Concepts in the Law of People Seeking Refuge and Sustenance in the Ancient Near East." *Zeitschrift für altorientalische und biblische Rechtsgeschichte* 8 (2002): 323–42.
Anbar, M. "L'influence deutéronomique sur le Code d'Alliance: le cas d'Exode 21:12–17." *Zeitschrift für altorientalische und biblische Rechtsgeschichte* 5 (1999): 165–66.
Aristotle, *Athenaion Politeia*, Aristotle in 23 Volumes, vol. 20, translated by H. Rackham. Cambridge, MA: Harvard University Press; London: William Heinemann, 1952.
Aristotle, *Rhetoric*, Aristotle in 23 Volumes, vol. 22, translated by J. H. Freese. Cambridge, MA: Harvard University Press; London: William Heinemann, 1926.
Arneth, M. *Durch Adams Fall ist ganz verderbt... Studien zur Entstehung der alttestamentlichen Urgeschichte*. Göttingen: Vandenhoeck & Ruprecht, 2007.

Asheri, D., A. B. Lloyd, and A. Corcella. *A Commentary on Herodotus I–IV.* Edited by O. Murray and A. Moreno, with a contribution by M. Brosius, translated by B. Graziosi. Oxford: Oxford University Press, 2007.
Auld, A. G. "Cities of Refuge in Israelite Tradition." *Journal for the Study of the Old Testament* 10 (1978): 26–40.
Bächli, O. *Israel und die Völker. Eine Studie zum Deuteronomium.* Abhandlungen zur Theologie des Alten und Neuen Testaments 41. Zurich: Zwingli, 1962.
Baentsch, B. *Exodus-Leviticus-Numeri.* Göttingen: Vandenhoeck & Ruprecht, 1903.
Baer, I. F. "The Historical Foundations of the Halacha." *Zion* 7 (1952): 1–55.
Barbiero, G. "Der Fremde im Bundesbuch und im Heiligkeitsgesetz zwischen Absonderung und Annahme." *Ricerche storico bibliche* 81–2 (1996): 41–69.
Barbiero, G. *L'asino del nemico. Rinuncia alla vendetta e amore del nemico nella legislation dell'Antico Testamento (Es 23:4–5; Dt 22:1–4; Lv 19:17–18).* Analecta Biblica 128. Rome: Pontificio Istituto Biblico, 1991.
Barbiero, G. *Studien zu alttestamentlichen Texten.* Stuttgart: Katholisches Bibelwerk, 2002.
Barmash, P. "Blood Feud and State Control: Differing Legal Institutions for the Remedy of Homicide During the Second and First Millennia B.C.E." *Journal of Near Eastern Studies* 63 (2004): 183–99.
Barmash, P. *Homicide in the Biblical World.* Cambridge: Cambridge University Press, 2005.
Bartelmus, R. *Einführung in das Biblische Hebräisch: Mit einem Anhang Biblisches Aramäisch.* Zurich: Theologischer Verlag, 1994.
Bartor, A. "Blood Guilt." In *The Oxford Encyclopedia of the Bible and Law,* edited by B. Strawn, vol. 1, 64–68. Oxford: Oxford University Press, 2015.
Bartor, A. "Narrative." In *Oxford Encyclopedia of the Bible and Law,* edited by B. Strawn, vol. 2, 125–33. Oxford: Oxford University Press, 2015.
Berger, K. *Die Gesetzesauslegung Jesu: ihr historischer Hintergrund im Judentum und im Alten Testament. 1, 1.* Neukirchen-Vluyn: Neukirchener Verlag, 1972.
Berges, U. *Das Buch Jesaja. Komposition und Endgestalt.* Freiburg: Herder, 1998.
Berlin, A. "Legal Fiction: Levirate cum Land Redemption in Ruth." *Journal of Ancient Judaism* 1 (2010): 3–18.
Berman, J. "Ancient Hermeneutics and the Legal Structure of the Book of Ruth." *Zeitschrift für die alttestamentliche Wissenschaft* 119 (2007): 22–38.
Berman, J. *Created Equal: How the Bible Broke with Ancient Political Thought.* Oxford: Oxford University Press, 2008.
Blum, E. "Der kompositionelle Knoten am Übergang von Josua zu Richter: Ein Entflechtungsvorschlag." In *Textgestalt und Komposition: Exegetische Beiträge zu Tora und Vordere Propheten,* edited by E. Blum, 249–80. Tübingen: Mohr (Siebeck), 2010.
Blum, E. *Studien zur Komposition des Pentateuch.* Berlin: de Gruyter, 1990.
Black-Michaud, J. *Cohesive Force: Feud in the Mediterranean and the Middle East.* New York: St. Martin's, 1975.
Block, D. I. *The Book of Ezekiel: Chapters 1–24.* Grand Rapids: Eerdmans, 1997.
Block, D. I. "Deuteronomic Law." In *The Oxford encyclopedia of the Bible and Law,* edited by B. A. Strawn, vol. 1, 182–95. Oxford: Oxford University Press, 2015.
Blundell, M. W. *Helping Friends and Harming Enemies: A Study in Sophocles and Greek Ethics.* Cambridge: Cambridge University Press, 1994.

Boecker, H. J. *Law and the Administration of Justice in the Old Testament and the Ancient Near East* (translated from the German). London: SPCK, 1980.
Boecker, H. J. *Redeformen des Rechtslebens im Alten Testament*. Neukirchen-Vluyn: Neukirchener Verlag, 1964.
Boegehold, A. L. "Perikles' Citizenship Law of 451/0 B.C.E." In *Athenian Identity and Civic Ideology*, edited by A. L. Boegehold and A. Scafuro, 57–66. Baltimore: The Johns Hopkins University Press, 1994.
Boehm, C. *Blood Revenge: The Enactment and Management of Conflict in Montenegro and Other Tribal Societies*. Second paperback edition with an extended Preface. Philadelphia: University of Pennsylvania Press, 1987. 1st ed. Kansas: University of Kansas Press, 1984.
Boehm, C. *Montenegrin Social Organization and Values: A Political Ethnography of a Refuge Area Tribal Adaptation*. New York: AMS Press, 1983.
Botica, A. *The Concept of Intention in the Old Testament, Philo of Alexandria and the Early Rabbinic Literature: A Study in Human Intentionality in the Area of Criminal, Cultic and Religious and Ethical Law*. Piscataway, NJ: Gorgias, 2011.
Botta, A. F. "Hated by the Gods and your Spouse: Legal Use of שׂנא in Elephantine and its Ancient Near Eastern Context." In *Law and Religion in the Eastern Mediterranean. From Antiquity to Early Islam*, edited by A. Hagedorn and R. G. Kratz, 105–28. Oxford: Oxford University Press, 2013.
Bourdieu, P. "The Sense of Honour." In *Algeria 1960: The Disenchantment of the World*, 95–132. Cambridge: Cambridge University Press, 1979.
Braulik, G. "Die dekalogische Redaktion der deuteronomischen Gesetze: Ihre Abhängigkeit von Levitikus 19 am Beispiel von Deuteronomium 22,1–12; 24,10–22 und 25,13–16." In *Bundesdokument und Gesetz. Studien zum Deuteronomium*, edited by G. Braulik, 160–61. Freiburg: Herder, 1995.
Braulik, G. *Die deuteronomischen Gesetze und der Dekalog: Studien zum Aufbau von Deuteronomium 12–26*. Stuttgart: Katholisches Bibelwerk, 1991.
Brewer, D. I. "Deuteronomy 24:1–4 and the Origin of the Jewish Divorce Certificate." *Journal of Jewish Studies* 49 (1998): 230–43.
Bultmann, C. *Der Fremde im antiken Juda. Eine Untersuchung zum sozialen Typenbegriff 'ger' und seinem Bedeutungswandel in der alttestamentlichen Gesetzgebung*. Göttingen: Vandenhoeck & Ruprecht, 1992.
Burnside, J. "Flight of the Fugitives: Rethinking the Relationship between Biblical Law (Exodus 21:12–14) and the Davidic Succession Narrative (1 Kings 1–2)." *Journal of Biblical Literature* (2010): 418–31.
Buss, Martin. "Logic and Israelite Law." *Semeia* 45 (1989): 49–65.
Carawan, E., ed. *The Attic Orators: Oxford Readings in Classical Studies*. Oxford: Oxford University Press, 2007.
Carawan, E. *Rhetoric and the Law of Draco*. Oxford: Clarendon, 1998.
Cartledge, P. A. "Metoikos." In *Brill's New Pauly*, vol. 8. Leiden: Brill, 2006.
Carmichael, C. M. *The Laws of Deuteronomy*. Ithaca, NY: Cornell University Press, 1974.
Carmichael, C. M. *The Origins of Biblical Law: The Decalogues and the Book of the Covenant*. Ithaca, NY: Cornell University Press, 1992.
Cazelles, H. *Études sur le Code de l'alliance*. Paris: Letouzey et Ané, 1946.
Cenival, F. de. *Les associations religieuses en Egypte d'après les documents démotiques*. Cairo: Institut français d'archéologie orientale, 1972.
Cenival, F. de, ed. *Papyrus démotiques de Lille (III)*. Cairo: Institut français d'archéologie orientale, 1984.

Chaniotis, A. "Asylon." *Brill's New Pauly*, vol. 2. Leiden: Brill, 2003.
Charlesworth, J. H., ed., *The Dead Sea Scrolls: Hebrew, Aramaic, and Greek Texts with English Translations.* Volume 2, Damascus Document War Scroll and Related Documents. Tübingen: Mohr Siebeck, 1995.
Chavel, S. *Oracular Law and Priestly Historiography in the Torah.* Tübingen: Mohr Siebeck, 2014.
Chirichigno, G. *Debt Slavery in Israel and in the Ancient Near East.* Sheffield: Sheffield Academic Press, 1993.
Cholewiński, A. *Heiligkeitsgesetz und Deuteronomium: eine vergleichende Studie.* Rome: Biblical Institute Press, 1976.
Christ, H. *Blutvergiessen im Alten Testament. Der gewaltsame Tod des Menschen untersucht am hebräischen Wort dām.* Basel: Friedrich Reinhardt, 1977.
Christ, M. R. *The Litigious Athenian.* Baltimore: The John Hopkins University Press, 1998.
Christ, M. R. "Response to E. M. Harris, Feuding or the Rule of Law?" In *Symposion 2001: Vorträge zur griechischen und hellenistischen Rechtsgeschichte (Evanston, Illinois, 5.–8. September 2001),* edited by R. W. Wallace and M. Gagarin, 143–46. Vienna: Verlag der Österreichischen Akademie der Wissenschaften, 2005.
Clines, D. J. A., ed. *The Dictionary of Classical Hebrew,* vol. 8. Sheffield: Sheffield Pheonix Press, 2011.
Cocco, F. *The Torah as a Place of Refuge: Biblical Criminal Law and the Book of Numbers.* Tübingen: Mohr Siebeck, 2016.
Cohen, D. "Crime, Punishment and the Rule of Law in Classical Athens." In *The Cambridge Companion to Greek Law,* edited by M. Gagarin and D. Cohen, 211–35. Cambridge: Cambridge University Press, 2005.
Cohen, D. *Law, Violence and Community in Classical Athens.* Cambridge: Cambridge University Press, 1995.
Cohen, M. "Le 'ger' biblique et son statut socio-religieux." *Revue de l'histoire des religions* 207 (1990): 131–58.
Collins, J. J. *Jewish Wisdom in the Hellenistic Age.* Louisville: Westminster John Knox, 1997.
Conrad, D. נכה. In *Theological Dictionary of the Old Testament* 9, edited by G. Johannes Botterweck, Helmer Ringgren, and Heinz-Josef Fabry, 415–23. Grand Rapids: Eerdmans, 1998.
Cowley, E. A. *Aramaic Papyri of the Fifth Century B.C.* Oxford: Clarendon, 1923.
Crüsemann, F. "Der Exodus als Heiligung: Zur rechtsgeschichtlichen Bedeutung des Heiligkeitsgesetzes." In *Die hebräische Bibel und ihre zweifache Nachgeschichte: Festschrift für Rolf Rendtorff zum 65. Geburtstag,* edited by E. Blum, C. Machholz, and E. W. Stegemann, 117–29. Neukirchen-Vluyn: Neukirchener Verlag, 1990.
Crüsemann, F. *The Torah: Theology and Social History of Old Testament Law.* Translated by Allan W. Mahnke. Minneapolis: Fortress, 1995.
Daube, D. "Direct and Indirect Causation in Biblical Law." *Vetus Testamentum* 11 (1961): 249–69.
Daube, D. "Law in the Narratives." In *Studies in Biblical Law,* 13–15. Cambridge: Cambridge University Press, 1969.
Daube, D. *Studies in Biblical Law.* Cambridge: Cambridge University Press, 1969.
Deissler, A. *"Ich bin dein Gott, der dich befreit hat." Wege zur Meditation über das Zehngebot.* Freiburg: Herder, 1975.

Delekat, L. *Asylie und Schutzorakel am Zionheiligtum: Eine Untersuchung zu den privaten Feindpsalmen.* Leiden: Brill, 1967.

Delkurt, H. *Ethische Einsichten in der alttestamentlichen Spruchweisheit.* Neukirchen-Vluyn: Neukirchener Verlag, 1993.

Demosthenes. A. T. Murray *Demosthenes with an English Translation.* Cambridge, MA: Harvard University Press; London: William Heinemann, 1939.

Dennett, D. *The Intentional Stance.* Cambridge, MA: MIT Press, 1987.

Derlien, J. *Asyl: Die religiöse und rechtliche Begründung der Flucht zu sakralen Orten in der griechisch-römischen Antike.* Marburg: Tectum, 2003.

Dietrich, C. "Asylgesetzgebung in antiken Gesellschaften." In *Gesetzgebung in antiken Gesellschaften: Israel, Griechenland, Rom*, edited by L. Burckhardt, K. Seybold, and J. von Ungern-Sternberg, 193–219. Berlin: de Gruyter, 2007.

Dietrich, W. "Rache, Erwägungen zu einem alttestamentlichen Thema." *Evangelische Theologie* 36 (1976): 450–72.

Dobbs-Allsopp, F. W. "The Genre of the Meṣad Ḥashavyahu Ostracon." *Bulletin of the American Schools of Oriental Research* 296 (1994): 49–55.

Dover, K. J. *Greek Popular Morality in the Time of Plato and Aristotle.* Oxford: Oxford University Press, 1974.

Edenburg, C. "Ideology and Social Context of the Deuteronomic Women's Sex Laws (Deuteronomy 22:13–29)." *JBL* 128 (2009): 43–60.

Eichler, B. L. "Exodus 21:22–25 Revisited: Methodological Considerations." In *Birkat Shalom: Studies in the Bible, Ancient Near Eastern Literature, and Postbiblical Judaism Presented to Shalom M. Paul on the Occasion of His Seventieth Birthday*, edited by Chaim Cohen, Victor Avigdor Horowitz, Avi Hurvitz, Yochanan Muffs, Baruch J. Schwartz, and Jeffrey H. Tigay, vol. 1, 11–29. Winona Lake, IN: Eisenbrauns, 2008.

Eichler, B. L. "Literary Structure in the Laws of Eshnunna." In *Language, Literature, and History: Philological and Historical Studies Presented to Erica Reiner*, edited by F. Rochberg-Halton, 71–84. New Haven: American Oriental Society, 1987.

Elliger, K. "Das Gesetz Leviticus 18." *Zeitschrift für die alttestamentliche Wissenschaft* 67 (1955): 1–25.

Elliger, K. *Leviticus.* Tübingen: Mohr Siebeck, 1966.

Elster, J. "Norms of Revenge." *Ethics* 100 (1990): 862–85.

Fensham, F. C. "Liability in Case of Negligence in the Old Testament Covenant Code and in Ancient Legal Traditions." In *Essays in Honour of Ben Beinart: Jura Legesque Antiquiores Necnon Recentiores*, edited by B. Beinart and Wouter De Vos, 283–94. Cape Town: Juta, 1978.

Fensham, F. C. "Das Nicht-Haftbar-Sein im Bundesbuch im Lichte der altorientalischen Rechtstexte." *Journal of Northwest Semitic Languages* 8 (1981): 17–22.

Fensham, F. C. "The Role of the Lord in the Legal Sections of the Covenant Code." *Vetus Testamentum* 26 (1976): 262–74.

Fichtner, J. J. "Der Begriff des Nächsten im AT." *WuD* 4 (1955): 23–52. Reprinted in J. J. Fichtner, *Gottes Weisheit. Gesammelte Schriften zum Alten Testament*, edited by K. D. Fricke, 88–114. Stuttgart: Calwer Verlag 1965.

Finkelstein, J. J. *The Ox that Gored.* Philadelphia: American Philosophical Society, 1981.

Finsterbusch, K. "Die Dekalog-Ausrichtung des deuteronomischen Gesetzes." In *Deuteronomium: Tora für eine neue Generation*, edited by G. Fischer et al., 123–46. Wiesbaden: Harrassowitz, 2011.

Finsterbusch, K. *Deuteronomium: Eine Einführung*. Göttingen: Vandenhoeck & Ruprecht, 2012.
Fishbane, M. *Biblical Interpretation in Ancient Israel*. Oxford: Oxford University Press, 1985.
Fischer, I. "The Book of Ruth: A 'Feminist' Commentary to the Torah?" In *A Feminist Companion to the Bible*, edited by A. Brenner, 24–49. Sheffield: Sheffield Academic Press, 1999.
Fistill, U. *Israel und das Ostjordanland: Untersuchungen zur Komposition von Num 21,21–35,13 im Hinblick auf die Entstehung des Buches Numeri*. Frankfurt: Peter Lang, 2007.
Fitzpatrick-McKinley, A. *The Transformation of Torah from Scribal Advice to Law*. Sheffield: Sheffield Academic Press, 1999.
Fleischman, J. "The Delinquent Daughter and Legal Innovation in Deuteronomy XXII 20–21." *Vetus Testamentum* 58 (2009): 191–210.
Fortes, Meyer. *Kinship and the Social Order: The Legacy of Lewis Henry Morgan*. With a new introduction by Lionel Tiger. New Brunswick, NJ: Transaction Publishers, 2006 (1st ed. 1969).
Fox, M. V. *Proverbs 1–9*. Anchor Bible 18A. New Haven: Yale University Press, 2000.
Fox, M. V. *Proverbs 10–31*, Anchor Bible 18B. New Haven: Yale University Press, 2009.
Fried, L. S. "A Religious Association in Second Temple Judah? A Comment on Neh 10." *Transeuphratene* 30 (2005): 77–96.
Frymer-Kensky, T. "Israel." In *A History of Ancient Near Eastern Law*, edited by R. Westbrook, vol. 2, 976–1046. Leiden: Brill, 2003.
Frymer-Kensky, T. "Tit for Tat: The Principle of Equal Retribution in Near Eastern and Biblical Law." *The Biblical Archaeologist* 43, no. 4 (1980): 230–34.
Frymer-Kensky, T. "Virginity in the Bible." In *Gender and Law in the Hebrew Bible and the Ancient Near East*, edited by V. H. Matthews, B. M. Levinson, and T. Frymer-Kensky, 79–96. Sheffield: Sheffield Academic Press, 1998.
Gagarin, M. *Drakon and Early Athenian Homicide Law*. New Haven: Yale University Press, 1981.
Gagarin, M. *Early Greek Law*. Los Angeles: University of California Press, 1986.
Gamberoni, J. חסה. In *Theological Dictionary of the Old Testament*, edited by G. Johannes Botterweck, H. Ringgren, and H.-J. Fabry, vol. 5, 64–75. Grand Rapids: Eerdmans, 1986.
Garner, B., ed. *Black's Law Dictionary*. 8th ed. Saint Paul, MN: Thomson, 2004.
Gass, E. "'Heilige sollt ihr werden. Denn heilig bin ich, Jahwe, euer Gott.' Zur Begründungsstruktur in Lev 19." *Münchener theologische Zeitschrift* 64 (2013): 214–31.
Gass, E. "Zum syntaktischen Problem von Lev 19,18." In *"Ich werde meinen Bund mit euch niemals brechen!" (Ri 2,1). Festschrift für Walter Gross zum 70*, edited by E. Gass and H.-J. Stipp, 197–216. Herder's Biblische Studien 62. Freiburg im Breisgau: Herder, 2011.
Gehrke, H.-J. "Die Griechen und die Rache: Ein Versuch in historischer Psychologie." *Saeculum* 38 (1987): 121–49.
Gerstenberger, E. *Leviticus: A Commentary*. Louisville: Westminster John Knox, 1996.
Gerstenberger, E. *Wesen und Herkunft des "apodiktischen Rechts."* Neukirchen-Vluyn: Neukirchener Verlag, 1965.
Gertz, J.-C. *Die Gerichtsorganisation Israels im deuteronomischen Gesetz*. Göttingen: Vandenhoeck & Ruprecht, 1994.

Gesenius, W. *Hebräisches und Aramäisches Handwörterbuch über das Alte Testament*. 18th ed. H. Donner, Berlin: Springer, 2013.

Gesenius, W., E. Kautzsch, and G. Bergsträsser. *Hebräische Grammatik*. 28th ed. Repr. Darmstadt: Wissenschaftliche Buchgesellschaft, 1995 (1909).

Gillihan, Y. M. *Civic Ideology, Organization, and Law in the Rule Scrolls: A Comparative Study of the Covenanters' Sect and Contemporary Voluntary Associations in Political Context*. Studies on the Texts of the Desert of Judah 97. Leiden: Brill, 2012.

Gilmer, H. W. *The If-You Form in Israelite Law*. Society of Biblical Literature Dissertation Series 15. Atlanta: Scholars Press, 1975.

Glotz, G. *La solidarité de la famille dans le droit criminel en Grèce*. Paris: A. Fontemoing, 1904.

Gödde, S. "Hiketeia." In *Brill's New Pauly*, edited by H. Cancik and H. Schneider, vol. 6, 323. Leiden: Brill, 2005.

Greenberg, M. "The Biblical Conception of Asylum." *Journal of Biblical Literature* 78 (1959): 125–32.

Gunkel, H., and J. Begrich, *Introduction to the Psalms: The Genres of the Religious Lyric of Israel*. Translated from German by J. D. Nogalski. Macon, GA: Mercer, 1998.

Haase, R. "The Hittite Kingdom." In *A History of Ancient Near Eastern Law*, edited by R. Westbrook, vol. 1, 619–56. Leiden: Brill, 2003.

Haase, R. "Körperliche Strafen in den altorientalischen Rechtssammlungen: Ein Beitrag zum altorientalischen Strafrecht." *Revue internationale des droits de l'antiquité* 3–10 (1963): 55–75.

Haase, R. "Zur Anzeigepflicht des Finders nach hethitischem Recht," *WO* 12 (1957): 378–81.

Hagedorn, A. *Between Moses and Plato. Individual and Society in Deuteronomy and Ancient Greek Law*. Göttingen: Vandenhoeck & Ruprecht, 2004.

Harris, G. "Feuding or the Rule of Law? An Essay in Legal Sociology." In *Symposion 2001. Vorträge zur griechischen und hellenistischen Rechtsgeschichte*, edited by R. Wallace and M. Gagarin, 125–41. Vienna: Österreichische Akademie der Wissenschaften, 2005.

Hartenstein, F., and B. Janowski. *Psalmen*. Neukirchen-Vluyn: Neukirchener Verlag, 2012.

Hartenstein, F. "Ein zorniger und gewalttätiger Gott? Zorn Gottes, ‚Rachepsalmen' und ‚Opferung Isaaks' – neuere Forschungen." *Verkündigung und Forschung* 58 (2013): 110–26.

Hartley, J. E. *Leviticus 1–27*. Dallas: Word 1992.

Heinemann, I. *Philons Griechische und Jüdische Bildung*. Breslau: M&H Marcus, 1932.

Heltzer, M. "Asylum on Alasia (Cyprus)." *ZABR* 7 (2001): 368–73.

Hempel, J. *Die Schichten des Deuteronomiums: Ein Beitrag zur israelitischen Literatur- und Rechtsgeschichte*. Beiträge zur Kultur- und Universalgeschichte 33. Leipzig: R. Voigtländer, 1914.

Herrmann, R. "Die Gemeinderegel von Qumran und das antike Vereinswesen." In *Jewish Identity in the Greco-Roman World: Jüdische Identität in der griechisch-römischen Welt*, edited by J. Frey, D. R. Schwartz, and S. Gripentrog, 161–203. Ancient Judaism and Early Christianity 71. Leiden: Brill, 2007.

Herrmann, S. "Weisheit im Bundesbuch. Eine Misszelle zu Ex 23,1–9." In *Alttestamentlicher Glaube und biblische Theologie. Festschrift für Horst Dietrich Preuß*, edited by J. Hausmann and H. J. Zobel, 56–58. Stuttgart: Kohlhammer, 1992.

Hignett, C. *A History of the Athenian Constitution to the End of the Fifth-Century B.C.* Oxford: Clarendon, 1952.
Hoebel, E. A. "Feud: Concept, Reality and Method in the Study of Primitive Law." In *Essays on Modernization of Underdeveloped Societies*, vol. 1, edited by A. R. Desai. Bombay: Thacker, 1971.
Hoffmann, D. *Das Buch Leviticus übersetzt und erklärt*, vol. 1, Berlin, 1905; vol. 2, Berlin: M. Poppelauer, 1906.
Hoffner, H. A. *The Laws of the Hittites: A Critical Edition*. Leiden: Brill, 1997.
Hölscher, G. "Komposition und Ursprung des Deuteromiums." *Zeitschrift für die Alttestamentliche Wissenschaft* 40 (1922): 161–255.
Holzinger, H. *Exodus*. Tübingen: Mohr Siebeck, 1900.
Horst, F. *Hiob*. Neukirchen-Vluyn: Neukirchener Verlag, 1963.
Horst, F. "Recht und Religion im Bereich des AT." *Evangelische Theologie* 16 (1956): 49–75.
Hossfeld, F. *Untersuchungen zur Komposition und Theologie des Ezechielbuches*. 2nd ed., Würzburg: Echter 1983.
Hossfeld, F. L., רצח. In *Theological Dictionary of the Old Testament*, vol. 13. Grand Rapids: Eerdmans, 2004.
Houtman, C. *Das Bundesbuch: Ein Kommentar*. Leiden: Brill, 1997.
Huffmon, H. B. "Ex 23:4–5: A Comparative Study." In *A Light Unto My Path: Old Testament Studies in Honor of J. M. Myers*, edited by H. N. Bream, R. D. Heim, and C. A. Moore, 271–78. Philadelphia: Temple University, 1974.
Hurvitz, A. "Linguistic Observations on the Priestly Term *'edah* and the Language of P." *Immanuel* 1 (1972): 21–23.
Jackson, B. S. *Essays in Jewish and Comparative Legal History*. Leiden: Brill, 1975.
Jackson, B. S. "Liability for Mere Intentions in Early Jewish Law." In *Essays in Jewish and Comparative Legal History*, edited by B. S. Jackson, 202–34. Leiden: Brill, 1975.
Jackson, B. S. *Semiotics and Legal Theory*. Repr., Wiltshire: Deborah Charles Publications, 1997; 1st ed., Routledge, Kegan Paul, 1985.
Jackson, B. S. *Theft in Early Jewish Law: An Historical Perspective*. Oxford: Clarendon, 1972.
Jackson, B. S. *Wisdom-laws: A Study of the Mishpatim of Exodus 21:1–22:16*. Oxford: Oxford University Press, 2006.
Jacobs, B. *Das Buch Exodus*. Stuttgart: Calwer, 1997.
Jacobsen, T. "Primitive Democracy in Ancient Mesopotamia." *Journal of Near Eastern Studies* 2 (1943): 159–72.
Jagersma, H. *Leviticus 19: Identiteit, Bevrijding, Gemeenschap*. Assen: Van Gorcum, 1972.
Janowski, B. *Arguing with God: A Theological Anthropology of the Psalms*. Louisville: Westminster John Knox, 2013.
Janowski, B. *Ein Gott der straft und tötet? Zwölf Fragen zum Gottesbild des Alten Testaments*. Neukirchen-Vluyn: Neukirchener Verlag, 2013.
Janowski, B. *Konfliktgespräche mit Gott: Eine Anthropologie der Psalmen*. Neukirchen-Vluyn: Neukirchener Verlag, 2003.
Jenni, E. *Die hebräischen Präpositionen. Band 3: Die Präposition Lamed*. Stuttgart: Kohlhammer, 2000
Jenni, E. "Zur Semantik der hebräischen Personen-, Tier- und Dingvergleiche," *ZAH* 3 (1990): 133–66.

Jenni, E., and C. Westermann. *Theological Lexicon of the Old Testament*, 3 vols. Peabody, MA: Hendrickson, 1997. Translated by M. E. Biddle from the German *Theologisches Handwörterbuch zum Alten Testament*, 2 vols., Munich: Chr. Kaiser, 1971/1976.

Jeremias, J. *Der Zorn Gottes im Alten Testament: Das biblische Israel zwischen Verwerfung und Erwählung*. Neukirchen-Vluyn: Neukirchener Verlag, 2009.

Johnson, B. משפט. In *Theological Dictionary of the Old Testament*, edited by G. Johannes Botterweck, Helmer Ringgren, and Heinz-Josef Fabry, vol. 9, 86–98. Grand Rapids: Eerdmans, 1998.

Jones, J. W. *Law and Legal Theory of the Greeks*. Oxford: Clarendon, 1956.

Joosten, J. *People and Land in the Holiness Code: An Exegetical Study of the Ideational Framework of the Law in Leviticus 17–26*. Leiden: Brill, 1996.

Kaiser, O. "Was ein Freund nicht tun darf. Eine Auslegung von Sir 27,16–21." In *Freundschaft bei Ben Sira. Beiträge des Symposions zu Ben Sira Salzburg 1995*, edited by F. V. Reiterer, 107–22. Berlin: de Gruyter, 1996.

Kaufman, S. A. "The Second Table of the Decalogue and the Implicit Categories of Ancient Near Eastern Law." In *Love and Death in the Ancient Near East: Essays in Honor of Marvin H. Pope*, edited by J. H. Mark and R. M. Good, 111–16. Guilford, CT: Four Quarters, 1987.

Keel, O. *Feinde und Gottesleugner. Studien zum Image der Widersacher in den Individual Psalmen*. Stuttgart: Katholisches Bibelwerk, 1969.

Keil, C. F. *Biblischer Commentar über die Bücher Moses. 2. Bd., Leviticus, Numeri und Deuteronomium*, 2nd ed., Leipzig: Dörffling und Franke, 1870.

Kellermann, D. רע. In *Theological Dictionary of the Old Testament* vol. 8, edited by G. Johannes Botterweck, Helmer Ringgren, and Heinz-Josef Fabry, 522–32. Grand Rapids: Eerdmans, 2004.

Kitz, A. M. "Naboth's Vineyard after Mari and Amarna." *Journal of Biblical Literature* 134 (2015): 529–45.

Klinghardt, M. "The Manual of Discipline in the Light of Statutes of Hellenistic Associations." In *Methods of Investigation of the Dead Sea Scrolls and the Khirbet Qumran Site: Present Realities and Future Prospects*, edited by J. J. Collins, M. O. Wise, N. Golb, and D. Pardee, 251–70. Annals of the New York Academy of Sciences 722. New York: Academy of Sciences, 1994.

Klopfenstein, M. *Die Lüge nach dem Alten Testament: Ihr Begriff, ihre Bedeutung und ihre Beurteilung*. Zurich: Gotthelf, 1964.

Knapp, D. *Deuteronomium 4: Literarische Analyse und Theologische Interpretation*. Göttingen: Vandenhoeck & Ruprecht, 1987.

Knight, D. A. *Law, Power, and Justice in Ancient Israel*. Louisville: Westminster John Knox, 2011.

Knohl, I. *The Sanctuary of Silence: The Priestly Torah and the Holiness School*. Minneapolis: Fortress Press, 1995.

Koch, K. "Gibt es ein Vergeltungsdogma im Alten Testament?" *Evangelische Theologie* 52 (1955): 1–42. Reprinted in K. Koch, *Um das Prinzip der Vergeltung in Religion und Recht des Alten Testaments*. Darmstadt: Wissenschaftliche Buchgesellschaft, 1972, 130–80.

Koch, K. "Der Spruch 'Sein Blut bleibe auf seinem Haupt' und die israelitische Auffassung vom vergossenen Blut." *Vetus Testamentum* 12 (1962): 396–416.

Kocher, A. "Sex or Power? The Crime of the Bride in Deuteronomy 22." *Zeitschrift für altorientalische und biblische Rechtgeschichte* 16 (2010): 279–96.

Köhler, Ludwig, and Walter Baumgartner. *Hebrew and Aramaic Lexicon of the Old Testament.* Leiden: Brill, 1983.

König, E. *Hebräisches und Aramäisches Wörterbuch zum AT.* Leipzig: Dieterich'sche Verlagsbuchhandlung Theodor Weicher, 1910. 6th, 7th eds. 1937.

Korošec, V. "Gesetze" In *Reallexikon der Assyriologie*, edited by R. Opificius, vol. 3, 288–97. Berlin: de Gruyter, 1966.

Kratz, R. G. "Psalm 1 und die doxologische Fünfteilung des Psalters." *Zeitschrift für Theologie und Kirche* (1996): 1–34.

Kugel, J. L. "On Hidden Hatred and Open Reproach. Early Exegesis of Leviticus 19:17." *Harvard Theological Review* 80 (1987): 43–61.

Lacey, W. K. *The Family in Classical Greece: Aspects of Greek and Roman Life.* Ithaca, NY: Cornell University Press, 1968.

Lang, B. "'Du sollst nicht nach der Frau eines anderen verlangen': Eine neue Deutung des 9ten und 10ten Gebots." *Zeitschrift für die alttestamentliche Wissenschaft* 93 (1981): 216–24.

Larson, E. W. "Greco-Roman Guilds." In *Encyclopedia of the Dead Sea Scrolls*, edited by L. Schiffman and J. C. VanderKam, vol. 1, 321–23. Oxford: Oxford University Press, 2000.

Levine, B. A. *Numbers 21–36.* New York: Doubleday, 2000.

Levinson, B. M. "The Case for Revision and Interpolation within the Biblical Legal Corpora." In *Theory and Method in Biblical Cuneiform Law*, edited by B. M. Levinson, 201–23. Sheffield: Sheffield Academic Press, 1994.

Levinson, B. M. "The First Constitution. Rethinking the Origins of Rule of Law and Separation of Powers in Light of Deuteronomy." *Cardozo Law Review* 27 (2006): 1853–88.

Levinson, B. M. "Is the Covenant Code an Exilic Composition? A Response to John Van Seters." In *In Search of Pre-exilic Israel: Proceedings of the Oxford Old Testament Seminar*, edited by John Day, 272–325. New York: T&T Clark, 2004.

Levinson, B. M. *The Right Chorale: Studies in Biblical Law and Interpretation.* Winona Lake: Eisenbrauns, 2008.

Lewis, D., ed. *Inscriptiones Atticae Euclidis Anno Anteriores, Vol. 1: Decreta et Tabulae Magistratuum.* 3rd ed. Berlin: de Gruyter, 1981.

Levy, J. עדה. In *Theological Dictionary of the Old Testament*, edited by G. Johannes Botterweck, Helmer Ringgren, and Heinz-Josef Fabry, vol. 10, 468–81. Grand Rapids: Eerdmans, 1999.

Liedke, G. *Gestalt und Bezeichnung alttestamentlicher Rechtssätze: Eine formgeschichtlich-terminologische Studie.* Neukirchen-Vluyn: Neukirchener Verlag, 1971.

Lipiński, E. נקם. In *Theological Dictionary of the Old Testament*, edited by G. J. Botterweck, H. Ringgren, and H.-J. Fabry, vol. 10, 1–9. Grand Rapids: Eerdmans, 1999.

Lipiński, E. רכל. In *Theological Dictionary of the Old Testament*, edited by G. J. Botterweck, H. Ringgren, and H.-J. Fabry, vol. 13, 498–99. Grand Rapids: Eerdmans, 2004.

Lipiński, E. שׂנא. In *Theological Dictionary of the Old Testament*, edited by G. J. Botterweck, H. Ringgren, and H.-J. Fabry, vol. 14, 164–74. Grand Rapids: Eerdmans, 1974.

Lippert, S. L. *Einführung in die altägyptische Rechtsgeschichte.* 2nd ed. Münster: LIT Verlag, 2012.

Loader, J. A. *Proverbs 1–9.* Leuven: Peeters, 2014.

Locher, C. *Die Ehre einer Frau in Israel. Exegetische und rechtsvergleichende Studien zu Deuteronomium 22,13–21.* Göttingen: Vandenhoeck & Ruprecht, 1986.

Löhr, M. *Das Asylwesen im Alten Testament*. Halle: Max Niemeyer, 1930.

Loomis, W. T. "The Nature of Premeditation in Athenian Homicide Law." *The Journal of Hellenic Studies* 92 (1972): 86–95.

Luciani, D. "Soyez saints car je suis saint: Un commentaire de Lévitique 19." *Nouvelle Revue Théologique* 114 (1992): 212–46.

Lüddeckens, E. "Gottesdienstliche Gemeinschaften im pharaonischen, ptolemäischen und christlichen Ägypten." *Zeitschrift für Religions- und Geistesgeschichte* 20 (1968): 193–211.

Lyons, M. A. *From Law to Prophecy: Ezekiel's Use of the Holiness Code*. London: T&T Clark, 2009.

Lysias. *Lysias. Speeches*, trans. S. C. Todd. Austin: University of Texas, 2000.

MacDowell, D. M. *Athenian Homicide Law in the Age of the Orators*. Manchester: University Press, 1963.

MacDowell, D. M. *The Law in Classical Athens*. London: Thames & Hudson, 1978.

Macholz, C. "Die Stellung des Königs in der israelitischen Gerichtsverfassung." *Zeitschrift für die Alttestamentliche Wissenschaft* 84 (1972): 157–82.

Magdalene, F. R., and B. Wells, "Law in the Writings." In *Oxford Encyclopedia of the Bible and Law*, edited by B. Strawn, vol. 1, 485–95. Oxford: Oxford University Press, 2015.

Madl, H. נטר. In *Theological Dictionary of the Old Testament*, edited by G. J. Botterweck, H. Ringgren, H.-J. Fabry, vol. 9, 395–401. Grand Rapids: Eerdmans, 1998.

Magonet, J. "The Structure and Meaning of Leviticus 19." *Hebrew Annual Review* 7 (1983): 151–67.

Maier, J. "Verleumder oder Verräter: Zur jüdischen Auslegungsgeschichte von Lev 19:16." In *Altes Testament. Forschung und Wirkung, Festschrift für H. Graf Reventlow*, edited by P. Mommer and W. Thiel, 307–11. New York: Peter Lang, 1994.

Malinowski, B. *Crime and Custom in Savage Society*. London: Kegan Paul, Trench & Trubner, 1926.

Marböck, J. קלה. In *Theological Dictionary of the Old Testament*, edited by G. J. Botterweck, H. Ringgren, and D. E. Green, vol. 13, 31–37. Grand Rapids: Eerdmans, 2004.

Marshall, J. *Israel and the Book of the Covenant: An Anthropological Approach to Biblical Law*. Atlanta: Scholars Press, 1993.

Martin-Achard, R. "גור *gûr* to sojourn." In *Theological Lexicon of the Old Testament*, edited by E. Jenni and C. Westermann, vol. 1, 307–10. Peabody, MA: Hendrickson, 1997.

Mathys, H.-P. *Liebe deinen Nächsten wie dich selbst: Untersuchungen zum alttestamentlichen Gebot der Nächstenliebe (Lev 19,18)*. Fribourg, Switzerland: Universitätsverlag, 1986.

Mayer, G. אוה. In *Theological Dictionary of the Old Testament*, edited by G. J. Botterweck, Helmer Ringgren, Heinz-Josef Fabry, vol. 1, 134–37. Grand Rapids: Eerdmans, 1974.

Mayer, G., and H. Fabry. יכח, *Theological Dictionary of the Old Testament*, edited by G. J. Botterweck, H. Ringgren, and D. E. Green, vol. 6, 64–71. Grand Rapids: Eerdmans, 1990.

Mayes, A. D. H. *Deuteronomy*. Grand Rapids: Eerdmans, 1981.

McBride, S. D. "Polity of the Covenant People. The Book of Deuteronomy," *Interpretation* 3 (1987): 229–44.

McKay, J. W. "Exodus XXIII 1–3, 6–8: A Decalogue for the Administration of Justice in the City Gate." *Vetus Testamentum* 21 (1971): 311–25.

Meinhold, A. *Sprüche*. Zürcher Bibelkommentare: AT, 16:1–2. Zurich: Theologischer Verlag, 1991.
Mendes-Flohr, P. *Love, Accusative and Dative: Reflections on Leviticus 19:18, The B.G. Rudolph Lectures in Judaic Studies*. Syracuse NY: University Press, 2007.
Merendino, R. P. *Das deuteronomische Gesetz. Eine literarkritische, gattungs- und überlieferungsgeschichtliche Untersuchung zu Dt 12–26*. Bonn: P. Hanstein, 1969.
Merz, E. *Die Blutrache bei den Israeliten*. Leipzig: Heinrichs, 1916.
Mieroop, M. Van De "Popular Participation in the Political Life of the Ancient Near East." In *Der Alte Orient und die Entstehung der Athenischen Demokratie*, edited by C. Horst, 1–10. Wiesbaden: Harrassowitz, 2020.
Miller, P. D. *The Ten Commandments*. Louisville: Westminster John Knox, 2009.
Mitchell, L. G. "New for Old: Friendship Networks in Athenian Politics." *Greece and Rome* 43 (1998): 11–21.
Milgrom, J. *Leviticus 1–16: A New Translation with Introduction and Commentary*. New York: Doubleday, 1991.
Milgrom, J. *Leviticus 17–22: A New Translation with Introduction and Commentary*. New York: Doubleday. 2000.
Milgrom, J. "Priestly Terminology and the Political and Social Structure of Pre-monarchic Israel." *Jewish Quarterly Review* 69 (1979): 65–81.
Monson, A. "The Ethics and Economics of Ptolemaic Religious Associations." *Ancient Society* 36 (2006): 221–38.
Moore, S. F., ed. *Law and Anthropology: A Reader*. Blackwell: Boston, 2005.
Morrow, W. S. "The Arrangement of the Original Version of Deuteronomy According to Eckart Otto." *Zeitschrift für altorientalische und biblische Rechtsgeschichte* 25 (2019): 195–206.
Morrow, W. S. *Scribing the Center. Organization and Redaction in Deuteronomy 14:1–17:13*. Atlanta: Scholars Press, 1995.
Morrow, W. S. "Tribute from Judah and the Transmission of Assyrian Propaganda." In *"My Spirit at Rest in the North Country" (Zechariah 6:8): Collected Communications to the XXth Congress of the International Organization for the Study of the Old Testament, Helsinki 2010*, edited by H. M. Niemann and M. Augustin, 183–92. Frankfurt: Peter Lang, 2011.
Muhs, B. "Membership in Private Associations in Ptolemaic Tebtunis." *Journal of the Economic and Social History of the Orient* 44 (2001): 1–21.
Murray, D. F. "MQWM and the Future of Israel in 2Sam VII." *Vetus Testamentum* 40 (1990): 309–19.
Muszynski, M. "Les 'associations religieuses' en Égypte d'après les sources hiéroglyphiques, démotiques et grecques." *Orientalia lovaniensia periodica* 8 (1977): 145–63.
Nelson, R. D. *Deuteronomy*. Louisville: Westminster John Knox Press, 2004.
Nielsen, E. *Deuteronomium*. Tübingen: Mohr Siebeck,1995.
Nihan, C. *From Priestly Torah to Pentateuch: A Study in the Composition of the Book of Leviticus*. Tübingen: Mohr Siebeck, 2007.
Noth, M. *Das Buch Josua*. Tübingen: Mohr Siebeck, 1953.
Noth, M. "Das Land Gilead als Siedlungsgebiet israelitischer Sippen." *Palästina-Jahrbuch* 37 (1941): 50–101. Repr. in M. Noth, *Aufsätze zur biblischen Landes- und Altertumskunde I*, edited by H. W. Wolff, 345–90. Neukirchener Verlag: Neukirchen, 1971.
Noth, M. *Exodus: A Commentary*. Philadelphia: SCM Press, 1962. Translated from the German, *Das zweite Buch Mose: Exodus*. Göttingen: Vandenhoeck & Ruprecht, 1959.

Noth, M. *Leviticus. A Commentary.* Philadelphia: SCM Press, 1965. Translated from the German, *Das dritte Buch Mose: Leviticus.* Göttingen: Vandenhoeck & Ruprecht, 1962.

Nutkowicz, H. "Concerning the Verb *śn'* in Judaeo-Aramaic Contracts from Elephantine." *Journal of Semitic Studies* 52 (2007): 211–25.

Oeming, M. צוד; ציד. In *Theological Dictionary of the Old Testament,* edited by G. J. Botterweck, H. Ringgren, and H.-J. Fabry, vol. 12, 270–75. Grand Rapids: Eerdmans, 2003.

Olson, D. T. *Deuteronomy and the Death of Moses: A Theological Reading.* Minneapolis: Augsburg Fortress, 1994.

Olyan, S. M. *Friendship in the Hebrew Bible.* New Haven: Yale University Press, 2017.

Olyan, S. M. "A Suggestion Regarding the Derivation of the Hebrew Noun *MĒRĒA'.*" *Journal of Semitic Studies* 56 (2011): 217–19.

Oswald, W. "Die politischen Konzeptionen des Deuteronomiums als Teil des politischen Denkens der antiken Mittelmeerwelt," in *Der Alte Orient und die Entstehung der Athenischen Demokratie,* edited by C. Horst, 55–68. Wiesbaden: Harrassowitz, 2020.

Otto, E. "Biblische Rechtsgeschichte als Fortschreibungsgeschichte." *Bibliotheca Orientalis* 56 (1999): 5–14. Repr. in E. Otto, *Altorientalische und Biblische Rechtsgeschichte,* 496–506. Wiesbaden: Harrassowitz, 2008.

Otto, E. "Book of the Covenant." In *The Oxford Encyclopedia of the Bible and Law,* edited by B. A. Strawn, 68–77. Oxford: Oxford University Press, 2015.

Otto, E. "Der Dekalog als Brennspiegel israelitischer Rechtsgeschichte." In *Alttestamentlicher Glaube und biblische Theologie,* edited by J. Hausmann and H.-J. Zobel, 59–68. Festschrift für Horst Dietrich Preuss zum 65. Stuttgart: Kohlhammer, 1992.

Otto, E. *Deuteronomium 12:1–23:15.* Freiburg: Herder, 2016.

Otto, E. *Deuteronomium 23:16–34:12.* Freiburg: Herder, 2017.

Otto, E. *Das Deuteronomium im Pentateuch und Hexateuch.* Tübingen: Mohr Siebeck, 2000.

Otto, E. "Deuteronomy." In *Religion Past and Present.* vol. III, edited by H. D. Betz, D. Browning, B. Janowski, and E. Jüngel, 786–88. Leiden/Boston: Brill, 2007.

Oswald, W. "Foreign Marriages and Citizenship in Persian Period Judah." *Journal of Hebrew Scriptures* 12, no. 6 (2012): 1–17.

Otto, E. "Gesellschaftsstruktur in der Hebräischen Bibel." In *Strafe und Strafrecht in den antiken Welten unter Berücksichtigung von Todesstrafe, Hinrichtung und peinlicher Befragung,* edited by R. Rollinger, M. Lange, and H. Barta, 233–47. Wiesbaden: Harrassowitz, 2012.

Otto, E. *Das Gesetz des Moses.* Darmstadt: Wissenschaftliche Buchgesellschaft, 2007.

Otto, E. "Gottes Recht als Menschenrecht." In *Rechts- und literarhistorische Studien zum Deuteronomium,* edited by E. Otto, 1–29. Wiesbaden: Harrassowitz, 2002.

Otto, E. "Das Heiligkeitsgesetz Leviticus 17–26 in der Pentateuchredaktion." In *Altes Testament. Forschung und Wirkung: Festschrift für Henning Graf Reventlow,* edited by P. Mommer and W. Thiel, 65–80. Frankfurt: Peter Lang, 1994.

Otto, E. "Innerbiblische Exegese im Heiligkeitsgesetz Levitikus 17–26." In *Levitikus als Buch,* edited by H. Fabry and H.-W. Jüngling, 125–96. Berlin: Philo, 1999.

Otto, E. *Körperverletzungen in den Keilschriftrechten und im Alten Testament: Studien zum Rechtstransfer im Alten Orient.* Neukirchen-Vluyn: Neukirchener, Butzon und Bercker, 1991.

Otto, E. "Zur Methodologie der Interpretation Biblischer Rechtsüberlieferungen. Diachronie und Synchronie im Depositenrecht des ‚Bundesbuches'." In *Altorientalische und Biblische Rechtsgeschichte*, edited by E. Otto, 486–95. Wiesbaden: Harrassowitz, 2008.

Otto, E. "Rechtshermeneutik in der Hebräischen Bibel. Die innerbiblischen Ursprünge halachischer Bibelauslegung." *Zeitschrift für Altorientalische und Biblische Rechtsgeschichte* 5 (1999): 75–98.

Otto, E. "Strafrechtstheorie und Rechtsanthropologie in Platons NOMOI und in der biblischen Tora des Buches Deuteronomium. Zweiter Teil: Strafrechtstheorie und Rechtsanthropologie im Buch Deuteronomium." *Zeitschrift für altorientalische und biblische Rechtgeschichte* 26 (2020): 161–234.

Otto, E. *Theologische Ethik des Alten Testaments*. Stuttgart: Kohlhammer, 1994.

Otto, E. "Verbot der Wiederherstellung einer geschiedenen Ehe. Deuteronomium 24,1–4 im Kontext des israelitischen und judäischen Eherechts." *Ugarit-Forschungen* 24 (1992): 301–10.

Otto, E. *Wandel der Rechtsbegründungen in der Gesellschaftsgeschichte des antiken Israel: Eine Rechtsgeschichte des „Bundesbuches" Ex XX 22–XXIII 13*. Leiden: Brill, 1988.

Papakonstantinou, Z. *Lawmaking and Adjudication in Archaic Greece*. London: Duckworth, 2008.

Patrick, D. *Old Testament Law*. Atlanta: John Knox, 1984.

Patterson, C. *Pericles' Citizenship Law of 451/0*. New York: Arno Press, 1981. Reprint: Salem, NH: Ayer, 1987.

Patterson, C. "The Hospitality of Athenian Justice: The Metic in Court." In *Law and Social Status in Classical Athens*, edited by V. Hunter and J. Edmondson, 93–112. Oxford: Oxford University Press, 2000.

Peels, H. G. L. *The Vengeance of God: The Meaning of the Root NQM and the Function of the NQM-Texts in the Context of Divine Revelation in the Old Testament*. Leiden: Brill, 1995.

Perlitt, L. "'Ein einzig Volk von Brüdern': zur deuteronomischen Herkunft der biblischen Bezeichnung 'Bruder'." In L. Perlitt, *Deuteronomium-Studien*, 50–73. Tübingen: Mohr Siebeck, 1994. Reprinted from *Kirche: Festschrift für Günther Bornkamm zum 75 Geburstag*, edited by D. Lührmann; G. Strecker, 27–52. Tübingen: Mohr Siebeck, 1980.

Petschow, H. "Zur Systematik und Gesetzestechnik im Codex Hammurabi." *Zeitschrift für Assyriologie* 57 (1965): 146–72.

Pfeifer, G., and N. Grotkamp, eds. *Außergerichtliche Konfliktlösung in der Antike. Beispiele aus drei Jahrtausenden*. Frankfurt: Max Planck Institute for European Legal History, 2017.

Phillips, A. *Ancient Israel's Criminal Law*. Oxford: Clarendon, 1970.

Phillips, D. D. *Avengers of Blood. Homicide in Athenian Law and Custom from Draco to Demosthenes*. Stuttgart: Franz Steiner, 2008.

Phillips, D. D. *The Law of Ancient Athens*. Ann Arbor: University of Michigan, 2013.

Phillips, D. D. "*Trauma Ek Pronoias* in Athenian Law." *Journal of Hellenic Studies* 127 (2007): 74–105.

Philo, *De Specialibus Legibus*. Trans. by C. D. Yonge, *The Works of Philo Judaeus, the Contemporary of Josephus*, vol. 3, London: G. Bell & Sons, 1855.

Pilch, J. J. *The Cultural Life Setting of the Proverbs*. Minneapolis: Fortress, 2016.

Pohlmann, K. F. *Der Prophet Hesekiel/Ezechiel Kapitel 20–48*. Göttingen: Vandenhoeck & Ruprecht, 2001.
Porten, B., J. J. Farber, C. J. Martin and G. Vittmann, eds. *The Elephantine Papyri in English: Three Millennia of Cross-Cultural Continuity and Change*. 2nd ed., Documenta et monumenta Orientis antiqui 22. Leiden: Brill, 2011.
Pressler, C. *The View of Women found in the Deuteronomic Family Laws*. Berlin: de Gruyter, 1993.
Preuss, H. D. *Deuteronomium*. Darmstadt: Wissenschaftliche Buchgesellschaft, 1982.
Propp, W. H. C. *Exodus 19–40*. Anchor Yale Bible Commentaries. New Haven: Yale University Press, 2006.
Rabinowitz, J. J. "Marriage Contracts in Ancient Egypt in Light of Jewish Sources." *Harvard Theological Review* 46 (1953): 91–97.
Ramirez-Kidd, J. E. *Alterity and Identity in Israel: The* גר *in the Old Testament*. Berlin: de Gruyter, 1999.
Reiterer, F. V. "Gelungene Freundschaft als tragende Säule einer Gesellschaft. Exegetische Untersuchung von Sir 25,1–11." In *Freundschaft bei Ben Sira: Beiträge des Symposions zu Ben Sira Salzburg 1995*, edited F. V. Reiterer, 133–69. Berlin: de Gruyter, 1996.
Rhodes, P. J. "Personal Enmity and Political Opposition in Athens." *Greece and Rome* 43 (1996): 21–30.
Richter, W. *Recht und Ethos: Versuch einer Ortung des weisheitlichen Mahnspruches*. Munich: Kösel, 1966.
Riede, P. *Im Netz des Jägers. Studien zur Feindmetaphorik in den Individualpsalmen*. Neukirchen-Vluyn: Neukirchener Verlag, 2000.
Rigsby, K. J. *Asylia: Territorial Inviolability in the Hellenistic World*. Berkeley: University of California Press, 1996.
Riley, A. J. *Divine and Human Hate in the Ancient Near East: A Lexical and Contextual Analysis*. Piscataway, NJ: Gorgias Press, 2017.
Ringgren, H. אלהים. In *Theological Dictionary of the Old Testament*, edited by G. J. Botterweck, H. Ringgren, H.-J. Fabry, vol. 1, 267–84. Grand Rapids: Eerdmans, 1974.
Ringgren, H. ינה. In *Theological Dictionary of the Old Testament*, edited by G. J. Botterweck, H. Ringgren, H.-J. Fabry, vol. 6, 104–106. Grand Rapids: Eerdmans, 1990.
Ringgren, H. ריב. In In *Theological Dictionary of the Old Testament*, edited by G. J. Botterweck, H. Ringgren, H.-J. Fabry, vol. 13, 473–79. Grand Rapids: Eerdmans, 2004.
Ringgren, H. שגב. In In *Theological Dictionary of the Old Testament*, edited by G. J. Botterweck, H. Ringgren, H.-J. Fabry, vol. 14, 34–36. Grand Rapids: Eerdmans, 2004.
Roberts, S. "The Study of Dispute: Anthropological Perspectives." In *Disputes and Settlements: Law and Human Relations in the West*, edited by J. Bossy, 1–24. Cambridge: Cambridge University Press, 1983.
Rofé, A. "The Arrangement of the Laws in Deuteronomy." *Ephemerides theologicae Lovanienses* 64 (1988): 265–87. Reprinted in A. Rofé, *Deuteronomy: Issues and Interpretation: Old Testament Studies*, 55–77. Edinburgh/New York: T&T Clark, 2002.
Rofé, A. "Family and Sex Laws in Deuteronomy and the Book of Covenant." *Henoch* 9 (1987): 131–59.
Rofé, A. "The History of the Cities of Refuge in Biblical Law." In *Studies in Bible*, edited by S. Japhet, 205–39. Jerusalem: Magnes, 1986, also in *Deuteronomy: Issues and Interpretation*, edited by A. Rofé, 121–47. Old Testament Studies. Edinburgh/New York: T&T Clark, 2002.

Römer, T. "La fille de Jephté entre Jérusalem et Athènes – Réflexions à partir d'une triple intertextualité en Juges 11." In *Intertextualités. La Bible en échos*, edited by D. Marguerat and A. Curtis, 30–42. Geneva: Labor et Fides, 2000.

Römer, T. "Why Would the Deuteronomist Tell About the Sacrifice of Jephthah's Daughter?" *Journal for the Study of the Old Testament* 77 (1998): 27–38.

Rosenbaum, S. H. "Israelite Homicide Law and the Term 'Enmity' in Gen 3:15." *Journal of Law and Religion* 2 (1984): 145–51.

Rost, L. *Die Vorstufen von Kirche und Synagoge im Alten Testament: Eine wortgeschichtliche Untersuchung.* Stuttgart: Kohlhammer, 1938.

Rothenbusch, R. *Die kasuistische Rechtssammlung im "Bundesbuch" (Ex 21,2–11.18–22,16).* Münster: Ugarit-Verlag, 2000.

Rouland, N. *Legal Anthropology.* Translated from the French by P. G. Planel. Stanford: University Press, 1994.

Ruffini, J. L. "Disputing over Livestock in Sardinia." In *The Disputing Process: Law in Ten Societies*, edited by L. Nader and H. F. Todd, 209–47. New York: Columbia University Press, 1976.

Ruschenbusch, E. "Φόνος: Zum Recht Drakons und seiner Bedeutung für das Werden des athenischen Staates." *Historia* 9 (1960): 129–54. Reprint in E. Ruschenbusch, *Kleine Schriften zur griechischen Rechtsgeschichte*, 32–53. Wiesbaden: Harrassowitz, 2005.

Ruwe, A. *"Heiligkeitsgesetz" und "Priesterschrift": Literaturgeschichtliche und Rechtssystematische Untersuchungen zu Leviticus 17,1–26,2.* Tübingen: Mohr Siebeck, 1999.

Sanchez, P. *L'amphictionie des Pyles et de Delphes. Recherches sur son rôle historique, des origines au IIe siècle de notre ère.* Stuttgart: Franz Steiner, 2001.

Sanders, J. T. *Ben Sira and Demotic Wisdom.* Chico: Scholars Press, 1983.

Sarna, N. H. *On the Book of Psalms. Exploring the Prayers of Ancient Israel.* New York: Schocken, 1993.

Saur, M. *Der Tyroszyklus des Ezechielbuches.* Berlin: de Gruyter, 2008.

Sauer, G. נקם *nqm* "to avenge." In *Theological Lexicon of the Old Testament*, edited by E. Jenni and C. Westermann, vol. 2, 767–69. Peabody, MA: Hendrickson, 1997.

Sayce, A. H. *Aramaic Papyri Discovered at Assuan*, with the Assistance of A. E. Cowley, and with Appendices by W. Spiegelberg and S. de Ricci. London: A. Moring, 1906.

Scharbert, J. זיד, זוּד. In *Theological Dictionary of the Old Testament*, edited by G. J. Botterweck, H. Ringgren, and H.-J. Fabry, vol. 4, 41–51. Grand Rapids: Eerdmans, 1980.

Scherer, A. "‚Sprich zur Weisheit: Meine Schwester bist du!' (Spr 7,4a): Weisheit in den Sprüchen Salomos." In *Die theologische Bedeutung der alttestamentlichen Weisheitsliteratur*, edited by M. Saur, 1–31. Neukirchen-Vluyn: Neukirchener Verlag, 2012.

Schiffman, L. H. *Sectarian Law in the Dead Sea Scrolls: Courts, Testimony and the Penal Code.* Chico: Scholars Press, 1983.

Schipper, B. *Proverbs 1–15: A Commentary.* Minneapolis: Fortress, 2019.

Schmid, H. R. מקלט. In *Theological Dictionary of the Old Testament*, edited by G. Johannes Botterweck, Helmer Ringgren, and Heinz-Josef Fabry, vol. 8, 552–56. Grand Rapids: Eerdmans, 1997.

Schmidt, L. "Leviten- und Asylstädte in Num XXXV und Jos. XX, XXI 1–42." *Vetus Testamentum* 52 (2002): 103–21.

Schrader, L. "Unzuverlässsige Freundschaft und verlässliche Feindschaft. Überlegungen zu Sir 12,8–12." In *Freundschaft bei Ben Sira*, edited by F. V. Reiterer, 19–59. Berlin: de Gruyter, 1996.

Schreiner, J. עוֹל. In *Theological Dictionary of the Old Testament*, edited by G. Johannes Botterweck, Helmer Ringgren, and Heinz-Josef Fabry, vol. 10, 522–30. Grand Rapids: Eerdmans, 1999.

Schreiner, J. *Die Zehn Gebote im Leben des Gottesvolkes: Dekalogforschung und Verkündigung*. Munich: Kösel, 1966.

Schultz, F. W. *Das Deuteronomium erklärt*. Berlin: Gustav Schlawitz, 1859.

Schulz, H. *Das Todesrecht im Alten Testament*. Beihefte zur Zeitschrift für die alttestamentliche Wissenschaft 114. Berlin: de Gruyter, 1969.

Schwartz, B. "Asylum." In *The Oxford Dictionary of Jewish Religion*, edited by R. J. Z. Werblowsky and G. Wigoder, 77. Oxford: Oxford University Press, 1997.

Schwertner, S., "אֱלִיל *'elîl* nothingness." In *Theological Lexicon of the Old Testament*, edited by E. Jenni and C. Westermann, vol. 1, 126–27. Peabody, MA: Hendrickson, 1997.

Schwienhorst-Schönberger, L. *Das Bundesbuch (Ex 20,22–23,33): Studien zu seiner Entstehung und Theologie*. Beihefte zur Zeitschrift für die alttestamentliche Wissenschaft 188. Berlin: de Gruyter, 1990.

Seaford, R. *Reciprocity and Ritual. Homer and Tragedy in the Developing City State*. Oxford: Oxford University Press, 1994.

Seeligmann, I. L. "Zur Terminologie des Gerichtsverfahrens im Wortschatz des biblischen Hebräisch." In *Hebräische Wortforschung. Festschrift zum 80. Geburtstag von Walter Baumgartner*, edited by B. Hartmann et al., 251–58. Leiden: Brill, 1967. Reprinted in I. L. Seeligmann, *Gesammelte Studien zur Hebräischen Bibel*, edited by E. Blum, 293–317. Tübingen: Mohr Siebeck, 2004.

Seidl, T. שָׁגָה/שָׁגַג. In *Theological Dictionary of the Old Testament*, edited by G. J. Botterweck, H. Ringgren, and H.-J. Fabry, vol. 14, 397–405. Grand Rapids: Eerdmans, 1980.

Seitz, G. *Redaktionsgeschichtliche Studien zum Deuteronomium*. Stuttgart: Kohlhammer, 1971.

Shields, M. A. "Syncretism and Divorce in Malachi 2:10–16." *Zeitschrift für die alttestamentliche Wissenschaft* 111 (1999): 68–86.

Sinn, U. "Greek Sanctuaries as Places of Refuge." In *Greek Sanctuaries: New Approaches*, edited by N. Marinatos and R. Hägg, 88–109. New York: Routledge, 1993.

Ska, J.-L. *Introduction to Reading the Pentateuch*, translated by Sr. Pascale Dominique. Winona Lake, IN: Eisenbrauns, 2006.

Smith, W. R. *Lectures on the Religion of the Semites*. 3rd edition. London: A & C Black, 1927.

Söding, T. "Feindeshass und Bruderliebe: Beobachtungen zur essenischen Ethik." *Revue de Qumrân* 16 (1993/1995): 601–19.

Stackert, J. "Holiness Code and Writings." In *The Oxford Encyclopedia of the Bible and Law*, edited by B. Strawn, vol. 1, 389–96. Oxford: Oxford University Press, 2015.

Stackert, J. *Rewriting the Torah: Literary Revision in Deuteronomy and the Holiness Legislation*. Forschungen zum Alten Testament 52. Tübingen: Mohr Siebeck, 2007.

Stamm, J. J. "Sprachliche Erwägungen zum Gebot ‚Du sollst nicht töten'." *Theologische Zeitschrift* 1 (1945): 81–90.

Stamm, J. J. *The Ten Commandments in Recent Research*. London: SCM Press, 1967.

Steck, O. H. "Der Rachetag in Jesaja 61:2. Ein Kapitel redaktionskritischer Kleinarbeit." In *Studien zu Tritojesaja*, 106–18. Berlin: de Gruyter, 1991.

Steck, O. H. *Studien zu Tritojesaja*. Beihefte zur Zeitschrift für die alttestamentliche Wissenschaft 203. Berlin: de Gruyter, 1991.

Steuernagel, C. *Das Deuteronomium*. Göttingen: Vandenhoeck & Ruprecht, 1923.
Strawn, B. A. "Intention." In *The Oxford Encyclopedia of the Bible and Law*, edited by B. A. Strawn, vol. 1, 433–46. Oxford: Oxford University Press, 2015.
Stroud, R. S. *Drakon's Law on Homicide*. Berkeley: University of California, 1968.
Sulzberger, M. *The Ancient Hebrew Law of Homicide*. Philadelphia: Julius H. Greenstone, 1915.
Szubin, H. Z., and B. Porten. "The Status of a Repudiated Spouse: A New Interpretation of Kraeling 7 (TAD B3.8)." *Israel Law Review* 35 (2001): 46–78.
Taubenschlag, R. *The Law of Greco-Roman Egypt in the Light of the Papyri, 332 B.C.–640 A.D.* 2nd ed. Warsaw: Panstowe Wydawnictwo Nankowe, 1955.
Thompson, T. W. "Punishment and Restitution." In *The Oxford Encyclopedia of the Bible and Law*, edited by B. Strawn, vol. 2, 183–93. Oxford: Oxford University Press, 2015.
Thür, G. "Dikasterion." In *Der Neue Pauly. Enzyklopädie der Antike*, edited by H. Cancik and H. Schneider, vol. 3, 567–69. Stuttgart: Metzler, 1997.
Thür, G. "Dikazein." In *Der Neue Pauly. Enzyklopädie der Antike*, edited by H. Cancik and H. Schneider, vol. 3, 570. Stuttgart: Metzler, 1997.
Tigay, J. H. "Deuteronomy." In *The Traditional Hebrew Text with the New JPS Translation*. Philadelphia: Jewish Publication Society, 1996.
Todd, S. C. "Law and Oratory in Athens." In *The Cambridge Companion to Ancient Greek Law*, edited by M. Gagarin and D. Cohen, 97–111. Cambridge: University Press, 2005.
Todd, S. C. *Lysias*. Translated by S. C. Todd. Austin: University of Texas Press, 2000.
Todd, S. C. *The Shape of Athenian Law*. Oxford: Clarendon, 1993.
Toorn, K. van der. "Ordeal Procedures in the Psalms and the Passover Meal." *Vetus Testamentum* 38 (1988): 427–45.
Treston, H. J. *Poine: A Study in Ancient Greek Blood-Vengeance*. London: Longmans, Green & Co., 1923.
Triandis, H. C., et al. "An Etic–Emic Analysis of Individualism and Collectivism." *Journal of Cross-Cultural Psychology* 24 (1993): 366–83.
Turner, B. *Asyl und Konflikt von der Antike bis heute: Rechtsethnologische Untersuchungen*. Berlin: Dietrich Reimer Verlag, 2004.
Van Seters, J. *A Law Book for the Diaspora: Revision in the Study of the Covenant Code*. Oxford: Oxford University Press, 2003.
Van Seters, J. "Cultic Laws and the Holiness Code." In *Studies in the Book of Exodus*. Bibliotheca Ephemeridum Theologicarum Lovaniensium 126, edited by M. Vervenne, 319–45. Leuven: Peeters, 1996.
Veijola, T. *Das 5. Buch Mose: Deuteronomium Kapitel 1,1–16,17*. Göttingen: Vandenhoeck & Ruprecht, 2004.
Verdier, R., G. Courtois, and J.-P. Poly. *La Vengeance. Études d'ethnologie, d'histoire et de philosophie*. 4 vols. Paris: Cujas, 1980–84.
Vittmann, G. *Der demotische Papyus Rylands 9: Teil 1, Text und Übersetzung*. Wiesbaden: Harrassowitz, 1998.
Wagner, A. *Emotionen, Gefühle und Sprache im Alten Testament: Vier Studien*. 2nd ed. Kleine Untersuchungen zur Sprache des Alten Testaments und seiner Umwelt 7. Kamen: Hartmut Spenner, 2011.
Wallace, R. W. "Private Lives and Public Enemies: Freedom of Thought in Classical Athens." In *Athenian Identity and Civic Ideology*, edited by A. L. Boegehold and A. C. Scafuro, 127–55. Baltimore: The Johns Hopkins University Press, 1994.
Walter, U. *An der Polis teilhaben. Bürgerstaat und Zugehörigkeit im archaischen Griechenland*. Stuttgart: Franz Steiner, 1993.

Weber, M. *Gesammelte Aufsätze zur Religionssoziologie, III, Das antike Judentum.* Tübingen: Mohr Siebeck, 1923.
Weinberg, J. P. "Das *beit 'ābōt* im 6.–4. Jh. v.u.Z." *Vetus Testamentum* 23 (1973): 400–414.
Weinfeld, M. *Social Justice in Ancient Israel and in the Ancient Near East.* Minneapolis: Fortress Press, 1995.
Weinfeld, M. *The Organizational Pattern and the Penal Code of the Qumran Sect: A Comparison with Guilds and Religious Associations of the Hellenistic-Roman Period.* Göttingen: Vandenhoeck & Ruprecht, 1986.
Wellhausen, J. *Die Composition des Hexateuch.* Berlin: G. Reimer, 1899.
Wellhausen, J. *Prolegomena zur Geschichte Israels.* Berlin: G. Reimer, 1883.
Wells, B. "Competing or Complementary? Judges and Elders in Biblical and Neo-Babylonian Law." *Zeitschrift für altorientalische und biblische Rechtgeschichte* 16 (2010): 77–104.
Wells, B. "The Cultic Versus the Forensic: Judahite and Mesopotamian Judicial Procedures in the First Millennium B.C.E." *JAOS* 128 (2008): 205–32.
Wells, B. "The Hated Wife in Deuteronomic Law." *Vetus Testamentum* 60 (2010): 131–46.
Wells, B. *The Law of Testimony in the Pentateuchal Codes.* Wiesbaden: Harrassowitz, 2004.
Wells, B. "Sex, Lies and Virginal Rape: The Slandered Bride and False Accusations in Deuteronomy." *Journal of Biblical Literature* 124 (2005): 41–72.
Wenham, J. G. "The Restoration of Marriage Reconsidered." *Journal of Jewish Studies* 30 (1979): 37–40.
Wesel, U. *Frühformen des Rechts in vorstaatlichen Gesellschaften. Umrisse einer Frühgeschichte des Rechts bei Sammlern und Jägern und akephalen Ackerbauern und Hirten.* Frankfurt: Suhrkamp, 1985.
Westbrook, R. "Cuneiform Law Codes and the Origins of Legislation." *Zeitschrift für Assyriologie* 79 (1989): 201–22.
Westbrook, R. *A History of Ancient Near Eastern Law.* 2 vols. Leiden: Brill, 2003.
Westbrook, R. "The Prohibition of the Restoration of Marriage in Deuteronomy 24:1–4." In *Studies in Bible*, edited by S. Japhet, 387–405. Jerusalem: Magnes, 1986.
Westbrook, R. "Reflections on the Law of Homicide in the Ancient World." In *Ex Oriente Lex: Near Eastern Influences on Ancient Greek and Roman Law*, edited by R. Westbrook, D. Lyons, K. Raaflaub, 194–219. Baltimore: The Johns Hopkins University Press, 2015. Originally *Maarav* 13 (2006): 143–47, 152–73.
Westbrook, R. *Studies in Biblical and Cuneiform Law.* Paris: Gabalda, 1988.
Westbrook, R., and B. Wells. *Everyday Law in Biblical Israel: An Introduction.* Louisville: Westminster John Knox, 2009.
Westbrook, R., and C. Wilcke, "The Liability of an Innocent Purchaser of Stolen Goods in Early Mesopotamian Law." *Archiv für Orientforschung* 25 (1974–77): 111–21.
Wevers, J. W. *Notes on the Greek Text of Leviticus.* Atlanta: Scholars Press, 1997.
Whitehead, D. *The Demes of Attica 508/7-Ca. 250 B.C.: A Political and Social Study.* Princeton: Princeton University Press, 1986.
Whitekettle, R. "Life's Labors Lost: Priestly Death and Returning Home from a City of Refuge in Ancient Israel." *Harvard Theological Review* 111 (2018): 333–56.
Whybray, R. *The Composition of Proverbs.* Sheffield: Sheffield Academic Press, 1994.
Whybray, R. *The Concept of Wisdom in Proverbs 1–9.* London: SCM Press, 1965.
Whybray, R. *Proverbs.* The New Century Bible Commentary. Grand Rapids: Eerdmans, 1994.

Whybray, R. "Thoughts on the Composition of Prov 10–29." *In Priests, Prophets and Scribes: Essays on the formation and Heritage of Second Temple Judaism, Festschrift for Joseph Blenkinsopp*, edited by E. Ulrich et al., 102–14. Sheffield: Sheffield Academic Press, 1992.

Wiener, H. M. "The Arrangement of Deuteronomy 12–26." *Journal of the Palestine Oriental Society* 6 (1926): 185–95.

Willis, T. *The Elders of the City: A Study of the Elders-Laws in Deuteronomy*. Atlanta, GA: Scholars Press, 2001.

Wilson, S. *Feuding, Conflict and Banditry in Nineteenth Century Corsica*. Cambridge: Cambridge University Press, 1988.

Wiseman, D. J. "Supplementary Copies of Alalakh Tablets." *JCS* 8 (1954): 1–30.

Wright, D. P. *Inventing God's Law: How the Covenant Code of the Bible Used and Revised the Laws of Hammurabi*. Oxford: Oxford University Press, 2009.

Yaron, R. R. "Aramaic Marriage Contracts from Elephantine." *Journal of Semitic Studies* 3 (1958): 1–39.

Yaron, R. R. "The Restoration of Marriage." *Journal of Jewish Studies* 17 (1966): 1–11.

Zenger, E. *A God of Vengeance? Understanding the Psalms of Divine Wrath*. Translated by L. M. Maloney. Louisville: Westminster John Knox, 1996.

Zobel, H. J. עמית. In *Theological Dictionary of the Old Testament*, edited by G. J. Botterweck, H. Ringgren, and H.-J. Fabry, vol. 11, 192–96. Grand Rapids: Eerdmans, 2001.

Index of References

Hebrew Bible/Old Testament

Genesis
3:5	78
3:15	32, 169
4:1-16	230
4:1	230
4:6-7	230
4:9-14	231
4:14	231
4:15	28, 230, 231
4:17-24	230
4:23-24	231
4:24	230, 231
4:25-26	230
6:5	76, 77
8:21	76
9:6	189, 234
10:9	171
11:3	39
11:7	39
13:7-8	52
15:10	40
18:15	216
22:1	34
23:4	178, 179
24:45	77
25:27	171
25:28	171, 238
26:20-21	52
26:26	138
27	171
27:3	171
27:5	171
27:7	171
27:19	171
27:25	171
27:30	171
27:31	171
27:33	171
29:18	238
29:30	238
29:31	120, 122, 123
29:33	120, 122, 123
31:5	100
31:42	226
31:36	52
31:44-45	52
34:3	238
37:3-4	238
37:16	173

Exodus
2:12	28
4:19	229
5:7-8	100
5:14	100
11:2	42
12:19	178
12:43-49	176
12:45	178, 179
12:48	178, 179
12:49	176
14:7	176
17:7	52
18:11	42
19:19	34
20:7	205, 216
20:10	175
20:12	206
20:15	216
20:16	39, 67, 80, 106, 137
20:17-18	206
20:17	39, 74, 77–80, 137, 252
20:20-21	34
20:23	8
20:24–22:26	9
20:24-26	8, 9, 35
20:24	36
21	42, 124, 167
21:1–22:6	54
21:1-11	125
21:2–22:6	9
21:2-12	131, 139, 159, 197, 251
21:2-11	8
21:6	34
21:12–22:19	9
21:12-36	45
21:12-35	37
21:12-34	36
21:12-32	34
21:12-27	37
21:12-25	31
21:12-17	9, 35, 37, 47, 90
21:12-15	26
21:12-14	21, 25, 27, 30, 31, 34–37, 52, 73, 75, 81, 86, 87, 89, 92, 96, 97, 100
21:12-13	38, 45

Index of References

275

21:12	8, 25, 26, 28, 29, 31–38, 49, 54, 64, 73, 75		74, 76, 80, 81, 85, 86, 101, 142, 196, 199, 252	21:35	36, 38, 39, 41, 54, 57, 106, 137
				21:36	38, 39, 47, 100
21:12	167, 168, 234	21:18-17	37	21:37–22:3	55, 216
		21:18	36, 38, 39, 41, 45, 47–51, 54, 101, 133, 137	21:37–22:2	22
21:13-17	8			21:37–22:1	134
21:13-14	25, 26, 28, 31, 35, 36, 38, 47, 63, 64, 72, 73, 76, 82–85, 96–98, 100, 105, 146, 252			21:37	55–57, 59, 60
				22:1-4	108
		21:19	47–49, 53	22:1-2	8, 26, 31, 55, 57–60, 63, 69, 72, 81, 83, 85, 142, 199, 252
		21:20-27	8		
		21:20-21	37, 38, 46, 229, 230, 234		
21:13	29–34, 36, 38, 44, 54, 99–101, 170, 172	21:20	28, 37, 38, 45, 48, 230		
				22:1	28, 56, 58, 60, 72
		21:22-25	38	22:2-3	59, 60
21:14	29–31, 34–36, 38–40, 42, 44–48, 54, 57, 60, 61, 63, 76, 78, 82, 99, 101, 124, 125, 137, 199, 217, 228, 251, 252	21:22-24	37, 39, 45	22:2	55–57, 59
		21:22-23	37, 101	22:3	55
		21:22	12, 38, 45, 50, 92	22:4-5	59, 60
				22:6-14	46, 60, 63, 81
		21:23-25	54	22:6-13	126
		21:23-24	92	22:6-8	106
		21:24-25	37	22:6-7	57, 60
		21:26-27	37, 38, 46, 230	22:6	39, 54, 60-62, 106, 137
		21:26	38, 45, 48		
		21:28-32	35, 37, 38, 74, 75	22:7-8	12, 34
21:15-32	37	21:28	38	22:7	60–62, 137
21:15-17	37	21:29	100		
21:15	35, 37, 38, 45, 47	21:30	8, 38	22:8	61, 62, 106, 108, 137
		21:31-36	8		
21:16	37, 38, 216	21:31	38		
		21:32	46	22:9-10	8
21:17	37, 38, 47	21:33–22:24	9	22:9	60, 137
21:18–22:13	8	21:33–22:14	46, 59, 90	22:10-15	72
21:18-35	37	21:33-36	37, 59	22:10	39, 60, 137
21:18-32	37, 46–48, 90	21:33-34	38, 41		
		21:33	38	22:11-12	60, 61
21:18-27	35, 37	21:34–22:14	22	22:11	61
21:18-19	26, 36-38, 45, 46, 48–54, 72,	21:34	72	22:12	61
		21:35-36	38	22:13	39, 60, 61, 137

Exodus (cont.)		23:5	67, 109, 237	5:2-4	109, 160
22:14	60, 61			5:2-3	160
22:15-16	8, 13, 90	23:6-8	9, 22, 52, 63–69, 91, 92, 237	5:2	109, 160
22:15	139			5:3	109, 160
22:17-19	90			5:4-5	160, 162
22:18-21	9	23:6	64–66, 108, 221, 222	5:4	109, 160
22:19	8			5:14-16	160
22:20-26	65			5:15	99, 160, 162
22:20-22	209	23:7-9	65		
22:20	179	23:7-8	65, 66	5:17-19	160
22:22-25	74, 80	23:7	64–67, 222	5:18	160, 162
22:24	132, 133			5:20-26	106, 216
22:25	39, 108, 137	23:8	52, 65, 67	5:20	160, 216
		23:9	65, 179	5:21-26	160, 216
22:28–23:12	9, 68	23:10-12	9	5:21-23	217
22:28-29	9	23:12	179	5:21-22 MT	216
23	68, 109, 237	23:13	8	5:21	216–18
		24:11	34	5:23	217, 218
23:1-8	9, 27, 52, 63–65, 68, 91, 206	24:13	34	6:2-3 ET	216
		25:7	150	8:3	181
		25:8	151	8:4	181
23:1-3	9, 22, 52, 63–69, 91, 92, 106, 237	25:21-22	72	8:5	181
		25:32	170	9:5	181
		27:21	239	10:6	181
		29:45-46	150, 151	10:17	181
23:1-2	44, 65–67	33:7	173	15–16	214
23:1	64–67, 90, 92, 109, 222	34:24	78	15	162
		37:18	170	15:15	214
				15:16	214
23:2-3	220–23	*Leviticus*		15:17-18	214
23:2	52, 64, 65, 67, 222, 224	1–16	211	15:17	214
		4	81, 162	15:18	214
		4:1–5:13	160	15:31	150, 151
23:3	52, 65, 66, 108, 221, 222	4:2	99, 160	16:5	181
		4:13-21	162	17–26	202, 210
		4:13	99, 109, 160, 162, 181	17	208, 211
23:4-6	65			17:1-7	96
23:4-5	9, 22, 31, 63–72, 81-83, 91, 106–10, 129, 142, 206, 232, 237, 252	4:15	181	17:3	176
		4:22-35	162	17:7	208
		4:22-23	160	17:8-9	175, 209
		4:22	99, 160	17:8	176
		4:27-28	160	17:10-12	209
		4:27	99, 160	17:10	176
23:4	67, 68, 109	5	81, 160, 162	17:12	153, 176
				17:13-14	209
		5:1-6	162	17:13	171, 176, 239
23:5-8	63	5:1	160	17:14	239

Index of References

17:15-16	209	19:11-18	7, 22, 41, 146, 147, 197–99, 201–205, 207, 209–16, 219, 221, 228, 237, 239–42, 244, 245, 247–50, 253		223–25, 228, 244, 245
17:15	178			19:17-18	22, 41, 108, 197, 202, 203, 206, 209, 213, 215, 219, 222, 225, 227, 229, 236–39, 242, 244, 249
18–20	206, 211				
18:1–20:27	247				
18:6-23	207				
18:6-17	176				
18:18-23	176				
18:19	207				
18:20	207, 228, 233				
18:21	208				
18:23	207				
18:25-29	150	19:11-17	202		
18:26	176, 178	19:11-14	213	19:17	41, 77, 209, 215, 219, 223, 225–29, 236–39, 253
18	54, 82, 162, 205, 210, 223, 245	19:11-12	213–16, 225, 253		
		19:11	41, 213, 214, 216, 217, 228, 244		
19	21, 22, 143, 202–206, 208, 210–12, 217, 220–22, 227, 228, 235–37, 239, 241, 244, 245, 247, 248			19:18-19	135
		19:12	205, 210, 213–16, 244	19:18	19, 39, 41, 137
				19:18	209, 210, 213, 215, 219, 225–29, 232, 234–39, 241, 244, 253
		19:13-14	213–15, 217–20, 225		
		19:13	39, 41, 137, 209, 214, 217, 218, 228, 244, 253		
19:1-18	204			19:19-22	204
19:1	211			19:19	203–205, 207, 208, 212, 237
19:2	181, 204, 205, 210, 211	19:14	206, 210, 213, 214, 217, 218, 253		
				19:20-36	212
19:3-18	212			19:20-26	204
19:3-4	203–205, 209, 213, 241	19:15-18	213, 221, 222	19:20-22	204, 212
		19:15-16	213, 215, 219–23, 253	19:23-25	204, 207, 212
19:3	206, 211, 213, 245			19:25	212
19:4	246	19:15	41, 65, 108, 213, 215, 219–25, 228	19:26-32	203, 204, 207, 208, 210, 212, 215, 247
19:5-10	204				
19:5-8	204, 212				
19:9-10	204, 207, 212	19:16	39, 41, 137, 209, 210, 213, 219, 221,	19:26-28	204, 207, 208
19:10	176, 179, 212			19:26	208, 247
				19:27	208
				19:28	208

Leviticus (cont.)

19:29	178	22:18	176	25:47	176, 179
19:30-37	204	22:23	185	25:55	175, 207
19:30	206, 245	22:32	239	26:1	246
19:31	208, 212	22:33	207	26:2	206
19:32	206, 213, 219	23:10	207	26:11	150, 151
		23:22	176, 179, 207	26:25	207, 232, 234
19:33-36	205, 209, 212, 213, 248	23:29	207		
		23:42	175, 178	*Numbers*	
		23:43	176	1–2	148
19:33-34	204, 205, 209, 223, 239	24:10-23	157, 182	1:2-3	181
		24:10-16	181, 183	5:3	150, 151
		24:10-13	182	9:14	176, 178, 179
19:33	208, 209, 212, 241	24:13	182		
		24:14	115, 181	10:11-12	148
19:34	41, 178, 209, 213, 248	24:16	178, 181	15:13	178
		24:17	28, 234	15:24	99
		24:18	207	15:27	99
19:35-36	204, 205, 223	24:20	175	15:28	99
		24:21	28, 207	15:29	99, 178
19:35	213, 220, 248	24:22	175, 178, 205	15:30	160, 162
				15:32-36	157, 181–83
19:36	204, 213	24:23	182		
19:37	204, 205	25	189, 208	15:33	182
20	210, 245	25:6	176, 179	15:35-36	115
20:1-6	208	25:14	209, 219, 228, 239	15:35	182
20:2-5	209			15:36	182
20:2	176	25:15	228	16:2	140
20:7	211	25:17	206, 209, 219	16:3	150, 151
20:8	211			16:5	184
20:10	39, 137, 228, 233	25:23	207	16:6	184
		25:25	239	16:11	184
20:15-16	207	25:26	135	17:16-26	182
20:22-26	207	25:31-34	207	20:1-13	148
20:26	211	25:35	179, 239	25–36	147
20:27	208	25:36	206, 219	25:1-5	149
21–22	208	25:39-46	176	25:6–36:13	148
21:1–22:16	211	25:39	176, 239	25:14-15	28
21:1–22:9	247	25:40-41	189	25:18	28
21:7	115, 122	25:40	179	25:32	185
21:10	151	25:41	189	26–36	147, 148, 183
21:14	115, 122	25:42	207		
22:10	179	25:43	206, 219	27	150, 172
22:13	115, 122	25:45	179	27:2	181, 183
22:14	160	25:46	135	27:12-27	181
22:17-30	211	25:47-55	176	27:12-23	183
22:18-19	209	25:47-54	175	27:12-13	148

27:20	183	35:11	28, 99,	35:20-23	173
30:9	115		148, 152,	35:20-21	152, 154,
31:2	234, 235		153, 156–		156, 157,
31:3	235		59, 161,		167–69,
32	149		162, 185,		194
32:2	181, 183		195	35:20	32, 156,
32:28-32	148	35:12	14, 148,		158, 167–
33:50-56	183		149, 152,		70, 172
33:51	150		153, 157,	35:21-22	32
34:16-19	148		158, 162,	35:21	28,
34:29	150		180–82,		154, 158,
35–36	183		185, 186,		167–69
35	6, 14, 22,		229, 253	35:22-33	156
	29, 32,	35:13	148, 153,	35:22-30	159
	36, 143,		185	35:22-23	152, 154,
	145–51,	35:14	153, 156,		155, 157,
	155–59,		157, 185		163, 167
	161–67,	35:15-29	152	35:22	32, 154,
	169, 170,	35:15-25	154, 155,		158, 159,
	172–74,		197		167–70,
	179–81,	35:15-23	159		172, 173,
	184–86,	35:15-21	157, 158		197
	189, 190,	35:13-15	152, 153	35:23	154, 158,
	193–96,	35:15-18	28		162, 170,
	198–201,	35:15	99, 148,		173, 197
	213, 249,		151–53,	35:24-29	152
	252		156, 158,	35:24-28	167
35:1–36:13	148		159, 161,	35:24-25	149, 154–
35:6	185		162, 167,		56, 162,
35:9-34	27, 96,		168, 174,		210
	100, 146–		178, 179,	35:24	28, 157,
	51, 157,		185, 186,		158, 174,
	162, 184		195		180
35:9-25	150	35:16-29	152, 186	35:25-34	195
35:9-15	149, 151–	35:16-24	149, 152,	35:25-32	149
	53, 155,		153, 155,	35:25-29	149, 152,
	184		187		153, 155,
35:9-14	152, 153	35:16-21	153, 154		159, 174,
35:9-12	158	35:16-19	152		181, 187,
35:9-11	152	35:16-18	154–57,		189, 190,
35:9-10	152		163, 167,		253
35:9	151–53,		168	35:25-28	188
	158	35:16	167	35:25	151, 157,
35:10-15	152	35:17-18	51		158, 180,
35:10	152, 153,	35:17	158		185, 187–
	158	35:19	180, 229		89
35:11-12	174, 210	35:20-24	152	35:26-34	157

Numbers (cont.)		4:42-43	27	12:20	96		
35:26-29	150	4:42	74, 90,	12:29	95, 151		
35:26-27	158		125	13:2-12	10, 89		
35:26	185	4:44-49	194	13:6	21		
35:27	140, 149,	4:44	194	13:7	39, 126,		
	160, 180,	4:45	194		137, 239		
	185, 188	5–11	194	13:9	97		
35:28	181, 185,	5:6	21	13:11	21		
	187–89	5:7	127	14:21	175		
35:29	151, 188	5:11	205, 216	14:22–15:23	89		
35:30-34	149, 150,	5:14	175	14:24	98		
	152, 153,	5:15	21	14:28–15:18	132		
	155	5:16	206	14:28-29	132		
35:30-33	152	5:17	139	14:29	175		
35:30	28, 140,	5:18	125	15–25	127		
	158, 183	5:19	216	15	131		
35:31	16	5:20-21	135	15:1-11	129–32		
35:32	158, 185,	5:20	39, 67,	15:1-3	131, 132		
	188		106, 125,	15:1-2	128, 130		
35:33	188, 189		137	15:1	131, 132		
35:34	150–52	5:21	39, 74,	15:2-3	131		
35:35	151		78–80,	15:2	39, 128,		
36	150, 172		125, 137,		130, 137		
36:1	182		206, 252	15:3	128, 131,		
		6:1	194		132		
Deuteronomy		6:12	21	15:4-6	131, 132		
1–3	148	6:19	168	15:4-5	131		
1:16	127, 175	6:21	21	15:4	132		
1:17	221, 222	7:1	95	15:6	131, 132		
1:27	168	7:8	21	15:7-10	131, 132		
1:28	127, 128	7:25	78, 79	15:7-8	128		
1:43	42	8:2-16	21	15:7	127, 131,		
2:4	127	8:14	21		132, 239		
2:8	127	9:7-12	21	15:9	128, 132		
3:12-20	195	9:28	168	15:11	128, 131,		
3:18	127	10:9	127		132		
3:20	127	10:18	238	15:12-18	130, 131		
4	145, 193–	10:19	175	15:12	128, 131,		
	95	11:2-4	21		132		
4:3-4	21	11:5-6	21	15:13-15	131		
4:32-40	21	12–27	125	15:13	131		
4:35	34	12–26	39, 88, 89	15:15	21		
4:39	34	12	95	15:16-18	131		
4:41-43	96, 194,	12:1–18:22	130	16–25	91		
	200	12:1	194	16	222		
4:41-42	194	12:13-27	10, 89	16:1-17	89		
4:41	195	12:13-19	96	16:1	21		

16:11	175		47, 150,		124, 125,
16:12	21		155, 158,		132, 143,
16:14	175, 176		159, 163,		145, 168–
16:18–21:23	11		173, 188,		70, 194,
16:18–18:22	88		194–97,		195, 252
16:18–18:5	89, 90, 92		199, 200,	19:5-6	103
16:18–17:13	11, 91, 97		234, 252	19:5	14, 51, 90,
16:18-20	220, 222,	19:1–25:19	130		94, 96–99,
	223	19:1–21:9	88		102, 104,
16:18-19	108	19:1-21	91, 92		105, 125,
16:18	95, 141,	19:1-13	89, 91,		156, 157,
	182, 222		141, 151,		195, 252
16:19	222		152, 156,	19:6	28, 92–94,
17:5	115		195, 196		96–98,
17:8-13	207	19:1-12	22, 27, 36,		103–105,
17:8-12	8		42, 86, 93,		129, 169,
17:8	11, 43, 52,		94, 96,		180, 195,
	129		100, 105,		252
17:9	11		124, 125,	19:7	90, 95, 97
17:10	11, 43		139, 140,	19:8-10	96
17:12-13	43		150, 157–	19:8-9	96
17:12	11, 43		59, 170,	19:8	91, 96
17:13	42, 43		180–82,	19:9-10	252
17:14-20	131, 207		200	19:9	96, 97
17:15	127	19:1-7	152	19:10	91, 97
17:17	95	19:1-3	90	19:11-13	97
17:20	127	19:1	95, 151,	19:11-12	90, 94,
18:1	128		156		96–98,
18:2	127	19:2-21	92		104, 105,
18:15-22	131	19:2-13	92		143, 252
18:15	95, 127	19:2-12	96	19:11	28, 87, 89,
18:16	11	19:2	93–98,		90, 93, 97,
18:18	127		100, 105,		99–102,
18:20	42		252		104, 105,
18:22	43	19:3-7	194		124, 125,
19–25	87–89,	19:3-6	97		129, 132,
	128	19:3	90, 91,		137, 140,
19–21	89, 93,		94–98,		145, 168,
	105		100, 105,		169, 195,
19	14, 29, 84,		139, 195,		252
	87, 89–93,		252	19:12	71, 98, 99,
	95–99,	19:4-7	129		105, 180,
	101, 105,	19:4-6	96, 97		182, 252
	119, 124,	19:4-5	137	19:13	90, 97,
	125, 129,	19:4	28, 87, 89,		129
	132, 139,		93, 94,	19:14	91, 125,
	140, 142–		96–105,		135, 137

Deuteronomy (cont.)		22	108–10, 119, 127, 237	22:19-20	112
19:15-21	67, 90–92, 103, 129, 132			22:19	115, 122
				22:20-21	111, 115
		22:1–24:5	11	22:21	113, 115, 143
19:15-17	129	22:1-12	91, 108, 237		
19:15	90, 92, 106, 158			22:22	233
		22:1-4	22, 87, 106–109, 111, 128, 129, 132, 140, 206, 232, 237	22:23-27	80, 125
19:16-21	92, 106			22:24	93, 115, 125, 137
19:16	67, 90, 92				
19:17	52			22:26	125, 137
19:18-19	129			22:29	93, 115, 122
19:18	90, 128, 132				
		22:1	107, 109, 110, 129, 194, 239	23:9-14	207
19:21	91, 92, 97			23:16-26	91
20:1	21			23:16	209
20:8	127	22:2-3	107	23:20-21	132, 133
20:10-20	207	22:2	107, 108	23:20	128, 135
21	87, 91–93, 107, 123	22:3	107–110, 127, 130, 133	23:21	128
				23:22-24	135
21:1-21	92			23:25-26	39, 135
21:1-9	92, 103, 207, 141	22:4	107, 109, 110, 129	23:25	125, 137
				23:26	125, 137
21:1	28, 92, 93	22:5-12	107, 108	24	88, 118
21:5	52	22:5	108, 237	24:1-4	88, 110, 111, 115, 116, 118, 123, 140, 141
21:7	93	22:6-7	108		
21:8	21, 93	22:7	108		
21:10–23:1	88	22:8	75, 108		
21:10-14	93, 207	22:9-11	108, 237		
21:10	93	22:12	108	24:1-3	114
21:12-14	132	22:13-29	108	24:1-2	116
21:14	93, 117	22:13-22	117	24:1	115, 117, 122
21:15-21	92	22:13-21	22, 87, 110–12, 114, 115, 123, 140, 141		
21:15-17	22, 87, 92, 93, 122, 123, 140, 142			24:3	110, 115–18, 122
				24:4	116, 118, 122
21:15	120, 142	22:13-17	111	24:5	48
21:17	142	22:13-14	112, 113	24:6–25:12	11
21:18-21	92, 93, 115, 141	22:13	110, 113, 114	24:6–25:4	91
				24:6-7	217
21:18	112	22:14	111, 113, 114	24:7	127, 216
21:19	112			24:10-22	217
21:20	112	22:16-17	115	24:10-17	88
21:21	92	22:16	110	24:10	125, 137
21:22-23	92, 93	22:17	111, 114	24:14-15	217, 218
		22:18-19	111, 112, 115	24:14	128, 135, 175, 218

24:15	127, 218	28:43-44	175	20:3	28, 99, 152, 185, 186, 194, 196
24:17	175, 205	28:43	175		
24:18	21	28:54	127		
24:19	175	29:4-5	21		
24:20-21	128	29:12-31	156	20:4-6	195
24:20	175	31:12	175	20:4-5	195
24:21	175	32:35	231, 233	20:5	14, 28, 99, 194–96
24:22	21	32:41	231, 233		
25	115, 128	32:43	231	20:6	152, 183, 184, 195
25:1-4	217	32:48-52	148		
25:1-3	133, 222	32:50	127	20:7-9	195
25:1	52, 133, 134, 221, 223	33:9	127	20:7-8	152
		33:16	127	20:7	95, 195
		33:24	127	20:8	195
25:2-3	133, 134	33:29	216	20:9	28, 99, 174, 183, 195
25:3	128, 134	34	148		
25:5-10	92, 115, 141	34:7-9	148		
				21	96
25:5-7	112	*Joshua*		21:13	185
25:5	127	7:11	216	21:21	185
25:6	127	7:21	78	21:27	185
25:7	112, 127	8:2	104, 140, 170	21:32	185
25:9-10	112			21:38	185
25:9	127	8:7	104	21:43-45	96
25:10	207	8:12	104, 140, 170	22:1	194
25:11-12	80, 92			22:23	229
25:12	97	8:14	104, 140, 170	23:4	95
25:13-16	220			24:27	216
25:13-15	207, 220	8:18-19	170		
25:15-16	220	8:19	104, 140	*Judges*	
25:16	220	8:21	104, 140, 170	4:22	173
26:2-13	89			7:3	128
26:8	21	8:30	194	9:24-25	107
26:13	175	8:33	178	9:25	170
27:9	162	9:4	30	9:53	168
27:16	134	9:27	29	14:4	173
27:17	125, 135, 137	10:11	168	14:11	138
		20	14, 27, 29, 96, 145, 148, 193–95, 200	14:15	139
27:19	175, 205			14:20	138
27:24	137			15:2	138
27:42	125			15:6	138
28:12-13	132			15:7	235
28:12	132	20:1-9	149, 195	16:4	238
28:15-46	175	20:1-3	184, 195	16:5	139
28:15	11, 89	20:1-2	152	16:9	104, 140
28:20-44	11, 89	20:2	185	16:12	104, 140, 170
28:29	217				

Judges (cont.)

16:28	235	24:12	32, 170, 171, 173, 233, 252	15:4	52
18:1	173			16:11	169, 173
20:29	104, 170	24:13	170, 235	17:3	173
20:33	104, 140	24:15	173	20:10	28
20:36-38	104	24:20	169	20:12	168
20:36	140	24:21-22	170	20:19	169, 173
20:37	140	25:22	233	21	16
20:38	140, 170	25:26-31	233	21:1-6	16
21:20	140	25:26	77	22:48	231
		25:29	77		

1 Samuel

1 Kings

1:13	77	25:39	229	1:50-51	97
4:7	100	26	170	2:28-35	97
10:11	40, 100	26:2	77	4:5	139
12:18	219	26:8	233	7:7	221
14:24-46	161	26:17-25	19	8:16	29
14:24	161, 235	26:20	77	8:17-18	76
14:32-35	208	26:21	161	8:21	29
15:5	140	27:1	77	8:29	29
16:7	76, 77	27:4	77	8:39	77
18:11	28	30:5	42	8:44	29
18:23	134			8:48	29
18:25	235	*2 Samuel*		9:3	29
19:2	77, 169, 173	1:15	28	9:7	29
		2:12-32	109	9:13	29
		3:8	138	9:32	29
19:10	28, 77	3:17	100	9:36	29
19:29	169	3:22-28	109	11:1	238
20:1	77, 169, 173	3:25	139	11:22	173
		3:27	28	13:18	216
20:33	28	4:2	229	14:21	29
21:6	100	4:7	28	15:22	48
22:8	104	4:8	77	17:1	179
22:13	104	6:9	219	20:7	173
22:23	77	7:10	29	21	93, 224
23:10	169, 173	9:7	208	21:13	115
23:14	77, 171	11:21	168	21:19	140
23:19	171	12:9	28	21:40	170
23:25	77	12:11	126		
24	170, 173	13:15	168	*2 Kings*	
24:1	171	13:23-29	227	2:3	40
24:2	77	13:28	28	2:5-6	107
24:8-21	19	13:37-38	185	4:13	247
24:9	77	14:6-7	28	4:27	168
24:10	169, 173	14:21	185	5:7	34
		15:1-6	8	6:26-30	8
		15:2	52	9:7	235

14:5-6	28	28:12	34	32:16	34
19:37	28	28:21	34	32:31	77
21:4	29	29:7	34	33:7	34
21:7	29	29:19	76, 179	33:13	34
23:27	29			35:8	34
25:21	28	*2 Chronicles*		36:16	34
		1:3-4	34	36:18-19	34
1 Chronicles		2:4	34		
6:33-34	34	3:3	34	*Ezra*	
6:42	185, 186	4:11	34	1:3-5	34
6:52	185, 186	4:19	34	2:68	34
9:11	34	5:1	34	3:2	34
9:13	34	5:14	34	3:8-9	34
9:26-27	34	6:30	77	6:22	34
11:7	171	7:5	34	7:26	185
12:9	171	8:14	34	8:31	104, 140
12:17	171	9:23	34	8:36	34
13:5-8	34	10:15	34	10:1	34
13:12	34, 219	11:2	34	10:6	34
13:14	34	13:12	34	10:9	34
14:11	34	13:15	34	20:9	215
14:14-16	34	15:18	34	20:20	215
15:1-2	34	18:5	34	20:22	215
15:15	34	19:3	34	22:16	215
15:24	34	19:8-11	8	22:26	215
15:26	34	19:10	8		
15:29	77	22:12	34	*Nehemiah*	
16:1	34	23:3	34	2:4	173
16:6	34	23:9	34	3:31-32	224
16:26	246	24:7	34	4:9	34
16:42	34	24:9	34	5:1-13	132
17:2	34	24:13	34	5:1-8	176
17:21	34	24:16	34	5:7	52
17:26	34	24:20	34	5:13	34
21:7-8	34	24:27	34	6:10	34, 97
21:15	34	25:7-9	34	7:2	34
21:17	34	25:24	34	8:6	34
22:1-2	34	26:5	34	8:8	34
22:19	34	26:7	34	8:13	182
23:14	34	28:24	34	8:16	34
23:28	34	29:36	34	8:18	34
24:5	34	30:12	34	9:7	34
25:5-6	34	30:16	34	9:16	43
26:20	34	30:19	34	9:29	43
26:32	34	31	34	10:15	182
27:33	139	31:13-14	34	10:29-30	34
28:3	34	31:21	34	11:11	34

Nehemiah (cont.)		24:16	56, 57	37:26	133
11:16	34	25:3	104, 170	37:32	169
11:22	34	30:12	140	37:35	178
12:24	34	31:28	216	39:12	226
12:36	34	31:33	99	44:17	233
12:40	34	35:16	99	44:22	76, 77
12:43	34	36:12	99	50:7	227
13:1	34	37:8	104, 140	50:16	227
13:7	34	37:24	219	50:18-20	227
13:9	34	38:12	99	50:21	227
13:11	34, 52	38:40	104, 140	54:5	42
13:17	52	40:2	226	55:2	109
13:20	224	40:23	218	55:12-14 ET	238
13:25	52	42:3	99	55:13-15 MT	238
				55:23	168
Esther		Psalms		58:2	76
4:2-3	182	3:7	219	58:3	220
8:13	235	5:23	161	58:10	233
8:16-17	182	7:4	220	59:13	216
8:29	182	7:10	76	60:10	168
10:16	182	8:3	233	62:11	217, 218
		9:29	170	66:18	76
Job		10:3	168	79:10	232
1:5	238	11:4-5	147	82:2	220
1:6	34	11:7	147	82:8	220
2:1	34	11:15	147	86:14	42
2:10	34	11:24	147	91:10	34
6:14	138	15:5	133	94:2	229
6:16	109	17:3	76	96:5	246
6:24	161	18:48	231	97:7	246
6:25	226	19	161	109	233
7:17-18	76	19:11	78	109:3	169
8:18	216	19:13	161	109:5	168, 169
9:33	227	19:14	43	94:11	77
9:35	219	24:4	76	112:5	133
10:13-16	171	24:19 LXX	168	116:3	171
13:4	246	25:19	168	119:21	43, 162
13:6	226	26:2	76	119:118	162
13:10	226	27:1	138, 219	119:121	43
16:21	126	28:3	40, 76, 238	119:122	42, 43
19:4	161			119:51	42, 43
19:6	171	28:4	229	119:69	42, 43
19:19	238	28:15	226	119:78	42, 43
20:27	140	35:10	218	119:85	42, 43
23:4	226	35:11	67	122:8	40
24:14	56, 57, 139	37:20	209	137:3	178
		37:25	173	138:22 LXX	168

139:1	76	11:9	40, 137, 138	20:19	224		
139:22	168			20:20	138		
139:23	76	11:12	40, 41, 137, 138	20:27	76		
141:5	226, 227			21:2	76		
146:8	238	11:13	224	21:10	136		
149:7	226	11:98	41	21:14	42		
		12:1	227	21:24	43		
Proverbs		12:6	140	22:11	137		
1–15	71	12:9	134	22:16	218		
1–9	40, 71	12:12	171	22:22	218		
1:4	30	12:21	34	22:23	185		
1:10	139	12:27	171	22:26	41		
1:11	140	13:9	138	22:28	93		
1:18	140	13:12	227	23:7	76		
1:23	227	13:18	227	23:10	93		
1:25	227	13:31	227	23:17	138		
1:30	227	14:19-21	137	23:18	138		
3:11	227	14:20-21	136	24:1	138		
3:28	139	14:20	40, 137	24:15-18	71		
3:29	41	14:21	139	24:15	71, 72		
3:31	138	14:31	218, 219	24:17-18	66, 69, 72		
5:12	227	15:5	227	24:17	72		
5:19-20	162	15:9	238	24:18	72		
5:23	161, 162	15:10	227	24:19-20	138		
6	230	15:11	76	24:20	138		
6:1-6	41	15:12	226, 227	24:23	221		
6:1-3	138	15:17	168	24:25	226		
6:1-2	40	15:32	227	24:28	40, 41		
6:1	40	15:33–16:9	71	24:28	139		
6:3	40, 41	16:2	76	25–29	72		
6:5	40	16:13	238	25–28	233		
6:23	227	16:29	137, 139	25–27	71		
6:25-33	233	17:3	76	25:8-9	40		
6:34-35	230	17:5	69, 219	25:8	41, 52, 138		
6:34	233	17:9	173				
6:35	169	17:17	40	25:9	41, 138		
8:5	30	17:18	40, 41, 136, 138	25:11-22	71		
8:12	30			25:12	226		
9:7-8	226, 227	17:19	173	25:15	139		
10:1–22:16	71	18:17	40, 126, 136, 138	25:16-17	136		
10:3	168			25:17	136		
10:12	168	19:4	138	25:18-20	70		
10:17	227	19:7	138	25:18-19	70		
10:18	169	19:25	226	25:18	40, 41, 70, 139		
10:18 LXX	168	19:27	161				
10:26	70	20:1	162	25:19	70, 72		
		20:18-19	224	25:20	70		

Proverbs (cont.)		7:26	34, 171	48:11	215		
25:21-22	27, 63, 66, 69–72, 252	7:29	34	49:8	231		
		8:12	34	50:1	115		
		8:15	34	50:8	224		
25:21	70	8:17	34	54:6	122		
25:22	71, 72	9:1	34, 168	57:11	219		
26:18-19	137	9:6	168	58:7	109		
26:19	139	9:7	34	59:13	216		
26:25	76	9:14	171	59:17	233		
26:26	168, 169	11:5	34	59:18	231		
26:27-28	72	11:9	34	61:1-11	231		
27:10	40, 137	12:7	34	61:2	231, 232		
27:14	40, 41, 137	12:13-14	34	61:8	218		
				63:1-6	231		
28:1	72	*Isaiah*		63:4	233		
28:3	218	1–66	231	63:10	169		
28:10	72	1:18	226				
28:16	72	1:24	232, 235	*Jeremiah*			
28:17-18	72	2:2-5	246	2:19	226		
28:17	218	2:4	226	2:25	238		
28:23	226	2:6-8	246	2:34	55		
28:24	218	2:8	246	3:1	115		
28:25	72	2:18	246	3:5	235		
28:27	109	2:20-21	246	3:6-12	235		
29:5	40, 137	2:20	246	3:8	115		
29:6	72	3:5	134	5:1	173		
29:15	226	5:8	93	5:9	232, 235		
29:23	72	10:10-11	246	5:12	216		
29:25	72	10:10	246	5:22	219		
29:27	220	11:3-4	226	5:29	232, 235		
		13:11	42	6:28	224		
Ecclesiastes		14:13	77	7:5	221		
2:24	34	14:28-31	246	7:6	218		
2:26	34	16:14	134	7:9	139, 216		
3:11	34	19	246	9:3	224		
3:14-15	34	19:1	246	9:7	104, 169		
3:14	34	19:3	246	9:8	232, 235		
3:16	221	28:6	221	11:20	76, 235		
3:17-18	34, 77	28:7	162	12:3	76, 77		
4:1	218	29:13	76	14:14	246		
4:17	34	29:21	218	15:15	235		
5:1	34	31:3	246	17:9	76		
5:5-6	34	31:7	246	20:10	139, 231, 235		
5:7	217	33:16	171				
5:17-19	34	34:8	231	20:12	76, 77, 235		
6:2	34	35:4	231, 233				
7:13-14	34	38:14	218	21:12	217		

22:3	209, 217	18:12	218	25:15	32
25:15	209	18:15-18	220	25:15	169, 231
26:1-19	8	18:16	218	25:17	226, 231, 235
26:10	8	18:18	217, 218		
26:11	92	18:24	220	27:3	223
26:16	92	18:26	220	27:12-25	223
29:21	28	20	215	27:13	223
30:17	171	22	240, 241, 245, 246	27:15	223
35	82, 205			27:17	223
35:6-7	54	22:1-16	240	27:20	223
43:2	42	22:1-12	146, 147, 240	27:22-24	223
44:30	169			28:18	220
46:10	231, 235	22:1-5	240	30:13	246, 247
46:16	209	22:1-2	240	31:13	246
48:41	171	22:1	240	33:2	235
50:15	209, 231, 235	22:2-4	244	33:3	220
		22:3-5	240	33:12	235
50:28	231	22:3	245	33:13	220
50:29	42, 43	22:6-12	197, 203, 211, 240–42, 244	33:15	220
51:6	231			33:17	235
51:11	231			33:18	220
51:12	104	22:6-7	240	33:25	208
51:30	171	22:7	179, 209, 240, 241	33:27	171
51:36	231			33:30	235
		22:8	245	34:6	173
Lamentations		22:9	224, 240, 244, 245, 247	34:21	168
3:10	140			35:5	32, 169
3:36	52			35:11	168, 169
3:60	231, 235	22:11	245	37:18	235
3:64	229	22:12	244, 245	44:22	115
4:18	171	22:17-22	240	45:8	209
		22:17	240	47:22	176, 178
Ezekiel		22:19	224		
2:6	219	22:23-29	240, 241	*Daniel*	
3:11	235	22:23	240	1:2	34
3:18	229	22:25	244	1:9	34
3:20	220, 229	22:26	109, 245	1:17	34
3:26	226	22:27	244	5:20	43
5:15	226	22:29	217, 218, 244, 245	9:3	34
13:13	246			9:11	34
13:18	172	23:29	168	9:25-26	188
13:20	172	23:45-46	233	12:1	235
16:38-40	233	24:1-14	232		
18	88	24:8	232	*Hosea*	
18:5-20	88	25:12	231, 235	3:1	238
18:7	218	25:14	231, 234, 235	4:1-3	216
18:8	220, 221			4:2	139, 216

Hosea (cont.)		2:16	110, 115, 117, 122	Qumran	
4:4	226			*1Q22*	
10:13	221	3:5	218	1.8	246
		3:15	42, 43		
Amos		3:19	42	*1QH*	
1:11	235	4:1 ET	43	5.25	224
4:1	218				
5:10	218	*Ecclesiasticus*		*1QM*	
		3:16	43	3.6	235
Obadiah		4:2	109	4.12	235
7	170	6:9	169	14.1	246
15	229	11:3	246		
		11:8	134	*1QS*	
Jonah		11:29	170	1.11	235
1:6	34	11:32	140	2.6	234
1:16	219	13:21-23	136	2.9	235
3:9-10	34	19:13-17	228	3.13–4.26	221
4:7	34, 229	20:2	228	4.9-11	221
		25:18	99	5.1	239
Micah		28:2	40	5.25	239
2:2	78, 79, 93, 217	29:14-16	41	6.1	226
		29:17-20	41	6.24–7.25	244
2:8	169	29:20	40	6.24-27	228, 241, 242
4:3	226	37:2	169		
5:14	231	42:10	139	7.8-9	240
7:17	219	45:15	188	7.8	236
7:20	140	46:1	235	7.15-16	224
Nahum		*1 Maccabees*		*1QpHab*	
1:2	231, 233, 235	9:40	170	9.2	235
		11:40	169		
3:6	168	11:69	170	*1QpPs*	
		13:17	169	37.3	209
Habakkuk				37.7	209
2:1	226	*2 Maccabees*			
2:18	246	1:10	188	*CD*	
		3:12	185	6.20–7.3	236, 240
Zechariah		4:33	185	7.2	236
7:9-10	205			8.5-6	235
7:10	218	*Jude*		8.5	236
11:17	246	50:15	235	8.11-12	235
13:7	228	50:38	235	9.1-8	240
		51:11	235	9.2-8	226, 236
Malachi				9.2-4	228, 241, 242
2:15	173				

Index of References

9.2	236	23.76	163	4.6	163, 164
9.3	236	23.50	59	4.9	164
9.4	236	23.60-61	59	4.13	164
9.5	235	24.113	58	4.18	164
9.6-8	228, 241, 242	24.65	58	4.19	164
		40.32	163, 164, 186	6.14	164
13.18	236			6.15	164
19.18	236	47	179	75	227
		47.68-73	180		

Philo
De Specialibus Legibus
3.104-107   196

54.18	163, 164		
54.19	164		
54.35	164		

Plato
Laws

865-874e2	166
874e-879b	164
874e-979b	166
874e5-7	166
876e-877a2	166
876e5-878b3	166
876e6-877a1	166
877a1-2-b4	166
877a7-b3	166
878b4-879b1	166
878c1-d6	166
879a2-b1	166
879b1-5	166
879d6-879a2	166

CLASSICAL SOURCES
Aeschines

1.91	58, 59
2.93	163, 164
3.51	163, 164
3.109	191
3.212	163, 164
3.244	163

Euripides
Ion
1314-1316   98

Herodotus

2.35	211
3.8	208
6.97	191
6.131	177

Aristotle
Athenian Politics

47.2	58
52.1	58
57.3	178
58	178, 180
58.2	177
1275a 14-16	177
1253a10-18	17
1253a32-40	17

Homer
Iliad
16:573-574   98

Odyssey
15.271-273   98

Thucydides

2.71	191
4.118.1	191
5.18.2	191

Constitutions of the Anthenians
27.3   164

Isocrates
18.52   163

Callimachos
Hymns
4.275-280   191

Lysias

1	78
1.27	163
1.50	58
3	165
3.1	164
3.28	164
3.38	164
3.41-42	164
3.42	164
4	165, 179
4.1	164

PAPYRI
PCaire

30605 1 19-20	245
30605 1 19	244
30605 1 20-21	244
30605 1 21	244
30605 5-6	245
31179 6	245
31179, 22	245

PLille

29.9	245
29.10	245
29.11-12	245

Demosthenes

21.43	58
23.22	164, 165
23.24	164, 165

PLille (cont.)			206-207	74	MAL	
29.11	245		206	49	29	118
29.14	244		229-230	75	37	118
29.15	244		244	60, 63	A 10	15
29.16	245		245	60	A 19	134
29.23-24	244		249	63	A 21	134
			250	75	B 15	134
PRylands			251	75	B 8	134
9	165, 248		266	60, 63	B 9	134
9.2.2.15-16	165		267	60	F 1	134
9.2.2.18	165					
9.17	138		CT		ND	
9.20	138		29 42	15	2307:47-48	121
ANCIENT NEAR EASTERN TEXTS			Codex Eshnunna		Sumerian Law Tablet	
			13	58	1–2	74
ADD						
321 2-6	15		Hittite Laws		TAD	
321 6-8	15		3–4	34	B2.4	121
			10–11	49	B2.6	121, 181
Amenemope			45	68	B2.4:8-9	119
6	93		71	68, 110	B3.3	121
21.17-20	69				B3.8	121
478	218		Laws of Eshnunna		B3.3:7-9	119, 121
			50	64	B3.3:9-10	121
CH			54	75		
1	28		56	75	TCL	
8	58		58	75	12 117	15
21	58					
48.59–49.17	64		LH			
153	28		116	230		
206-208	34		229-230	28		

Index of Authors

Achenbach, R. 33, 148, 149, 181–83
Adam, K.-P. 161, 162, 240
Albertz, R. 148–50, 185, 206
Altman, A. 191
Anbar, M. 36
Arneth, M. 230
Asheri, D. 211

Baentsch, B. 57, 176
Baer, I. F. 193
Barbiero, G. 64–69, 107, 109, 176, 204, 213, 221, 232, 238
Barmash, P. 13–16, 32, 100, 151–53, 157, 159, 173, 181, 186, 231
Bartelmus, R. 100
Bartor, A. 21, 235
Baumgartner, W. 185
Begrich, J. 19
Berger, K. 139
Berges, U. 246
Bergsträsser, G. 100
Berman, J. 183
Black-Michaud, J. 68
Block, D. I. 10, 240
Blum, E. 67, 149
Boecker, H. J. 7, 8, 21, 23, 170, 226
Boegehold, A. L. 177
Boehm, C. 4, 5
Botica, A. 54, 76, 77, 79, 81, 147, 160, 161, 165, 170
Botta, A. F. 119, 121, 122
Bourdieu, P. 179
Braulik, G. 88, 237
Bultmann, C. 176, 209
Burnside, J. 19, 143, 144
Buss, M. 26
Carawan, E. 27
Carmichael, C. M. 33, 88
Cartledge, P. A. 177, 178

Cazelles, H. 23, 30
Cenival, F. de 243, 244
Chaniotis, A. 98
Charlesworth, J. H. 236
Chavel, S. 182
Chirichigno, G. 229
Cholewiński, A. 206, 223
Christ, H. 201, 231
Christ, M. R. 20
Clines, D. J. A. 159, 186
Cocco, F. 152, 159, 181, 182, 186, 187
Cohen, D. 17, 18, 20, 83, 84, 179, 201, 218
Cohen, M. 175
Conrad, D. 28
Corcella, A. 211
Cowley, E. A. 119
Crüsemann, F. 160, 207

Daube, D. 33, 143, 231
Deissler, A. 139
Delekat, L. 186
Delkurt, H. 226
Dennett, D. 73
Derlien, J. 184, 191
Dietrich, W. 185, 186, 190, 191, 235
Dobbs-Allsopp, F. W. 14

Edenburg, C. 114
Eichler, B. L. 37
Elliger, K. 82, 160, 162, 175, 181, 185, 205, 208, 216, 221, 228, 237
Elster, J. 2, 3

Fabry, H. 67, 181, 182, 184, 226, 227
Fensham, F. C. 25, 33, 34, 51
Fichtner, J. J. 39, 40, 137
Finkelstein, J. J. 74
Finsterbusch, K. 88, 89

Fishbane, M. 10
Fistill, U. 149
Fitzpatrick-McKinley, A. 89
Fleischman, J. 114
Fortes, M. 5, 68, 69
Fox, M. V. 138
Fried, L. S. 243
Frymer-Kensky, T. 106, 112–14, 170

Gagarin, M. 27, 28, 165
Gamberoni, J. 186
Garner, B. 74, 75
Gass, E. 41, 219, 238, 239
Gerstenberger, E. 26, 54, 82, 205, 247
Gertz, J.-C. 11, 35, 43, 57, 95–98, 100, 101, 105, 111, 115, 134, 140, 141, 153, 156, 162, 181, 182, 184, 188, 195
Gesenius, W. 100
Gillihan, Y. M. 242
Gilmer, H. W. 65
Gödde, S. 98
Greenberg, M. 100
Grotkamp, N. 12
Gunkel, H. 19

Haase, R. 68, 80, 134
Hagedorn, A. 82
Harris, G. 20
Hartenstein, F. 232
Hartley, J. E. 216, 218
Heinemann, I. 81
Heltzer, M. 98
Hempel, J. 95
Herrmann, R. 66, 242, 244
Hignett, C. 178
Hoebel, E. A. 3
Hoffmann, D. 208
Hoffner, H. A. 110
Hölscher, G. 107, 135
Holzinger, H. 54
Horst, F. 126, 232, 234
Hossfeld, F. 139, 240
Houtman, C. 25, 30, 35, 37, 48
Huffmon, H. B. 68
Hurvitz, A. 181

Jackson, B. S. 13, 23–26, 30, 33, 37, 53, 54, 56, 57, 78–80, 89, 143, 145, 158, 169, 172, 196, 230

Jacobs, B. 64
Jacobsen, T. 182
Jagersma, H. 233
Janowski, B. 19, 233
Jenni, E. 238
Jeremias, J. 233
Johnson, B. 221
Jones, J. W. 165
Joosten, J. 179, 190, 207, 210, 212, 247

Kaufman, S. A. 88
Kautzsch, E. 100
Keel, O. 19
Keil, C. F. 208
Kellermann, D. 39, 126, 137, 138, 175, 176, 179
Kitz, A. M. 224
Klinghardt, M. 242, 243
Klopfenstein, M. 106
Knight, D. A. 184
Knohl, I. 148, 150–52, 176, 212, 247
Koch, K. 72, 180, 231, 233
Kocher, A. 114
Koehler, L. 185
König, E. 171
Korošec, V. 35
Kugel, J. L. 228

Lacey, W. K. 212
Lang, B. 78
Larson, E. W. 242
Levine, B. A. 159, 189
Levinson, B. M. 55, 57, 100, 183
Levy, J. 181, 182, 184
Lewis, D. 28
Liedke, G. 47, 51
Lipiński, E. 110, 122, 223, 224, 229, 234, 235
Lippert, S. L. 138, 165
Lloyd, A. B. 211
Loader, J. A. 41, 233
Locher, C. 114
Löhr, M. 186
Loomis, W. T. 58, 165
Luciani, D. 204
Lüddeckens, E. 242
Lyons, M. A. 211, 240

Index of Authors

MacDowell, D. M. 27, 58, 59, 165, 191, 201
Macholz, C. 8
Madl, H. 236
Magdalene, F. R. 21
Magonet, J. 204
Maier, J. 225
Malinowski, B. 4
Marböck, J. 134
Marshall, J. 65
Martin-Achard, R. 177, 178
Mathys, H.-P. 126, 204, 221, 228, 234–36, 238, 240, 242
Mayer, G. 79, 226, 227
Mayes, A. D. H. 111
McBride, S. D. 183
McKay, J. W. 64, 65
Meinhold, A. 70
Mendes-Flohr, P. 238
Merendino, R. P. 134
Merz, E. 234
Mieroop, M. Van De 183
Milgrom, J. 148, 160, 181, 182, 184, 205, 206, 208, 210, 211, 216, 218, 221, 223, 224, 226, 227, 229, 234–36, 245
Miller, P. D. 78
Monson, A. 243
Morrow, W. S. 11, 88, 89, 130
Muhs, B. 242
Murray, D. F. 29
Muszynski, M. 242, 243, 246, 247

Nelson, R. D. 91–93, 133–35, 194, 220
Nielsen, E. 107, 135
Nihan, C. 148, 176, 204–11, 217, 218, 222, 237
Noth, M. 65, 148, 176, 208, 227, 233
Nutkowicz, H. 121

Oeming, M. 171, 172
Olson, D. T. 88
Olyan, S. M. 19, 138
Oswald, W. 174, 183
Otto, E. 7–9, 11, 13, 23, 25, 26, 31, 33, 38, 43, 46–48, 55, 57, 59–62, 64, 67, 68, 88–93, 97, 98, 106–108, 110, 118, 120, 129, 130, 132, 148, 151, 166, 193, 194, 204, 206, 210, 216–18, 237

Papakonstantinou, Z. 28
Patrick, D. 21
Patterson, C. 178, 180
Peels, H. G. L. 231, 232
Perlitt, L. 127, 128, 130, 131, 135
Petschow, H. 88
Pfeifer, G. 12
Phillips, A. 25, 111, 180
Phillips, D. D. 18, 20, 27, 28, 51, 54, 78, 83, 144, 163–66, 175, 179, 189, 192, 218
Pilch, J. J. 4, 10
Pohlmann, K. F. 240
Porten, B. 119, 120, 181
Pressler, C. 112
Preuss, H. D. 88
Propp, W. H. C. 55

Rabinowitz, J. J. 120
Ramirez-Kidd, J. E. 176
Richter, W. 205
Riede, P. 171
Rigsby, K. J. 185, 190–93
Riley, A. J. 19, 110
Ringgren, H. 34, 53, 67, 181, 182, 184, 186, 209
Roberts, S. 5
Rofé, A. 88, 96, 100, 111, 149, 152, 184, 188, 193
Römer, T. 163
Rosenbaum, S. H. 169
Rost, L. 181
Rothenbusch, R. 23, 57
Rouland, N. 2
Ruffini, J. L. 5
Ruschenbusch, E. 27, 58
Ruwe, A. 213

Sanchez, P. 191
Sarna, N. H. 147
Sauer, G. 229
Saur, M. 223
Sayce, A. H. 119
Scharbert, J. 42
Scherer, A. 71
Schiffman, L. H. 226, 234
Schipper, B. 138
Schmid, H. R. 185
Schmidt, L. 151

Schreiner, J. 220
Schultz, F. W. 88
Schulz, H. 47
Schwartz, B. 189
Schwertner, S. 246
Schwienhorst-Schönberger, L. 8, 35, 36, 48, 51, 54–58, 60, 64, 65, 230
Seeligmann, I. L. 226
Seidl, T. 159
Seitz, G. 88, 95–98, 114, 130, 134
Shields, M. A. 117
Sinn, U. 98, 193
Ska, J.-L. 64
Stackert, J. 35, 36, 100, 101, 145, 148, 151–53, 158, 182, 189, 211, 223
Stamm, J. J. 78, 139
Steck, O. H. 231, 232
Steuernagel, C. 130, 135
Strawn, B. A. 73–75, 77–80
Stroud, R. S. 27
Sulzberger, M. 180
Szubin, H. Z. 120

Taubenschlag, R. 165
Thompson, T. W. 235
Tigay, J. H. 88
Todd, S. C. 20, 51, 201, 227
Toorn, K. van der 147
Treston, H. J. 54
Triandis, H. C. 82
Turner, B. 98

Van Seters, J. 100
Veijola, T. 89
Verdier, R. G. 2
Vittmann, G. 248

Wagner, A. 110, 186
Wallace, R. W. 84
Walter, U. 177
Weber, M. 240
Weinberg, J. P. 182
Weinfeld, M. 98, 243
Wellhausen, J. 65, 97
Wells, B. 12, 13, 21, 67, 89, 106, 113, 114, 120, 122, 123, 170, 201, 216
Wenham, J. G. 116
Wesel, U. 4, 24
Westbrook, R. 12, 16, 21, 25, 55, 74, 75, 89, 116, 118, 120, 122, 230
Wevers, J. W. 209
Whitehead, D. 177
Whitekettle, R. 158, 189
Whybray, R. 71, 136
Wiener, H. M. 88
Wilcke, C. 74
Willis, T. 141
Wilson, S. 5, 12, 184
Wiseman, D. J. 120
Wright, D. P. 24, 25, 28, 30, 32, 36, 49, 50, 56–58, 64, 65

Yaron, R. R. 116, 117, 182

Zenger, E. 233
Zobel, H. J. 228

Index of Subjects

prohibitives 9, 22, 54, 79, 88, 109, 128, 146, 197, 201–203, 205–206, 210, 212, 215–17, 219, 220, 225, 226, 229, 235, 236, 238, 250
protasis 29, 39, 41, 47, 54, 90, 96, 100–102, 111, 113, 115, 117, 131–33, 154–56, 163, 167, 168
Ptolemaic 138, 165, 193, 197, 242, 243, 253

reconciliation 20, 188, 190, 227, 228, 240
regulatory statutes 181, 187, 188, 190, 253
religious associations 7, 203, 242–47, 249, 253
revenge 1–3, 5, 14–16, 21, 26–28, 35, 36, 39, 87, 98, 102–103, 124, 129, 153, 174, 180, 181, 199, 200, 212, 225, 226, 229–38, 240, 244, 249, 252
robbery 218, 220

Sabbath 175, 183, 203, 204, 213, 224, 241, 245
slanderer 214, 220, 223, 224, 244
slave 8, 37, 38, 45–48, 121, 125, 130, 131, 166, 177, 180, 190, 191, 210, 229, 230

slavery 8, 9, 21, 125, 128–33, 176, 189, 229, 230
sojourner 8, 151, 154, 156, 159, 174–76, 179, 208, 209, 212, 240

Tebtunis 242, 243
theft 55–63, 78, 79, 106, 127, 128, 134, 199, 206, 216, 217, 244, 252, 253
theocracy/theocratic 22, 33, 88, 146, 148–51, 172, 181–84, 190, 193, 197, 200, 249, 252
trauma ek pronoias 51, 163, 164, 166, 167
trial 12–14, 18, 21, 26, 28, 33, 44, 47, 48, 51, 52, 58, 60, 65, 67, 68, 72, 78, 83, 84, 86, 90–92, 97, 113–15, 128, 129, 140, 149, 152, 153, 163, 165, 166, 174, 179, 180, 183, 192, 201, 214, 219–24, 226, 232–34, 237, 244, 245, 253

vengeance 2, 3, 12, 15, 48, 54, 189, 201, 222, 229, 231–36

yiqtol 39, 42, 45, 47, 49, 50, 102, 125

Index of Hebrew Terms

אהב 19, 137, 209, 238, 239, 253
אח 107, 124, 125, 133, 217, 222, 228, 248
איב 18, 19, 93, 252
איבה 32, 77, 107, 154, 155, 158, 168–70, 172, 173
אוה 78, 79
אזרה 178
אלהים 34, 117, 133
אלילים 213, 246, 247
ארב 71, 94, 104, 124, 125, 140, 169
אשם 160
בני עמיך 228, 248
בקש 77, 155, 169, 170, 172, 173, 229
גבול 91, 125, 187
גר/גור 41, 135, 151, 154, 156, 174–80, 208, 209, 212, 217
גזל 79, 216–18, 244
דל 65, 221, 222
דם, דמים 11, 93–95, 154, 155, 187, 196, 224
הדר 94, 221, 222
זיד/זוד* (hi.) 42, 43, 45
דל 65, 221, 222
הדף 154, 155, 168–70
זדון 42, 43
זדים 42, 43,
זמם 77
חטא 160
חמד 76–80, 202, 252
חמס 67, 90, 209, 220, 224
טמא 116, 118
יכח (hi.) 226–28, 253
כפר 16, 230
יצר 77, 170
לב 76, 77, 94, 170, 138
מוכיח 227
מות 28, 44, 45, 50, 60, 94, 98, 116, 124, 129, 139, 154–56, 167, 187, 229
מחסה 186

מנוס 186
מעוז 186
מרעים 138
משגב 186
משפט, שפט 43, 94, 98, 129, 155, 182, 187, 218, 220–23
מִתְּמוֹל שִׁלְשֹׁם 94, 101, 102, 170, 252
נטה 222
נטר 229, 234, 235, 236, 240, 253
נכה 28, 67, 104, 167, 168
נקמה, נקם 226, 229–35, 240, 253
עדה 148, 151, 152, 155, 157, 158, 162, 167, 174, 180–85, 187, 197, 210, 211, 253
עול 220–23
עלם 109, 160
עמד 224
עמית 41, 212, 216, 219, 221, 222, 226–28, 248
עשק 42, 43, 79, 179, 217, 218, 244
צדה/צדיה 32, 34, 36, 77, 101, 154, 155, 158, 169–73, 252
צעק 231
צר 19
קלה 134
רבים, רב 43, 67, 222, 235
ריב 11, 39, 49, 52, 53, 66, 138, 222
רכיל 223
רע (רעהו .incl) 30, 39–42, 44, 47, 50, 60, 61, 77, 78, 90, 94, 104, 106, 124–26, 136–39, 168–70, 194, 196, 199, 212, 217, 220, 228, 237, 239, 248, 252
רצח 90, 94, 139, 140, 149, 152, 154–56, 187, 194–96, 252
שחד 230
שגגה, שגה 77, 152, 154, 156, 158, 159–62, 173, 195, 196, 252
שגגה/שגג 159–63, 172, 173
שוב 116, 187, 189, 229
שלח 95, 115–17, 122, 133
שלם, šallem yᵉšallem 55, 57, 60, 70

שֶׁקֶר 65, 90, 216
שׂנא 19, 94, 100, 101, 104, 107, 110, 111, 117, 119, 121, 122, 124, 125, 168–70, 194–96, 226, 239, 252, 253
שִׂנְאָה 77, 116, 154, 158, 168, 169, 172, 252
תּוֹכַחַת 226, 227, 232, 239
תּוֹשָׁב 154, 156, 174, 178, 179

Index of Subjects

26th dynasty 138, 247, 248

alterity 151, 175, 176, 202, 205–11, 215, 239, 247
apodictic law 9, 13, 82, 109, 205
apodosis 29, 41, 96, 100–102, 111, 115, 118, 131, 133, 154–57, 209
associations 7, 17, 67, 91, 136, 203, 242–47, 249, 253
asylum 6, 27, 29, 30, 32–34, 36, 44, 45, 76, 87, 89, 90, 92, 93, 95–100, 102–106, 125, 129, 132, 140–42, 145–52, 154–59, 165, 170, 171, 174, 178, 181, 182, 184–86, 188–97, 199–201, 252, 253
avenger of blood 14, 84, 94, 95, 99, 103, 154–56, 158, 180, 181, 186–88, 195, 196, 200, 230, 231, 233, 252

benevolence 1, 7, 22, 89, 91, 93, 107–108, 129, 134–37, 140, 147, 198, 200, 202–206, 209, 210, 212, 215, 221, 223, 226, 227, 229, 235, 237–41, 244, 248–50, 253
bloodshed 8, 93, 129, 141, 150, 240, 241, 244, 245
brother 10, 22, 40, 41, 77, 82, 86, 90, 92, 97, 106–10, 124–36, 139, 175, 176, 199–203, 205–207, 209–11, 213–15, 217, 219, 221, 223, 225–29, 235, 237, 239, 241, 243, 245, 247–50
burglar/burglary 21, 26, 55–57, 59, 60, 142, 252

case/counter-case 3, 8, 9, 11–15, 17, 18, 20, 22, 23, 25–33, 36, 37, 40–51, 53–63, 65–70, 72–78, 80, 81, 83–85, 87, 90–94, 96–106, 108–24, 126–39, 141–43, 152–58, 160–67, 170, 172, 174–76, 178–85, 187, 188, 191–93, 197–201, 211, 215, 216, 218, 221, 223, 224, 228, 230, 231, 233–35, 237, 238, 243–45, 247, 249, 252–53
casuistic law 8, 13, 37, 54, 62, 65, 112, 176, 204, 212
Covenant Code/CC 6–12, 21, 23–28, 31–33, 36, 39, 40, 43–46, 49, 51, 52, 54, 55, 59, 61, 63, 65, 81–87, 89–92, 100, 106, 108, 124–26, 128, 131, 132, 135, 137, 139, 142, 146, 196, 197, 199, 223, 251
cities of refuge 96, 100, 142, 146, 147, 152, 153, 174, 180, 184, 187, 188, 190, 192–95
compatriot 41, 106, 209, 214–16, 219, 224–28, 237, 239, 241, 248, 250

Demotic 120, 138, 243, 244, 248

Egypt/Egyptian 21, 42, 69, 120, 121, 147, 165, 175, 192, 193, 204, 207–209, 211, 243, 246–48
enemy/enemies 2, 5, 9, 17–22, 25, 37, 39, 42, 44, 45, 50, 51, 53, 56, 64–72, 84–87, 90, 91, 93, 95, 100, 101, 103–107, 110, 126, 129, 139, 140, 142, 143, 145, 154–56, 162, 165, 168, 169, 172, 173, 186, 196, 216–19, 227, 229, 231–33, 235–38, 246, 249, 251–53
ethics 2, 11, 66, 89, 106, 108–109, 193, 201, 203, 227, 232, 234, 243, 249
Exodus 11, 13, 19, 21, 26, 32–34, 37, 42, 45, 48, 50–52, 54–55, 57, 59, 63–67, 69, 72, 91, 100, 106, 107, 133, 144, 176, 180, 202, 204, 206–208, 211, 221

fairness 22, 127, 135, 204, 206, 217, 218, 223, 224

feud/feuding 1–8, 10–18, 20, 21, 24, 27, 31, 39, 44–46, 48, 52, 63, 67, 68, 72, 83, 84, 86, 87, 91, 98, 102, 105–107, 109, 124, 126, 139–45, 150, 151, 174, 180, 183, 184, 187, 189, 196, 199, 201, 203, 211, 216, 227, 231, 235, 237, 251, 252
friendship 1, 19, 21, 44, 67, 136, 137, 142, 143, 146, 147, 197, 198, 200, 202, 203, 225, 238, 249, 253

Hellenistic 42, 53, 80, 136, 140, 145, 158, 161, 162, 167, 174, 182, 184, 185, 190–93, 196, 197, 210, 219, 227, 229, 231, 241–43
Holiness Code/H 5, 7, 13, 19, 21–23, 34, 39, 41, 47, 53–55, 58, 65–68, 77, 81, 82, 88, 108, 110, 112, 119–21, 125, 126, 130, 137, 146–48, 150–52, 169, 170, 174–76, 178–81, 185, 186, 189–90, 198, 202–12, 217, 219–23, 225–28, 231–36, 239–41, 245–49, 253
homicide 2, 3, 6, 12–16, 18, 19, 21, 22, 25–37, 42–49, 51, 52, 54–60, 63, 69, 73–77, 80–87, 89–93, 96, 97, 99–103, 105, 119, 124–26, 129, 130, 132, 139–43, 145–47, 149–53, 155–67, 169, 170, 172–75, 178, 180–89, 191–201, 203, 219, 228, 231, 234, 235, 249, 251–53

identity 10, 22, 69, 81, 84, 110, 150, 151, 175–77, 183, 206–208, 210, 215, 216, 225, 228, 239, 242, 247, 249
indictment 113, 209
injury 3, 9, 21, 26, 27, 31, 36, 37, 43, 45, 46, 48–55, 57, 61, 76, 80, 81, 86, 87, 97, 101, 126, 142, 143, 164, 167, 175, 196, 199, 200, 203, 234, 252
intent 19, 25, 27, 29–33, 36, 42, 49, 51, 55, 58, 62, 73, 75–80, 83, 85–87, 98, 99, 105, 107, 109, 113, 118, 123, 124, 130, 140, 143, 146, 149, 154, 156, 158, 159, 161–73, 192, 195, 199, 202, 206, 213, 220, 233, 236, 237, 242, 252
intentionality 26–30, 32, 33, 49, 54, 58, 72–81, 83, 85, 103, 104, 142, 143, 145, 146, 154, 156, 159, 160, 164, 165, 167, 170, 200, 251, 252

kinship 1–3, 5–14, 16, 17, 21, 22, 24, 26, 30, 45, 47, 52, 54, 67–69, 73, 75, 81–87, 89–93, 97–99, 103, 105, 107–10, 114, 126–36, 139–46, 149–51, 157, 174, 180, 182–85, 197–201, 205–206, 209–13, 218, 221, 228, 230, 237, 239–41, 247, 249, 251–53

legal anthropology 1–5, 10, 12, 16, 24, 73, 81, 83, 85, 87, 119, 184, 234, 251, 253
love 9, 19, 22, 41, 86, 88, 91, 93, 106, 108–109, 121, 122, 124, 129, 137, 142, 143, 175, 197–203, 205–207, 209–11, 213–15, 217, 219, 221, 223, 225–27, 229, 231, 233, 235–45, 247, 249, 250, 253

marriage 5, 6, 22, 87, 93, 102, 105, 110, 111, 113, 115–25, 127, 141–43, 150, 168, 174, 177, 182, 184, 197, 202, 220, 245, 251, 253
metic 174–76, 178–80, 197, 204, 205, 209, 223, 244, 248

oppression 209, 217–19, 240, 244, 253

Papyrus Lille/P. Lille 29 244, 245
Papyrus Rylands 138, 165, 248
parents 37, 112–14, 204, 213
patriarchal 6, 7, 69, 202, 215, 245
personae miserae 65, 66, 69, 217
plaintiff 44, 92, 170, 172, 248, 249, 252
polity 5, 7, 18, 22, 41, 82–84, 93, 145–47, 149, 150, 174, 175, 177, 182–84, 187, 201, 202, 210, 221, 235, 237, 239–42, 249, 253
premeditation 25, 26, 28, 30, 34, 57, 58, 145, 146, 159, 161, 164, 165, 167, 173
priestly/P 2 6, 9, 10, 13, 14, 16, 21, 22, 24, 29, 32, 34, 36, 42, 43, 68, 67, 73, 76, 78, 100, 106, 109, 126, 134, 138, 140, 144, 153, 155, 157, 159–63, 165, 167–71, 173–79, 181–83, 185, 187–91, 193, 195, 197, 199, 211, 216–18, 220, 222–27, 230–33, 235, 237, 238, 240, 242, 247–52

www.ingramcontent.com/pod-product-compliance
Lightning Source LLC
Chambersburg PA
CBHW070751020526
44115CB00032B/1614